Human Beginnings in South Africa

Uncovering the Secrets of the Stone Age

H.J. DEACON & JANETTE DEACON

ALTAMIRA
PRESS

A Division of Sage Publications, Inc.

Walnut Creek, CA • London • New Delhi

Front cover illustrations. *Background*: Rock engraving from the Northern Cape.
Clockwise from top left: Khoekhoe pot with pointed base and lug; handaxes from
the Western Cape; a bored stone; shell pendants and beads from the Western Cape;
bone fish gorges from Nelson Bay Cave.
Back cover. *Above*: The Howiesons Poort artefacts at Klasies River
occur stratified in a sequence of dark carbonised and ash layers.
Below: Rock painting of a procession of hunters.

First published 1999 in southern Africa by David Philip Publishers (Pty) Ltd,
208 Werdmuller Centre, Claremont 7708;
in the United States of America by AltaMira Press,
A Division of Sage Publications, Inc.,
1630 North Main Street, Suite 367, Walnut Creek, CA 94596;
and in the United Kingdom by Sage Publications,
6 Bonhill Street, London EC2A 4PU, United Kingdom;
and in India by Sage Publications India Pvt. Ltd.
M-32 Market, Greater Kailash I,
New Delhi 110 048, India

ISBN 0-86486-417-5 (David Philip)
ISBN 0-7619-9086-0 (AltaMira Press)

Library of Congress Cataloging-in-Publication Data
are available upon request from the publisher

99 00 01 02 03 6 5 4 3 2 1

Text design by Abdul Amien
Layout by Michelle Willmers
Cover by Abdul Amien

Reproduction by Hirt & Carter, Cape
Printed by Creda Communications, Eliot Avenue, Eppindust II,
Cape Town, South Africa

Contents

Acknowledgements

This book reflects our different yet complementary interests in the Stone Age archaeology of South Africa. We shared the writing equally, with HJD responsible for the first half and JD for the second, bringing together the experiences of our respective professional careers.

Between us we have had the privilege of studying under the founders of South African archaeology, A.J.H. Goodwin and C. van Riet Lowe, and to have had this interest nurtured by a long and close association with Ray Inskeep. C.K. Brain, Basil Cooke, Desmond Clark, Brian Fagan, Richard Klein, David Lewis-Williams, Berry Malan, Revil Mason, Philip Rightmire, Phillip Tobias, John Vogel, Patricia Vinnicombe and numerous other colleagues, collaborators, students and friends have contributed to the research and ideas expressed in this book. Some but not all of their names feature in the bibliography. Many have shared the rigours of fieldwork and taxing hours in the laboratory that are part of learning about the past. To Boy Adams, Mary Leslie-Brooker, Vera Freyer-Geleijnse and Ria Schuurman we owe a special debt of gratitude. HJD expresses his thanks to colleagues Sarah Wurz, Tanya Harris and Ryno Goosen and students who have helped search the literature and who have played an essential part in writing the book. It is for their generation that the book has been written. Janette's work at the National Monuments Council has been greatly enriched by colleagues who have given freely of their time assisting with hands-on conservation such as the removal of graffiti from rock paintings and the stabilisation of sites like Matjes River. Henry Bredekamp, Peter Farmer, Ron Martin, Shireen Martin and numerous members of the A-team deserve special mention.

The research reported here has been assisted by a number of agencies. These include the institutions to which we are attached, the University of Stellenbosch and the National Monuments Council, and funding bodies such as the Foundation for Research Development, the Centre for Science Development, the Wenner-Gren Foundation, the L.S.B. Leakey Foundation and the Swan Fund, which were generous in their support.

Martin West suggested we write this book. Russell Martin of David Philip Publishers waited patiently through its gestation. In preparing the text and illustrations we depended greatly on the computing skills of Andrew Deacon and thank him for his willingness to help. James Mills-Hicks was also of great help with the diagrams and maps. Melissa Deacon lived with us.

A number of colleagues have read and commented on a draft of the book and we would like to thank Jan Boeyens, Marie van der Ryst, Lyn Wadley, Tony Humphreys, Ray Inskeep, Mary Leslie-Brooker, Judy Sealy, John Vogel, Ron Clarke, Kathy Kuman and Carmel Schrire. We owe a particular debt to Carmel Schrire who undertook the role of a publisher's reader and who was able to suggest many ways in which we could improve the clarity of the text.

Special thanks are due to the following authors who gave permission for their illustrations to be used: Stephen Townley Bassett, E. Eastwood and W. Fish, S.L. Hall, R.R. Inskeep, A. Jerardino, R.G. Klein, T. Maggs, A. Manhire, C.G. Sampson, J. Sealy, S. Talma, A. Traill and J.C. Vogel. Permission to reproduce photographs is gratefully acknowledged from the Jagger Library at the University of Cape Town, (Figure 1.3 and Figure 1.4), M. Scott (Figure 8.4), H. Opperman (Figure 8.9), Pitt-

Rivers Museum, Oxford (Figure 8.14), H.P. Steyn (Figure 8.5), Cedric Poggenpoel (Figure 8.18, right) and Lita Webley (Figure 10.15). We are especially grateful to Chloë Buckland whose illustrations of primates greatly improved Chapter 3.

All photographs were taken by ourselves unless otherwise acknowledged.

Grateful acknowledgements are due to the Mauerberger Trust for financial assistance in the publication of this volume.

In 1870, a San man from Lesotho named Qing was asked by Magistrate J.M. Orpen where /Kaggen, the San deity who made all things, came from. Qing replied: 'I don't know ... but now you are asking the secrets that are not spoken of ... only the initiated ... know these things.'

The Stone Age of South Africa holds many secrets and this book initiates readers into the fascination of archaeology and the information we have inherited from the past. It describes how researchers have discovered evidence for human beginnings and have devised ways to decode some of the finds.

We would like to dedicate this book to Qing and the /Xam San, as they shared knowledge of a period of South African history and of a heritage that for too long has been a secret which has not been spoken of. The period occurred before formal histories were written and the heritage is all that remains of human endeavour from those times.

CHAPTER ONE

Learning about the past

History from page one: the Stone Age

This book is a history of the earliest people of South Africa. It is based on archaeological evidence for the emergence of humanity and traces the long period of settlement by hunters and gatherers who relied mainly on stone for their tools. It ends with the introduction of farming and iron technology. This precolonial past is conventionally known as the 'Stone Age'. Because there are few written accounts or folk memories, archaeology is the single most important source of information for human activities of those times.

The oldest recognised stone artefacts are some two and a half million years old. Although we still use stone today, 'living in the Stone Age' has become a metaphor for all that is primitive. Yet it is worth reflecting that our immediate ancestors were Stone Age people who thought, spoke and acted like us and who were just as intelligent. It is their creativity that paved the way for our modern technology, and their history is thus far from trivial. If our Stone Age ancestors had the opportunity to comment, they might not be too impressed by some of our achievements, in particular how we have changed the world.

The term 'Stone Age' may mask more than it illuminates, however. For example, it excludes the history of creatures with an anatomy related to ours and ancestral in the sense of belonging to the same family, but who did not have stone tool technology. These proto-humans are of considerable scientific interest in the human story, as are apes, monkeys and other human look-alikes, and we have therefore included something of their story in this book too.

The term also masks the fact that the material evidence from the Stone Age includes the association not only of stone tools, but also of all the things that were made and used by people and that were abandoned, thrown away or lost. Such things are called artefacts. Indeed, the principle that artefacts and their associations carry information about people and past events forms the basis of archaeology.

Artefacts – things that were artificially made and were not formed naturally – include the widest variety of items. They may be objects that were used in day-to-day living such as knives, spoons, tables and chairs, or they may be works of art, ritual objects, structures and buildings. Because artefacts are or were made by people in a social context, they can also give information about past societies, communities or individuals as well. They are therefore not only tangible, but also reflect intangibles, things that cannot be touched, like the behaviour, beliefs, thoughts and aspirations of their makers.

Much of this information is to be found in the details of the associations of the artefacts, their dating and their location. This is known as their context. The associations are the things and features found with the artefacts. Dating places the artefacts in a time dimension and location places them in space. The better the associations between artefacts are known and the better the time and space dimensions are known, the more information can be gained. On the other hand artefacts from contexts that are not known or are poorly known are less informative. Many people collect artefacts and in doing so take them away from their contexts and therefore destroy most of the evidence. The recording of the contexts of artefacts is a vital part of archaeological research.

The identification of artefacts as things that have been made is obvious where they are familiar objects. But where materials and artefacts are no longer in common use identification is less obvious. Identification of stone artefacts depends on records or direct observations of stone artefact makers and on knowledge of the mechanical properties of stone coupled to experimentation. Replication experiments are valuable in showing not only how stone artefacts were made but how they may have been used and how effective they were. The same approach can be followed to study artefacts in other materials such as wood, bone and metal. Identification and description of an artefact may require chemical analysis of the material used, possibly to indicate its source, and microscopic study of any marks that may indicate use or function.

Not all artefacts can be collected and taken to the laboratory for study, though. Some can only be mapped and studied in the field: these are called features. A 100 000-year-old circular layer of ash, which is all that remains of a cooking hearth, the fireplace of a woman living with her family in the shelter of a cliff on the Tsitsikamma coast, is one example. A pit dug for the grave of a child 5000 years ago is another. Artefacts like rock paintings and rock engravings take time to record accurately. They are often best left in place with their location and interpretation recorded on paper or computer so that they can be interpreted again by future generations.

Historically, according to the record, Khoekhoe (Hottentot, Khoikhoi) and San (Bushman) communities in South Africa relied on stone rather than metals for making tools for use in everyday life. They were the last representatives of the Stone Age. Because South Africa was relatively distant from the centres where metal technology developed, the primary use of stone persisted longer here than in many other parts of the world. Ten thousand years ago, for people everywhere in the world, stone was the most important raw material for fashioning a wide range of sharp cutting tools that could not be made in alternative materials like bone or wood. More than five thousand years ago metals like copper and bronze came into use in a limited area of the globe, where the ores were available. But it was the spread of iron-smelting technologies in the last three thousand years that

reduced the value of stone as a raw material. The working edge of iron tools is not initially sharper than the edge on stone tools but, with use, stone tools lose the sharpness of their edges sooner than iron tools. It is for this reason that iron with its alloys has replaced stone for the majority of the artefacts in current use.

Stone is a very durable material and stone artefacts often survive where bone and wood have decayed. Stone artefacts lying in the landscape or on the surface or buried are markers or visiting cards of people who were present there but have long since died. These are often the only clues we have for understanding who the tool-makers were. This explains the emphasis given by archaeologists to the use of stone.

The evidence archaeologists recover has to be interpreted and the interpretation depends on who is interpreting it and what biases they bring to it. Any interpretations made by different individuals will reflect how they see the past. Whatever the biases we bring to our archaeological perspective of the Stone Age, the purpose of this book is to encourage others to develop an interest in discovering something about the peopling of South Africa, in the sincere hope that they may improve on our scholarship.

The challenge is to glimpse beyond the earliest European records, which date from AD 1488, to discover where we have all come from. We all have a past and therefore own the past. As individuals we need to claim the past that is important to us and through communication, make it accessible to others. This book is therefore our own perspective on the precolonial past of South Africa.

Development of archaeological studies in South Africa

It was the remarkable wealth of stone artefacts in the landscape and a Victorian yen for collecting curiosities that gave the initial impetus to archaeological studies in South Africa. Thomas Holden Bowker is credited with being the first person to recognise and make a collection of stone artefacts. In 1858 he discovered some stone artefacts among the sand dunes near the mouth of the Great Fish River in the Eastern Cape. In 1866, a collection of 41 of these artefacts was donated to the Royal Artillery Museum at Woolwich, London, where

Figure 1.1: *Thomas Holden Bowker, the first collector of stone artefacts in South Africa.*

they were kept for almost a hundred years before being returned to South Africa. John Hewitt, who was director of the Albany Museum in Grahamstown, learnt of the donation from studying the Bowker family records. He organised their return and they now form part of the collections of this museum.

Once stone artefacts were recognised as such, Victorian collectors recorded them from many different parts of the country. The active collectors were professional people such as school teachers and medical doctors. Later, geologists joined them as the country was opened up to prospecting for diamonds and other minerals. What motivated these collectors? The ability to recognise stone artefacts gave an educated elite knowledge of technology dating from a time before written history began; in some sense, they were able to control that forgotten past through their knowledge. They knew South Africa had a precolonial past.

There are no dominating archaeological features in the South African landscape like the pyramids of Egypt or Stonehenge, which drew attention and demanded interpretation. Instead, there are numerous shell middens along the coast in positions far above the reach of the sea. Yet it took many years of debate to resolve whether these piles of shells were natural or due to the activities of people. The shell midden controversy can be traced back to an exchange between two early travellers, the Englishman John Barrow (1801:58), and the Swedish naturalist Henry Lichtenstein (1928:219), at the beginning of the nineteenth

century. Neither seems to have been aware of Van Riebeeck's journal (Thom 1958), which referred to people at the Cape whom he called 'Strandlopers' and who harvested shellfish for food. Almost fifty years later, the same debate was taken up in the pages of the *Cape Monthly Magazine* but by this time it was known that the heaps contained not only shellfish but also animal bones and even human burials, and the piles were the food remains discarded at living sites. Many such midden deposits have been destroyed in the development of coastal resort towns, especially since the 1960s, by an affluent society that has trivialised the past.

In the last decades of the nineteenth century there were attempts by Dunn, Gooch, Stow and others to write archaeologies of South Africa. Stow's book, *The Native Races of South Africa*, published in 1905, is a good example of the state of contemporary knowledge. The book holds that until recent times the 'Bushmen' had been stone tool-makers and that they represented a people long resident in southern Africa. Other peoples are seen as later immigrants. Shrouded in mystery were the people who may have preceded the 'Bushmen'. A map reproduced in this book illustrates Stow's migration model. The map is a mass of arrows showing waves of migrations from eastern Africa of San painter and sculptor 'tribes' who were responsible for the rock art in the region, of Hottentot (Khoekhoe) herders and of different siNtu-speaking (Bantu-speaking) groups into southern Africa. Stow projected into the past the

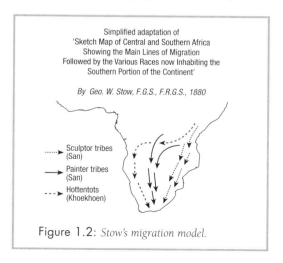

Simplified adaptation of
'Sketch Map of Central and Southern Africa
Showing the Main Lines of Migration
Followed by the Various Races now Inhabiting the
Southern Portion of the Continent'

By Geo. W. Stow, F.G.S., F.R.G.S., 1880

Sculptor tribes (San)

Painter tribes (San)

Hottentots (Khoekhoen)

Figure 1.2: *Stow's migration model.*

ethnic diversity as understood in his own times and assumed that these social, political and linguistic divisions had gone unchanged. Yet individuals and communities interact constantly and so social groupings are continuously changing or transforming. For this reason Stow's migration model (Figure 1.2) is too simple. However, the importance of Stow's work cannot be underrated because his was a pioneering attempt to explain the peopling of South Africa. Migration is a valid process, people do move – if not *en masse,* at least in smaller groups – and migration models not as extreme as Stow's have remained a popular form of explanation in South African archaeology.

Stow is also remembered as a pioneer recorder of rock art although he was not the first to make field copies. Several of the early European travellers had reported and made copies of rock paintings and engravings. Barrow, for example, on a visit to the Graaff-Reinet area in the early nineteenth century commented that the paintings were so fresh that they must have been made very recently. Rock art became known as 'Bushman paintings' and stone artefacts as 'Bushman implements'.

Without any reliable estimates of the timescale of precolonial history or knowledge of 'pre-Bushman' peoples, archaeology could not develop as a discipline. Many of the finds of stone artefacts occurred on the modern surface, not deeply buried, and this was taken to indicate that they were relatively recent and that most, if not all, artefacts were of the same age. Comparisons could be made with the deeply buried and undoubtedly ancient stone artefacts, associated with extinct kinds of animals, that were found in Europe. Were the South African finds much younger? Penning, a geologist of Stow's generation, appreciated that this need not be the case. The land surfaces in southern Africa were not glaciated in the Ice Age as in Europe and therefore were not covered with glacial debris. In other words, artefacts occurring on the surface here might be tens and even hundreds of thousands of years old.

Perhaps the clearest statement on the ages of artefacts in the South African landscape came from Louis Péringuey, a French-trained entomologist. Péringuey's work took him to the vineyards around Stellenbosch, where artefacts are regularly

• A new science •

The first publication on South African archaeology appeared in the *Cape Monthly Magazine* in 1870 and was written by Langham Dale. He was the Secretary for Education in the colonial government and wrote under the pseudonym 'Delta'. His short but informative publications told his readers about local finds and explained what archaeology was about:

'Archaeology is arranging its facts and pointing to important inferences from what it has to teach about primitive Man. A new science interposing between Geology and History, is collecting many a ray of light, apparently converging from many regions towards a focus in the remote past, and constructing a history of Man, in his earliest condition, from the contemplation of his works, his dwellings, and his implements.'

And again, in referring to land now occupied by the inner suburbs of greater Cape

Town like Maitland and long since built over, he wrote:

'The largest variety of South African stone implements has been found on the Cape Flats on the margins of the great vleys, or in the open spaces between the sand-hills, where the drift-sand has blown off by the summer S.E. winds or washed off by the winter floods, leaving the natural soil bare: loosely imbedded in this soil have been brought to light lance-heads, arrow-heads, axe-heads, scrapers, and sling-stones, and flakes of several shapes applicable to many uses. No excavations of the soil have been made. Some of these specimens show by the careful chipping and neatly serrated edges that considerable labour was expended on them. Nuclei or cores from which flakes have been chipped off are numerous.'

ploughed out of the ground. The artefacts he collected included distinctive large almond-shaped tools, called handaxes, which were also known to occur in great quantities in the gravels mined for diamonds along the Vaal River and had been found as far afield as Swaziland and the Victoria Falls. Péringuey appreciated that similar kinds of stone artefacts were known from the oldest deposits in France, and in a paper, 'Notes on stone implements of Palaeolithic (Old Stone Age) type found at Stellenbosch and vicinity', delivered to the South African Philosophical Society in 1900 and reported in the proceedings of the society and in the publication *Nature*, he claimed that the stone artefacts from Stellenbosch were as old as the most ancient in Europe. At the turn of the century it was a revolutionary idea that people may have had as long a history of living in Africa as in Europe. We now know that human beginnings took place in fact in Africa, not Europe, and we accept that the age of the artefacts collected by Péringuey from Stellenbosch is half a million or more years old. They are indeed as old as and older than any in Europe.

Péringuey became the director of the South African Museum and, from the turn of the century, with the growth of museums in South Africa, he and other museum directors were active in promoting archaeological studies. The museums became the storehouses for collections. The close association between archaeology and museums has continued to the present. One of Péringuey's counterparts was John Hewitt, who trained as a zoologist in England and came to South Africa in 1910 from an appointment in Sarawak. Lower vertebrates, snakes, tortoises, frogs and the like were his main research interest at the Albany Museum in Grahamstown but he also spent weekends and holidays investigating archaeological sites. In collaboration with Jesuit priests who taught at St Aidan's College and with local farmers, Hewitt made collections from coastal shell middens and excavated a number of rock shelters. His most important excavations were in rock shelters on the farms 'Wilton' near Alicedale, 'Howiesons Poort' near Grahamstown and 'Melkhoutboom' in the Suurberg. These were among the first systematic excavations undertaken in South Africa. Although trained as a natural scientist and not an archaeologist, Hewitt brought a new rigour to the fledgling

Figure 1.3:
John Goodwin.

Figure 1.4:
'Peter' van Riet Lowe.

subject of archaeology.

The first South African to be trained as an archaeologist was Astley John Hilary Goodwin. Born in Pietermaritzburg in 1900, John Goodwin studied archaeology under Miles Burkitt at Cambridge, returning in 1923 to South Africa. He gave himself the task of making archaeology a more systematic study. Existing museum collections had been accumulated casually rather than systematically but they represented a body of information that needed to be put in order. In a series of publications in journals and in the press in the 1920s, Goodwin developed and publicised his ideas. The culmination was the 1929 publication of the *Stone Age Cultures of South Africa* in the Annals of the South African Museum, written in collaboration with Clarence van Riet Lowe. While the concept of the book owed much to Goodwin, Van Riet Lowe supplied the information on the archaeology of the interior of the country that he had gathered while working as an engineer engaged in building bridges.

The 1929 publication had a long-lasting influence on the development of archaeology in South Africa. It proposed a three-stage division of the Stone Age into the Earlier, Middle and Later Stone Ages. Although subsequently some archaeologists have referred to these divisions as Early, Middle and Late Stone Age, Goodwin deliberately selected the former terms to emphasise that his scheme could date the stages only relative to each other and not in absolute terms such as Early or Late.

The Earlier Stone Age (ESA) is characterised by large bifacial (flaked over both faces) artefacts,

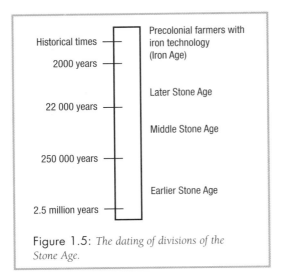

Figure 1.5: *The dating of divisions of the Stone Age.*

with handaxes (like those collected by Péringuey) being the diagnostic form. The Middle Stone Age (MSA) was characterised by the use of cores – pieces of stone skilfully prepared to produce flakes of regular triangular or parallel-sided shape. The definition of the Later Stone Age (LSA) suggested a technology designed to produce microlithic (small) tools and blades, but stressed the association with the San rock art and burials. The Later

Stone Age therefore provided the link with historical times.

Goodwin and Van Riet Lowe had no means of establishing the time ranges of these stages but this proposed division was a considerable advance, and collections and archaeological sites could at least be ordered in broad time units even if they could not be defined in social terms. The Later Stone Age was thought to date to the last 2000 years, with the Middle Stone Age extending back perhaps a further 2000 years. It was not until the advent of radiocarbon dating in the 1950s that more precise estimates of age ranges could be obtained. The radiocarbon revolution, complemented by other dating techniques, has shown that the guesstimates of the pioneers were out by a factor of at least 10. Thus 20 000 years is a better estimate for the duration of the Later Stone Age than the guess of 2000 years, while the Middle Stone Age began about 250 000 years ago (Figure 1.5).

A further legacy of the Goodwin and Van Riet Lowe publication was the terms derived from the names of places where type or reference collections were found. The type site name has been conventionally used as a label to identify similar artefacts at other sites. Goodwin and Van Riet Lowe's underlying assumption was that differences

Figure 1.6: *Pioneer archaeologists set out: a group led by C.H.T.D. Heese from the University of Stellenbosch in the 1930s.*

in artefacts denoted people of different culture, language or tribe. It is now known that much of the variability in the stone artefacts had to do with successive innovations. These were reflected in the choices people made about the raw materials they used and about changing styles of tool manufacture. Such changes were widespread and at any one time similar artefacts were made over much of southern Africa. The archaeological record, for the most part, is too indefinite to distinguish social or linguistic groupings.

Some labels continue to be used as an archaeological convenience. An example is the term Wilton, named for a rock shelter near Alicedale in the Eastern Cape. This name was adopted by Goodwin and Van Riet Lowe as one of the two main components (cultures) of the Later Stone Age, the other being the Smithfield. In current usage, the label Wilton refers to that part of the Later Stone Age sequence, dating to the last 8000 years. Characteristic artefacts from this period – small-shaped tools of similar design that were mounted in handles – are found at sites throughout southern Africa. It was a widely shared technology at the time, much like electronics in the present. In function the artefacts were used for tasks like making skin clothing, beads and arrows.

Goodwin and Van Riet Lowe were the dominant figures in South African archaeology from the 1920s to the 1950s. Goodwin carried out extensive fieldwork in the southern Cape in the 1930s aimed at investigating the divisions of the Middle and Later Stone Ages. After the interruption of the war years he devoted himself more to the promotion of archaeology through the founding of the South African Archaeological Society in 1945 and editing the *South African Archaeological Bulletin*, the main publication of the society. Van Riet Lowe became the director of the Archaeological Survey. Apart from being the spokesperson on archaeological concerns in the country, he made a major contribution through his studies of the Earlier Stone Age gravel deposits of the Vaal River. Van Riet Lowe died in 1957, a year after his retirement, and Goodwin in 1959. In two short years South African archaeology lost its leading authorities.

The Archaeological Survey was disbanded in 1962. A former student of Goodwin who had worked in the Survey, B.D. Malan, became Secretary of the Historical Monuments Commis-

Figure 1.7: *Van Riet Lowe with Raymond Dart, Robert Broom and Henri Breuil.*

sion, now the National Monuments Council. Another of Goodwin's students, Revil Mason, became the founding staff member of a new Department of Archaeology at the University of the Witwatersrand. Goodwin's teaching position at the University of Cape Town was filled by Ray Inskeep, who had been involved in research in Tanzania and Zambia. Through their teaching, Inskeep, Mason and those that followed were instrumental in training a number of archaeologists to fill the new posts that became available in the 1960s and 1970s. From a complement of about six professional archaeological posts in the early 1960s the number has grown to over 60 in the 1990s, with more than 100 graduates from five different university teaching departments in the country practising as professional archaeologists.

The economic boom of the 1960s saw archaeology enter a growth phase worldwide. It emerged from being a subject concerned with documenting and ordering artefacts into periods so as to construct histories of cultures, to a concern with the processes leading to cultural changes in the past. Heralded as the 'New Archaeology', the processual movement became the paradigm of the 1960s. The mood was reflected not only in popular culture but also in a positive approach to the natural and human sciences. Because the past was knowable, the challenge of the archaeologist became a matter of asking the right questions and designing appropriate research to find the answers. As a result of

Figure 1.8:
Ray Inskeep.

this movement archaeology became more rigorous and scientific in its practice and more aware of theory. The past could not be understood by making more and more finds of the same kind. Archaeologists had to unravel the past by constructing and testing hypotheses.

The positivist approach of processual archaeology and the agenda which this movement proposed for research provoked the criticism that its explanations were too deterministic and did not take human agencies sufficiently into account. This criticism spawned a competing post-processualist theoretical movement in archaeology. The post-processualists adopt a more humanistic or relativist stand arguing that the past is interpreted rather than explained through the not-unbiased eyes of the archaeologist living in the present. The past is thus created out of the present and there cannot be a single authoritative past. It has been a concern of post-processualists to show that constructions of the past have been manipulated so as to disadvantage and undervalue the role of some groups like women and ethnic minorities. These are philosophical and real concerns of modern

society at large, and critical discussion of the way archaeologists engage with the past has parallels in other subjects like history.

South African archaeology has been influenced by theory in European and North American archaeology. In turn it has made a contribution to world archaeology proportionate to the size of its community of practitioners. In the 1940s scientists worldwide first came to appreciate the importance of fossil sites of early representatives of humankind in South Africa. New insights into the expanding collection of fossils continue to focus international interest on the country. Archaeological sites of all ages are known to be numerous and are a considerable cultural resource of more than national significance. This resource includes more than 10 000 rock art sites. While rock art is universal, that of South Africa is amongst the most impressive anywhere. Through this art the archaeology of South Africa has become accessible to the wider community. Documenting, managing and interpreting this archaeological heritage is no mean task.

The reason why much of Stone Age history has remained a secret for so long is not that it may not be told or that it has not been told in other books, but rather that it has to be individually discovered. Because we are remote from the past, we have to find it and immerse ourselves in it, if we wish to understand it and unlock its secrets. Pursuing the past is rewarding, and we hope it is a challenge more will follow.

Figure 1.9: *Map of South Africa showing the provinces*

CHAPTER TWO

Environments of the past

The idea that environments have changed is difficult to grasp. Some of the most important fossils of creatures called mammal-like reptiles have been found in the Karoo, a word that means dryness in a Khoisan language. These creatures, very distantly related to us, lived in swampy areas, some 200 million years ago, under very different conditions from the present. How do we know? Their fossilised bones are encased in mudstone, very old mud turned into rock. The mud came from fine clay particles weathered from older rocks and washed by rivers and streams into a large inland basin from surrounding highlands. Finding fossils of creatures in the Karoo mudstones tells us something we cannot deny: that climates have changed through the ages. The Karoo was once a swampy place like the modern Okavango Delta in Botswana, but on a much larger scale. This was a long time ago, before there were people on earth, but there have been many wetter and drier climate pulses since then which have changed the environment.

Even more difficult to grasp is the idea that the world has been through several Ice Ages. We know that Antarctica is the coldest place on earth and covered with kilometre-thick ice. This is understandable because the continent is at the South Pole and the polar regions receive less heat from the sun than the tropics. We also know that high mountains like the Himalayas are permanently snow-capped and climbers have to negotiate mountain glaciers – streams of ice – when they try to reach the summits of the peaks. Both the ice sheets on Antarctica and the glaciers on the Himalayas are reminders of the present Ice Age. About 250 million years ago, when the southern part of Africa drifted close to the South Pole, ice once covered much of what we now identify as South Africa. This is apparent in the ice-scratched rock pavements that underlie the fossil-bearing Karoo mudstones; they are being uncovered by erosion in the bed of the modern Vaal River at Nooitgedacht near Kimberley. There have been repeated Ice Ages in the history of the earth. The present Late Cainozoic Ice Age is the most recent of these and we are currently living in a brief warmer interval, an interglacial period, of this Ice Age.

What does living in an Ice Age mean? At times climates were several degrees cooler at the equator and several tens of degrees cooler in the high latitudes than is the norm for geological history. The present Ice Age started with the growth of an ice sheet on East Antarctica, about 13 million years ago, and entered its current mode, some 3 million years ago, when ice sheets developed in the northern hemisphere. The oceans of the world became cooler and, with less evaporation from the oceans, the continents became drier. An Ice Age is associated not only with extremes of temperature but, above all, with aridity. Although, in the present Ice Age, glaciation has occurred only on a few of the higher mountains in East Africa, the drying of the continent has shrunk forests and expanded savannas, deserts, shrub and grasslands. Humankind emerged in Africa under the selective regime of Ice Age drought rather than of cold.

It was Louis Agassiz, a Swiss palaeontologist who spent his later years at Harvard, who publicised the concept of an Ice Age. In the nineteenth century the thought that the earth had been through an Ice Age seemed revolutionary. For many the biblical flood was an idea hard to dispel and evidence for the flood could be found in the surface mix of clays and boulders, then known as 'diluvium'. Yet as Agassiz realised, this was clearly the 'muck', the outwash of ground-up pieces of rock, transported and dumped where the glaciers melted. Only glaciers can transport clay-sized particles and rock blocks as big as houses in the same motion: wind- and water-transported materials are much better sorted according to size. Agassiz recognised the glacial signature in large areas of Europe and North America, which had once been covered by ice. It was also discovered that people had been living in the Ice Age because their artefacts and bones are to be found in places buried by glacial deposits. This was the first realisation that people had inhabited the earth for many thousands and even millions of years. Agassiz, the enthusiastic promoter of the Ice Age, would have delighted in the knowledge that humans are very much the children of the Ice Age (Stanley 1996). How this might be so is explored in the present and following chapters. [HJD]

Global perspective

The human story starts some millions of years ago and has been played out in a world different from the modern one we know. At times animals, only some of which we would recognise, populated the world, and the vegetation and climates were very different from the present. Part of understanding how and why humans became what we are lies in the knowledge of the ways environments have changed. Environments of the past – what we refer to as palaeoenvironments – are of interest in many fields including archaeology. The special interest of archaeologists is human palaeoecology, the ways people interacted with their environments in the past.

Our habitat is the place where we live. There are physical factors that affect habitats, like the landscape, soils and the many parameters of climate often simplified as temperature and rainfall. In addition there are biotic factors that have an influence on the habitat: they are due to all the living organisms, from microbes to large animals and trees, that interact because they share and use the same habitats. Some habitats, like forests, woodlands and grasslands, may be rich in the number of different kinds of organisms found there and therefore have relatively high biotic diversity. By contrast deserts are habitats with much lower diversity because moisture, from rain, dew or fog, is limited. Some habitats suit one life form better than others do.

Humans are large-bodied, ground-living, general feeders who have invaded all available habitats on the earth. However, our ancestors were restricted to equatorial habitats and occupied a narrow niche. Today the niche modern humans occupy has become so broad that the continued existence of many other organisms is threatened. The human story is one of increasing control over the environment. This control is not total, however, and we are vulnerable to natural disasters, like floods, droughts or volcanic eruptions, in addition to hazards of our own making.

One reason for the strong interest in palaeoenvironments and human palaeoecology is that humankind is potentially threatened with extinction in the future through the progressive deterioration of global environments. The pollution we generate and the rate at which we are destroying natural ecosystems and reducing biodiversity are all cause for alarm. To face the threat to the survival of future human generations and to find ways of countering this threat, international research programmes, like the International Geosphere–Biosphere Programme (IGBP), have been launched. These programmes aim at understanding how the earth and its ocean–land–atmosphere systems work. Predicting the future requires us to look back to determine the rate and scale of environmental and ecological changes over hundreds and thousands of years. Archaeology in particular can tell us something of how people have coped with these changes.

Geological timescales

Earth history is divided into aeons, eras, periods and epochs (Figure 2.1). The age of the earth is about 5000 million years. When a little more than 1000 million years old, the young earth was cool and wet enough for the emergence of life. At that time simple single-celled organisms, like bacteria, composed the living world but in their ability to reproduce under the control of DNA (the genetic material called deoxyribonucleic acid) they carried the makings of all living things, humankind not

excepted. The same 20 amino acids form the building blocks of the proteins found in the cells of bacteria, mice and humans. This supports the idea of a common ancestry from those remote times. It took aeons for living forms to diversify and, from the shelter of the seas, for some forms to invade the land and the air. The myriad of creatures now found on earth, both single-celled like bacteria and multi-celled like humans, have thus evolved through the millions of years of geological time.

The Cainozoic (Cenozoic) (65–0 million years) is the youngest era in geological time (Figure 2.2) and it is this, the era of mammals, which most concerns us. In the older literature, the Cainozoic was divided between the Tertiary (65–1.8 million years) and the Quaternary (the last 1.8 million years). These terms are still used. However, current practice is to refer to the first period of the Cainozoic (65–23.3 million years) as the Palaeogene, made up of the Palaeocene, Eocene and Oligocene epochs, and the latter part of the Tertiary as the Neogene, comprising the Miocene and Pliocene epochs (23.3–1.8 million years). The Quaternary (or, less often used, Pleistogene) would then include the Pleistocene and Holocene epochs. The Holocene is defined by convention as the last 10 000 radiocarbon years, and the base of the Pleistocene to almost 1.8 million years. In the Pleistocene, the time units Early (1 800 000–700 000), Middle (700 000–125 000) and Late (125 000 –10 000) Pleistocene are recognised. All these divisions of the Cainozoic, formulated in the last century from changes in fossil marine shells in the Mediterranean Basin, were meant to mark the progressive appearance of modern species. Although the terms have local rather than global relevance, they are the standard time units for discussing human fossil history and global climatic changes.

Dating methods

Dates may be relative (A is older than B) or chronometric, measured on a scale equivalent to solar years (A is 10 500 years old and B is 9500 years old). Most chronometric methods have as their basis the radioactive decay isotopes. Radioactive decay proceeds at a constant rate, irrespective of external conditions, and where the rate

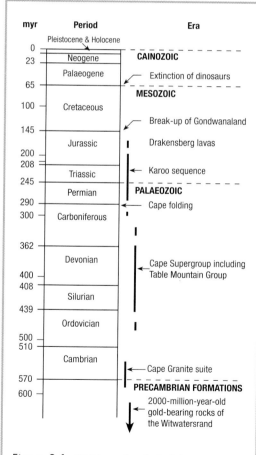

Figure 2.1: *Divisions of geological time.*

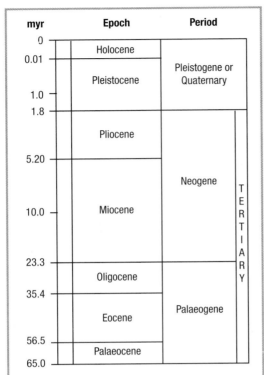

myr	Epoch	Period

Figure 2.2: *The Cainozoic, the last 65 million years of geological time.*

of decay is known, measurement of the ratio of the mother and daughter products can be used to estimate the age. Relative and chronometric dating techniques may be employed together to increase the precision (rather than accuracy) with which ages can be estimated.

Stratigraphic dating. The law of superposition states that in a layered deposit the older materials occur in the lower layers and the younger materials occur in the upper ones. A relative age can thus be given to finds ordered in a stratigraphic sequence. In a single layered deposit it is possible to observe stratigraphic positions directly. Composite sequences involving more than one deposit may be constructed by correlation, or matching strata according to common items of content such as artefacts or fossils. In this way longer temporal sequences can be built up. Culture stratigraphies refer specifically to the relative order in which different types, classes or sets of artefacts occur in time. Biostratigraphies are

similarly the order in which plant or animal (faunal) fossils occur in time. Stratigraphic dating is a very powerful tool, especially when allied to chronometric methods.

Radiocarbon dating. Radiocarbon dating is a well-established method of chronometric dating and numbers of laboratories worldwide offer a routine service. A recent development has been the use of particle accelerators instead of conventional gas (Geiger) or liquid scintillation counters to make the radiocarbon measurements. The advantage of this is that samples of milligram size can be dated, whereas conventional radiocarbon dating requires samples of 6 or more gram mass.

The radiocarbon dating method is widely applicable because carbon of mineral or organic origin is a common element in materials. The radioactive isotope ^{14}C is formed in the upper atmosphere by the bombardment of nitrogen by cosmic rays and immediately combines with oxygen to form carbon dioxide. As carbon is cycled through the atmosphere, ocean and land systems, all materials containing carbon become weakly radioactive due to ^{14}C. Cycling and mixing maintain the level of radioactivity until the carbon is removed from the system through, for example, the death of an animal or plant or the deposition of a carbonate mineral. Thereafter the specific radioactivity of that material decreases at a constant rate, known as the half-life.

The half-life of radiocarbon has been estimated at 5730 years. In other words, after the elapse of this period only half of the original number of radiocarbon atoms will remain, after double this period a quarter will remain, and so on. From a knowledge of the mass of carbon, the half-life and the specific radioactivity, the age of a sample can be calculated. With material of about 40 000 years or older in age, the radioactivity is too low to measure. There is also a constraint on dating very young samples because, among other reasons, the industrial revolution has pumped enormous quantities of old and non-radioactive carbon from fossil fuels (coal and oil) into the atmosphere. Age estimates obtained are in radiocarbon, not truly calendar, years.

For the period for which there are tree ring sequences that can be cross-dated by radiocarbon, a calibration curve, which equates radiocarbon and calendar years, has been constructed. A portion of the curve for the southern hemisphere can be used to calibrate radiocarbon dates from South Africa. This is of primary importance for dates that fall within the last 300 years, when solar activity caused marked fluctuations in ^{14}C production in the atmosphere. For earlier prehistoric times the systematic differences in age between radiocarbon and calendar years are not so important for most problems. An example of the scale of difference is that at 7000 radiocarbon years, this dating method underestimates the tree ring or calendar age by some 800 years.

Radiocarbon dates are reported with the laboratory identification and sample description, the radiocarbon age estimate and a plus-minus value that represents a statistical estimate of the standard error of the measurement. An example of a reported radiocarbon date run by the laboratory at the CSIR in Pretoria for the Matjes River Rock Shelter, near Plettenberg Bay, might be: Pta-6688 (=Pretoria laboratory number) Matjes River La (=site name and square number) SL16 (=layer number) 7920 (=age in radiocarbon years) ± 100 (=standard error in years) BP (= years before the present, i.e. before AD 1950).

Laboratories routinely make corrections for carbon isotope fractionation. This may be important because some organisms discriminate between the different carbon isotopes, which may lead to an error of several hundred years in the estimated age. The dates can, however, be adjusted by measuring the $^{13}C/^{12}C$ ratios in the samples. Charcoal is the best material to submit for dating but wood and other plant tissues, bone, shell, carbonate rocks and soils can also be used. There is an added complication in dating shell. Shell carbonate is formed from materials dissolved in the water in which the organism lives and the carbon isotope ratios of the water will not be the same as in atmospheric carbon dioxide. This is because the rate at which decayed radioisotopes are replaced is faster in the well-mixed atmosphere than, for example, in the ocean. Modern sea shells may have an apparent age of 500 years and the radiocarbon age estimates have to be reduced by this amount.

In South Africa there is a long-established radiocarbon facility in the Quaternary Dating Research Unit (QUADRU) at the CSIR in Pretoria. This is able to provide some 250 age determinations a year. In the Schonland Research Centre of the University of the Witwatersrand a further facility provides a limited service.

Potassium/argon (K/Ar) dating. Like radiocarbon dating, this is a well-established chronometric dating method and has wide application in the geological sciences. It has been used to establish the age of 4000 million-year-old moon rocks and samples of archaeological interest that are only a few hundred thousand years old. Conventional K/Ar dating depends on the ability to measure the quantity of the gas argon (^{40}Ar) produced from the decay of the radioactive isotope of potassium (^{40}K); the ratio is a measure of the age. The development of the single crystal fusion argon/argon method, whereby the isotope of potassium (^{39}K) is irradiated to an isotope of argon (^{39}Ar), makes it possible to measure the ratio in smaller and younger samples with greater precision. In view of the fact that samples from archaeological deposits are relatively young, this is an important technical development. As the age measured is the age when the mineral containing the potassium formed, the application of the method in archaeology is restricted to places where there has been recent volcanic activity. This excludes South Africa but vulcanism is associated with the East African Rift Valley where there are important archaeological and palaeontological sites that can be correlated biostratigraphically with sites in South Africa.

Alternative radioisotope methods. There is a suite of methods, still under development and less routine in application, that is alternative to radiocarbon and potassium/argon. They can be used to provide chronologies for occurrences that are too young to date by potassium/argon, yet are beyond the 40 000-year limits of radiocarbon.

Uranium disequilibrium (Ionium) dating depends on the principle that uranium is soluble though some of the products of radioactive decay in the uranium series, like the thorium isotope (^{230}Th), are not. The ratio of parent uranium to the daughter product (^{230}Th) changes as a function of time. Disequilibrium methods have been used to date coral, bone, teeth and speleothems (stalagmites and other cave formations). In the example of speleothems the calcite (calcium carbonate) crystals forming from drip water will contain uranium isotopes but no initial thorium. The conventional method has been to determine the isotope ratios by alpha counting; a recent advance is the

2

• Mass extinction •

Palaeontologists, constructing the story of life on earth from fossil remains, have found that with time animal and plant species change through migration, evolution and extinction. The changes or biotic turnover may proceed gradually or in spurts ('punctuated evolution'). Catastrophic events can lead to the mass extinction of a number of species and their replacement by others. The best-known episode of mass extinction is that which led to the disappearance of the dominant large land-living animals, the dinosaurs, and many marine and terrestrial organisms, at the end of the Cretaceous (65 million years ago).

What killed off the dinosaurs? There is a clue in the end-Cretaceous sedimentary layers containing anomalous quantities of a chemical element, iridium. Iridium is not a common element in earthly rocks and this has encouraged speculation that the mass extinction was caused by the impact of an iridium-rich asteroid from space. It is reasoned that the dust thrown up into the atmosphere following the impact would have caused a sudden major climatic change, an 'impact winter', by reflecting back the heat of the sun and cooling the globe. There are several known impact sites of the right age: a crater over 100 km in diameter in Yucatan, Mexico, and another some 30 km in diameter in Iowa; the identification of these lends strong support to the impact hypothesis. It seems possible that an asteroid 10–20 km in size broke up as it closed on earth, causing several impacts in quick succession. In 1994, telescopes were trained on the impacts made by pieces of an asteroid, essentially large dirty snowballs, on the planet Jupiter. This showed very dramatically that missiles from space do strike the planets from time to time.

One effect of the end-Cretaceous event seems to have been the disappearance of the dinosaurs, which made it possible for the mammals to inherit the earth. The mammals have filled the large land animal niche vacated by the dinosaurs. One consequence of the diversification of the mammals has been the evolution of humankind. The 'impact winter' of the end-Cretaceous is a warning of what might happen should an atomic war create a 'nuclear winter'.

introduction of mass spectrometric methods for higher precision in dating. The limits are 1–350 000 years. In South Africa a uranium disequilibrium dating facility exists in Pretoria.

Luminescence dating depends upon the fact that many minerals contain traces of the radio-isotopes of uranium, thorium or potassium as impurities. The nuclear radiation emitted by these impurities leads to electrons being trapped at defects in the crystal lattice of the mineral; such 'radiation damage' increases as a function of time. To be useful in dating, the electron traps need to have been emptied and the 'clock' set to zero. This can happen, for example, with the release of such stored energy by heating in a fire or exposure to sunlight before burial. In the laboratory, under controlled conditions, the glow of energy due to radiation damage – the luminescence – emitted by a sample can be measured by appropriate photo-electric detectors. The luminescence can be related to the age of the sample if the sensitivity of the material and the radiation dose rate are established through additional measurements. Two luminescence dating techniques, thermoluminescence (TL) dating and optically stimulated luminescence (OSL) dating, are finding applications that use materials ranging from pottery and burnt stone artefacts to sands and sediments with minerals like quartz and feldspar. At the Quaternary Dating Research Unit in Pretoria, scientists are developing OSL dating of feldspathic sands by the use of infrared stimulation. This technique has potential for dating the movement of dunes in desert and coastal regions and sediments in archaeological sites, among other applications. The dating range is about 350 000 years or beyond.

Electron spin resonance (ESR) spectroscopy is a further technique that can measure the radiation damage caused by the dislocated electrons in the lattice of crystalline material. As with luminescence dating, the intensity of the ESR signal is related to the radiation dose and time. Tooth enamel has proved the most suitable material for dating. However, as enamel is not a closed system, due allowance must be made for the rate of uptake of uranium after burial. No ESR dating service currently exists in South Africa and it is done in collaboration with overseas laboratories.

Chemical dating. An important chemical method with South African applications is amino acid dating. Amino acids occur in two spatial configurations, known as L- (left-handed) and D- (right-handed). The L-amino acid configuration normally occurs, but by racemisation or epimerisation reactions a mixture of D- and L-configurations can be produced. The speed of these chemical reactions is a function of time and temperature. If the temperature variable can be estimated or the rate of the reaction calibrated from analysing radiocarbon-dated samples, then samples of unknown age can be dated. The epimerisation of the amino acid isolucine in samples of ostrich eggshell and marine shell produces consistent results. There is currently no facility for amino acid dating in South Africa but a service is available through laboratories overseas.

Cainozoic climates

At the end of the Jurassic (140 million years ago) and the beginning of the Cretaceous, the southern landmass, or supercontinent, known as Gondwanaland began to separate into its component continents – Antarctica, Australia, India, Africa and South America. Propelled by convection currents below the crust of the earth, these portions of Gondwanaland (Figure 2.3) started their slow movement or drift towards their present positions. It was at this stage that the outlines of the southern coast of South Africa were formed. The westward drift of South America and the more limited northward drift of Africa led to the opening up of the South Atlantic Ocean and a seaway connecting the Atlantic to the Pacific via the Indian Ocean to

the east. One Gondwanaland fragment, Antarctica, drifted towards the South Pole. In the course of this movement it became separated from Australia, in the Eocene (55 million years ago). A continent in a polar position has a cooling effect on the earth because it reflects back more of the incoming solar radiation than ocean waters. The circumpolar seaway that developed with the separation and isolation of Antarctica feeds dense cold waters into the oceans, transmitting the cooling effects globally. These are some of the reasons why Cainozoic climates have shown a progressive decline in temperatures relative to the Cretaceous. The drift of Antarctica started the cooling process: this continent became the refrigerator of the world and was eventually buried under ice.

Mountain glaciers were extensive in the Eocene; in the Oligocene they may have reached the coast of Antarctica. However, plants, which included proteas and even trees like yellowwoods, survived in places until at least the early Miocene (20 million years ago). Progressive deterioration of climates culminated in the growth of the eastern Antarctic ice sheet in the Miocene, some 13 million years ago. This marked the beginning of the Late Cainozoic Ice Age, the most recent of a series of Ice Ages in earth history, known to have occurred before the break-up of Gondwanaland and even earlier. We are at present living in the Late Cainozoic Ice Age and there is no reason to think it is near its end.

Although both the eastern and western Antarctic ice sheets developed during the Miocene,

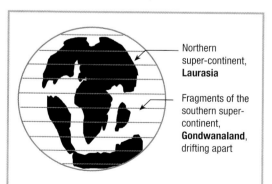

Northern super-continent, **Laurasia**

Fragments of the southern super-continent, **Gondwanaland**, drifting apart

Figure 2.3: *Following the break-up of Gondwanaland, Antarctica drifted to a position over the South Pole and separated from Australia to become the refrigerator of the globe.*

between 13 and 6 million years ago, a delay occurred in the formation of sea ice at the North Pole and continental ice sheets in the northern hemisphere until the later Pliocene (2.5–3 million years ago). The reason is that although there are large continental areas at high latitudes in the northern hemisphere, there are none in a polar position. The continental ice sheets were created with the blocking of effective heat transfer along seaways between the warm Pacific and Arctic oceans. What also contributed to the cooling of the northern hemisphere were changes in atmospheric circulation caused by the uplift of continental mountain ranges like the Rockies, the Alps, and the Himalayas and the Tibetan Plateau. The continental ice sheets in the northern hemisphere have grown and shrunk in cyclic fashion: these cycles have been the engine of climate and environmental change in human times.

In the last 2.5 million years, including the whole of the Quaternary (Pleistocene and Holocene), the rhythmic pulsing of continental ice sheets in the northern hemisphere has changed from a periodicity of 41 000 years to a 100 000-year cycle in the last 900 000 years. Each 100 000-year cycle has been made up of 90 000 years of conditions cooler than the present and 10 000 years of conditions like the present, when the extent of global ice has been at a minimum. These are known as glacials and interglacials respectively. We are living at the close of the twentieth century AD in an interglacial that corresponds to the Holocene. The present time is near the end of the current interglacial and it can be predicted that, in the future, global climates will become cooler than now, unless the natural earth rhythm is disturbed by global warming caused by atmospheric pollution. Part of current concern about global warming is that we do not fully understand its precise effect on the glacial–interglacial cycling of the earth.

During the cooler glacial episodes of the Quaternary, large parts of North America, to the latitude of New York, and of Europe, almost to the latitude of London, were ice-bound. The ice sheets were kilometres thick, spreading from centres like the Rockies and Hudson Bay in North America and the North Sea and Scandinavia in western Europe. Siberia, in continental Eurasia, where the snowfall was not sufficient to allow the formation of an ice sheet, became a frigid desert. This zone of permanently frozen ground in Siberia occasionally gives up the perfectly preserved and still edible carcasses of woolly mammoths, a kind of elephant that became extinct many thousands of years ago.

In view of its stability the Antarctic ice sheet did not get bigger under glacial conditions although, as a result of a higher rate of calving of the glaciers reaching the sea, more sea ice was to be found in its surrounds and icebergs floated further north in the South Atlantic. These icebergs did not, however, reach the South African coast because South Africa lay north of the subtropical convergence – the ocean boundary between cold sub-Antarctic and warm subtropical waters. While Marion Island, a South African territory and weather base in the South Atlantic, carried mountain glaciers during glacial times, South Africa itself was not glaciated though it had cooler climates. The subcontinent is not far enough south and the mountains of the Drakensberg and the Cape, even under the coldest conditions, were not high enough for permanent snow to accumulate and form glaciers, unlike the equatorial mountains of Kilimanjaro and Mount Kenya.

The general trend towards cooler temperatures in the Cainozoic, and the waxing and waning of ice sheets in the later part of this era, have had major effects on world climates. Although mean annual temperatures at the equator have decreased by only a few degrees relative to the Cretaceous, the higher latitudes towards the poles have become much colder. As the weather in the atmosphere is driven by hot equatorial air moving polewards and cold polar air moving equatorwards, atmospheric circulation and wind strengths have increased especially in glacial episodes. Another result has been to make the world more arid. Ice Age aridity can be ascribed to the fact that there is less evaporation from the cooler oceans and therefore less water vapour in the air to fall as rain on the continents. It is the increased aridity, in addition to reduced temperatures, that has most relevance to the latitudes of southern Africa during glacial cycles (Deacon, J. & Lancaster 1988).

The pulse of Quaternary climates

The cyclic Quaternary (Pleistocene and Holocene) climate changes, most marked in the periodic expansions and retreats of ice sheets and mountain

3 • Climate and evolution: Vrba's 'turnover pulse hypothesis' •

Elisabeth Vrba (1985, 1988, 1992, 1996), a South African-trained palaeontologist now based at Yale University, has argued that speciation in African mammals has occurred in evolutionary spurts ('punctuated evolution') driven by abrupt changes in global climate. She holds that when environments are stable there is little or no evolutionary change, and equilibrium is reached. But an environmental change and the consequent need to adapt to new conditions will then cause a turnover, a change in the composition of the biota, including both the fauna and flora. Some species may respond by dispersal to new areas, others may become extinct or undergo speciation.

Vrba's own particular interest is in the antelopes. Antelopes, like the alcelaphine tribe to which the wildebeest, hartebeest and the blesbok–bontebok belong, are specialised in their diets: they are grass-eaters. In Vrba's argument the success of this antelope tribe has been located in the evolution of new species better adapted to life on the expanding African savannas as climates became drier in the later Cainozoic. A contrast can be drawn with other antelopes that are less specialised in their diet. One example is the impala, an animal of riverine open woodland habitats, that feeds goat-like on grasses, leaves, flowers, fruits and seeds, shifting with the seasons between being mainly a grazer and mainly a browser. This antelope, an early offshoot of the alcelaphine tribe, is represented by a single species over a geographical range from South Africa to Kenya. The same species has been in existence for 3 million years. From such evidence one can draw the principle that environmental change is more likely to promote the formation of new species in groups of dietary specialists than in those groups that are generalists. Animals as different as pigs and humans would be rated as generalists.

The question posed by Vrba and others is whether there is a cause and effect relationship between major climatic changes and evolutionary spurts not only in tribes of African antelopes but also in other families like that to which humans belong. The alcelaphines first appear in the fossil record at the end of the Miocene at about 6 million years ago, along with a number of other antelope tribes. Indications that this was an episode of marked global climate change are provided by the formation of the West Antarctic ice sheet and the shift towards the equator of the boundaries between the cold Antarctic and the warm subtropical water masses in the southern oceans. Later chapters in this book discuss the appearance of the first human ancestors, adapted to moving two-legged on the ground, at about this time. The end of the Miocene does seem therefore to have been a period of significant change.

Between 3 and 2.5 million years ago there is again evidence for large-scale changes in global environments. The continental ice sheets were forming in the northern hemisphere, and global cooling intensified. This was the onset of 'Ice Age aridity' which marked the Pleistocene. Vrba has shown that a number of new species in different families of animals make their appearance in this period, an era which provides some of the best support for the idea of a turnover pulse. Fossils of true humans, members of our own genus *Homo*, and fossils of a near relative, *Paranthropus*, first appear in the record about this time.

Most scientists would accept that climate forcing is an important factor in causing habitat changes. However, they would be reluctant to support the idea that a single cause is enough to explain the emergence of humankind. Supporters of the turnover pulse hypothesis are engaged in systematically gathering data on the links between changes in earth and biological systems, with the ultimate goal of learning how evolution operates. The work has encouraged more precise dating and measurement of the scale of climatic events, on the one hand, and has kept alive the debate on gradual and punctuated evolution, on the other.

glaciers in the high latitudes, can be explained by orbital forcing. As John Imbrie and his daughter Katherine (1979) have explained, the weak gravitational pull of the moon and the planets causes periodic variations in the parameters of the orbit of the earth. The scale and timing of these variations, known as perturbations, can be calculated mathematically. The earth moves in a slightly elliptical orbit: the eccentricity – the departure from a circular orbit – varies between 0.05 per cent, almost circular, and 6 per cent, slightly elliptical (Figure 2.4). The full cycle of variation is completed over a period of 100 000 years. The axis of the earth is tilted relative to the plane of the orbit, presently 23.5° (Figure 2.5). With a periodicity of 41 000 years the tilt changes between about 22° and 24.5°. There is a slight wobble in the spin of the earth, which causes the direction in which the axis points to change following a circular path (Figure 2.6). This is known as the precession of the equinoxes (Figure 2.7); it takes about 22 000 years to describe the full circle. The combined effect of these perturbations – known as Milankovitch factors after the Serbian mathematician who spent a lifetime studying the relation between planetary orbits and seasonal climates – is to cause changes in the amount of solar energy received at different latitudes over time. The effect on the total amount of energy received globally is not significant. But changes in the distribution of the sun's energy (sunshine) over the surface of the earth due to orbital forcing are important in providing an explanation for the cyclical climates of the Quaternary.

The three Milankovitch factors working together reinforce at times and diminish at other times

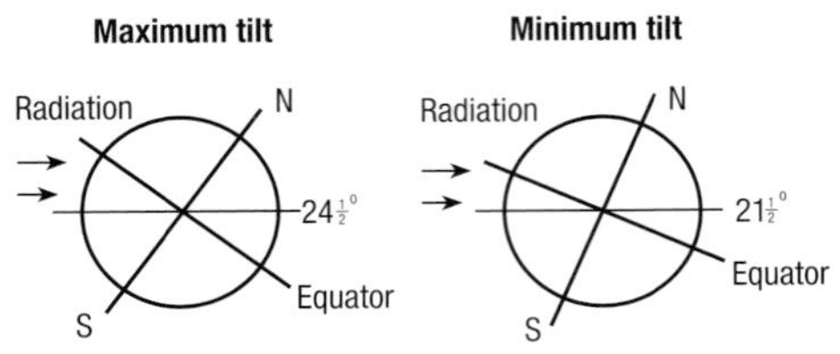

Figure 2.5: *Axial tilt of the earth changes with a periodicity of 41 000 years. A decrease in tilt decreases the radiation in the polar regions and conversely an increase in tilt increases radiation there. The effects of changes in tilt are more important in the higher latitudes.*

their individual effects. The greater part of the variance in Quaternary climates can be explained by the tilt and precession factors; eccentricity is a weaker force. Tilt affects the intensity of differences between summer and winter; moreover, changes in tilt have the most marked effect in the high latitudes. Precession, on the other hand, determines whether the northern or southern hemisphere is closer to the sun in summer and has a more marked influence on climatic change in the low latitudes. As a result of the different periodicities and different influences on seasonality, as they relate to latitude, the Quaternary climate changes in different regions of a continent like Africa, which covers a large latitudinal range in two hemispheres, were at times similar and at times opposite.

When continuous, well-dated sequences in the floor of the deep ocean became available for study, it was possible to test the Milankovitch astronomical hypothesis. Research has shown that climatic changes inferred from analyses of fossil shells and measurements of oxygen isotopes on shells are in accord with the periodicities predicted by the Milankovitch factors. This constitutes proof of the importance of the Milankovitch factors in explaining the pulse of the Ice Age. But the Milankovitch factors do not explain why the Ice Age began. For this we have to look to the positioning of the continents, the transport of heat by ocean currents and the elevation of mountains for the ultimate reasons why the earth was plunged into an Ice Age. The state of the earth would also explain why the beat of the Ice Age changed from an initial 23 000

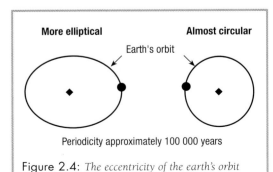

Figure 2.4: *The eccentricity of the earth's orbit around the sun. (Redrawn after Imbrie & Imbrie 1979)*

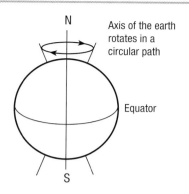

Figure 2.6: *Like a spinning top with a wobble, the earth rotates on its axis over a cycle of 23 000 –19 000 years. The direction in which the axis points when the earth is closest to the sun affects the length of the seasons. Known as the precession of the equinoxes, it has effects that are most important in the equatorial latitudes.*

in modes, the geologists Wally Broecker and George Denton (1990) have proposed a model. Their model emphasises the role played by ocean currents as they are driven by differences in the temperature, salinity and density of water masses and as they function like conveyor belts in distributing heat around the globe. Broecker and Denton suggest that there are glacial and interglacial modes for their conveyor belt system, with the Milankovitch factors acting to favour one mode over the other. The Broecker and Denton model, while not the final answer about the way these factors force global climates to change, yet carries the prediction that the change from one mode to the other can occur in decades rather than centuries or millennia. The result of such a rapid change from the present interglacial to a glacial mode would be catastrophic because it would throw the world economy into turmoil.

Quaternary climates in southern Africa

Southern Africa is dominated now, as in the past, by two weather systems. The frontal systems, generated in the sub-Antarctic, sweep like global windscreen wipers across the South Atlantic, flicking the southern tip of the continent in winter. They bring cold air and winter precipitation but pass too far south in the summer to influence the subcontinent. The second system is linked to the

–19 000 cycle of years prior to 2.8 million years ago, to the 41 000-year cycle and, some 900 000 years ago, to a 100 000-year cycle (DeMenocal 1995). At times, it appears, one Milankovitch factor has had a greater effect in the timing of climatic changes than the other factors.

There are suggestions that the Milankovitch factors may be linked to cyclic changes in the quantities of carbon dioxide, a greenhouse gas, in the atmosphere–ocean systems. The oceans are the biggest store of carbon dioxide. Carbon dioxide, taken up in the building of the shells of marine organisms, is removed from circulation when these organisms die and their shells are deposited on the ocean bottom. In this way the oceans cleanse the atmosphere. From air bubbles trapped in old ice layers drilled in Antarctica and Greenland, it is known that the carbon dioxide levels of the warm interglacial atmosphere are much higher than in the cool glacials. The publicity given to global warming makes us conscious of the importance of carbon dioxide cycling in the heating and cooling of the earth. We have still much to learn about how the Milankovitch factors regulate the carbon dioxide levels of the atmosphere.

The earth's climate system is both complex and finely balanced. It has shifted repeatedly from a glacial to an interglacial mode. To explain this shift

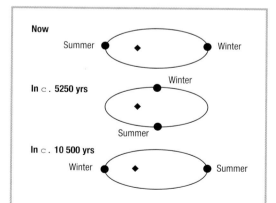

Figure 2.7: *Precession of the equinoxes in the southern hemisphere. In the current part of the cycle the earth is closest to the sun in the southern summer. (Redrawn after Imbrie & Imbrie 1979)*

circulation around the high-pressure cells, the South Atlantic high off the west coast and the Indian high off the east coast. The anticlockwise or anticyclonic movement of air around these subtropical highs is responsible for the larger part of the region receiving summer precipitation. While the fronts travelling over the ocean are not disturbed by landmasses and are reliable and predictable, the anticyclonic circulation, by contrast, is much more complex, affected as it is by the positioning of the highs in relation to ocean and land, waveforms in the upper atmosphere and interaction with tropical air masses. It is therefore less reliable and less predictable.

Several lines of evidence show that while under glacial conditions these atmospheric circulation systems may have increased in intensity but they did not move more than about one degree of latitude equatorwards. It was once proposed that under glacial conditions and colder polar regions, climate zones contracted in the lower latitudes. This held the prospect that the present winter rainfall zone of the Cape would have been displaced northwards as far as Gauteng and the Cape would have had a cold and all-seasons rainfall climate like Marion Island, situated as it is in the belt of the westerlies.

The westerlies are the major winds in our lower atmosphere and coincide in the southern oceans with the position boundary between the cold waters of the sub-Antarctic and the warm waters of the tropics – the subtropical convergence. By collecting cores of sediments from the ocean bottom, dating the sediments and determining from shell microfossils the relative numbers of sub-Antarctic and subtropical species present, we can map changes in the position of the convergence zone. Between the maximum of the Last Glacial and the present the displacement off South Africa was about one degree. The belt of the westerlies even under the extremes of the Ice Age was far to the south.

Complementary evidence that climate zones did not simply shift equatorwards under glacial conditions comes from the imprint of the anticyclonic circulation on the alignment of dunes. The central interior of South Africa is a sag in the crust, occupied by the sands of the Kalahari. In the arid core of the country these sands are mobilised as dunes by the winter dry-season winds. The winter winds

blowing around the anticyclone high-pressure cell trace a pattern that curves from northern Botswana through Namibia and into the southern Kalahari. The position of this cell under the coldest glacial conditions, when subtropical deserts worldwide expanded and wind speeds were highest, is marked by lines of now-vegetated dunes. These fossil dune alignments are clearly visible on satellite images of southern Africa and they show that the high-pressure cell, though larger, was displaced little more than a degree of latitude towards the equator.

Knowing how climate works, one can construct mathematical models that not only forecast the weather in the future but also run backwards and retrodict past climates. In the light of the many variables that have to be taken into account, the models, running on even the most powerful computers available, are very simplified approximations of the real world. Most efforts in modelling exceptionally long-term climate changes have been put into investigating how world climate systems have operated under contrasting glacial and interglacial conditions. These are known as General Circulation Models, or GCMs. The present state of

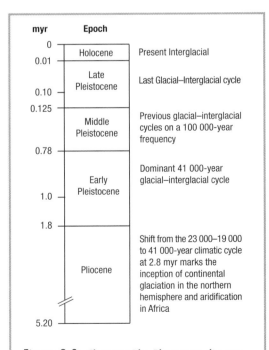

Figure 2.8: *Changing Plio-Pleistocene climates.*

development of these models allows some general predictions or retrodictions of trends in climate change, as they would have affected southern Africa. An example from one model is that under maximum glacial conditions the precipitation in southern Africa would have been reduced by 30–40 per cent. A reduction of that order would have made southern Africa very arid. Modelling climate change in the short and long term has considerable social and economic significance for us and much effort is being put into developing better models. To create confidence in models that predict the unknown future, they have to be able to simulate conditions known in the past.

The influence of past climates is recorded in the ground and in fossils of various kinds. From such proxy information it is possible to show the changes that have taken place on timescales of thousands of years. Archaeological deposits are a major source of such information. The best resolution is for the last 40 000 years, for which radiocarbon chronologies are available (Deacon, J. & Lancaster 1988).

In the last 5000 years southern Africa has enjoyed the most favourable climates of recent times. Temperatures fluctuated around the norm for the present warm interglacial period, and seasonal differences were marked. Precipitation in the summer rainfall area increased, reaching a peak between 2000 and 3000 years ago. These conditions are indicated by more water in pans, extension of forest and the range of forest animals, and the expansion of subtropical pioneer plant species. There were climate changes on a similar scale in South America and Australia in the last 5000 years: this suggests the forcing factor of the changes was the hemisphere-wide El Niño–Southern Oscillation (ENSO), which has operated in the present mode only since the later Holocene. High and low phases of ENSO account for much of the year-to-year variability in the climates of South Africa: for example, devastating drought was followed by floods in KwaZulu-Natal in the 1970s and 1980s.

The temperature optimum – the warmest episode of the Holocene interglacial – occurred about 6000 years ago when temperatures were 1–2°C above the present. Sea levels along the coast were higher by 1 m, indicating a correspondence between global warming and the freeing of some

of the waters locked up in the ice sheets. These may have been the hottest and driest conditions of the generally dry earlier Holocene (10 000–5000 years ago).

In contrast to the dryness in South Africa 12 000–5000 years ago, lake levels in the East African rift system and the southern margin of the Sahara were full to overflowing. To maintain these lakes at this level required an estimated 50 per cent more precipitation than occurs now. The cause of the eastern African and Saharan pluvial (or period of higher rainfall) was a stronger tropical or monsoon circulation. The strengthening of the monsoon circulation can be predicted by the Milankovitch hypothesis and was due to differential heating of land in those latitudes, causing hot air to rise and moist ocean air to be drawn in. The effects of stronger tropical circulation appear to have been felt in Central Africa as far south as Zimbabwe. In this period climates were very different in the various regions of the continent; the contrast was between a strong tropical circulation and a weak anticyclonic circulation.

Before 12 000 years ago, climates were cooler than the present and were at a minimum at the Last Glacial Maximum (LGM), 18 000 years ago, when continental ice sheets in the northern high latitudes reached their greatest extent. There were no glaciers, but frost heaving of the ground occurred, and frost-shattered scree of periglacial (or near glacial) conditions existed in the Drakensberg and the Cape mountains at the LGM. The climate was generally cold and mean annual temperatures were some 5°C lower. It was also dry and windy at the LGM, but amelioration of the harsh conditions had begun by 16 000 years ago. From this time some pans in Botswana and the Northern Cape–Free State acquired more permanent water, suggesting higher precipitation and less evaporation. By 12 000 years ago the shift to the present interglacial mode of climate was completed.

Significant climatic changes also occurred in tropical Africa between the LGM and the present but they tend to contrast with, rather than parallel, those in South Africa. Glaciers on the high volcanic peaks like Kilimanjaro extended 1000 m lower at the LGM, lake levels were low, the rainforest was reduced in extent, and the margin of the Sahara was some 600 km south of its present posi-

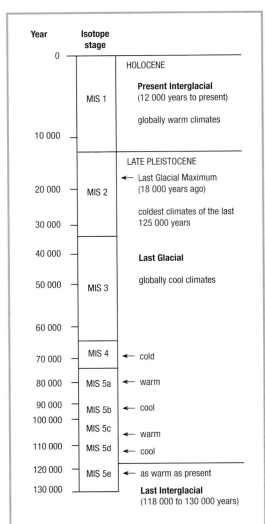

Year	Isotope stage	
0		HOLOCENE
	MIS 1	**Present Interglacial** (12 000 years to present) globally warm climates
10 000		
		LATE PLEISTOCENE
20 000	MIS 2	← Last Glacial Maximum (18 000 years ago) coldest climates of the last 125 000 years
30 000		
40 000		**Last Glacial**
50 000	MIS 3	globally cool climates
60 000		
70 000	MIS 4	← cold
80 000	MIS 5a	← warm
90 000	MIS 5b	← cool
100 000	MIS 5c	← warm
110 000	MIS 5d	← cool
120 000	MIS 5e	← as warm as present
130 000		**Last Interglacial** (118 000 to 130 000 years)

Figure 2.9: *The Late Pleistocene includes the Last Interglacial–Last Glacial cycle and the Present Interglacial is the Holocene. Marine isotope stages (MIS), numbered 1–5e and defined from studies of deep-sea cores, are measures of the volumes of global ice, at a minimum in the warm interglacials MIS 5e and MIS 1, and greatest at the Last Glacial Maximum in MIS 2 and in MIS 4.*

Tanzania to Chad.

During the Last Glacial there was a series of short milder episodes, called interstadials. The best evidence is centred on 32 000 years, the boundary between marine oxygen isotope stages (MIS) 2 and 3. There is an earlier interstadial that roughly corresponds with the oxygen isotope boundary between MIS 3 and 4, some 60 000 years ago. Well recorded in deep-sea cores are the interstadials following the Last Interglacial (MIS 5e at 130 000–118 000 years) and associated with the MIS 5c (103 000 years) and 5a (84 000 years). These were milder oscillations of climate in the early part of the Last Glacial, with MIS 4 corresponding to a period almost as cold as the LGM.

The trends that can be seen in the oxygen isotope record, itself a reflection of the amount of global ice, are paralleled in other measures of climate change deduced from cave sequences. An example is Boomplaas Cave near the Cango Caves, where thousands of small shrews' and rodents' bones accumulated as a result of owls roosting in the cave. Margaret Avery (1982) undertook the task of identifying and counting the numbers of each species of these small mammals present in each layer in the sequence. When climates were favourable there were as many as 20 species present, represented by many individuals. This is the same as saying the diversity was high. At times of less favourable climates fewer species were present and the diversity was reduced. From these data a plot of diversity indices can be made; the plot mimics the trends seen in the deep-sea record from MIS 5a to 1. The last time that climates in the oceans or on land were as warm as, or even possibly warmer than, the present was 120 000 years ago in the Last Interglacial. We still have little knowledge of conditions in southern Africa during the earlier cycles of glacials and interglacials of the Pleistocene.

Case study: Cango stalagmite

Siep Talma and John Vogel (1992) undertook a study of a stalagmite collected from the deeper part of the Cango Caves, the best-known South African tourist caves near Oudtshoorn. These deeper recesses, more than 1 km from the entrance, are not open to the public. However, for the scientist they present a natural laboratory.

A deep cave provides a constant environment:

tion. From 12 000 to 5000 years ago, the African monsoon strengthened, making this a wet or pluvial period when the underground water aquifers of the Sahara recharged and lakes filled from

4

• Sea levels •

Sea levels are controlled by the shape of the ocean basins and the amount of water available to fill them. In the Late Cainozoic Ice Age the amount of water locked up in the ice sheets varied, resulting in relatively rapid rises and falls in sea level. These are known as glacial eustatic sea-level changes. Changes in sea level due to glacial eustasy are registered by fossil dunes, beach deposits and marine erosion features, above and below the present-day sea level. The South African coast has been relatively stable for the past several million years.

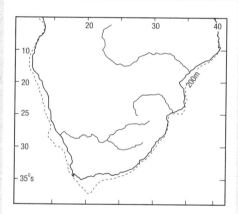

Figure 2.10: *The 200 m offshore contour indicates areas of coast most affected by lower sea levels.*

The sea level was 140 m lower at the LGM, 18 000 years ago, than it is today. This low sea level exposed much of the Agulhas bank so that between Cape Agulhas and Plettenberg Bay the coastline lay 100 km or more south of the present-day position (Figures 2.10 & 2.11). Along other sections of the coast with a steeper offshore profile, coastlines were displaced by shorter distances. Off Cape Point, for example, the

shoreline was displaced only a few kilometres south but False Bay was dry land. With the reduction of global ice after the LGM, sea level rose rapidly, reaching levels close to the present by 12 000 years ago and slightly above the present at 6000 years. Sea levels have stayed put at the modern level for the last 4000 years.

The relation that exists between global ice volumes and sea level means that should ice volumes decrease as a result of future global warming (there is evidence that this is already happening), sea levels will rise. Some parts of the world with large populations in low-lying coastal areas will be more affected than South Africa but some projections of a sea-level rise of 1 m or more in the next century would destroy many waterfront developments. Major cities of the world from Venice to London would be affected as would concentrations of coastal populations in countries like Bangladesh.

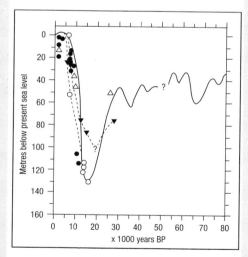

Figure 2.11: *A plot of radiocarbon-dated shells dredged from known depths offshore shows the ups and downs of sea levels on a scale of thousands of years.*

5

• Oxygen isotopes and deep-sea cores •

The oxygen isotopic analysis of deep-sea cores was pioneered by Cesare Emiliani and has been developed by N.J. Shackleton of the University of Cambridge and other researchers since the 1960s as an important tool in understanding the Late Cainozoic Ice Age.

The element oxygen occurs in three isotopic forms in nature. All three isotopes are stable (non-radioactive). The commonest isotope has an atomic mass of 16 (16 times the mass of a hydrogen atom); ^{16}O makes up 99 per cent of the oxygen in the atmosphere and the oxygen that is bound up with other elements. The other isotopes of oxygen have atomic masses of 17 (rare) and 18. Although the differences in mass between the lightest (16) and heaviest (18) isotope are small, any selection for one isotope over the other can be measured with the aid of sensitive instruments. Evaporation from the ocean, for example, will favour the lighter ^{16}O over the heavier ^{18}O isotope. As a result the water vapour that falls as rain or snow on land will be isotopically lighter relative to the ocean water. This has significance because during glacial periods in earth history, when large volumes of water were locked up in the global ice sheets, the oceans became slightly depleted in the lighter ^{16}O isotope. Marine

organisms like tiny foraminifers with calcium carbonate ($CaCO_3$) shells take up oxygen isotopes in equilibrium with the isotopic composition of the ocean water in which they live. The shells of many generations of foraminifers that have lived in the past accumulate in the layered sediments on the ocean floor. These layers of shells thus preserve a record, over many thousands of years, of changes in the oxygen isotope ratios of the ocean water.

Cores of sediments from the ocean floor are collected regularly by research ships. By analysing the oxygen isotope ratios in the foraminifers, scientists can measure the changing volumes of global ice between glacial and interglacial periods (Figure 2.12). The oxygen isotope ratios in closely spaced samples collected down the length of a core are plotted as a saw-toothed diagram. Marine isotope stages (MIS) numbered from 1 at the top, as in Figure 2.9, are defined from the peaks and troughs in the diagram.

Oxygen isotope measurements can also be made on terrestrial samples, such as land shells, cave formations (speleothems) and ice cores drilled in the Arctic and Antarctic, to reveal the natural rhythms of the climates of the earth and information about future global warming.

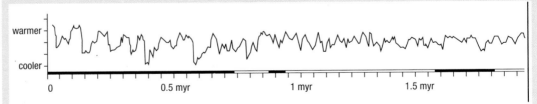

Figure 2.12: *The oxygen isotope record from deep-sea core V28-239 (after Shackleton & Opdyke 1976) shows the wiggles of temperature (amount of global ice) through the Pleistocene. At about 900 000 years ago there was a change from the 41 000- to the 100 000-year Milankovitch cycle of glacial and interglacial climates. The solid bars represent normal magnetic polarity and the open bars represent times when rocks like lavas and deep-sea sediments show that the magnetic north and south poles of the earth were reversed.*

the temperature of the air is the mean annual temperature, as the summer and winter fluctuations are averaged out. Today the temperature is a constant 17.5°C. Stalagmites, like the one analysed, are formed by rainwater soaking into the soil, percolating through the rock roof and dripping into the cave. In the soil zone, the rainwater takes up additional carbon dioxide from plant roots. Percolating downwards, as a weak carbonic acid, it is able to dissolve calcium carbonate in the limestone roof. The calcium is held in solution as bicarbonate in the percolating waters. However, in the chamber of the cave, the vapour pressure is reduced, dissolved carbon dioxide is lost and insoluble calcium carbonate is precipitated where the drips fall. In this way, at a rate of a fraction of a millimetre per year, a stalagmite grows towards the roof, with the oldest layers at the base and the youngest at the top, as in any stratified sequence. There are numerous stalagmites and other formations in Cango but for Talma and Vogel only one appeared suitable in diameter and length for analysis.

As the Cango Caves are a national monument special permission had to be obtained for the study to proceed. The stalagmite was removed from the cave and sliced along its length in the laboratory. One half was used to provide samples for dating; from the other half, a series of closely spaced samples was drilled along the stalagmite's length for the measurement of the carbon and oxygen isotope ratios (Figure 2.13). Radiocarbon dating was possible because carbon is present in calcium carbonate. Calcium carbonate minerals are also acceptable materials for uranium disequilibrium dating. This independent dating technique was used to check the radiocarbon chronology and to date sections of the stalagmite that are too old to date by radiocarbon.

A mass spectrometer was employed to measure the stable isotope ratios of oxygen and of carbon. Because temperature determines the isotope fractionation that occurs during precipitation as a result of the difference in mass of the two oxygen isotopes, one can use the oxygen isotope ratios $^{16}O:^{18}O$ in carbonates precipitated from water to calculate the temperatures at the time of precipitation.

Certain conditions have to be met to allow the calculation of temperatures. One must know the oxygen isotopic content of the water from which

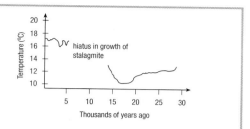

Figure 2.13: *Changes in mean annual temperature in the Cango Valley over the last 30 000 years inferred from oxygen isotope measurements of stalagmite samples.*

the carbonate was precipitated, and precipitation must have taken place in isotopic equilibrium with the drip water. Further, the stalagmite should not have suffered chemical weathering and re-solution by younger dripping water or changes in the ventilation of the cave.

In this study, Talma and Vogel relied on the isotopic composition of radiocarbon-dated artesian waters in the Uitenhage aquifer to provide an estimate for changes in the isotopic composition of the drip water back to 30 000 years, the limit to which temperature calculations can be made. The aquifer, a porous underground layer of sediments, is charged by water falling as rain in the mountains around Uitenhage. These waters seep into the porous layers at the edge of the aquifer and travel slowly towards the sea below thick non-porous clays. They are therefore not contaminated by younger surface water.

In sectioning the stalagmite it was evident from growth lines that the initial precipitation took place on the central 'flat top'; further precipitation took place on the sloping sides as the drip water ran off and evaporated. Restricting the sampling to the central 'flat top' areas ensured that precipitation had occurred under equilibrium conditions; this was confirmed by comparing plots of isotope measurements of oxygen against carbon at different growth lines.

The radiocarbon measurements place the LGM at between 15 000 and 18 000 years, when the mean annual or cave temperature determined isotopically was some 12°C, or 5–7° C lower than present. In his study of the fossil waters in the Uitenhage aquifer Heaton, working in association with Vogel and his colleagues, obtained estimates

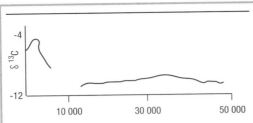

Figure 2.14: *The carbon isotope ratios in the Cango speleothem show a shift in the last 5000 years from C_3 to C_4 grasses growing in the valley.*

of a 5°C reduction in mean annual temperature for the LGM. The solubility of gases in water is temperature dependent and the measurement of concentrations of noble gases ('noble' because they are chemically inert) was chosen in Heaton's study because noble gases would not be affected by chemical reactions. From another study, of glacial deposits on the high mountains of eastern Africa, extending about 1000 m below their modern extent, it has been calculated that at the LGM the mean annual temperature there was reduced by 6°C: this value is close to that obtained in the South African studies.

The Cango stalagmite shows a break in growth between 14 000 and 5000 years but outside this range it provides a detailed palaeotemperature record to 30 000 years ago. Temperatures in the last 5000 years show fluctuations of about 1°C above and 2°C below the present-day mean. Although Holocene interglacial temperatures were constantly higher than in the Last Glacial, they were not constant. By comparison with those that occurred in the later Holocene and Late Pleistocene, year-to-year variations in mean temperatures recorded at weather stations in the country are small. We only know the scale of these past changes in temperature in South Africa from studies like that of the Cango stalagmite.

The stable carbon isotope ratios $^{12}C:^{13}C$, measured in the Cango stalagmite (Figure 2.14), provide as a bonus the opportunity to learn about changes in the local vegetation, primarily the types of grasses that grew in the soil above the roof of the cave. The drip water that built the stalagmite originally fell as rain and exchanged carbon dioxide with the plants in the root zone before percolating downwards into the cave. Grasses that grow under temperate climates, as in the winter rainfall area of the Cape, use the same type of metabolism to fix

Figure 2.15: *Collecting the Cango stalagmite.*

6 • Stable isotopes of carbon •

Carbon occurs in three isotopes, ^{12}C, ^{13}C and ^{14}C; the last is radioactive but the two lighter isotopes are stable. Isotopic fractionation – deviation from the ratios of the stable isotopes of carbon in the well-mixed atmosphere – is caused by the metabolism of plants. The South African scientist J.C. Vogel (1983) was the first to use stable carbon isotope ratios in fossil bones and teeth to learn about the foods animals were eating and, by extension, the vegetation on which they lived.

Carbon is a component of all living organisms but only plants are able to take up carbon from the atmosphere during photosynthesis and produce the organic molecules necessary for life. There are different metabolic pathways used by plants to fix carbon. The pathway used determines the isotopic ratio. Most plants, trees, shrubs, temperate grasses and marine plants use the C_3 pathway. Tropical grasses that grow under conditions of high summer temperatures, on the other hand, follow the C_4 pathway. Plants like succulents, adapted to extreme water stress, follow yet another pathway. Some plants like the spekboom are very adaptable and can shift between the C_3 and C_4 pathways according to growing conditions. In the food chain, animals like grazers and browsers live on the plant tissue of the primary producers, and other animals like carnivores and humans consume these secondary producers. Stable carbon isotope ratios in tissue like fossil bone can therefore be used as an environmental and dietary indicator.

One example of how this works is given here. Zebras are exclusively grazers: the isotopic ratios in their bones and teeth will indicate the proportion of temperate C_3 or tropical C_4 grasses in their diet because of the isotopic fractionation associated with the different metabolic pathways. Samples of fossil zebra teeth have been analysed from radiocarbon-dated levels in the Lesotho cave of Melikane. At present this is a summer rainfall area and C_4 grasses dominate the vegetation. The results show that 1500 years ago only 35 per cent of the graze consisted of C_3 grasses but this percentage increased to 75 per cent and 84 per cent at 20 000 and 35 000 years ago. This means that C_3 grass species, now growing on the cooler Drakensberg uplands, were able to grow at lower elevations in earlier times. The implication is that summer temperatures were lower and climates cooler. The results from Melikane can be compared to samples from another cave, Apollo 11, in southern Namibia. This is an area close to the boundary between C_3 winter rainfall areas and C_4 summer rainfall areas. Analyses of the carbon isotopes in recent and fossil zebra teeth found here, which were dated to 7000, 20 000 and 70 000 years, show only a moderate increase in C_3 grasses in the diet, from 36 per cent to 53 per cent. From these results John Vogel has inferred that the summer rainfall boundary was not displaced further westwards in the past.

Carbon and other stable isotopes used in imaginative ways are an important source of information about past environments and the diet of animals, including humans.

carbon in living matter as trees and shrubs. Tropical grasses that grow in the hot season use another metabolic pathway. The differences in the way carbon is fixed can be detected in measuring the ratios of the two carbon isotopes (see Box 6).

The carbon isotope ratios indicate that tropical grasses have increased markedly in the last 5000 years. This increase indicates higher summer temperatures and therefore more seasonal climates. It can also be associated with an increased component of summer rainfall. At nearby Boomplaas Cave, fossil charcoals show that, at this time, the thorn tree *Acacia karroo* invaded the Cango Valley. Like subtropical pioneer grasses, it requires more summer rainfall to compete successfully with plants that grow mainly in the winter season. This evidence for greater seasonality and greater summer precipitation from the Cango Valley, on the boundary between the winter and summer rainfall areas, adds to our understanding of climate change in South Africa. The climates of the last 5000 years have been different from any in the time range covered by the stalagmite (Deacon, H.J. 1995).

Climates and human populations

From year to year the global climate is remarkably constant and the mean annual temperature varies by as little as a few tenths of a degree. Even this low level of variability has a large effect on food production worldwide, determining whether there are surpluses or shortfalls and profits or losses. On longer timescales the global climate, as shown in the regional example of the Cango Valley, has been much more variable and so has food production from natural and agricultural ecosystems.

Until 2000 years ago, people living in southern Africa as hunters and gatherers were entirely dependent on which edible plants and animals were available in their habitats. None practised significant food storage. 'Farming' with fire was the only means of controlling the production of foodstuffs. Amongst modern hunter-gatherers, the limiting factor for local populations is coping with shortages in the scarce season, usually immediately before the onset of the rains. At greatest risk from food shortages are the young and mothers who are

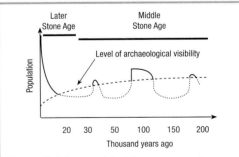

Figure 2.16: *A model of changes in population density in time. Fluctuations in populations inferred from the numbers of archaeological sites from different periods show a shark-fin pattern. Better-preserved younger sites have higher archaeological visibility.*

feeding their infants. In the short term, risks can be reduced by using alternative foods and extended visits to other groups. But in the long term, risks are less easily overcome. Under conditions where environments over large areas have deteriorated for extended periods, as has happened in the past, fertility levels have been lowered and mortality levels increased. The result has been a periodic thinning out of populations.

These contractions and expansions of populations can be correlated with the lows and highs in archaeological visibility. The concept of archaeological visibility is simply the ease or difficulty that archaeologists have in finding sites in a region in a particular time range.

Archaeological sites, or scatters of artefacts, mark places where people camped at some time in the past. Although it is individuals that make artefacts, these individuals live in local communities that are themselves part of a network of communities. In this way the distribution and dating of archaeological sites carry information about populations in the landscape. With the advent of radiocarbon dating, it has been possible to show that archaeological sites form patterns in time and space. Thus there have been periods when archaeological sites were widespread and other periods of thousands of years when large parts of southern Africa contained few sites. What all this implies is that the differences between very high and very low archaeological visibility reflect changes in population densities (Figure 2.16).

The most striking pattern to emerge from the archaeological record of South Africa is the expansion of populations in most areas, excluding the highveld of the interior, in the late Holocene or the last 5000 years. Sites of this time range are the most recent and therefore well preserved and most visible but they do represent a significant increase over those of the immediately preceding time. Prior to 5000 years ago the Karoo and much of the interior plateau in the early Holocene (8000–5000 years ago) were depopulated, as the distribution of radiocarbon-dated sites well documents. This pattern is consistent with environmental indicators that conditions during the last 5000 years were less arid and among the most favourable for human occupation in southern Africa in the Quaternary. By contrast, the earlier Holocene was relatively arid, and hence much of the interior of South

Africa was not habitable. During the latter part of the Late Pleistocene (60 000–10 000 years ago), populations in southern Africa appear to have been very fragmented and densities relatively low.

From the Cape to Zimbabwe, many cave sequences have a distinct break between Later Stone Age deposits, dating to younger than 22 000 years, and the underlying Middle Stone Age deposits, which mostly date from 60 000 years back to the beginning of the Last Interglacial (130 000 years). The Last Interglacial, associated with the main Middle Stone Age occupations, was warmer than the present. Both this period and the series of warm interstadials that followed it were times of population expansion in southern Africa, as in the Present Interglacial in the late Holocene. In older Middle and Early Pleistocene times, the patterning is less clear because sites are difficult to date with precision and populations appear to have been relatively small and largely confined to valley habitats.

In sum, the population history of South Africa, as understood from the archaeological record, is one of expansions and contractions that are relat-ed to environmental conditions. It is relevant that 6000 years ago, when mean annual temperatures were almost 2°C warmer than the present, well within the current predictions for future global warming, much of the interior of South Africa had been abandoned by hunter-gatherers. Although modern-day agriculturists armed with selectively bred crops cope better than hunter-gatherers, global warming, although not all of our own doing, may hold serious consequences for the population of South Africa.

The future can only be predicted by knowing the past. Uncovering the secrets of the past in the rhythms of ocean, land and atmospheric climates, as they affect our future, must be a priority for research. The worst scenario, by analogy to the temperature optimum of the Holocene, is that global warming in the future holds the prospect of extended droughts and lower crop production. Global warming is something that is happening now, in our lifetime, and not in the dim and dis-tant future.

CHAPTER THREE

Primate ancestry

Each year students in our undergraduate archaeology course on human origins were taken to the Tygerberg Zoo. Going to the zoo? For archaeology? John Spence, the curator, has managed to keep the zoo going over the years only through immense dedication and it is to his credit that it remains an educational asset and makes learning fun. The tour starts with the reptiles, which generate reactions of revulsion and fascination. Then there are spotted eagle owls and barn owls gazing at the group from their perches. They are a bit like humans in the position of their eyes in the middle of the face. And what do owls do for a living? They catch mice and insects at night, remarks one attentive student, and the discussion turns to whether in the deep, dark, murky past we got our 3-D vision from an ancestor that spent its time grabbing at tasty insect morsels.

Tucked in among the aviaries full of noisy exotic birds are cages housing different creatures. These are primates, our nearest relatives in the animal kingdom. The reaction is: you have got to be joking. That little animal with a foxy face, striped fur and a tail sticking up like a periscope? A relative? 'Ring-tailed lemur from Madagascar' says the label on the cage, and the talk is about whether they have flat nails like us rather than claws, apparently a good way to recognise a primate. But our trip is all about monkey business and monkeys there are aplenty in all shapes and sizes. This is called diversity and monkeys are clearly very diverse. Everybody oohs and ahs about the fist-sized marmosets with their bald faces and serious expressions, all the way from South America. We become excited about a lion-maned tamarin from Rio in Brazil, which is an endangered species. Zoos perform a valuable service in conserving species threatened with extinction in the wild. All monkeys have tails but some of the South American monkeys use their tails as a fifth hand. That's cool.

The procession moves onward past more caged monkeys, more familiar ones from the Old rather than the New World; and there are the baboon and the small, nervous vervet. The nostrils of their noses point downwards like ours, not sideways like New World monkeys; this makes them closer to human ancestry, the group is told. Still, perhaps because of their size, they do not look as 'human' as the funny-faced New World monkeys. It is all about common ancestry and inheritance. In explaining the idea of evolution the point is made that people are not descended from monkeys but that shared special features like the form of the nostrils show that long, long ago, there was a common ancestor for the evolutionary branches that led to monkeys and to humans. Someone asks how you can know humans are related to monkeys. Back comes the reply that Old World monkeys share 90 per cent of their DNA with humans. And on the same scale, New World monkeys share only 84 per cent while chimpanzees are a close 98 per cent.

Embarrassed laughs break out as the group lines up in front of a large new enclosure and gazes puzzled at the mayhem inside the cage. Chattering chimps are tearing around attempt-

ing to annihilate each other. Innocent of the intentions of an old male with puffed-out cheeks who entices the group to come nearer, some stand close to the wire netting and get showered with water. There are squeals and the wily old male goes back to the water trough to get another mouthful to spray at the unwary. Too many and too confined is the overall impression of the students, who discuss what being caged does to active, intelligent animals. Too hairy to look really human, and they have awfully long arms. The students tick off the now familiar primate characteristics of flat nails, opposable thumbs and soft pads on the fingers. And a few new ones: no tail, knuckle-walking and – watch out, here comes another shower of water – complex behaviour.

What's all this got to do with archaeology? Well, archaeology is about people, and to understand them we have to know where they have come from. This is the drift of conversation as the band of near-chimpanzees climb into the steel cage and drive off.

Evolution has not been taught in schools in South Africa, and is still considered a sensitive topic. At university level students are supposed to be mature enough to be exposed to the idea that humans may be related to other living creatures. This is very hard to deny when in the name of medical science animals are used for testing the safety of drugs meant for humans, and bone for bone the skeletons of other mammals can be matched with the human skeleton. The pet dog suckles its pups in the same way a human mother breast-feeds her baby; after all, they are both mammals. What, then, is dangerous about the idea of evolution? It is seen to conflict with the religious doctrine that humans were made in the likeness of the Great Creator. Darwin, the founding figure in evolutionary biology and a religious man, saw no conflict between religion and science. Indeed, there is none because they are about different truths. This is how Darwin expressed his thoughts on the matter in his famous book On the Origin of Species, *published in 1859:*

'There is grandeur in this view of life, with its several powers, having been originally breathed by the Creator into a few forms or into one; and that, whilst this planet has gone cycling on according to the fixed law of gravity, from so simple a beginning endless forms most beautiful and most wonderful have been, and are being evolved.'

This chapter introduces some wondrous creatures whose continued existence we threaten through ignorance and greed but who are legitimately members of the same club, the primate club, as we are. To study them is part of understanding ourselves. [HJD]

What is a primate?

In the Cainozoic, the last 65 million years, mammals have become the dominant class of large land vertebrates (backboned animals), making earth the planet of the mammals. Animals as diverse as elephants, zebras, hyenas, antelopes and humans are all products of the divergent evolution that has taken place in different zoological orders of placental mammals. In contrast to the diversity of placental mammals, the marsupial mammals, of which kangaroos are the best-known example, are dominant only on the island continent of Australia, and egg-laying mammals, monotremes, like the duck-billed platypus, are also found only there.

By the beginning of the Cainozoic, flowering plants, which co-evolved with the insects needed to pollinate them, were represented by many modern families. This marked the inception of a world different from that over which the dinosaurs had reigned; their extinction allowed the rise of the placental mammals. To have been born and nurtured through a placenta attached to the mother's womb has proved more efficient than starting life in a pouch as marsupials do, or as an egg laid in the nest of a monotreme.

The classification of biological specimens began in the eighteenth century with the publication of *Systema Naturae* by Carl Linné, whose name is usually written in the Latin form of Linnaeus. Although the Linnaean system has been developed and extended, it remains the basis of classification. The system is hierarchical and has rules for the naming of plants and animals, each of which is given a unique double name indicating the genus (spelled with a capital letter) and species (spelled with a lower-case letter) to which it belongs (Figure 3.1). This scientific name in its Latinised form, like *Homo sapiens*, is universal whereas the common name will vary from place to place and from language to language. It was Linnaeus who proposed the name 'primate' for humans and their look-alikes.

Humans are classified in the placental mammal order, the primates. There is a major division in

Kingdom:	Animalia (animals)
Phylum:	Chordata (spinal cord)
Subphylum:	Vertebrata (backbone)
Class:	Mammalia (suckle young)
Order:	Primata (primates include lower and higher primates)
Suborder:	Anthropoidea (anthropoids or higher primates are the monkeys, apes and humans)
Infraorder:	Catarrhini (includes Old World monkeys, apes and humans)
Superfamily:	Hominoidea (hominoids include apes and humans but exclude monkeys and lower primates)
Family:	Hominidae (hominids are living and extinct members of humankind but exclude the apes and other primates)
Genus:	*Homo* (true humans)
Species:	*H. sapiens* (all living humans)

Figure 3.1: Humans classified in a Linnaean hierarchy.

this order between lower primates, Prosimii (prosimians, meaning 'before the simians, or the monkeys and apes'), and the higher primates, the Anthropoidea. Grouped among the lower primates are the lemurs and bushbabies (loris), which do not particularly resemble people. The tarsiers, small woolly animals with enormous eyes and a very restricted distribution on islands in south-eastern Asia, are usually considered to be lower primates. Like the higher primates, tarsiers are haplorhines (with internally moist noses) and not strepsirhines (with externally moist noses like a dog or a cat), as are other lower primates. The anthropoids, on the other hand, include humans and their look-alikes, the New World and Old World monkeys and the apes.

Most primates are tree-living; their ancestors evolved in competition with other very successful mammal orders, like the rodents (mice and rats) and the insectivores (shrews). Characteristic of the primate order are grasping five-digit hands and feet, with flat nails on sensitive pads, forward-pointing eyes giving three-dimensional vision, and relatively large brains. Primates are social animals, living in groups, showing strong mother–infant bonds and relatively complex behaviour. These distinctive characteristics, it is assumed, were inherited from an ancestor adapted to life in the trees.

Other groups of animals share some of these characteristics although not in the same combination, and they are not necessarily tree-living. As Matt Cartmill, an evolutionary biologist at Duke University has argued, owls and cats for instance also have eyes close together in the middle of the face and they are nocturnal predators. Cartmill has suggested that the ancestral true primates were predators too, using their grasping hands to catch insects in the forest undergrowth and in the forest canopy. Others suggest that the shared primate characteristics may have to do with an ancestral habit of feeding on fruit that was difficult to get to at the ends of high branches in the forest. Recent comparative studies of different forest-living animals are helping to explain the significance of the basic primate characteristics. Not only are we, like any other animal, a product of what we eat but we were moulded by the way some distant mouse-sized ancestor lived in the Cretaceous forest.

Since the time of that ancestral true primate, the

7 • Why do we look like chimpanzees? •

Any objective observer will admit that chimpanzees look more like humans than any other animal. We can read their body language and hence chimpanzees are often used in advertising. Because they are embarrassingly like humans, advertisers use them to make us laugh at ourselves. The theory of evolution offers a reasonable explanation as to why humans and chimpanzees look so alike. Chimpanzees did not get left behind in the progress of evolution, however, and humans are not descended from chimpanzees. Chimpanzees and humans look alike because at some point in the past, perhaps as recently as 6 million years ago, they shared a common ancestor. At a more remote time, some 30 million years ago, both shared a common ancestor with monkeys. In evolutionary terms, monkeys, apes and humans are neither inferior nor superior to one another, just different. Although we may think of ourselves as the high point of evolution, evolution by natural selection has no goal or direction. There can be no perfection in nature, just endless variety, from bugs to humans. Like it or not, we are part of that variety – the human variety as opposed to the chimpanzee variety.

process of natural selection has operated to generate variations on the same basic primate theme. The differences between bushbabies and monkeys, or apes and humans, are all examples of these variations. It was Charles Darwin, the zoologist more interested in barnacles than primates, who introduced the concept of natural selection as the driving force of evolution. Darwin's lasting contribution was to show how evolution works (see Box 8).

Fossil representatives of true primates (Figure 3.2) are relatively abundant from the Eocene onwards. This was the warmest and wettest period of the Cainozoic, with tropical conditions and forest habitats extending to high latitudes. It was in these habitats that the lower primates represented by the fossil group known as the lemur-like adapids and a second group, the tarsiers and their close fossil relatives, the omomyids, were particularly successful. Until now, the main fossil finds have come from North America and Europe, regions that have been best explored though they may have been marginal to primate distribution at that time. Recent finds from south-eastern China and North Africa show that Africa and Asia were important centres for primate evolution and suggest that, by the early Eocene (55–50 million years ago), a third group, ancestral to the anthropoid higher primates, had already diverged. The common ancestor of these three divergent primate groups lived still earlier in time, probably in the late Cretaceous in Africa. Palaeontologists now know where and in what age strata to search.

Lower primates, the prosimians

Living representatives of one major group of lower strepsirhine primates, the lemurs, are to be found on the tropical island of Madagascar, where, apart from people, they have no other primate competition. The equivalent group found in continental habitats, in tropical Africa and parts of Asia, are the loris. The loris are all nocturnal because they

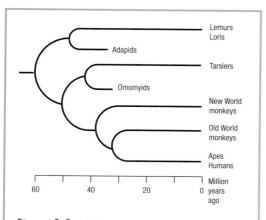

Figure 3.2: *The last 60 million years of primate evolution.*

8 • Theory of evolution by natural selection •

The theory of evolution by natural selection was first set out in 1859 in the book *On the Origin of Species* written by Charles Darwin. In the century and a half since the publication of this book, the theory, constantly updated as new knowledge has become available, has remained central to the biological sciences. Evolution is about change: Darwin was concerned with explaining how simpler life forms changed or evolved into more complex ones. He was impressed that organisms produced more offspring than could survive. The concept of natural selection which he introduced implied that in nature those individuals best suited to the total environment would survive and produce the most offspring at the expense of the less fit. Biologists are still exploring the ways in which natural selection works and helping us to understand what Darwin saw as the wondrous natural order of living things.

have direct competition from diurnal monkeys.

Madagascar is a fragment of the African continental plate that drifted away from the mainland perhaps 100 million years ago, before the evolution of the primates. One or more founding populations of strepsirhines were able to reach the island by chance or long-distance dispersal or via a land bridge. It is possible that they were transported on a float of vegetation washed out to sea from the mouth of one of the coastal African rivers. Such chance events were rare because monkeys and apes, which later became dominant on the mainland, were not able to colonise Madagascar. In the varied habitats on this large island, evolution has produced some 30 species in five families, and there were half again as many species at the time when humans first arrived on the island 1500 years ago. Extinction has taken, and is taking, its toll. The main cause is the destruction of the lemurs' habitats in the course of clearing the forest for agriculture and the use of fire to create pastures for domestic animals.

Lemurs range in size from mouse-like (50 g) to monkey-like (10 kg); body sizes in turn relate to differences in diet and behaviour. The smaller species (less than 1 kg) tend to be nocturnal; those of intermediate size (1–3 kg) are active at times in the day and night; and the larger species (more than 3 kg) are diurnal. All are vegetarians but insects are an important component in the diet of the smaller-body-sized lemurs. Fruit, flowers, young or mature leaves, tree-gum and bamboo shoots are all eaten by the mix of species, some of whom are dietary specialists while others are more generalised in their diet. As many as ten species may inhabit the same forest. Under natural selection, competition between species has led to the evolution of different activity patterns, ways of feeding and moving, and social groupings. Lemurs are unusual in that sexual differences in body size are not marked in any of the species; this may be linked to the fact that all the smaller species are solitary as well as nocturnal and some of the other species form pairs or pairs within groups.

Figure 3.3: *The lower front teeth of a bushbaby form a dental comb (top). The orbit shows the size of the tarsier's eye relative to the brain case (bottom).*

9 • Phillip's guest •

Phillip Hammel found a bushbaby on his doorstep. It seemed to be lifeless and he brought it to the Archaeology Department, where he was a student. An eyelid fluttered when it was laid in the sun to be photographed. It was rushed to the local vet and pumped full of medicine. It survived. Perhaps it had been kept (illegally) as a pet and had escaped. Whatever had happened thereafter, it landed on Phillip's doorstep in a state of deep shock. Until it could be handed over to Nature Conservation it became Phillip's guest. Bushbabies are attractive pets but Phillip soon learned that looking after a nocturnal animal, one that moreover moves by leaping and clinging rather than walking, has some disadvantages. For a bushbaby it is one step from the floor to the

Figure 3.4

pelmet above the window, and curtains are great to grab. Up and down, here, there and everywhere: befriending a bushbaby is not conducive to a good night's rest but this good deed was a better learning experience than any lecture or book.

Lemurs share common characteristics. They are vocal, making noises to announce their presence either to bond with their own group or to warn off others. They are also territorial and mark their home ranges with urine or scent. Most retain a dental comb used in grooming, which is formed by the lower front teeth projecting forward. Lemurs have a built-in capacity for night vision. In a special layer in the eye they have an equivalent of the yellow-lensed glasses which we use to see better at night. Lemurs share these characteristics with their continental counterparts, the loris.

10 • The species concept •

Linnaeus, the eighteenth-century Swedish botanist, devised a system to classify all living things. The unit of classification in the Linnaean system is the species. A species is a reproductive unit. Members of the same species can interbreed but are normally reproductively isolated from members of different species. This poses a problem for the palaeontologist for the obvious reason that fossils cannot breed. In classifying fossils into species or higher groups the similarities and differences in anatomical characters, or morphology, have to be taken into account. The task is made difficult because in some cases individuals of the same species may show marked morphological variation and in other cases individuals of different species may not look very different. Sexual dimorphism – the differences between the two morphs, male and female – is a further source of variation to consider. The difficulties of defining palaeospecies from often fragmentary and scarce fossils can lead to vigorous debates on details of the relationships between groupings of fossils. Such debates are an essential part of weighing up the possibilities and alternatives.

11 • Old World monkeys •

The Old World monkeys divide into two families. The colobus monkeys of the equatorial forests of Africa and Asia are leaf-eaters and their stomach is specially adapted to digest leaves. The other family is the cercopithecids. They use their cheeks as food pouches. This family includes genera that are arboreal and others that have become primarily ground-living. The vervet monkey (Afrikaans, *blouaap*) is arboreal, while the baboon is ground-living. Both these monkeys have a wide distribution in South Africa. Many more species of monkeys are found in the tropical latitudes of Africa than in South Africa. Like humans, the Old World monkeys have been able to range beyond the tropics and are now found from the Cape to Japan.

On the African mainland the loris equivalents are the potto and the bushbabies. The bushbabies, with their long hind legs and a leaping and fast running locomotion through the trees, are found as far south as subtropical South Africa. They have long tails and projecting snouts and their ears are large relative to those of monkeys, signifying a greater reliance on the senses of smell and hearing in their night-time activities. The Afrikaans name, *nagapie* (nocturnal small monkey), is apt but they are not monkeys. Bushbabies feed on insects and other small prey, the nectar of flowers, gum and fruit. Social groups are composed of closely related females and their offspring – small matrilineal groups that occupy a shared territory. Individual dominant males occupy larger territories and mate with the females of more than one group. As males leave their maternal group when they reach sexual maturity, they have to compete with other males to establish their own territory. This is how natural selection works to ensure that the genes of the males most fit to breed are passed on to future generations.

The potto is confined to the equatorial regions and rainforest habitats of Africa. Being slow-moving climbers, their hind limbs are not as elongated as bushbabies and the tail, not needed for balancing, is short. Unlike the bushbabies they do not build nests or form social groups. In these respects they are more limited in their behaviour. The potto and the other living prosimians from Madagascar, Africa and Asia are all important for the clues they provide about the diverse ways primates live, in a variety of body forms and with different diets and behaviour. The lower primates are not simply living examples of the early stage in the ancestry that we share with them, for they too have evolved special adaptations. However, comparative studies of

12 • Pioneer studies of baboon behaviour •

Two South Africans, Eugène Marais and Solly Zuckerman, were among the pioneers in the study of baboon behaviour. Eugène Marais (1871–1936) was a lawyer and writer who became a naturalist and studied baboon troops in their natural habitat. Solly Zuckerman (1904–93) trained as an anatomist and later became an eminent scientist in Britain. His interest began when he collected baboon skulls in Middelburg, Cape, and he chose to study the behaviour of a colony of London Zoo animals. Marais has been dismissed as a romantic who was not scientifically objective. In contrast, Zuckerman went about his study in a thoroughly scientific manner but the deviant behaviour of the zoo baboons reduced the value of his conclusions. Both, in their way, made a recognised contribution in showing something of the complexities of life in a troop. In South Africa baboons are hunted as vermin and captured for use as laboratory animals. They deserve better protection in legislation as animals with rights to 'humane' treatment.

the lower primates provide valuable models for primate beginnings.

The 35-million-year-old Eocene fossils of tarsiers are remarkably similar to the living form. They are nocturnal predators with a diet of insects and small vertebrates and are unique among the primates in not eating fruit, leaves or any plant foods. They have enormous eyes, each larger in size than their brain. Being specialised in diet, body form and behaviour accounts for their being little changed since the Eocene. Today they are the sole representatives of a primate branch, different from the higher primates and the strepsirhines. Once they were widespread, but they now survive only on a few tropical islands.

Anthropoids: the higher primates

In the late Eocene and in the Oligocene there existed monkey- and ape-like animals. The fossil evidence comes principally from the Fayum, now a desert area, south of Cairo in Egypt. But in those times tropical forests and swamps fringed drainage channels across a coastal plain bordering an inlet of the Sea of Tethys, a forerunner of the Mediterranean Sea. Some 300 m of fossiliferous sediments, dated to 33–36 million years ago, were deposited there. These sediments have been exposed by erosion in the floor and on the margins of a large pan-like depression. The depression is now many kilometres inland because of subsequent changes in the position of the coastline and of the drainage. Among the plant and animal fossils preserved are primates, both anthropoids and prosimians. Anthropoids can be distinguished from prosimians in a number of characteristics: for example, bone completely closes the back of the eye socket; the forehead is made up of a single bone, the frontal; and the jaws and teeth are adapted for powerful chewing. There are very early anthropoids in the oldest layers; we can see from their teeth that they fed on insects and fruit. Most of the higher primate fossils from the upper layers, none weighing more than 12 kg, can be grouped into two families. One family is the parapithecids, which were a monkey-like side branch. The other is the propliopithecids (dawn apes), which were like Old World monkeys and apes, and were the possible ancestors of the catarrhines.

The importance of the Fayum fossils lies in the fact that they provide the best evidence for dating the emergence of true anthropoids. This site records a time close to the divergence of the ancestors of the New World and Old World monkeys and apes.

There are three superfamilies into which living

---

13 • Distinguishing Old World monkeys and hominids •

Although grouped together as catarrhines, Old World monkeys differ from apes and humans, the hominoids, in being four-footed and having tails. Forest-dwelling monkeys have long tails, which they use to help them keep their balance when walking along branches. Ground-living baboons have stumpy tails, but tails nonetheless. Apes and humans lack tails. As a way of protection against dangerous carnivores and rivals competing for the same resources, catarrhines live in large complex social groups. This explains why catarrhines have relatively large brains and are very intelligent. Old World monkeys have a social organisation that is derived (or modified from the ancestral form). This is a matrilineal system where females stay in the group into which they were born. Baboons and their allies have added a rigid hierarchy of male dominance to this matrilineal base. Individuals in a baboon troop, male and female, 'know' their place. For apes and humans, who have a less derived social organisation, selection for larger brains may be linked to the continual need for individuals to negotiate a place in the community. Monkeys and hominoids have solved the stresses of living in large groups in different ways.

14 • New World monkeys •

The New World monkeys are found in the equatorial forests of South America and are mostly cat-sized creatures. The positioning of the nostrils is a characteristic that separates the New World monkeys (platyrrhines) from the Old World monkeys, apes and humans (catarrhines) in the suborder Anthropoidea. A further distinction is that New World monkeys retain three pre-molar teeth whereas the catarrhines have only two. The New World monkeys include the tamarins and marmosets, with claw-like nails, and a second group among which are the capuchin, squirrel and spider monkeys. All are favourites of zoo-keepers. The ancestors of the New World monkeys reached South America from Africa in the Oligocene by log-rafting and island-hopping across what was then a narrower and shallower Atlantic. In the expanse of equatorial forests of South and Central America, New World monkeys underwent a radiation on a more impressive scale than, but of similar kind to, that of the lemurs on Madagascar. As the New World monkeys evolved in parallel with Old World monkeys and apes in similar habitats, they provide evolutionary biologists with comparative models for understanding the workings of natural selection. Both groups faced the same problems of making a living with the foods available to them. Especially illuminating are the differences as much as the similarities in physical characteristics, like body size, length of the stomach, tooth form and social organisation.

anthropoid primates are classified: the Ceboidea (New World monkeys), the Cercopithecoidea (Old World monkeys) and the Hominoidea (apes and humans). In the beginning of the Miocene, the hominoids – ancestral in a general sense to modern apes and humans, which were to emerge later – were particularly successful in the equatorial forests of Africa. The success of the hominoids may have delayed radiation in the lineage of the

Old World monkeys, for the latter achieved their greatest distribution and diversity in the last 5 million years. The New World monkeys evolved in isolation in the Americas, much as the lemurs did on Madagascar. Of the three superfamily groups, the hominoids are central to any discussion of human origins.

Hominoids

The climates of the early Miocene (23.3–16 million years ago) were almost as favourable as in the Eocene, and the wide zone of equatorial rainforest provided habitats in which the hominoids prospered. As many as ten genera, ranging in body size from that of a vervet monkey to near gorilla-size, have been recognised in the palaeontological finds, mainly in deposits in eastern Africa. The best known are the fossils classified in the genus *Proconsul*. The genus was named after a captive chimpanzee in a Manchester zoo, called Consul, who, in the latter part of the last century, shocked and delighted his visitors with antics that made him famous. The scientific name for the fossils was proposed as a joke although the implication that the proconsulids were the ancestors of the chimpanzees was serious enough. The proconsulids and their Miocene contemporaries were ape-like in some characteristics of the jaw and teeth but they were four-footed and more like monkeys than living apes in the way they moved in the trees. They show none of the derived or special characteristics that link them directly to the ancestry of living apes.

In the mid-Miocene (16–12 million years ago) hominoid diversity decreased in Africa. Genera like the chimpanzee-sized *Kenyapithecus* came to inhabit woodland habitats as the extent of lowland forest in eastern Africa began to shrink with the Late Cainozoic cooling (Benefit & Mc Crossin 1995). The semi-terrestrial *Kenyapithecus* was once considered by Louis Leakey to have been a possible early human ancestor. It has thick tooth enamel – an adaptation to a diet of hard fruits – which is also found in orang-utans and humans but not in gorillas and chimpanzees, which feed on foliage and soft fruits. However, the post-cranial anatomy of *Kenyapithecus* is unlike that of the living apes; these share derived characteristics of the vertebral column and upper limbs, which point to descent from an ancestor that was a below-branch feeder. The straight back and shoulder joints that can bowl a cricket ball and play netball derive from that ancestor's ability to hang suspended by its arms. The ancestor was a *Kenyapithecus*-like ape rather than *Kenyapithecus* itself.

One new *Kenyapithecus*-like fossil found in 1991 by an American–French team of scientists (Conroy *et al.* 1993) comes from an area of southern Africa that has not previously yielded any Miocene apes. The 13-million-year-old jaw, classified as *Otavipithecus namibiensis* (the ape from Otavi in Namibia), was found in rocks discarded on a mine dump; a lower jaw and some limb bones were also discovered. The relatively thin cheek-tooth enamel is chimpanzee-like. In 1996 even older dental material was recovered from a diamond mine at Hondeklip Bay in Namaqualand on the west coast of South Africa. This is encouraging of the prospect, that as more areas of Africa are explored scientifically, geographical as well as temporal gaps in the African Miocene record will be filled (see Box 17).

The hominoids spread beyond Africa in the mid-Miocene with the progressive closing of the Tethys seaway between Africa and Eurasia. The present-day Mediterranean and Caspian seas are relics of this seaway, which had once been a barrier to the migration of land animals between the continents. But the barrier disappeared as the northward-drifting African plate collided with the Eurasian plate, creating a land bridge. Among the animals to migrate out of Africa were the elephants and the apes. Other species made the reverse journey in the faunal interchange. In Eurasia, apes known to science as *Dryopithecus* from Spain, France, Germany and Hungary, *Ouranopithecus* from Greece, and *Sivapithecus* and *Gigantopithecus* from Asia were widespread until 8 million years ago, when their habitats shrank with uplift along the Himalayan–Alpine axis. The near-absence of finds of fossil apes from Africa in the time range after 12 million years gives the Eurasian finds added significance. With the possible exception of *Ouranopithecus*, none would seem to represent the African ape–human lineage. As we shall see, the few living species of apes are confined to the limited extent of equatorial forests of Asia and Africa (Figure 3.6). Ancestral humans, like the Old World monkeys, responded to the shrinking size

Figure 3.5: *The long-armed gibbon.*

and lower plant diversity of the forests by successfully invading non-forest environments.

Living apes

In south-eastern Asia there are six or more species of lesser apes, the small-bodied gibbons and siamangs (10 kg or less), and the larger, more ponderous orang-utans ('men of the forest'). The lesser apes are thought to have evolved a number of derived characteristics like smaller body size and their arm-swinging, or brachiating, locomotion. The orang-utan has been linked to the Miocene sivapithecines (Box 15) but the facial characters that have been suggested to support this relationship are possibly ancestral rather than derived. The post-cranial anatomy of the sivapithecines is very different from that of the orang-utan.

The gibbons and siamangs are classified in a single genus in a separate family, the Hylobatidae. The hylobatids are found on the mainland from eastern India to southern China and on the islands of Java, Sumatra and Borneo. They are noteworthy on several counts. They mate for life and the social grouping, like the human family, is a pair of adults and their immature offspring. Their diet is primarily fruit although they eat some foliage and insects. Like all apes and humans they can only digest ripe fruit and they feed on soft fruits, the larger species

15 • The God apes •

Named for the Hindu gods Siva and Rama, important ape fossils have been recovered from the Miocene deposits (12–7 million years old) of the Siwalik Hills on the Indo-Pakistan border. They include a number of fossil species of baboon size and larger. Collectively they are known as the siva-pithecines. One of the sivapithecine species, formerly named *Ramapithecus punjabicus*, was suggested as a possible early human ancestor on the basis of finds of fragmentary jaws. At the time too much was made of too little evidence, and we now accept that the human lineage had no such early roots.

including more leaf material in their diet. Their small body size allows them to feed on clusters of ripe fruit at the end of branches reached by brachiation high up in the forest canopy. Gibbons use their hind legs to 'walk' on the ground and along thicker branches, keeping the trunk of the body upright; they illustrate the ancestral body posture that humans have perfected. Feeding is not a group activity but members of the family usually remain in close proximity within a defined territory and announce their position by calls. Once numerous in the forests of south-eastern Asia, the

gibbon finds its habitat is under threat from the demand for timber, primarily by distant first-world countries like Japan.

The orang-utan has been traditionally classified in the family Pongidae along with the African great apes. In view of anatomical and molecular biological evidence that the African apes are more closely related to humans than they are to orang-utans, some recent classifications place the African apes and humans in the same family, the Hominidae, traditionally reserved only for humans and their direct ancestors. The orang-utans would in this scheme be the sole representatives of the Pongidae. Still other recent classifications group all the large-bodied apes and humans, the large hominoids, in the family Hominidae. To avoid any confusion, the traditional classification is followed here because the informal term hominid (derived from Hominidae) is widely used to refer only to human ancestors.

Orang-utans, now restricted mainly to the Indonesian islands of Borneo and Sumatra, probably number fewer than 30 000 individuals. Whereas gibbons are fine feeders, very selective in what they eat, the large-body-sized orang-utans, with stronger jaws and thicker tooth enamel, have to be able to cope with coarser and harder shelled items in addition to soft fruit, among the several hundred plant species in their diet. They supplement this diet with small mammals and birds.

Orang-utans are the least social of the apes. A female and her immature young constitute the

16 • On being a giant •

Gigantopithecus, literally meaning 'giant ape', is known from the Miocene of the Siwalik Hills and in the giant form from the Pleistocene in southern China and Vietnam. The fossils indicate a gorilla-like body size. As in the case of the gorilla, large body size would have been insurance against predators but at the cost of its being a bulk feeder. This means feeding on a diet of plants with high availability but low nutritional value. Giant apes like gorillas and, by inference, *Giantopithecus* cannot afford the feeding time

to seek out ripe fruits when scarce.

Gigantopithecus has a more trivial claim to fame as it first became known to science from collections of teeth among the medicines of Chinese traditional healers. It has been speculated that stories of the Yeti, the 'abominable snowman' and 'big foot', refer to *Gigantopithecus*. It seems rather that human myths need weird and wonderful creatures, bogey men and animals. *Gigantopithecus* became extinct many thousands of years earlier than the stretch of folk memories.

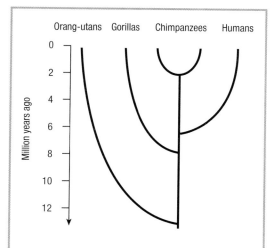

Figure 3.6: *The divergence of apes and humans, the large hominoids, in the last 14 million years.*

single form of social grouping. Males only associate with females during mating and, as the birth spacing is as much as eight years, this is infrequent. The asocial behaviour of orang-utans – a derived and not an ancestral character – may relate to reduced biodiversity in their habitats under conditions of Pleistocene aridity and a need for feeding space. A male commands a territory that includes those of several females. Because of limited visibility in the forest, he uses calls or 'songs' to announce his presence to females and potential male competitors. Infanticide has not been observed in the wild but such details of social relationships are difficult to observe among solitary apes.

Orang-utans in captivity perform well on intelligence tests and have proved adept tool-users, being even able to make stone flakes. The ability shown by the orang-utan to learn to make and use tools appears to go with another ability, self-recognition in a mirror. Orang-utans and chimpanzees recognise themselves but normally gorillas do not.

The lowland gorillas occur in two populations, one in eastern Zaire and the other in West Africa, separated by a distance of almost 2000 km. The separation may be of long standing because the two areas correspond to the main rainforest refugia of higher plant diversity, where rainforest survived even under drier Pleistocene climates. These larger refugia would last have been joined

some 2.5–3 million years ago; the genetic differences between the two populations are consistent with long separation (Morell 1994). The western population, or subspecies (*Gorilla gorilla gorilla*), is more numerous than once thought, comprising about 30 000 individuals, and is centred on Gabon. The second population (*G. g. graueri*) of some 4000 lowland gorillas is found in eastern Zaire.

The mountain gorilla (*G. g. beringei*) is best known from the studies of George Schaller, described in *The Mountain Gorilla* and *The Year of the Gorilla* in the 1960s, and through the work of Dian Fossey in the 1970s and 1980s. Her book *Gorillas in the Mist*, published in 1983, was made into a film with the same title. Mountain gorillas may now number less than 500. They occur in the lushly vegetated habitats of the volcanic mountain slopes on the Rwanda–Zaire–Uganda border region and are essentially herbivores, subsisting mainly on leaf and stem plant materials. In view of their abundant food supply, mountain gorillas have a smaller daily range and live in larger groups, up to ten individuals, than the lowland gorillas, whose diet includes more fruit. Lowland gorillas have a larger daily range, about 4 km, because they must search for ripe fruit in season, but when fruit is less available they eat more foliage. Large body size means gorillas feed mostly at ground level.

The social norm is a group made up of several unrelated females, their immature offspring and a dominant silver-backed male. The sexual dimorphism, or difference in the body size between males and females, is very marked. The larger males have to establish and keep their harems. Ritualised displays of aggression, like chest-beating and hooting and even fights, are linked to inter-male competition. Gorillas lack natural enemies and Schaller's studies promoted the view that gorillas were gentle creatures living in relatively stable groups. Subsequent longer-term studies, like those of Fossey, have shown a higher level of group instability and inter-male aggression, possibly the result of increasing disturbance of habitat and human interference. The displacement of one dominant male by another may lead to infanticide as the new male asserts his breeding rights.

When a female becomes sexually mature she leaves her natal group and chooses a mate with an

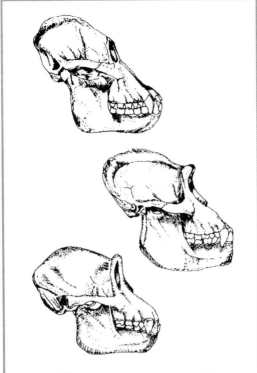

Figure 3.7: *Comparison of the crania of the orang-utan (top), gorilla (middle) and chimpanzee (bottom).*

established territory and the ability to protect her offspring. Although matrilineal groupings of one or other form are found in animals as diverse as elephants, lions, bushbabies and monkeys, the females in a gorilla harem are unrelated. Mature male offspring live alone until they can show their fitness by establishing their own harems. The uniform non-seasonal habitat in which gorillas live is the usual explanation of why they show a more limited repertoire of behaviour than the common chimpanzee. For example, gorillas have not been observed to use tools in the wild.

The chimpanzees are classified in two and sometimes more species. The 'common' (i.e. better-known) chimpanzee (*Pan troglodytes*) is found north of the Congo River, and the pygmy chimpanzee (*Pan paniscus*), or bonobo (a name of dubious origin), is found in swamp and lowland forests, south of the middle reaches of the Congo. The Congo River has thus acted as a barrier: the

two sections of a common ancestral population have diverged since being separated by the development of the modern Congo drainage system some 1.5–2.5 million years ago. Species formed in this way are known as vicariant species.

The Kyoto University primatologist Takayoshi Kano, a pioneer in research on the pygmy chimpanzees, has pointed out that while there is considerable overlap in size and a 15 per cent difference in body mass between the species, the pygmy chimpanzee should be better known as the slender chimpanzee. He has pointed to other differences, in coloration, facial hair, skull morphology and limb proportions. For example, the back legs of the pygmy chimpanzee are relatively long so that in knuckle-walking the body is held horizontal to the ground rather than semi-upright, as with the common chimpanzee. Some characteristics that distinguish the two species have to do with the pygmy chimpanzee's retaining more juvenile features in the adult stage. This principle is known as neoteny. Humans are an even more extreme example of neoteny, with the result that juvenile chimpanzees 'look' more human than adults of either chimpanzee species.

The common chimpanzee is found in a wide range of habitats, from humid forest to the drier forest–savanna margins. The distribution is from Guinea in West Africa (*P. t. verus*) to Cameroon–Gabon in West–Central Africa (*P. t. troglodytes*) to the Congo, Uganda and Tanzania (*P. t. schweinfurthi*) in Central–East Africa. This geographic range, like that of the gorilla, is so wide that the three subspecies form long-separated populations. In Gabon, their range overlaps with that of the gorilla and they may inhabit the same area of forest, even though they compete for some of the same foods.

The common chimpanzees are among the most intensively studied primates. While interest initially centred on their general social organisation and ecology, studies have come to include aspects like the use of tools and hunting behaviour and to focus on detailed comparisons of geographically isolated communities. As for the pygmy chimpanzees (White 1996), they occupy less accessible swamp-forest habitats south of the Congo River. They are more arboreal and are less easy to study. There are notable differences in behaviour between the two species.

Chimpanzees, unlike the heavier gorillas, feed and build their nests high above the ground. They are able to move or stand on their hind legs in an upright position; locomotion on the ground is, however, normally by knuckle-walking. They are primarily fruit-eaters but their diet includes a variety of other plant foods, the soft piths of herbs rather than leaves, as well as honey, termites and animals as large as monkeys. Because fruit ripens seasonally, trees bearing ripe fruit have to be sought. Thus although fruit is a higher-quality item of diet than most other plant foods, there are costs in being a fruit-eater.

The common chimpanzees meet these costs by being very fluid in their social groupings: their society is usually characterised by fission (splitting up) and fusion (coming together). Females and their infants split off and forage for food independently, though within the group territory. While males of both species remain members of the communities into which they were born, all-male parties are found among common chimpanzee communities. These parties are co-operative alliances of males whose role is to defend the communal territory in which individual females have established their own smaller territories.

Pygmy chimpanzee groups show more cohesion and sociable interaction between members than are found among the common chimpanzees (White 1996). The reason is that food sources are more abundant, less patchy in distribution and less seasonally variable. In this habitat it does not pay males to form 'clubs' for defending territories and attracting females, and male bonds are weak. Associations of females in communities are common and males are less dominant over females. Young females of both species disperse to other communities as they mature sexually, a characteristic common to gorillas. In human terms the equivalent is marrying out, or exogamy. This mating pattern was inherited from the common large hominoid ancestor and has the selective advantage of avoiding incest.

The famous primatologist Jane Goodall, who is well known for her books *In the Shadow of Man*, *The Chimpanzees of Gombe* and *The Chimpanzee: The Living Link Between 'Man' and 'Beast'*, recorded some 30 years ago chimpanzees using grass stalks or sticks to 'fish' for termites and leaves as sponges to mop up water to drink. This showed that mak-

ing and using tools were not unique to humans. These pioneering observations have been amply confirmed in many studies since. Perhaps the most impressive example is the nut-cracking behaviour of the chimpanzee community of the Taï National Park in the Ivory Coast, documented by Hedwige and Christophe Boesch of the University of Basle. The chimpanzees carry stone or wooden hammers and nuts, collected on the ground or in the trees, to a suitable root, which serves as an anvil, and the nuts are cracked open by pounding. The nut-meat is consumed immediately. This activity may go on for several hours a day for the four months of the year when the two main nut-bearing tree species are producing. At other times of the year nuts from other species are prepared and eaten in the same way but on a lesser scale. Nut-meat is nutritious and is an important source of food for the mothers and their infants. Sharing nut-meat binds the mother to her offspring for some eight years until the young chimpanzee has the strength and dexterity to cope for itself. Older juveniles learn the skills for cracking nuts through imitation. A mother may leave a suitable hammer on an anvil or allow a juvenile to crack the nuts she has collected. Nut-cracking is a good example of behaviour that is learnt in the social environment of the community and has spread from group to group. It is a behaviour that is only practised by some communities in West Africa and not by all chim-

Figure 3.8: *Chimpanzee.*

panzees living where trees bearing hard-shelled nuts are abundant. For Hedwige and Christophe Boesch the nut-cracking of this and other West African chimpanzee communities is evidence for social learning and a capacity for culture.

W.C. McGrew in his book *Chimpanzee Material Culture* has surveyed the range of about a dozen tools used by the different communities of chimpanzees in the wild. Not all chimpanzee use tools, however. The notable exception among the common chimpanzees is the Kibale Forest community in Uganda. Like the pygmy chimpanzees, they live in a habitat with plentiful food sources and this may explain why they do not have to rely on tools. Chimpanzees demonstrably share with humans the ability to design tools to suit a particular task; any difference in tool-making is one of degree, not kind. Humans have developed this basic ability: our aeroplanes and computers had beginnings in simple tools like hammerstones and termite fishing sticks.

There is still much to be learnt from studies of chimpanzees and, indeed, all living primates before the populations living in the wild are reduced to the few in nature reserves. Only those in zoos or private research centres have a guarantee of survival. Long-term studies of individuals and communities show there is considerable variability in behaviour. Each individual and each community has a unique history. It is this level of knowledge and understanding that is in danger of being lost with the destruction of their natural habitats.

Studies of primates in the wild have been complemented by studies of captive animals in research centres. Controlled conditions make it possible to compare the abilities or intelligence of different primates in solving problems. The reward for doing a task is normally some choice food item. Relatively large-brained primates like chimpanzees perform exceptionally well and are very intelligent. Attempts have been made to teach chimpanzees raised in captivity to communicate with ASL (American Sign Language), the sign language used by people with hearing and speech impediments.

Initial optimism that painstakingly tutored individual chimpanzees showed an ability to communicate using signs was dampened by criticism that the animals were responding to unconscious prompts from their trainers rather than showing any linguistic abilities. In spite of this criticism, research into testing and teaching communication between humans and chimpanzees has gone ahead. The most notable success story is that of a pygmy chimpanzee called Kanzi, which was detailed in *The Last Chimpanzee: Ape on the Brink of the Human Mind* by his mentor Sue Savage-Rumbaugh and the science journalist Roger Lewin. Kanzi shows an awareness of self, not least when he watches TV films with chimpanzee characters, especially ones with action and danger, or homemade ones in which he himself features. Kanzi's upbringing was different from that of his predecessors in that he grew up in a learning environment: his mother was in language training. He learnt to communicate the way a human child does. On a computerised keyboard he punches out abstract signs – symbols for words he has learnt – and he is able to make specific requests and indicate his intentions. He also shows comprehension of a number of spoken words. Chimpanzees lack the vocal apparatus to speak like humans because with the tongue wholly in the mouth cavity they cannot form consonants to separate vowel sounds.

Attempts have been made to teach Kanzi to make stone tools in a human way by using a hammer stone held in one hand to knock flakes from a block or core of stone held in the other hand (Toth *et al.* 1993). These attempts have failed miserably. Kanzi worked out that by throwing the stone on the cement floor of his room or, when put outside, against another block of stone, he could get small sharp splinters of stone that would cut through the cord around the reward, in this case a box of fruit. He was not interested in chancing bruised thumbs or fingers to please some humans in their experiment. He solved the problem of getting the reward in his own way. The humans went away happy because they thought stone splinters might provide the earliest evidence of stone tool-making, and Kanzi drew more immediate benefits. Kanzi has revealed the mind (or soul) of an ape, the holy grail sought by Eugène Marais.

Molecular clock

Animals that share a recent common ancestor will be genetically more similar that those that are distantly related. This is because mutations – spontaneous changes in the DNA that arise mostly when being copied in sex cells – occur at roughly similar rates in mammals. The process is somewhat slower for long-lived animals like humans than for small mammals like mice, which breed faster. In the 1960s, the Nobel laureate Linus Pauling suggested that genetic differences between species, accumulated with time through mutation, could serve as a biological clock to date the branching times of different lineages. One can give a scale for the clock by some palaeontologically dated event. A common practice is to assume the clock was set 30 million years ago with the divergence of New and Old World primates.

Genetic distances between the primates were initially investigated by means of immunological techniques, similar to those used in matching tissues in organ transplants, to analyse protein albumins. In 1967 Vince Sarich and Alan Wilson of the University of California, Berkeley, made the surprising finding that the African apes and humans may have diverged as recently as 5 million years ago. Until then palaeontologists, particularly those who had accepted *Ramapithecus* as a possible human ancestor, thought that humans and apes had diverged much earlier, perhaps 18 million years ago. Palaeontologists have thus been forced to reassess the status of *Ramapithecus* (see Box 15) in the light of the genetic evidence and new, more complete fossil finds, and they now accept the younger dating as a better estimate. The molecular biologists have won this scientific battle.

Advances in molecular biology have made it possible to use other genetic markers, like sequences of nuclear and mitochondrial DNA, to assess the relatedness among primates. Consistently, humans can be shown to be closely related to chimpanzees and gorillas and more distantly related to orang-utans and gibbons. Despite reservations about the precision of the molecular clock and in the absence of good palaeontological evidence, scientists have ascribed the branching of the gibbon line to the early Miocene (about 20 million years ago) and the separation of the orang-utan line to the mid-Miocene (about 14 million years ago). Estimates of the branching times of the gorilla–chimpanzee–human lineages are in the range of 4–10 million years. Some authorities, for example Bailey (1993), argue for a three-way split between the gorilla, chimpanzee and human lineages, implying that the three lineages are equally

distantly related. The majority view is that the gorilla lineage branched off earlier, at 6.7–10 million years (Ruvolo *et al.* 1991), and the human and chimpanzee lineages later at 4–6 million years (Stoneking 1993). The molecular clock has also been used to date the emergence of modern humans, as we shall see in Chapter 6.

Primate perspective

The first primates were one of many evolutionary experiments in different orders of placental mammals in the late Cretaceous world, which was still dominated by the dinosaurs. From fossil finds, from characteristics shared by living primates and from comparison with other orders that evolved in parallel, an educated guess can be made as to how the first true primates looked and how they lived. They would have been small, with a body mass probably less than 500 g. Climates were tropical into high latitudes and habitats forested, and they would have lived on the forest floor and in the trees. The increasing importance of flowering plants and co-evolving insects would have offered new opportunities for making a living. By analogy with small-bodied primates, such as the lemurs, the first primates may have fed on insects, fruit and nectar and have been nocturnal and possibly solitary. The characteristics shared by all primates, such as flat nails and sensitive pads on the digits, were established in the way the first primates moved and fed in the forest. These were not auspicious beginnings but they carried the elements of success because members of the order survived and diversified in the Cainozoic.

In the available fossils the ancestors of the lemur–loris, tarsiers and simians can be identified by the early Eocene (55–45 million years ago). In that period the lower primates, or prosimians, were the dominant suborder represented by many genera and were spread over much of the world. In the late Eocene (40–34 million years) the higher primates, or anthropoids – diurnal rather than nocturnal, and social rather than solitary – evolved separate branches, which led to New and Old World monkeys and hominoids (apes–humans). One indicator of the fact that the stem simians – the ancestors of monkeys, apes and humans – were diurnal is sexual dimorphism. Palaeontologists can demonstrate this in the catarrhine-like *Aegypto-*

17 • Gaps in the fossil record •

The richness of the fossil record of hominoids in the early–middle Miocene (23–12 million years) in Africa contrasts with the near-absence of fossils from this continent dating from 12–4 million years ago. The apparent gap in the African record is simply related to available exposures of sediments of the right geological age. The preservation of fossils is a chance affair, depending on rapid burial in ground that is not too acid to destroy bone, and then on re-exposure by erosion so that the finds can be made. Very few of the animals that have lived at any one time become preserved after death as fossils.

Many important find sites occur along the length of the rift valley in eastern Africa, because different episodes of rifting have created basins in which fossils have become buried and later re-exposed for palaeontologists to examine. There are sediments containing fossils that still lie buried and others that have eroded away so that their fossil content has been lost. Fossil evidence is not available on demand. Science can help in suggesting areas for search where fossils of the appropriate age may be found. There is a continuing effort to fill the gaps in the record, using advanced techniques like satellite images of earth structures so as to indicate likely locations. This has to be followed by systematic search on the ground. Looking for the proverbial needle in the haystack, the searchers use the clues of a fragment of skull bone or tooth to locate specimens. Good anatomical knowledge rather than luck is the key ingredient for success.

pithecus from the late Eocene at sites like Fayum. Although the oldest-known fossil remains of monkeys in the New World date from the late Oligocene (25 million years), long-distance dispersal of their ancestors from Africa would have occurred much earlier.

In the late Oligocene and the Miocene, ancestral apes diversified: they were able to inhabit most of Africa and spread to Europe and Asia. In the late Miocene (10–5.2 million years ago) suitable habitats for hominoids decreased in number or were fragmented as a result of changes in physical geography, glaciation of Antarctica, uplift of mountain chains and the closure of the seaway through the Mediterranean. This set the stage for the radiation of the Old World monkeys. It was at this time too that the last common ancestor of the gorillas, chimpanzees and humans lived in Africa.

This ancestor would have been an arboreal forest creature that was hairy, standing no more than 1 m high, small-brained and looking more like a pygmy chimpanzee than any person walking the streets of Cape Town or New York. Adrienne Zihlman (Zihlman *et. al.* 1978) in particular has argued that the pygmy chimpanzee is a good model for the last common ancestor between the apes and humans. It would have been a social creature living in a group for protection and subject to all the demands that group-living places on the individual.

The pattern common to gorilla and chimpanzee societies is for males to remain in their natal groups and for females to disperse. In multi-male groups of common chimpanzees, males may establish alliances and dominance hierarchies, and defend communal territories with the food resources to attract females. The females in these groups are unrelated, and to gain acceptance they have to be tolerant of others. By contrast, through alliances with other males and strong individual bonds with their mothers, the males are more dominating and aggressive. This basic social pattern, inherited by apes and humans from the last common ancestor, is expressed in a more extreme form among the strongly male-dominated common chimpanzee communities than among the more sociable pygmy chimpanzees. Female associations formed to counter male dominance are observed among the latter. In *Demonic Males: Apes and the Origins of Human Violence*, Richard Wrangham and Dale Peterson argue that human violence is rooted in the Miocene, and draw heavily on the evidence for violent encounters observed among the common chimpanzee at Gombe. It is possible, as Adrienne Zihlman (1996) argues, that the pygmy chimpanzee, being more concerned with love than war, provides a better model than the common chimpanzee for the behaviour of the last common ancestor of apes and humans.

Since the Miocene, habitats have changed. The equatorial forests of Africa are not as rich in species as the equivalent forests of the Amazon or Malaysia and the biodiversity of all rainforests has decreased, making them poorer habitats. Although continuing to occupy these seasonally uniform equatorial habitats as frugivores, the large-bodied hominoids have been forced to become more terrestrial. For the human lineage the shift to ground-living, in more seasonal and open habitats, required a different set of adaptations. This had consequences for the way we move, sit and stand, for what we eat, and how we look, think and behave. These are the characteristics that make humans what they are and different from the apes. Without examples of living apes and other primates or knowledge of the fossil record it would be impossible to understand in which precise ways humans are different. This is

CHAPTER FOUR

Human beginnings

One of the kindest people we have met was also one of the 'three wild men' identified by Robert Ardrey in his book African Genesis. *They were all 'wild' in the enthusiasm they showed for their mission to track down the origins of humankind. Robert Broom and Louis Leakey were two of them and the mild and generous third was Raymond Dart. Completely out of character, Raymond Dart came up with the most bloodthirsty scenario for human origins. As Ardrey saw it, Dart was suggesting that the first human-like creatures had the mark of Cain because they were killers not only of antelope but also of baboons and their own kind. But the associations of fossil bones in the underground solution caverns or caves on which Dart based his 'killer' scenario can be explained better in other ways: it turns out that those human-like creatures were the innocent victims and not the real killers. Killing was not an original sin that burdened human beginnings.*

Ardrey's 'wild men' were full of ideas, some dead wrong like this example, but others brimming with insight. There is no denying Dart's insights. In 1924, he identified one of the most important hominid fossils ever found and recognised its importance. This find, made in a chance collection of bones from a remote mine at Taung, showed that it was possible to learn about human beginnings from the fossil record. It also focused attention on Africa as the birthplace of humankind.

In a paper published in 1925 in the scientific journal Nature, *Dart announced the find. In spite of the florid tooth and nail (or claw) prose, he argued for predation by dangerous beasts as driving selection for smarter (bigger-brained) ancestors. The importance of living in large protective groups to avoid being eaten is still debated among scientists interested in the emergence of humankind. Through his insight Dart was an initiator of this debate. Dart wrote:*

'In anticipating the discovery of the true links between apes and man in tropical countries, there has been a tendency to overlook the fact that, in luxuriant forests of the tropical belts, Nature was supplying with profligate and lavish hand an easy and sluggish solution, by adaptive specialization, of the problem of existence in creatures so well equipped mentally as living anthropoids are. For the production of man a different apprenticeship was needed to sharpen the wits and the higher manifestations of intellect – a more open veldt country where competition was keener between swiftness and stealth, and adroitness of thinking and movement played a preponderating role in the preservation of the species. Darwin has said "no country in the world abounds in a greater degree with dangerous beasts than Southern Africa," and, in my opinion, Southern Africa, by providing a vast open country with occasional wooded belts and a relative scarcity of water, together with a fierce and bitter mammalian competition, furnished a laboratory such as was essential to this penultimate phase in our evolution.' [HJD]

What makes humans different?

Humans differ from apes in some obvious ways, in being two-legged (bipedal) and in having naked skins. They also grow up slower, develop larger brains and live for a longer time (Hill 1993). It is important to appreciate that these differences have come about through natural selection: humans have become different and did not start out as a new kind of being. They have evolved their own unique recipe for life.

The end-Miocene (6 million years ago) date ascribed to the split between chimpanzee and human lineages is broadly contemporary with a period of global climatic change marked by the formation of the West Antarctic ice sheet. Strong selection – a species turnover pulse, at that time – could account for the lineage split. Yves Coppens, the eminent French palaeoanthropologist, has also linked the emergence of a separate human lineage to environmental changes but more specifically to those caused by the earth movements that formed the rift valleys and pushed up the eastern African landscape (Figure 4.2). The oldest-known fossils of bipedal ancestors, from earlier than 4 million years ago, have been found in the eastern rift valley deposits in northern Tanzania, Kenya and Ethiopia. Eastern Africa was the probable centre of human evolution.

Climate changes and earth movements may have contributed to the emergence of a human lineage by fragmenting the Miocene forest habitat of the last common ancestor. Vicariance is a term used to describe the division of an ancestral population by barriers, physical or ecological, and vicariance in a fragmented habitat is a plausible explanation as to why apes and humans diverged. Gorillas, chimpanzees and humans are vicariants, variations on the same theme brought about through separation. In the previous chapter it was suggested that the chimpanzees represent two vicariant species. Impressed by their close genetic relationship to chimpanzees, Jared Diamond has termed humans the third chimpanzee. Vicariance in the end-Miocene may explain why human DNA differs so little from that of the common and pygmy chimpanzees.

One of the fundamental differences between apes and humans is locomotion, the way of getting about. The last common ancestor would have been

Figure 4.1: *Monkeys are quadrupedal, apes are knuckle-walkers and humans are bipedal.*

capable of climbing with the body held upright, swinging the arms, and hanging by the arms below branches. Monkeys, by contrast, are quadrupedal, and walk on all fours on top of the branches. In becoming more terrestrial and having to move on the ground, the African great apes have developed a semi-upright, knuckle-walking type of quadrupedal locomotion. On the other hand, humans have become dedicated bipeds. Animals move faster on four feet than on two on the ground, and bipedalism is the unusual option. Bipedalism retains the ancestral way in which the body was held hanging vertically in the trees. However, in

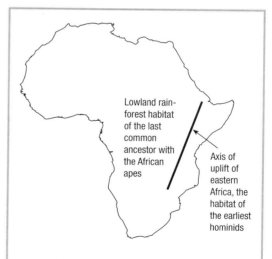

Lowland rain-forest habitat of the last common ancestor with the African apes

Axis of uplift of eastern Africa, the habitat of the earliest hominids

Figure 4.2: *Fragmentation of the habitat of the last common ancestor through uplift and climatic change at the close of the Miocene explains the divergence of early hominids and African apes.*

adapting to walking there have been major changes in the human skeleton to strengthen the lower limbs.

Long hours of observation of chimpanzees by Kevin Hunt of the Peabody Museum, Harvard University, has shown that 84 per cent of the incidences of bipedalism occur when feeding. This is strong circumstantial evidence that selection for bipedalism was related to the posture adopted when gathering fruit and moving between fruiting trees. Hunt makes an important distinction between an initial stage, lasting some millions of years, of 'postural bipedalism' and a second stage of 'locomotory bipedalism', the ability to walk with a striding gait rather than a waddle, and to run and jump. Postural bipedalism was a compromise between retaining an ability to climb in the trees for shelter and protection, and feeding at ground level. The progression from the occasional bipedalism, which living apes retain, to postural bipedalism can be detected in fossils in the shape of the pelvis. One of the bones of the pelvis, the iliac, is much shorter in bipeds than in knuckle-walkers. As walking on the hind legs places unique stresses on the knee joint and the foot bones, the form of these bones where preserved provides conclusive proof of bipedalism. The earliest bipeds, at some 4 million years, would fit Hunt's category of postural bipeds: their long fingers aid climbing and their long toes make a modern striding gait impossible.

At 1.6 million years ago, ancestral humans were fully bipedal like us. Selection for locomotory bipedalism may have been driven by the challenges of occupying open habitats in what were then expanding savannas. The benefits of full bipedalism lie in freeing the arms for carrying food and young, and in freeing the hands for manipulating artefacts. Some of the advantages of bipedalism are highlighted by debates on whether the male role in carrying food to feed the female, burdened with dependent infants, was more significant in selection for bipedalism than the female's need to use her arms to carry infants. Other reasons suggesting why bipedalism may have given a selective advantage are that it allows a head-up view to spot dangerous predators and to track and follow scavengers like vultures to food sources.

Peter Wheeler, the English physiologist, has offered further reasons for the adaptive advantages of locomotory bipedalism. Central to his argument

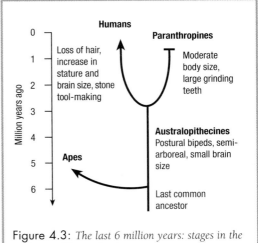

Figure 4.3: *The last 6 million years: stages in the evolution of humankind.*

is that an upright creature presents a smaller target for the sun's rays, which cause heat stress. A further element of his argument is that moving on two legs over longer distances generates less heat in the muscles than moving on four legs. Bipedalism became of particular importance in the course of evolution, as the heat-sensitive organ, the brain, increased in volume. Raising the brain higher above the ground, and thus in the zone of higher wind speeds, enhanced the cooling effects. Then again, humans have only vestigial hair on certain parts of the body. According to Wheeler the loss of long body hair developed as a way of increasing the efficiency of cooling the body, including the brain, by allowing sweat to evaporate from the skin. One consequence of the loss of hair was that the infant had to be carried on the hip and supported by an arm rather than clinging to the mother's fur. This was part of the price to pay for becoming fully bipedal and having an abnormally large brain.

Bipedalism promoted changes to the soft as well as bony tissues of the body. Soft tissues do not fossilise but we can infer that upright posture may be related to sexual displays, like enlarged female breasts and protruding male penises, which are not shared with knuckle-walking apes and four-legged monkeys. Male and female sexual displays in turn relate to the evolution of sexual behaviour. In the human female ovulation is concealed and there is not the obvious swelling of the genitalia that females of many primate species show when they are on heat. Concealed ovulation is found in other species of primates. The advantage it offers is in reducing infanticide, for a male cannot be certain that any offspring is not his. The male also derives the added assurance of parenthood if he belongs to a species that forms pairs as humans do. This is known as pair bonding.

The adoption of bipedalism was a pre-adaptation for later selection for large brain size. This increase in the brain relative to body size is an evolutionary trend in the mammals and has been most pronounced in monkeys, apes and humans. The part of the brain that expanded is the neocortex, the 'new' covering layer. In mammals the neocortex envelops the inner brain, which was inherited from the common mammal–reptile ancestor. In most mammals the neocortex makes up a third of the volume of the brain but in baboons it is 60 per cent, in chimpanzees it is 70 per cent and in humans it is 80 per cent.

Robin Dunbar (1992, 1995) has established that there is a direct relationship between the volume of the neocortex and group size in primates. Sociality – living in large groups, as monkeys, chimpanzees and humans do – has an advantage in protection. However, there are costs in terms of the squabbles and scrambling for position that arise in large groups. All primates are capable of intentional deceptions (De Waal 1992) and cunning ploys, if not outright cheating, to manipulate their worlds and they put their brains to use in outsmarting their fellows.

From their studies of vervet troops in Kenya, Robert Seyfarth and Dorothy Cheney (1992) have suggested that while monkeys have an acute awareness of social position, they lack a theory of mind. This is the ability to know and act on what they think is the emotional state and knowledge of another. Chimpanzees and humans with a less derived social structure than monkeys, such as baboons, need all the social manipulative skills they can muster for group living. Chimpanzees have a well-developed sense of self, as the mirror test shows. What needs research is whether, in contrast to monkeys, they possess the human equivalent of the sense of other, a theory of mind. Either way, the prime reason for the evolution of the large human brain was social rather than economic. It involved humans getting on with each other rather than getting more food.

In chimpanzees the adult brain is twice as large as that of the new-born infant whereas in humans there is a three- to four-fold increase in brain size by adulthood. Strong selection for the large human brain is evident only in the last 2 million years, long after evidence emerges for bipedalism. There is a physical limit on the size of the brain at birth because the head of the foetus has to pass through the birth canal of the mother – the opening in the pelvis modified for bipedalism. The foetus does this by performing a half-twist to avoid getting the head and shoulders stuck and greets the world helpless and needing parenting. Increase in brain size was only possible through the development of social behaviour that allowed both parents to be involved in rearing offspring over the lengthened period of dependency. This is where pair bonding becomes important.

The brain is an expensive organ of the body to

Species	Age (myr)	Region	Site(s)
Ardipithecus ramidus	4.5	E. Africa	Awash River
Australopithecus anamensis	4.1–3.9	E. Africa	Turkana
Australopithecus afarensis	3.8–3.0	E. Africa	Hadar, Laetoli
Australopithecus africanus	3.0–2.5	S. Africa	Gauteng, Taung
Paranthropus aethiopicus	2.5	E. Africa	Turkana
Paranthropus robustus	2.0–1.0	S. Africa	Gauteng
Paranthropus boisei	2.2–1.0	E. Africa	Olduvai, Turkana
Homo spp. (species)	2.5–0	World	—

Figure 4.4: *A listing of hominid fossil species, their age range and distribution.*

maintain. The way humans have met this cost is by having what is termed a cheap gut. Animals that eat low-quality foods, like leaves, from which it is difficult to extract life-sustaining energy, need long intestines in their gut. By having a short or cheap gut, essentially one that can only process high-quality foods, humans have been able to afford the costs of larger brains (Milton 1993). The earliest stages of human evolution were played out in fruit-rich woodlands. Dispersal into new and more open habitats, as environmental conditions changed, meant that more use had to be made of other food sources to maintain a quality diet. Chimpanzees eat some small animals and a wide range of plants but remain dependent on the availability of ripe fruit as the high-quality item in their diet. Under more seasonal climates in less predictable environments where fruit was not as abundant, early humans, some 2.5 million years ago, responded by increasing their reliance on meat and fat. It is generally assumed that becoming proficient stone tool-makers was directly linked to the need to cut into animal carcasses and to break open marrow-rich bones.

What makes humans unique is the evolution of a mix of characteristics, none unique but all in a unique combination. The initial stage (Figure 4.3 & Figure 4.4) in human evolution is documented in the fossil record by small-bodied and small-brained bipeds, which are known as the australopithecines. Popularly dubbed man-apes or ape-men, they are extinct representatives of humanity; in their own right they were an evolutionary success. Knowledge about the australopithecines was first developed in South Africa and their discovery is one of the major achievements of South African science. The australopithecines were ancestral to two branches of humanity that emerged about 2.5 million years ago. One branch includes all species classified in the genus *Homo*, and they are the subject of following chapters. The other branch marked the evolution of a kind of near-humans rather than ape-men, known to science as the paranthropines, from their classification in the genus *Paranthropus*. The paranthropines, also called robust australopithecines and considered by some to be an australopithecine species, were an evolutionary experiment that took a different course. In the paranthropine lineage, large grinding teeth show a dietary specialisation that is not

evident in the *Homo* branch. Like the australopithecines they retained the ancestral chimpanzee-sized body while humans increased in stature. Although the paranthropines evolved in parallel with the direct ancestors of modern humans and were immensely intelligent creatures with brains larger than any living apes, they became extinct about 1 million years ago. It is convenient to discuss the paranthropines along with the australopithecines in this chapter because their remains were initially discovered at the same set of sites though in younger layers.

Discovery of the australopithecines and paranthropines

The name *Australopithecus africanus* was given to a fossil discovered in 1924 in the Buxton limestone quarry near Taung, 130 km north of Kimberley (Tobias 1984). The name means 'southern ape' and it was coined by Raymond Dart in 1925 when he was Professor of Anatomy in the Medical School at the University of the Witwatersrand. Dart, who was a graduate of the universities of Queensland and Sydney, and who had furthered his education in England, developed a research interest in the evolution of the primate brain (Dugard 1993). It was because of this interest that he was shown a fossil baboon skull that had been recovered from the infilling of an underground cave exposed in the quarry. Reasoning that the lime-rich deposit could preserve human fossils, as was the case with the finds made in 1921 at Kabwe (Broken Hill) in Zambia, Dart asked a geological colleague, R.B. Young, to visit the site. Fortunately other fossils had also been saved and these were sent to Dart for study.

Among the material Dart received were two natural casts of the interiors of skulls. The smaller one was of a baboon-sized brain but the second was appreciably larger and comparable in size to the brain of an ape. The larger cast could be joined to a cemented block in which a broken lower jaw was visible. Careful chipping away of the cemented lime of the block revealed, after some weeks, the almost entire face of a juvenile individual.

Five years later, with further preparation, it was possible to free the jaw and confirm the juvenile age from the teeth. Despite its young age, Dart considered the individual had a large and complex brain. From the central position of the opening for the spinal cord, in the base of the skull, he concluded that it was also bipedal. Furthermore, in details of the morphology of the face and jaw, there were human-like characters. The next year, Dart (1925) published an account of the find in the scientific journal *Nature*. In this paper he claimed the specimen was important because 'it exhibits an extinct race of apes intermediate between living anthropoids and man' and he tentatively proposed that a new family, the Homo-simiadae (man-apes), be created to accommodate this and similar fossils that might be found in the future.

Dugard has summarised the reasons why scientific opinion of the time was not disposed towards accepting Dart's claims for the importance of the Taung specimen. The combination of a relatively small brain and human-like teeth was a contradiction of the features shown by a fossil, the Piltdown skull, found a decade earlier in England and then accepted as heralding the dawn of mankind. A clever hoax, the Piltdown skull combined a recent human skull with the tampered jaw of an orangutan; only in 1953, through a battery of chemical tests, was it finally unmasked as a fraud. In the 1890s the find of a skullcap and leg bone in Java by the Dutch doctor Eugène Dubois seemed to point to Asia, not Africa, as the human homeland. The scenario of the hominids evolving under the selective pressures of the African savannas, which Dart argued, appeared to be speculative and did not help his cause. Had good plaster casts been available to send to anatomists overseas to study, the reception that greeted the announcement of the Taung skull find might have been more favourable. As it was, the plaster cast of the specimen that Dart was asked to have made was poor; it went on display in the South African Pavilion at the British Empire Exhibition held at Wembley in 1925. Coupled to doubts about the age of the specimen, this appeared to convince the leading authority of the time, Sir Arthur Keith, that the fossil was nothing more than an ape. It took more than 20 years, and the recovery of further specimens, for the scientific significance of the Taung discovery to become accepted. With hindsight, the Taung child is arguably the most important hominid fossil that has been found because it gave a direction to the study of human origins that is still being followed.

In 1935 Robert Broom took on the task of searching for adult specimens. Broom, a Scottish-trained medical doctor, had achieved considerable renown as a palaeontologist studying Gondwanaland-aged mammal-like reptiles (250 million years old) from the geological strata of the Karoo. He had retired from his medical practice and launched on this new career. His search started at the limeworks on the farm Sterkfontein near Krugersdorp. Lime was being quarried there, as at Taung, and fossilised baboon skulls had been found in the deposits. With the assistance of the mineworkers, Broom was able from 1936 to obtain samples of the hominid fossils and these proved to include the adult specimens he was looking for. The limeworks on the nearby farm Kromdraai produced in 1938 further material, which Broom recognised as different and classified as *Paranthropus robustus*.

The Second World War interrupted the search, but it resumed immediately after the war. The Sterkfontein site was particularly productive: an important find was the near-complete skull of an adult australopithecine female, dubbed 'Mrs Ples' (an abbreviation of Broom's scientific name) by the media. As significant were finds of skeletal parts other than crania. A pelvis from Sterkfontein provided conclusive evidence for bipedalism. In 1947 the University of California African Expedition explored the limeworking on a farm, Swartkrans, across the valley from Sterkfontein, without any success. However, in the following year, Broom extended his activities to Swartkrans. This has proved to be a prolific source of paranthropine fossils. Further afield, the dumps of the limeworks in the Makapan Valley near Potgietersrus yielded bone-rich samples, which were sorted and analysed by the Karoo palaeontologist James Kitching and by Alun Hughes, under the direction of Dart. Since 1947 Makapansgat Limeworks has become an established find site. The specimens of so-called gracile australopithecines from Taung, Sterkfontein and Makapansgat, and the 'robust' paranthropines from Kromdraai and Swartkrans, were both the product of a marvellous phase of discovery, which ended with Broom's death in 1951. Detailed studies of the sites and their fossil contents, animal as well as hominid, have continued. In the process the collections have been increased in size. Studies are now sufficiently

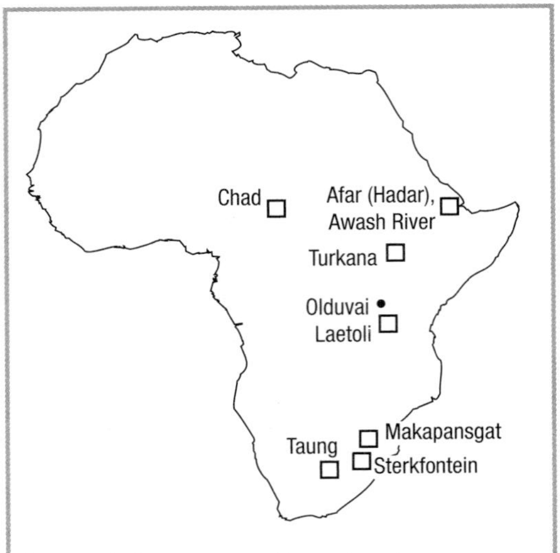

Figure 4.5: *Find sites of* Australopithecus *spp. Olduvai Gorge, near Laetoli, and sites in the Turkana area have yielded younger paranthropine fossils as have Swartkrans and Kromdraai, near Sterkfontein.*

advanced to enable scientists to begin the search for new fossil-bearing deposits. Gladysvale and Drimolen in Gauteng have been added to the list of potentially important find sites.

All the South African hominid sites are underground solution caverns in dolomite (a calcium–magnesium carbonate rock type), which have become filled with soil washed in from the surface. Where the infilling is bone-rich it is known as bone breccia. The exception is Taung, where the site formed as a cavity in a tufa limestone deposited by spring waters from a dolomite source. Subsequent finds of similar fossils made in eastern Africa come from a different geological context, namely lake and river sediments (Figure 4.5).

Until 1959, with the exception of an upper jaw fragment from Garusi in Tanzania, early hominid fossils were known only from South Africa. That year marked the first major find from East Africa. Mary Leakey made the discovery at the site of Olduvai Gorge in Tanzania, where she was working with her husband, Louis Leakey. This initial find was followed by others at Olduvai, and in the following years many new fossil-rich localities in Tanzania, Kenya and Ethiopia have been discovered. All are associated with the eastern branch of

the rift valley that runs from central Tanzania to the Red Sea.

In 1966 the joint French and American team participating in the Omo Research Expedition transformed the eastern African research into an international effort. The Omo River drains into the northern end of Lake Turkana on the Ethiopia–Kenya border. Although the Omo localities yielded new australopithecine fossils, these are fragmentary because they came from a high-energy riverine environment. Nevertheless, the Omo deposits have provided a wealth of information on Plio-Pleistocene stratigraphy, large mammal fauna and dating. Following from the Omo research, deposits to the east, west and south of Lake Turkana have been investigated with considerable success by teams from the National Museum in Kenya and its overseas associates. In Ethiopia the focus of research shifted to the sediments exposed along the Awash River, which flows into the Afar Depression, in the north-east of the country. The Institute for Human Origins and the University of California, Berkeley, in particular, have provided financial and technical support in developing co-operative research with colleagues from Ethiopia. The Ethiopian deposits have yielded some of the oldest and most complete remains.

The association of these East African finds with rifts and vulcanism made it possible to obtain chronometric dates for the sites. In particular, the extensive use of potassium/argon dating techniques has yielded a comprehensive timescale for

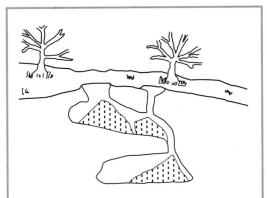

Figure 4.6: *The main South African early hominid sites are associated with underground solution caverns – sink-holes – that have become filled with bone-rich soil.*

the hominid and associated faunas. Biostratigraphic correlations can also be made between the mammal faunas from the East African and South African sites and in this way suggest chronometric ages for the South African deposits.

While a recent discovery in Chad by Brunet and colleagues (1995) has extended the known geographic range of the australopithecines to western Africa, there are no certain finds of australopithecines or paranthropines outside sub-Saharan Africa. It would seem that the early stages of human evolution were played out in Africa south of the Sahara and in relatively drier habitats. There are no finds from the better-watered and -forested western rift valley in East Africa; moreover, equatorial Central Africa may not have been a suitable habitat for early hominids. Many areas in sub-equatorial Africa have been explored scientifically at a reconnaissance level or not at all, and deposits in southern Angola, Namibia, Zambia, Zimbabwe and Mozambique may still yield fossil sites. In Malawi deposits on the 'arid corridor' described by Balinsky (1962), a route for the interchange of arid-adapted animals between southern and eastern Africa, have produced some early hominid remains. While they are claimed to be those of the oldest-known true human, they are perhaps too fragmentary for certain identification. However, for many parts of sub-Saharan Africa the discovery phase has yet to begin.

Classification of the australopithecines and paranthropines

Australopithecus africanus is the genus and species name that Dart proposed for the Taung child. The adult specimens found by Broom at Sterkfontein were given the scientific name *Plesianthropus transvaalensis* (now sunk or grouped into *A. africanus*). The fossils he found at Kromdraai were designated *Paranthropus robustus* and very similar fossils from Swartkrans were named *Paranthropus crassidens*. The reason for this plethora of names has to do with precedence. Until it could be satisfactorily established that different finds belonged to the same palaeospecies or genus, names were applied so as to establish precedence. In zoological nomenclature, the first name given to a valid species is the one by which that species becomes known. Revisions of earlier classifications may

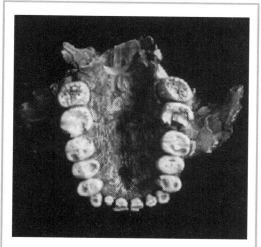

Figure 4.7: *The upper dentition of Zinj, OH5, showing the large molars (cheek teeth) and premolars and the much reduced canine and incisors (front teeth), which John Robinson (Box 18) immediately recognised as paranthropine. Note that the wisdom teeth that erupt at about 19 years in humans are only coming into wear, showing that this was a young individual. (Photo from cast)*

result in the 'sinking' of one name into another or the resurrection of an earlier name for a different grouping of specimens. For a pioneer in Broom's position it made sense to emphasise the differences in case, through further study, these anatomical differences should prove significant.

Broom's contribution was to show that more than one kind of 'ape-man' could be recognised. It was Broom's co-worker and successor, John Robinson, who undertook the systematic revision of the South African fossils and laid the foundation for their current understanding. Robinson was able to show that these early hominids differed not only in their anatomy but also in their dating and diet. Importantly, he was also able to show that the paranthropines were the contemporaries of stone-tool-making true humans, members of the genus *Homo*. Most researchers would follow Robinson in accepting that the difference between the australopithecines and paranthropines is at the genus level. However, some, notably Phillip Tobias, Dart's successor in the Anatomy Department at the University of the Witwatersrand, have preferred to lump the australopithecines and paranthropines in the same genus, *Australopithecus*.

Leakey named the 1959 East African find – OH 5 (Olduvai hominid 5) – *Zinjanthropus boisei*: Africa was known as the land of Zinj to travellers from the Mediterranean in Classical times, *anthropos* means human and the Boise Fund sponsored Leakey's work. Because stone artefacts were found in the same bed of deposit and as the ability to make and use tools was then accepted as a unique attribute of true humans, *Zinjanthropus* was labelled human. But the specimen, a well-preserved near-complete cranium and upper dentition of a 19-year-old (in human years), is that of a paranthropine male and not a true human (Figure 4.7) Robinson predicted from the Swartkrans evidence that, in addition to *Zinjanthropus*, the remains of a true human tool-maker would be found in Bed l at Olduvai. In the next year this proved to be the case. Revisions have subsequently sunk the name *Zinjanthropus boisei* into *Paranthropus (Australopithecus) boisei*.

The East African paranthropines are even more robust than the South African specimens. They are known from two localities in Tanzania, from a number of Kenyan sites near and around Lake Turkana, and from the Ethiopian sites on the Omo River. The so-called black skull, with the Kenya National Museum number KNM-WT 17000, from West Turkana and some materials from the Omo River, which are half a million years older than the other paranthropine finds, are usually referred to as *Paranthropus aethiopicus*.

There are a few fossils that have been considered to indicate the presence of *Australopithecus africanus* in East Africa. On the whole, however, the fossil record of the period to which such fossils would be expected to date, between 2.5 and 3 million years, is poor relative to the preceding and succeeding periods. Clarity on the presence or absence of this species of australopithecine will depend on better sampling of this period.

There are, nevertheless, two important groups of fossils from earlier time ranges assigned to the genus *Australopithecus*. *A. afarensis* was defined in 1978, its definition the result of the collaborative study of materials from Laetoli in Tanzania and Hadar in the Afar Depression of Ethiopia (Johanson & White 1979). The recognition of this, a species with relatively 'primitive' features of the skull, jaw and teeth, provided a potential ancestor

for all later australopithecines; however, the presence of other advanced features makes this less certain. The expectation that older australopithecine specimens would be found has been vindicated in the finds, designated *A. anamensis* (Leakey, M. *et al.* 1995), at Kanapoi and Allia Bay near Lake Turkana, by a team from the Kenya National Museum. Even more ape-like and older are finds from the the Afar region in Ethiopia (White *et al.* 1994), now named *Ardipithecus ramidus*. (*Ardi* means 'earth', *pithecus* means 'ape', *ramid* means 'root' in the Afar language; the scientific name translates as 'the ground ape at the root of our ancestry'.) Although a new genus has been erected to accommodate the *A. ramidus* material, the relationship to the australopithecines remains open. All the same, the ardipithecines trace our human ancestry a step closer to the last common ancestor between African apes and humans.

Ardipithecus ramidus

The Afar Depression in Ethiopia is formed by a junction of three lines of rifting, where the eastern African rift valley meets the Red Sea rifts. Erosion by the modern Awash River and its tributaries has exposed fossiliferous lake and river sediments, which have accumulated in the depression. The reason why deposits of ages ranging over several million years occur there is uplift and geological faulting in this unstable part of the earth's crust. In the Middle Awash research area, in the drainage of the Aramis tributary, the remains of *A. ramidus* have been discovered. The finds date to almost 4.5 million years. The specimens, all surface finds, are mainly teeth but include jaw (mandible) and skull fragments, bones of the arm and a partial skeleton: together they represent 20 or more individuals. Features like tooth-enamel thickness indicate that the specimens are intermediate between the relatively thinner chimpanzee and thicker, later australopithecine values. Although the proportions and morphology of the deciduous pre-molar tooth are chimpanzee-like, the specimens are australopithecine-like in the reduced size of the canine teeth, the morphology of the molar teeth, and the shape of the base of the cranium or skull. The estimated body mass of more than 30 kg would be within the lower part of the range for the australopithecines. What are lacking are hind-limb bones

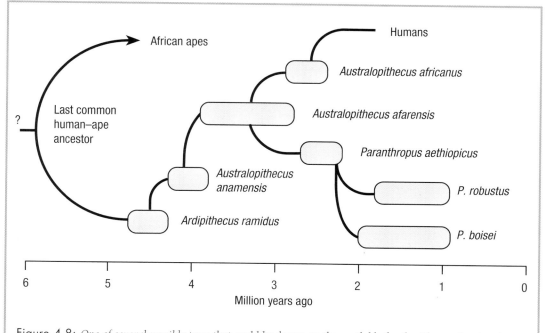

Figure 4.8: *One of several possible trees that could be drawn on the available fossil evidence, showing the relationship between ardipithecines, australopithecines, paranthropines and humans.*

which would confirm that the remains are those of a bipedal true hominid.

There are some pointers to the habitat in which *A. ramidus* lived. The area was a flat plain covered with woodland vegetation. Preserved in an associated fossil soil are thousands of *Canthium* (Rubiaceae) seeds. These seeds probably owe their preservation to burial by ants. The most common large mammal fossils are of a colobine (arboreal leaf-eater) monkey species, and the main antelope represented is a kudu species: this supports the contention of a closed woodland habitat. In this habitat the largest carnivore was a bear, *Agriotherium*, which has also been recorded from Pliocene deposits at Langebaanweg in the Western Cape. There were other carnivores present; carnivore tooth marks were found on the hominid and other bone. The carcasses of the animals that were killed or died in this habitat were torn apart by carnivores and the bones scattered in no particular pattern. This ecological information suggests that the ardipithecines preferred the safety of closed habitats. The fossils of later hominids are found in habitats that were more open.

Australopithecus anamensis

Lake Turkana is a large rift valley lake in northern Kenya, bordering on the Sudan and Ethiopia. In a zone up to 50 km wide around the present shore there are uplifted, faulted and eroded ancient sediments of the lake, interbedded with soil horizons and volcanic ash layers. Erosion by rain exposes fossil bone, and careful collecting from different localities over many years has provided a rich harvest of hominid remains. The *A. anamensis* (*anam* means 'lake' in Turkana) remains were mostly collected in 1994 and come from two horizons at Kanapoi on the southern margin and the Allia Bay area on the east. The dating is between 3.9 and 4.1 million years. A tibia, the larger lower leg or shinbone, from Kanapoi is direct evidence for bipedalism because of its distinctive form. The teeth are thick-enamelled in contrast to the ardipithecines. The canines are relatively large and the palate shallow. The estimated body mass of 55 kg is on the higher part of the range for australopithecines. *A. anamensis* may represent an intermediate species in a single lineage that evolved from *A. ramidus* to

A. afarensis, or it may be one of a number of evolutionary experiments, branches of hominid bipeds, only one of which could have been a direct human ancestor.

The associated fauna from Allia Bay includes woodland species like kudu and the colobine monkey but also small mammals, like the gerbil, that occupy grassland and relatively dry areas. This suggests a habitat of riverine woodlands with open grassland between the drainage lines.

Australopithecus afarensis

The Hadar research area adjacent to as well as north of the Middle Awash area in the Afar (Kimbel *et al.* 1994) produced a sample of 250 hominid fossils during exploration in the 1970s. They included 40 per cent of a female skeleton, AL 288-1, informally known as 'Lucy', and the remains of some 13 individuals, popularly referred to as the 'first family', from AL 333. Political upheavals stopped any further internationally sponsored searches there until 1990. As of March 1994, renewed efforts added a further 53 new specimens from this, the richest locality for finds of *A. afarensis*. The Hadar remains are well dated to 2.92–3.4 million years. New finds that date in the 3.4–4 million-year interval have also been made in the Middle Awash research area. At Maka, in addition to a femur reported in 1984, several mandibles and arm bones have been recovered, and at Belohdelie the frontal bone of a skull was found (BEL-VP-1/1). They are as old as or older than those from Laetoli, which have been dated to 3.6 million years. The eroded lake sediments at Laetoli, near Lake Eyasi, south of Olduvai Gorge in central Tanzania, produced not only a number of jaw fragments with teeth in position but also two trails of hominid footprints.

The species *A. afarensis* was defined from the Laetoli and Hadar finds. Size differences between the individuals in the sample raised questions about the possibility of there being more than one species represented in the combined sample. Sexual dimorphism was proposed to explain this size variability. With the new finds mentioned in the previous paragraph, the diagnostic anatomical details of the cranium can be established by the essentially complete skull of a larger, probably male individual and the face of a similar, but smaller, probably female individual. Previously the best available was a composite reconstruction of an adult male cranium. This was less satisfactory because it could not demonstrate that, for instance, the reconstructed cranium would have matched a small gracile skeleton like that of Lucy. The majority view is that Lucy is the skeleton of a female of this single dimorphic population. Comparisons of the admittedly few post-cranial remains, like the upper and lower arm bones, suggest that the degree of sexual dimorphism between smaller and larger individuals was no larger than that found among paranthropines. The fossils ascribed to *A. afarensis* are of a single species.

The newer finds confirm a picture of a sexually dimorphic, terrestrial biped, with powerful upper limbs and relatively long digits (fingers and toes) for climbing. The brain capacity, at about 400 cm³, is chimpanzee-sized. There is a compound nuchal–temporal bony crest at the rear of the skull, which is present as well in chimpanzees but is not found in *A. africanus*. The canines are large relative to later hominids; because of this a gap, called a diastema, to accommodate the canine is frequently present in the upper jaw, the same as with the apes, which have even larger canines. The emphasis in the dentition is on the front teeth and is associated with a protruding lower face. Well-developed front teeth are an indication that fruit was an important item in the diet. The wear on the premolars is not as flat as in *A. africanus*, suggesting that the diet was not rich in fibrous foods.

Whether a small hominid with long toes, like Lucy, or another larger, more bipedal and contemporary form was responsible for the footprints fossilised at Laetoli again raises the debate about the number of species in the taxon *A. afarensis*. It has been argued that the two or possibly three lines of footprints, preserved along with the tracks of other animals in the volcanic ash, are those of creatures with more of a striding gait than a Lucy-type waddle. Harder evidence than smudgy spoor will be needed to prove that the footprints were not made by *A. afarensis*.

Australopithecus africanus

A. africanus has enjoyed a special status as a model of the australopithecine forerunner of *Homo*. In some phylogenetic trees it is shown closer to the

18

• Dietary hypothesis •

What did the australopithecines eat? This was the question addressed by John Robinson in his study of australopithecine dentition. In Robinson's reasoning the dentition of the paranthropines, with their large molars and pre-molars, indicated that they were specialised vegetarians. The dentition of A. africanus was more like that of true humans, he argued, and indicated omnivory, a generalised diet. The difference in the damage observed on the crowns of the teeth of the two species was offered as supporting evidence. This dietary hypothesis has been productive in stimulating research and in offering new interpretations. Under the dietary hypothesis, for example, the paranthropine and vegetarian Zinjanthropus (P. boisei), found in association with animal food remains and stone tools in the same horizon at Olduvai, would not have been the diner but part of the dinner of another creature. Robinson argued this other creature was Homo.

The initial tests of the dietary hypothesis focused on studies of the differences in crown damage conducted under conventional light microscopes. With the development of scanning electron microscopes (SEM), it has been possible to examine the contrasts in tooth-crown wear in the different species under high magnifications. Acetate peels that replicate the tooth surfaces are made and photographed in the SEM. These reveal very clearly the wear facets and striations on the teeth. To interpret the SEM photographs reference can be made to wear patterns on the teeth of species of animals with known dietary preferences. Microscopic traces of

wear on the teeth have suggested to the anatomist Fred Grine that both P. robustus and A. africanus were eating plant foods but, as the wear facets are not the same, different kinds of plants are indicated. More pits on the paranthropine teeth suggest their diet included hard items, possibly seeds, pods and nuts, whereas A. africanus may have had more access to fleshy fruits. Using as an index the proportion of antelope species that browse on the leaves of trees and shrubs to the species that graze on grasses, Elisabeth Vrba (1975) has been able to show that A. africanus lived in relatively wooded habitats and P. robustus in open grassland. In such contrasting habitats dietary differences would be expected.

Other methods have been developed to test the dietary hypothesis. By measuring the stable isotopes of carbon in tooth enamel, Julia Lee-Thorp and co-workers from the University of Cape Town have shown that as much as 30 per cent of the paranthropine diet came from grasses or possibly from animals that ate grass. Independently, through the analysis of the strontium–calcium ratio in the skeletons of both Paranthropus and Homo at Swartkrans, Andrew Sillen has come to the same conclusion, arguing that the paranthropines were not exclusively vegetarians and that they also ate animal foods. Chimpanzees hunt, and there seems no reason to infer that paranthropines were not capable of hunting and scavenging. Nevertheless, those heavy jaws and large crushing teeth evolved for a purpose, which had nothing to do with carnivory. They were for munching plant foods.

human lineage and in others it is placed at the base of the paranthropine branch, where it splits from the human line. While showing more derived features than A. afarensis, it retains a generalised morphology that would be expected in the ancestor of both paranthropines and humans. The vault of the

cranium is high and rounded, so bony crests for muscle attachment are absent. The face is protruding and the teeth larger than in later representatives of the genus Homo but similar in their proportions. While A. africanus is the most human-like of all the australopithecines known, a brain capacity of some

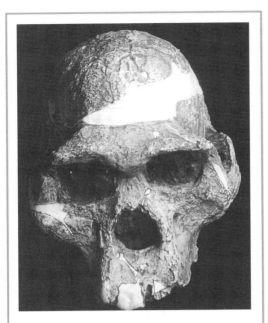

Figure 4.9: Australopithecus africanus *from Sterkfontein, dubbed Mrs Ples. (Photo from cast)*

early members of the genus *Homo* in the species *H. habilis*. We are still learning about the complexities of early human origins.

Paranthropines

The paranthropines show a number of specialised or, more properly, derived features ('apomor-phisms' in cladistic terminology), notably in the cranium. They have dished or concave faces, very large cheek (molar) teeth, large pre-molars that are in effect additional molars, stumpy front incisor teeth and canines, a heavy jaw and well-developed bony crests on the skull for attachment of the jaw muscles. The architecture of the skull is designed to support the muscles necessary for powerful chewing and crushing with the back teeth.

The massive chewing jaws of the paran-thropines, different in shape but equivalent in cross-section area to the jaws of a gorilla, suggest sturdy bodies. The label 'robust' conjures up the picture of a hominid equivalent to the gorilla. As more post-cranial remains have become available for study, it seems that the paranthropines had what Henry McHenry of the University of California at Davis describes as petit bodies (McHenry 1991a). Different estimates of body mass have been obtained by using measurements from the fore or hind limb and making comparison with

440 cm³ places it in the same league as the apes. The limb proportions and the whole post-cranial anatomy show this species to be as at home in the trees as on the ground. If the bones of the Sterkfontein fossil dubbed 'Little Foot' by Phillip Tobias and Ron Clarke can be referred to *A. africanus*, then, as we shall see, this creature was adapted to climbing. The animal fossils associated with *A. africanus* are also those belonging to a closed rather than open environment.

The species is known with certainty only from southern Africa and from a time range centred on 2.8 million years. Specimens referred to this taxon have been recovered from the sites of Makapansgat Limeworks, Taung, Sterkfontein and possibly Gladysvale. Given that only a small fraction of the individuals that lived have contributed to the fossil record, the number of specimens recovered – more than 500 and mostly from Sterkfontein – is impressive. An intriguing possibility, supported by Ron Clarke among others, is that the descendants of this *A. africanus* may have survived after 2 million years ago. They may be represented by specimens from Olduvai Gorge (OH 62) and Sterkfontein, which are usually included with

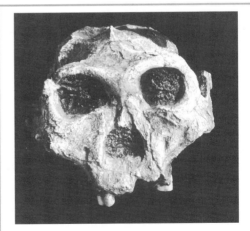

Figure 4.10: Paranthropus robustus *from Swartkrans showing the broad, dished face and bony crest on the top of the skull, an architecture 'designed' for the attachment of strong muscles to work heavy jaws. (Photo from cast)*

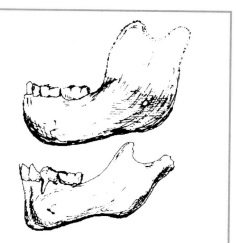

Figure 4.11: *The paranthropine mandible (above) is deeper and thicker and the ascending ramus is broader and more vertical than in modern humans (below). (Broom & Robinson 1952)*

modern humans or apes. On all estimates the paranthropines are comparable in their body mass to the australopithecines as well as to living chimpanzees (McHenry 1992). Estimates show that *P. robustus* tipped the scales at 40 kg for males and 32 kg for females. These estimates use a formula based on the relationship of human hind-limb joint size to mass; the estimate would increase by some 30 per cent if the comparison were made with the ape hind-limb proportions. The estimates for *A. afarensis* (45 and 29 kg), *A. africanus* (41 and 30 kg), and *P. boisei* (49 and 34 kg) are of a similar order. All would be petit by modern human standards and in comparison with members of the genus *Homo* dating younger than 1.5 million years. Stature can be estimated from the length of the femur. McHenry (1991b) estimates that *P. robustus* males stood 1.32 m tall and the females 1.1 m. *A. africanus* was equally short in stature and well below the 1.8 and 1.6 for males and females of later African members of the genus *Homo*.

A precise date for the extinction of the paranthropines has yet to be established in either eastern or southern Africa. In both regions it is probable that they became extinct prior to 1 million years ago. Suggestions as to why these dietary specialists became extinct range from habitat changes, forced by Pleistocene climate changes, to competi-

tion with true humans occupying an increasingly wider ecological niche.

Case study: Makapansgat Limeworks and the osteodontokeratic culture

Makapansgat is an historical cave in the Northern Province where, in 1854, Mokopane, an Ndebele clan leader, and his followers took refuge from a Boer commando. Besieged for almost a month, many of the clan members died or were killed and others were taken captive. In the same valley are the Cave of Hearths (Mason 1962, 1988a), an important excavated Pleistocene site, and the Makapansgat Limeworks site, which is of concern here. This is a solution cavern system that became filled with sediments cemented by lime deposits. Researchers have recognised five layered sedimentary units, called members 1–5 from the bottom to the top. The thinnest is Member 3, informally known as the grey breccia; this is particularly rich in bone. Researchers have taken blocks of lime-cemented soil infilling and, by the careful chipping away of the matrix around the bone, revealed a mass of jaw and limb bone fragments, mostly from antelopes. It is this member that has produced the remains of a dozen or more australopithecine individuals. Dart originally proposed the name *Australopithecus prometheus* (after the Roman god of fire) for these specimens, under the mistaken impression that the black staining in the deposit was traces of fire. However, the ground water percolating through the rock carries traces of manganese; this may be deposited on exposed surfaces and even on bones, so that superficially it looks like soot. A simple chemical test (Oakley 1957) was able to show the stain was manganese. The hominid remains are now classified as *Australopithecus africanus*.

The dating evidence indicates an age of about 3 million years, based on geomagnetic reversal chronology. At this, but at none of the other australopithecine sites in South Africa, the sediments were sufficiently rich in magnetic minerals to preserve a detectable signal of their orientation to the direction of the earth's magnetic field at the time of deposition. The technique, widely used in dating volcanics and deep-sea sediments, depends on knowing the sequence in which the earth's magnetic field has reversed direction through 180°.

The earth is like a giant but unstable bar magnet: when polarity reverses, a magnetic compass that once pointed to the north magnetic pole would point to the south pole. The instability in the magnetic field is related to disturbances deep down in the earth's core. Potassium/argon dating, particularly of lavas, has provided the timescale for what are random changes of the polarity in the earth. The dating depends on being able to match the sequence of magnetic polarity measurements in borehole cores of sediments from the site, to the established universal pattern. The fossil fauna indicates an age close to 3 million years and the magnetics support this age. On this evidence Makapansgat Limeworks is the oldest of the South African australopithecine occurrences.

The dumps of bone-bearing sediments too impure to feed into kilns at the limeworks were good places to search for australopithecines. Miners had done the initial work. It remained for James Kitching and Alun Hughes, working under the direction of Raymond Dart, to sort through the debris they had left. From five tonnes of bone-rich blocks collected from the miners' dumps Kitching and Hughes were able to obtain a large sample of the kinds of animals that shared the australopithecine habitat. They took a quantitative approach, collecting all the bone fragments without selection and identifying them as far as possible, first to the part of the body and then to species. In so doing, they set a standard for the analysis of South African fossil faunas and made a fundamental contribution to studies of how and why fossil bones accumulate at a site. This is known as the study of taphonomy.

The paranthropines with their large blunt molars were not candidates for meat-eating, but could the gracile australopithecines have been carnivores and engaged in hunting? Dart argued that the fauna associated with the australopithecines at Makapansgat Limeworks indicated 'yes' on both counts. He assumed that the site was a home to the australopithecines. It followed logically that the bones were the remains of meals, and that *A. africanus* was indeed a hunter and carnivore. The bones of australopithecines in the fauna suggested to Dart that they were also cannibals. The australopithecines were not equipped with claws or sharp canine teeth to kill and tear apart the carcasses of wild animals, and, so Dart reasoned

further, they would have had some form of tools.

Counting the body parts in the bone sample suggested a solution to the problem. Some body parts of the mammal skeletons, like jaws and teeth, were over-represented and others, like vertebrae, were under-represented. To explain the puzzle of the body parts, Dart proposed that australopithecine hunters made use of bone, teeth and horns as tools for slaying animals as well as the occasional member of their own species. He used the term 'osteodontokeratic culture' to describe such tools. The implication was that the man-apes were killers and that, in more ways than one, humankind had a skeleton in the proverbial ancestral cupboard. This is what Robert Ardrey in *African Genesis* referred to in dramatic biblical terms as the mark of Cain.

But what if the site had been the home of other animals? Had carnivores used it as a den for raising their cubs or pups? If so, the australopithecine bones were carnivore food remains and many of the inferences drawn by Dart about tool-using would have fallen away. What was needed was a more convincing explanation of the pattern for the skewed distribution of body parts of the animal skeletons found in the bone samples.

C.K. Brain decided to test Dart's hypothesis by analysing the bones accumulated around a Topnaar Khoekhoe settlement on the Kuiseb River in Namibia. He noted that the bones from goats that had been slaughtered were cooked and eaten. They were also broken open for marrow and fed to the dogs. Trampling and weathering on the surface of the ground had further damaged what remained. The bones collected from around the encampment had very similar body-part proportions to those in the Makapansgat Limeworks sample. In sum, then, what Dart, Hughes and Kitching had established had little or nothing to do with the dietary habits of the australopithecines. However, they had established an important taphonomic principle: the hardest parts of the skeleton survive the best and are likely to be more common in bone accumulations where carnivores or hominids have had a role.

Although Brain's study did not confirm or refute the Dart hypothesis, it made it plausible that carnivores other than hominids had been the bone accumulators. The best candidates in Member 3 at Makapansgat Limeworks are possibly hyenas.

Hyenas feed their pups in their dens and in this way accumulate bones there; the frequency of hyena bones at the site indicates that they sometimes died there too.

When it was still assumed that australopithecines used Makapansgat as a home base, it seemed logical to search the stony rubble for stone tools that may have been used by them. Of the many pieces of stone debris included in the deposit, there is a very small proportion that arguably may be simple artefacts made by percussion flaking. However, at this and other sites of *A. africanus* there is no convincing evidence for the making of stone artefacts, and the doubtful artefacts from Makapansgat Limeworks can be explained away as naturally fractured stones.

From studies of plant and animal remains from the site, Dick Rayner and his team from the University of the Witwatersrand have shown that the australopithecines lived in a subtropical forest habitat. This would be consistent with the proposition that australopithecines are chimpanzee-like in their ecology and as much at home in the trees as on the ground. They must be seen as dubious candidates for either stone tool-makers or 'killers'.

Case study: Sterkfontein

Sterkfontein is an eroded cavern system that developed along an extended fissure in the dolomite. The original underground solution cavity was filled by a series of cones of soil and rock debris of different ages that slumped through surface openings. Of the six stratigraphic members that have been defined, Member 4 is a prolific source of the remains of *A. africanus*. Although the bulk of the hominid remains are of this species, there is a possibility that a larger form (or morph) is present. Clarke (1994) considers this to be an ancestral paranthropine. In a bed between Member 4 and Member 5, there is fossil material that has been attributed to *H. habilis* or a late form of *A. africanus*. From Member 5, new finds include teeth of *Paranthropus*, previously not known in this member, and stone tools. The top member is significantly younger than 700 000 years and has yielded no human remains.

The deposits below Member 4 have not been as intensively studied. Amongst some samples collected 20 years ago from these older deposits, and

Figure 4.12: *Ron Clarke, with a cast of the Taung child, stands in front of piles of breccia at Sterkfontein.*

possibly dating as early as 3.5 million years, four foot bones that articulate have been recently recognised as hominid and were dubbed 'Little Foot' by Phillip Tobias and Ron Clarke. These are a significant find because they are the bones of the big toe

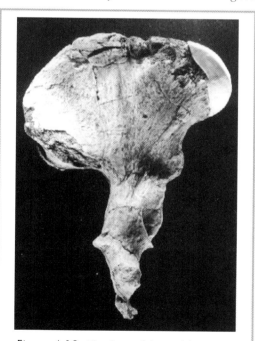

Figure 4.13: *The shape of the Sterkfontein innominate (pelvis) is incontrovertible evidence for a form of bipedalism. (Photo from cast)*

and show this to be more mobile, as with apes and unlike the modern human toe. 'Little Foot' is the foot of a postural rather than a locomotory biped, a creature able to climb rather better than later flat-footed humans.

The dating of Member 4 is estimated at between 2.4 and 2.8 million years on the evidence of the Bovidae (the family that includes buffalo and the antelopes) found there, at 2.5–2.8 million years on the evidence of the species of monkeys, mainly fossil baboons, and at 2.1 ± 0.5 million years by ESR dating (Schwarcz *et al.* 1994). The ESR date, the mean of 20 determinations on specimens of tooth enamel, underestimates the faunal age, possibly because some teeth are from Member 5, not 4. A plot of the age measurements shows two peaks, one at 2.4 million years, an approximation to the age of Member 4; the other, at 1.7 million years, would fall within the expected age range for Member 5. This is a good illustration of the fact that even the most sophisticated modern dating techniques depend on knowing the stratigraphic provenance of the materials dated. At Sterkfontein and at the other sites, the collections made in the pioneer phases of exploration were not as well controlled stratigraphically as those made since the geology has become better understood. The current best estimate for the dating of Sterkfontein is 2.6–2.8 million years (Clarke & Tobias 1995).

Case study: Taung and the death of a child

A little over 100 km north of Kimberley are the Buxton Limeworks at Taung. At the limeworks, sheets (or carapaces) of lime tufa are mined. The tufa is formed by the deposition of lime from spring waters issuing from the dolomite rocks of the Gaap (Kaap) Plateau; mats of algae growing in the waters here precipitate the lime. Four different tufa carapaces have been recognised (Peabody 1954) and the Taung skull came from oldest, the Thabaseek tufa. Early reports show this to have contained numerous cavities formed either primarily by growth of tufa or secondarily by solution within the carapace. These cavities became filled with soil. The fills are rich in bone from animals using the openings as dens or shelters. In the quarrying operations from 1919 onwards, collections of bones were made on a casual rather than systematic basis and were given to various scientists

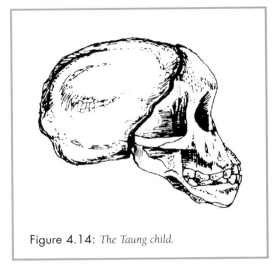

Figure 4.14: *The Taung child.*

to describe. The sample from which Dart extracted the near-complete Taung child skull in 1924 was one of these collections. It was, however, Ales Hrdlicka, a noted American physical anthropologist, and not Dart, who made the first attempt to establish the provenance of the skull by visiting the quarry in 1925 and collecting further bone material from adjacent and possibly slightly younger caverns. More detailed study of the deposits was only undertaken during the University of California African Expedition of 1947–8. Study has continued to the present although now only remnants have survived and mining has destroyed the original find locality.

Attempts to date the Taung skull on geological grounds have not provided convincing results, nor have the attempts made thus far with uranium disequilibrium dating. The faunal associations (McKee 1993) from the original collection, from Hrdlicka's site and from newly excavated deposits indicate an age at least as old as 2.4 million years and possibly as old as 2.8 million years. An extinct baboon, *Parapapio broomi* ('Broom's near baboon'; *Papio* is the genus name of the extant baboon), is known only from the original skull site. In what are stratigraphically younger deposits this species is replaced by *Parapapio antiquus* and an early ancestral true baboon, *Papio izodi*. The primate fossils provide good evidence that the Taung site is of the same order of age as the other *A. africanus* occurrences at Makapansgat Limeworks and Sterkfontein.

Taung is the most westerly of the australopithecine sites and, given the strong east-to-west rainfall gradient in southern Africa, was certainly the driest. Dart originally described the environment as open savanna; the modern hot and dry climate of the site suggests that hominids in this time period were able to range into open habitats. Although the faunal associations are not complete enough to reconstruct the past habitat conditions in detail, proximity to the Harts River suggests a complex vegetation mosaic including woodlands. It may be misleading to assume that the Taung find shows *A. africanus* was able to live in open country but the Taung find may represent the southwesterly limits of the distribution of this species.

Taung has produced a single australopithecine find, the remains of a juvenile. How did these remains get into a cave deposit along with baboon, dassie, rodent and antelope fauna, all small animals? It is unlikely to be the sad story of a child that lost its way and crept into a shelter and died. More probably it was a case of predation by a small predator. The skull is reasonably intact: this rules out any of the large cats or a hyenid. As agent of accumulation the likely candidate is a small cat or a bird of prey. There are scratch marks on the skull that are consistent with the claw marks of an eagle, and the fauna associated with it is similar to that found below the nests of eagles (Berger & Clarke 1995). This is strong circumstantial evidence that a large bird of prey like the crowned eagle, *Stephanoaetus coronatus*, carried the skull to its nest. This does not necessarily mean the eagle snatched the child from its mother's arms or from the ground where it was walking. An eagle the size of the crowned eagle would not be able to lift a creature with a body mass of 10–12 kg, as estimated for the Taung child. What this means is that if the crowned eagle was involved (Hedenström 1995), the body had been dismembered, perhaps by a carnivore, before the skull was taken to the eagle's nest. McKee suggests that the bones, including the Taung skull, were accumulated in a tufa carapace overhang rather than in an underground solution cavity in the tufa mass; presumably the eagle nest was positioned above the overhang. The bony litter from the nest accumulated in the overhang and would have become sealed and buried as the tufa continued to grow.

The skull is remarkably complete and includes the face, mandible and most of the vault. A cast (endocast) is preserved of the imprint of most of the right side of the brain on the inner wall of the skull. This means there is direct evidence of the size and external morphology of the brain. The volume of the brain, at 400 cm³, is the same as that of a new-born human child and about 100 cm³ more than that of a juvenile chimpanzee. Thus, although Dart was correct in pointing to relatively large brain size as a human-like feature, study of the endocast (Falk *et al.* 1989) shows it to be more ape-like than human in shape and in the pattern of sulci (folds) of the outer surface of the cerebral cortex.

The teeth allow an estimate of age at death. If one assumes the tooth eruption sequence was the same as in modern humans, the age is estimated at 5–6 years. In humans the brain increases four-fold in volume from birth to adulthood but in apes and other mammals it doubles. To allow for the extra development of the brain, juvenile humans mature more slowly and tooth eruption is thus delayed relative to chimpanzees. The smaller brain of *A. africanus* as compared to modern humans points to maturation rates closer to apes than humans. The age at death of the Taung child would have been somewhat less than that estimated in human years. A more precise estimate can be made from a technique that studies growth increment lines in milk teeth (Bromage 1985); the results reduce the estimate to 2.7–3.7 years – young enough and small enough to be defenceless if it strayed from its parent. The death of this child, registered in the chance preservation and discovery of its remains in what became a limestone quarry in modern times, provides us with a precious glimpse of the past.

Case study: Swartkrans and paranthropine behaviour

Swartkrans lies across the Blaaubank Valley and within sight of Sterkfontein. It was one of the sites worked by Broom and Robinson from 1948 to 1953 and provided the first evidence for the co-existence of the paranthropines and *Homo*. In 1965 a long-term research project was initiated by C.K. Brain. The first task was clearing the site of rock and breccia from the mining operations. Bone-rich blocks of breccia had to be sorted out

Figure 4.15: *Congress participants wind their way across Sterkfontein valley up the hill to Swartkrans.*

and the fossils recovered either by mechanically chiselling away the matrix or by dissolving the calcified matrix with acids. Clearing the site of rubble and, later, excavation in areas of softer, naturally decalcified breccia gave better exposures of the *in situ* deposits. This made it possible to develop more complete models of the formation of the site, understand the details of the stratigraphy, and improve the explanations for the associations of fossil bones, artefacts and other finds.

The investigation of any major palaeontological or archaeological site progresses through both knowledge of specific detail and appreciation of the general principles of how sites are formed. The investment of 30 years in research at Swartkrans has paid off in the generation of stimulating scientific thought on broader issues concerned with environmental change, taphonomy, and paranthropine and human behaviour, issues which are not specifically related to the site.

The Swartkrans depository is a solution cavern system made up of an upper chamber divided into the Outer and Inner caves by a large collapsed roof block, which plugs the opening to the Lower Cave, the hole that drains to the present water table. As with all such features the cavern system was formed by solution-widening fissures in the

dolomite. As underground cavern development proceeded, erosion took place as a result of waters flowing through shaft-like openings, known as avens, connecting to the surface. Limestone formations like stalagmites, stalactites and flowstone – collectively called speleothems – occurred by chemical deposition from the lime-charged waters dripping into the cavern. Speleothems draped the walls, floor and roof of the original chamber at the stage when enlarged avens allowed hillslope soils to begin filling the Outer and Inner caves. Such filling took place in a series of pulses as soils washed in through openings created by roof collapse to occupy empty spaces or channels caused by erosion of older fills. Subsequent erosion has lowered the ground level: little thus remains of the original roof of the depository, and the breccia fills are exposed at the surface.

Careful mapping has distinguished five stratigraphic members, 1 to 5, oldest to youngest. Paranthropine specimens have been found in the lower three members, and specimens referred to *Homo* in the lowest two members and Member 5. The absence of any human remains from the intervening members is a quirk of sampling. However, the absence of paranthropine fossils from deposits younger than Member 3 is due not to sampling but to extinction of this lineage.

The dating of Member 5 is 11 000 radiocarbon years and Member 4 is Late Pleistocene, on the basis of the included artefacts. Of more interest here is the dating of the older members that are associated with paranthropines. These are broadly in the 1.8–1 million year range. Because of the episodic filling of the depository, different slices of this time range are represented but they cannot as yet be dated with great precision. The Acheulian artefacts found in Member 3 would date to less than 1.5 million years and may be as young as 1 million years. The faunal remains suggest that the stratigraphically oldest deposits in Member 1 are not significantly older than 1.8 million years and the dating of Member 2 is estimated at 1.5 million years.

At Swartkrans the initial focus of interest was in showing that the paranthropines were contemporary with *Homo*. The human remains were initially referred to *Telanthropus capensis* but they are now classified in the genus *Homo*. Although the finds are fewer than of those of paranthropines, the presence of humans is supported by the occurrence of artefacts. In order to explain how *A. africanus*, the omnivore from the older Sterkfontein site, could be ancestral to *Homo* and how *Paranthropus*, known from a few individuals from Kromdraai (*P. robustus*), but mainly from Swartkrans (*P. crassidens*), was a side branch to humanity, the dietary hypothesis (see Box 18) was developed.

The second focus of interest was taphonomic and was directed at explaining how the bones of the animals represented in the bone breccias got into the site. This set the predation hypothesis of Brain up against the osteodontokeratic hypothesis of Dart. For a number of reasons – because leopards are well represented among the carnivores at Swartkrans and because the puncture marks on one paranthropine cranium match the spacing between the canines of a leopard – Brain has favoured this carnivore as the main predator on the paranthropines at Swartkrans. This does not exclude the possible role of other carnivores, particularly *Dinofelis*, an extinct cat with sabre-like teeth. Such a role is supported by the modern analogue of a leopard under competition from hyenas that stores its kills in a tree. *Celtis* trees are frequently found growing round solution caverns in the otherwise treeless highveld, and this could explain how the bones from kills stored in trees fell into the site.

What this scenario does not explain is the high frequency of primates and particularly paranthropines found at the site. In the modern situation, primates represented by baboons may make up 5 per cent of the prey of a leopard and antelope, and small game like dassies the rest. Modern leopards, the same species as occur in the Swartkrans deposits, are not specialised predators of primates. Even with a more diverse primate fauna in earlier times it is unlikely that leopards or sabre-toothed cats targeted primates as their main prey. However, special circumstances may have existed at Swartkrans that drew the paranthropines to this location and made them vulnerable to predation. The modern analogue of troops of baboons sheltering from winter frost in caverns suggested a shelter hypothesis to Brain. Paranthropine remains in the site could be found in high frequency because these creatures regularly visited there, either for shelter or access to water. The loss of an individual to predation every now and then would have been offset against the benefits of shelter, which contributed to the survival of the group. It was a cost paid not only by paranthropines but also by individuals of several species of baboons and rare humans. In an underground shelter used as a den by different carnivores, one would have expected to find the bones of animals other than primates. The counts of minimum numbers of individuals of all the large animals do suggest, however, that the main drama played out a million and more years ago at Swartkrans involved paranthropines and leopard predation.

With the erosion of the roof, areas of breccia – lime-cemented soil, rock and bone – have become decalcified by the naturally acid ground waters draining through the site. The advantage to the investigator is that such parts of the site can be excavated by a trowel in a more controlled manner than is possible in rock-hard cemented breccia. This has allowed Brain to explore other interesting lines of thought. One way in which hominids can compete with large cats for shelter in dark places is by having control of fire. In this type of deposit any ash from a fire would not have survived leaching. The evidence must be more circumstantial and occurs in the form of burnt bones. In the exca-

Figure 4.16: *Fragments of burnt bone come from the deep section in the foreground at Swartkrans.*

vation of Member 3, Brain noted that some of the bone fragments were burnt. In collaboration with Andrew Sillen he has shown that some 270 pieces out of a total of more than 50 000 are indeed burnt. The burnt pieces occur through the full thickness of the 6 m of deposits that formed at this time and occupy an eroded gully along the western wall. That burnt bones have not been found in the very large collection from the lower members is strong evidence that fire-tending, if not fire-making, started from this time. While paranthropine fossils occur in this member, so do advanced stone artefacts, and the presumption is that true humans were the fire-tenders.

The evidence for using fire is not as incontrovertible as that of the numerous hearths to be seen in sites dating to the last 100 000 years. At these younger sites, the ability to make fire at will, presumably by using fire sticks, is not in doubt. There are archaeological sites that may be as old as half a million years at which evidence for hearths has been claimed, and purposeful fire-making may have such antiquity. However, scientists are reluctant to interpret the occurrence of some dispersed million-year-old burnt bones at Swartkans as more than fire-tending. This would mean getting and keeping alight burning wood from veld fires. Burnt bones are known from older contexts, such as the 4.5 million-year-old palaeontological site of Langebaanweg near Saldanha, which is too early for any human involvement: here the burning is thought to be due to natural causes. Could natural fires also be the answer at Swartkrans? This remains a possibility until it can be shown that there is similar evidence from other million-year-old sites. Another test would be to show that from this time the increase in the frequency of fires caused more erosion, ecological changes and even the extinction of some animal species. It is possible that extinction of the paranthropines was the result of fire-induced ecological changes.

The pioneering excavations at Sterkfontein extension site produced undoubted examples of artificially shaped bone tools. Bone was used as a material for making tools from early times. Excavations in the decalcified breccias of members 1–3 at Swartkrans produced some 60 examples of pointed shaft-bone fragments with striations and polish. Confirmation that these are indeed artefacts is provided by study under the electron microscope, which gives highly magnified three-dimensional pictures of details of the surfaces. The striations and polish visible on these bones were not produced naturally. Through experiment, by using shaft-bone fragments to dig for bulb-like corms of the plant *Hypoxis* on the rocky hillside near the cave, Brain has been able to replicate the striations and polish on the tools, thereby suggesting they were used in the gathering of plant food. As with any replication study the burden of disproof lies in providing a more plausible alternative explanation. None has been offered thus far.

No one questions the ability of true humans to make bone tools. But could these tools be the equipment of paranthropines, as Brain has proposed? Tool-making is well documented among chimpanzees and there is no reason to deny some level of tool-making ability to the paranthropines. As a large part of the production of edible plants in the relatively open habitats in which they lived would have taken place underground, digging equipment may have been important to paranthropine survival. If they are considered candidates for making bone tools, then they are also candidates for making stone tools. Conventional wisdom assumes that the kind of stone artefacts found in members 1–2 – small flakes and cores described as the Oldowan industry – were made by true humans. Yet, the level of skill in percussion flaking required to make such stone artefacts is quite basic, and it is conceivable, even if unlikely, that the paranthropines and early humans had indistinguishable stone toolkits.

Bones of the hand have been found, which have been attributed to *Paranthropus* by the anatomist Randall Susman: he claims that these show sufficient manual dexterity to make and use tools at more than a rudimentary level. The attribution of the hand bones to *Paranthropus* has not gone unquestioned. This highlights the problem of how to distinguish who did what when two advanced hominids were living in the same area and visiting the same locations. Recent research at Swartkrans has re-opened the discussion of the potential skills the paranthropines possessed but it is premature to conclude that they, rather than the contemporary humans, had a 'hand' in making the bone or stone tools found there. Their coexistence for one million years or more suggests that the paranthropines and true humans occupied different niches, and that they had different tasks in life. This may be the strongest argument against expecting close parallels between their respective abilities. The paranthropines and early humans were different kinds of humanity.

Ape-men and ape-women

The discovery at Taung in 1924 opened up the world of the australopithecines to science. Until then, it was presumed that brain expansion preceded reduction of the canine teeth: this is indeed what the Piltdown hoax tried to promote. Instead, what the Taung child showed was a creature that had human-like teeth and an ape-like brain and was bipedal. The australopithecines – as they have come to be known from the increasing number of finds in the time range of 4.5 to 2.5 million years from eastern and southern Africa – were a distinct kind of humanity. Being bipedal gave them membership of the human family but they retained many characteristics of the common ancestor with the apes. Most significant is that their post-cranial anatomy shows they were partly arboreal. Just as their bipedalism can be related to feeding on the ground, their climbing abilities would have been related to the need to escape predators by being able to flee into the trees and by building their sleeping nests high off the ground. The main predators of those times were not the large African cats but sabre-toothed cats and a diverse assortment of hyenas. Predation pressure may have been a reason why the australopithecine brain size was not significantly larger than the apes. The evolution of larger brains only became possible when infants could sustain high foetal rates of brain growth after birth for more than the few months sustained by chimpanzees (Smith & Tompkins 1995). The australopithecines matured at rates more comparable to apes than humans and could not afford the cost of extended infant helplessness. Australopithecine infants like those of monkeys and apes would have had to be able to cling to their mothers when climbing into the safety of the trees.

Whether it was that Ice Age aridity became more severe between 3 and 2.5 million years, or more gradual deterioration of woodland habitats occurred, environmental change spelled the end of the australopithecine success. Two very different life forms emerged to replace them. These were true humans and the paranthropines. Evolution early in the paranthropine lineage of dental specialisation – with the molars and pre-molars forming grinding surfaces for chewing – shows them to have been dietary specialists. Conservatively retaining the australopithecine body size as they did, their life history from birth through childhood to adulthood and age at death was probably australopithecine-like. Dietary specialisation may have been the reason for their eventual extinction because it made them become vulnerable to ecological changes in the Pleistocene. While the paranthropines succumbed, true humans have survived.

CHAPTER FIVE

The first true humans

There are any number of myths or stories about the origin of humans. Every traditional community in the world has its own version. Many tell about a man and a woman who came out of the ground or out of a tree or out of a reed growing in the ground. These are essentially similar to Adam and Eve eating an apple in the Garden of Eden. Snakes, universal symbols of fertility, give such stories an extra twist and embellishment. How have Khoisan peoples seen human beginnings?

The anthropologist Mathias Guenther has recorded versions of the myths from Nharon informants in Botswana. These tell of an ancient order when there were people-like animals and ill-mannered people, but in the new order that replaced it the roles were reversed and the people-like animals became people and people became animals. The beliefs of the Khoisan interlink the spirit world and that of humans and animals in a profound way. Origin myths are beliefs sacred to those who hold them, and in that respect they are the truth.

Science wants more than moral explanations or beliefs designed to keep communities together. It requires hypotheses that can be tested by observation and experiment. Evolutionary biologists arguing from a Darwinian perspective look to the workings of natural selection to explain the emergence of humankind. Every human fossil known to science has come under the close scrutiny of physical anthropologists, who far outnumber the subjects of their study. When true humans appeared on the earth they left a trail of artefacts for archaeologists to follow. It is through the study of artefacts and their context that peoples of the past live again. [HJD]

True humans

Extinction has claimed not only all the australopithecine and paranthropine species but also all other species of our own genus, *Homo*, true humans. Opinions differ on the number of species that can be recognised in the genus *Homo* from the fossil evidence. Some authorities 'lump' all the available fossil finds into as few as three species while others 'split' the finds among as many as nine species. The divergent views on the number of valid species show just how continuous the process is of assessing the significance of new finds and re-evaluating older finds in the light of advances in ideas of how evolution works. However, all would accept that members of the genus *Homo* are distinct from australopithecines and paranthropines in their anatomy and in their ability to make stone artefacts. Large brain size and small teeth, set in a broad short tooth row, are among the obvious anatomical characters that distinguish early true humans from the australopithecines and paranthropines.

Lumpers' list of species in the genus *Homo*	Splitters' list of species in the genus Homo
H. habilis	H. habilis
	H. rudolfensis
H. erectus	H. ergaster
	H. erectus
	H. antecessor
H. sapiens	H. heidelbergensis
	H. helmei
	H. neanderthalensis
	H. sapiens

Figure 5.1: *Listing of the minimal (lumping) and the extended (splitting) number of species recognised in the genus* Homo.

True humans became reliant on stone artefacts in obtaining and processing food to an extent not approached by the australopithecines. As stone artefacts are virtually indestructible, they are the most important trace fossils of true humans. Other examples of trace fossils are dinosaur footprints and the burrows of lower animals from some ancient time preserved in rock; they show where and, if dated, when the animals lived. Finds of early human fossils will always be rare because the chances of preservation are low. But stone artefacts, quickly blunted, had a high throw-away rate, and they are the most abundant 'spoor' indicating where people lived in the past.

The oldest find of stone artefacts is at Gona in the Awash Valley of Ethiopia. Some 3000 well-made artefacts occur there and are dated to 2.5 million years old. Gona is close to the Hadar area where many fossil hominids from strata older than 3 million years have been found, but these strata contain no artefacts. In November 1996 the find was announced of an upper jaw of a true human in the Hadar area, AL 666, dated to 2.3 million years and in proximity to stone artefacts of the same age. These datings are the best approximations we now have for the time when true humans emerged.

Fossil evidence

True humans evolved in Africa. However, the first finds of fossil human remains to be recognised as different from modern people – now known to science as the Neanderthals (also spelt Neandertals) – were made in Europe in the last century. They represent a species, *Homo neanderthalensis*, that lived in Europe and western Asia until about 27 000 years ago. Still older are the finds that were made by Eugène Dubois in Java at the end of the last century. These were labelled *Pithecanthropus erectus* (now classified as *Homo erectus*); the name translated literally means 'upright ape-man'. The finds crowned Dubois's search for the so-called missing link.

The idea of there being a missing link, a hypothetical creature that linked humans and apes, followed from the publication of Darwin's *On the Origin of Species*. This idea, popular in the last century, was sufficient to motivate Dubois to search for such a creature. There are many forms of humanity that link modern humans to the last common ancestor with the apes, and in that sense the idea of a missing link is simplistic. Dubois and many others of his time assumed that Asia was the birthplace of humanity. Research in the early decades of this century produced more pithecanthropine fossils from the famous Zhoukoudian Caves near Beijing and again from Java. Until the hominid status of the australopithecines was accepted and even older fossil remains of true humans were found in Africa, the Asian pithecanthropines held the centre of the stage. In the decades since the Second World War, however, new finds and better dating have shifted the focus to Africa, where the oldest human fossils and artefacts have been found.

Homo habilis and the habilines

In 1964 a new species, *Homo habilis*, was described by Phillip Tobias from material found by Louis and Mary Leakey at Olduvai Gorge in Tanzania. The scientific name means 'the human that was able'. Its ability was to make the stone tools found in the same layers, 1.8 million years old, at Olduvai.

Further fossils described as *Homo habilis* have been found at Olduvai and notably at Lake Turkana in northern Kenya. The specimens include individuals with large brains and large faces and specimens with small brains and small faces. The KNM-ER (Kenya National Museum–East Rudolf) 1470 skull, representative of the large form, had a brain size of about 800 cm³. On the evidence of the relatively complete skeleton, OH (Olduvai hominid) 62, the small form, with brain size in the 650 cm³ range, had the post-cranial anatomy of an arboreal australopithecine-like creature. As we have noted, some authorities like Ron Clarke believe the small morph represents a late form of *A. africanus* and not *Homo*. Most accept that the two forms appear to represent different species rather than, as a minority argue, different sexes of the same species. The large form has been labelled *Homo rudolfensis* (after Lake Rudolf, the old name for Lake Turkana) while the small form retains the name *Homo habilis*. Informally they are referred to as habilines. The initial stage of human evolution may have seen a number of short-lived evolutionary experiments at being human and only one of the habiline species may have been ancestral to later humans. The oldest known habiline fossil, dated to 2.1–2.4 million years, is possibly one from Malawi but this is rivalled as the oldest human by AL 666 from Hadar, which is yet to be given a species designation.

In the ongoing excavations at Sterkfontein, Ron Clarke and Kathy Kuman have shown that the cranium described as *Homo habilis* from this site comes from a breccia occurring stratigraphically between Members 4 and 5 rather than from Member 5. The dating would be between 2.6 million years, the age of Member 4, and 2 million years. This is older than has been assumed. A representative of the small form, this may in Clarke's view turn out to be a late form of *A. africanus* rather than a member of the genus *Homo*. No habiline finds have been reported from Asia: this evolutionary stage may have been played out entirely in Africa.

Beginnings of technology

It is generally assumed that flaked stone artefacts indicate the presence of true humans. Stone is flaked by percussion: this involves the use of a hammer, usually a pebble or small cobble, to strike a piece, called a flake, from a block of stone, called a core. Although the process is simple, it requires an appreciation of geometry and mechanics that is not inborn. Most would-be artefact-makers when they are first faced with the task of striking off a flake in a practical class find difficulty in directing the hammerstone at the correct angle and following through with the blow. When correctly struck, the flake is released with a cluck-like sound. Like many skills, percussion flaking is more easily learnt by imitation and becomes routine through practice. Being able to strike small flakes from a core with some degree of control puts one at the same level of technology as the earliest artefact-

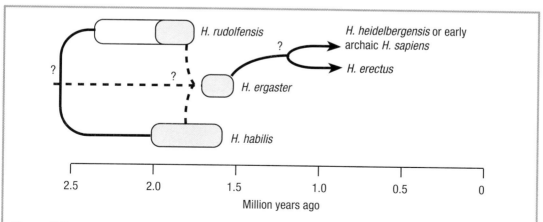

Figure 5.2: *The first members of the genus* Homo, *some 2.5 million years ago, were the habilines. One habiline species would have been ancestral to* H. ergaster, *the putative ancestor of all later humans. The shaded box shows the more certain estimated age range.*

makers at about 2.5 million years ago. It should not be surprising that the oldest known artefacts are competently made because they simply show mastery of the basic skill.

To be suitable as a raw material, stone needs to be hard, even brittle, and fine grained. Vein quartz, chalcedonies, lavas, sedimentary rocks like quartzites and hornfels, and fossil soils like silcretes are some of the rock types used for raw materials in southern Africa. Flint, a raw material widely used in some other parts of the world, is absent in southern Africa, as is obsidian, the volcanic glass, which is perhaps the ideal raw material.

The form in which raw material is found is also important for tool use. Naturally flat or rounded surfaces of a block or cobble are of limited use for cutting, although they can be used for grinding or pounding. To create a cutting edge involves percussion flaking. The process of flaking usually requires a series of flake removals from the core of raw material to produce a usable artefact. This activity produces many pieces of flaking debris that cannot be used. Archaeologists call these products 'waste'. The sheer volume of waste produced makes the activity easier to detect.

The edge of a stone flake is as sharp as the edge of a steel knife blade, but will dull with one cutting stroke. Although edges can be resharpened, it is as easy to make a new artefact. As soon as early humans began to use stone artefacts they created an ancient trail, which modern archaeologists can follow.

Stone artefact technology may have developed out of a capacity for using and making tools from various natural materials, like plant stems, wood, bone and stone, at a level similar to or in advance of the capabilities shown by chimpanzees. Stone is not freely available everywhere. In areas of deep chemical weathering and lateritic soils, such as may be found under a rainforest, there are few stone outcrops. In younger eroded landscapes, such as those created by uplift and rifting of the eastern side of the African continent, rock outcrops abound. Here weathered mantles of rotten rock have been stripped away by erosion to expose fresh raw material and the landscapes, peppered with volcanoes and covered by extensive sheets of plateau lavas, provide plentiful raw materials. It is in these settings that the earliest traces of stone tools have been found; they are the kind of settings which encour-

aged the initial attempts at flaking stone.

Stone artefacts are relatively permanent markers of a human presence in the landscape. After extended periods, artefacts may have been moved by erosion, water and wind action from where they were originally made and used, to where they have become incorporated in the subsoil. However, the places where they are found are still a good approximation of the areas over which people once ranged. Artefacts occur in localised concentrations – what we refer to as archaeological sites – and they are assumed to mark camps (home bases) or tool-manufacturing sites. Isolated artefacts outside such concentrations – what the archaeologist Glynn Isaac has called the scatters between the patches – then become discards from activities or tasks carried out away from the camp sites. The camp sites of contemporary San hunter-gatherers living in the Stone Age tradition have been studied by ethno-archaeologists like John Yellen (see Chapter 8). These camp sites, occupied over a period of weeks, have defined boundaries and can be recognised by the concentration of discarded artefacts long after the sites have been abandoned. Because such modern camp sites are occupied by co-operative family or kin groups, the question arises whether a similar social organisation is implied by the earliest-known artefact occurrences.

From his interest in the implications that living in a home base carried for food sharing and the sexual division of labour, Glynn Isaac was led to formulate the home base hypothesis. This has stimulated much of the research on early human behaviour. To avoid falling into the trap of assuming that the earliest human groups lived like modern hunter-gatherers in camps or home bases, archaeologists have become involved in testing ways in which localised concentrations of artefacts may form under natural conditions. It is only appropriate to use analogies from modern hunter-gatherers to interpret the earliest archaeological sites if one can show that natural agencies like running water and soil creep do not simulate concentrations of artefacts, which could be misinterpreted.

Alternatives to the home base hypothesis

The home base hypothesis is a simple but not simplistic explanation of the roots of human behav-

19 • Home bases •

The home base hypothesis was formulated by the South African-born archaeologist Glynn Isaac to explain why, in layered old-lake deposits, like at Olduvai Gorge, concentrations of artefacts and bones occurred in localised patches where they were subsequently exposed by erosion or through excavation. At Olduvai Gorge, the principal excavator, Mary Leakey, interpreted the artefact concentrations and associated animal remains as relatively undisturbed living floors, old camping places or homes. Isaac extended this interpretation and reasoned that to form localised concentrations of artefacts and bone representing food waste, people must have repeatedly returned to these locations. He inferred that sharing of food in a group, a human attribute, would explain the behaviour of repeatedly returning to the same location. Among chimpanzees,

food – particularly meat – is shared, but it is at a level that was described by Isaac as 'tolerated scrounging'.

Natural selection works to emphasise behaviours that have an advantage. In the human lineage, as brain size increased, food sharing would have been essential to offset the burden on the mother in raising children who were maturing at a slower rate than the young of apes. Food sharing means males had a role in provisioning the female, and implies pair bonding and some degree of division of labour. The home base concept or, as it later became labelled, the central place foraging hypothesis, argues that this level of what Isaac classed as proto-human behaviour set the stage for the later development of cultural rules and language that characterise humans.

iour. It has been criticised for projecting what we know of the base-camp-living and food-sharing behaviour of modern hunter-gatherers back to the beginnings of emerging humanity. If people in remote times were not living in home bases to share food, how else can the scatters and patches of artefacts and bones in the landscape be explained?

Considerable research effort by students of Isaac and others has gone into the study of the association between the bones and artefacts at early sites like Olduvai and around East Turkana. Some sites have suffered disturbance by the natural elements like running water but at others there is convincing evidence of direct associations in the refitting of flakes onto cores and the presence of cut and percussion marks made by stone tools on bones. Without doubt such occurrences mark localised places where stone tools were used to get meat. Direct evidence for what else the early humans may have been doing at these locations is lacking primarily because of the poor preservation of plant materials. The general assumption is that any patterning in the distribution of these sites in the

landscape must be related to features like the position of shade and shelter trees along stream beds and around water holes. The question remains, Were these sites home bases?

The idea that the earliest humans were scavengers rather than hunters has gained general acceptance over the hypothesis, which was popular until the 1960s, that becoming hunters played the major role in human evolution. In arguing against the hunting hypothesis and the home base hypothesis, Lewis Binford has sought to explain the concentrations of artefacts and bones as marking places where people went to scavenge the minimal leftovers from carnivore meals. In his argument, these places do not indicate food-sharing behaviour, for the leftovers would have been in parcels too small to share. This thesis casts early humans in the role of daytime scavengers and foragers, following their route across the savanna, keeping an eye on the vultures and other indicators for available carcasses, and gathering plant foods on the way. The idea of routed foraging as the initial stage on the way to becoming human has its adherents but few would follow Binford in holding that humans remained locked into the scavenging niche for much of their history.

George Schaller, who is known for his studies of the mountain gorilla and for his book *The Serengeti Lion*, showed that in the course of traversing an area in Serengeti by foot a number of animal carcasses from natural deaths or kills may be encountered on the way. Robert Blumenschine has been able to provide more quantitative information on the availability of carcasses for scavenging in the Serengeti. In environments with many trees, carcasses are not easily spotted by carnivores or even vultures, and are in some relative sense plentiful.

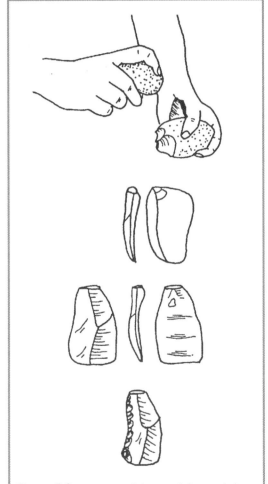

Figure 5.3: *Percussion flaking. A flake struck from a core through the use of a hammerstone can be recognised by the features illustrated.*

They would have been more plentiful if early humans had engaged in what Henry Bunn classes as confrontational as opposed to passive scavenging – chasing carnivores off their kills (Bunn & Ezzo 1993). Bunn would also allow opportunistic hunting: as chimpanzees engage in purposeful hunting, it is difficult to exclude this from the capabilities of early humans.

The downside of scavenging was the potential competition from dangerous carnivores. For those equipped with a basic Oldowan technology but lacking control of fire, predation by sabre-toothed and modern large cats and by hyenas would have posed a significant threat and encouraged living in larger groups. Some of the ways early hominids may have reduced the threat of carnivore predation are indicated by noisy chimpanzee groups crossing open places and, where necessary, wielding branches and throwing handfuls of earth.

Pertinent to explaining why the artefacts may be concentrated in localised patches is the stone cache idea of Richard Potts. He argues that some places are revisited time and again because they are close to regular kill sites. In the process these locations would accumulate re-usable artefact raw materials and bone debris but would not be living places because they would attract predators. Another idea, proposed by Jeanne Sept, is that artefact and bone accumulations mark locations below tree nests: she has looked to the nest-building behaviour of chimpanzees for analogies.

Lisa Rose and Fiona Marshall (1996) have recently revived a version of the home base idea, suggesting home bases were focal sites with shelter trees, water and access to plant foods, which could be co-operatively defended against carnivores and other hominid groups. These would be places to which meat could be transported and at which bones and artefacts would accumulate. Their resource-defence model, as they term it, accepts carnivore predation as the prime reason for promoting group living or sociality. However, they do not take living in a group to imply either monogamy (pair bonding) or well-defined sexual division of labour, both of which were implicit in the original strong form of the home base hypothesis.

If there were a progression from routed foraging in groups to living in and moving between defensible central places, this has still to be documented archaeologically. As the resource-defence model suggests, group size would have been vital as humans left the shelter of the trees and became ground-dwellers. The need to cope with living in large social groups for defence would have propelled selection for increased intelligence. Social intelligence of this kind could have been applied in other domains and one of these was in the making of stone artefacts.

Oldowan artefacts

The name 'Oldowan' derives from Olduvai Gorge in Tanzania and is used to label the kinds of artefacts found at the earliest archaeological sites. Characteristic are large numbers of flakes of irregular shape, consistently smaller than 100 mm, and fewer chunky cores showing the scars of flake removals and, in some cases, battering, which suggests use in pounding or chopping. Mary Leakey devised a classification of the Oldowan artefacts according to which a number of different design classes or types could be recognised. This implied that the Oldowan artefact-makers were capable of mentally picturing standard designs of tools for specific tasks, a mental ability that other researchers argue developed only later. The weakness of the Leakey classification was that it grouped the chunkier core-like pieces into classes of choppers and ignored the more abundant, but variable, flake products. The Oldowan artefacts should rather be seen as a starter-level stone toolkit that reveals little control over design, other than reducing cores to flakes. This kind of toolkit is the minimum required to be effective: as a result the Oldowan stone technology was the only one used for the first million years. The 2.5 million-year-old artefacts from Gona (noted above) are not obviously more rudimentary than those dating to 1.8 million years at Olduvai.

Apart from occurring in the lower beds at Olduvai Gorge, Oldowan artefacts are also known from sites along the eastern rift valley from Tanzania to Ethiopia and from Malawi and South Africa. Because Oldowan technology is so basic and might be mistaken for the by-products of later traditions, Oldowan occurrences can only be identified with assurance at sites known to be appropriately old. In South Africa, artefacts that may be Oldowan have been reported from the gravel deposits of the Vaal River and elsewhere. However,

definite occurrences have been found at the sites of Sterkfontein and Swartkrans, where the associated fauna confirms their age. Even these two occurrences are sufficient indication that a population of Oldowan artefact-makers was present in South Africa because anything less than an established population would not leave findable archaeological traces. However, on this basis we cannot know how large or widespread that population was. The Oldowan artefacts recovered by Kathy Kuman and Ron Clarke from their large excavation in Member 5 at Sterkfontein date to the earliest Pleistocene between 1.7 and 2 million years – a reasonable estimate for the dating of the appearance of true humans in South Africa.

Descendants of the first true humans

It was the descendants of one habiline species that colonised the whole of the African continent and all other parts of the world. The initial dispersal, sometimes called 'Out of Africa 1', occurred between 1 and 2 million years ago. New dates (Tattersall 1997) for deposits containing fossils and artefacts in Java and China suggest the initial dispersal may have been almost 2 million years ago. At Dmanisi in Georgia, on the way out of Africa through western Asia, a human mandible is said to date to 1.6 million years, a further hint of high antiquity for the dispersal. However, these new datings need confirmation. Even if the older dating for the Asian fossils are substantiated, the pithecanthropines of Java and China, the classic representatives of *H. erectus*, are younger than the earliest fossils of *Homo* from Africa. The most economical hypothesis is that the early humans from Asia, the pithecanthropines, represent a human population whose founders moved out of Africa.

Dispersal events, which are really range expansions, are documented in many species at different times. The immediate cause of dispersal may not be obvious. Alan Turner, who developed an interest in studies of Pleistocene carnivore ecology while working with C.K. Brain at Swartkrans, has argued that the human expansion out of Africa paralleled the range expansion of African carnivores, thus linking human expansion to the emergence of hunting abilities.

As the number of African finds has grown, the question has been asked whether these fossils represent an African form of *H. erectus* or an ancestral species. A new scientific name, *H. ergaster*, has been proposed to accommodate African fossils that might have been the ancestors of *H. erectus* and later species of *Homo*. The best-known example is the 'Turkana boy', WT-15000 from Kenya, a very complete skeleton of a tall, 12-year-old youth dated to 1.7 million years and found in 1984; other well-preserved crania come from East Turkana. Among fossils now classified as *H. ergaster* by Bernard Wood of George Washington University, who has been influential in revising hominid taxonomy, is the find from Swartkrans originally labelled *Telanthropus capensis*.

Colin Groves, a biological anthropologist at the Australian National University, considers that among the older African fossils only OH 9 – a 1.4 million-year-old cranium from Olduvai Gorge – shows the specialised characters that link it with *H. erectus* from Asia. This implies that *H. erectus* represents a separate Asian branch of humanity, poorly represented, if at all, in Africa. Philip Rightmire, a leading authority and former student of John Robinson at the University of Wisconsin, takes a more conventional and widely accepted view that would lump the early descendants of the habiline ancestor in Africa and Asia in a single species, *H. erectus*. However, he would accept that in the Middle Pleistocene (after 700 000 years ago) *H. erectus* continued to inhabit Asia long after a different species had emerged in Africa and Europe.

The extensive areas in Europe of limestone, favourable for the preservation of bone, have been well explored. Although Europe, in more temperate latitudes, was marginal to the distribution of early humans, the search here has provided a number of important human fossil finds. None are as old as those from Africa or Asia and none date with any certainty to more than 800 000 years, although there are artefact occurrences that may be as much as 1 million or more years old. The Mauer jaw, from a quarry near Heidelberg in Germany, is one of the best-known fossil finds from Europe and may date to between 400 000 and 500 000 years. Other similar finds come from Petralona in Greece and Arago in France. In the Atapuerca hills of northern Spain at Sima de los Huesos (the 'pit of bones'), there are finds, dated to 400 000 years, comparable in morphol-ogy to other fossils from Europe. At a separate site, Gran Dolina, there are finds, including the face of a child, that are twice this age. The latter, labelled *H. antecessor*, have been heralded as representing a possible ancestor of all later humans.

In the early part of the century a new species, *H. heidelbergensis*, was proposed to accommodate the Mauer fossil. This name enjoys priority in labelling the species that shows more derived anatomical features than *H. ergaster* and *H. erectus,* on the one hand, and features that are less derived than modern humans, on the other. Some researchers prefer the informal descriptive label 'archaic' *H. sapiens* to any formal designation until better understanding emerges of Middle Pleistocene human variability in Europe as well as in Africa.

The African representatives of the early archaic *H. sapiens* (*H. heidelbergensis*) group include a skullcap from Elandsfontein, a farm between Hopefield and Langebaan in the Western Cape; the Kabwe finds (originally named *H. rhodesiensis*) from a lead–zinc mine in Zambia; the fossil from Lake Ndutu near Olduvai in Tanzania; and the very broad-faced find from Bodo in the Afar region of Ethiopia. These specimens date to the Middle Pleistocene, between 600 000 and 300 000 years ago. The parietal bones placed on the sides of the skull are more vertical than in *H. erectus;* this gives more vault to the cranium. In this and in other characteristics of the skull they differ from the contemporary Far Eastern *H. erectus* finds from China. It is early archaic *H. sapiens* that is the probable ancestor of later humans.

There is another source of information on the human story, and that is the archaeology. Do the artefacts tell the same story as the fossils? The answer must be an uncomfortable no. Although mental or cognitive abilities would be set at the time of speciation, their potential would only be realised sometime after the event. This means that the emergence of a new species would not be marked by a set of novel behaviours which archaeologists could document. This would explain why the basic Oldowan technology persisted until after humans more advanced than the habilines had emerged. Archaeologists have documented Acheulian technology associated with the descendants of *H. ergaster* and early archaic *H. sapiens* (*H. heidelbergensis*) in Africa. To archaeologists, Acheulian technology indicates a new level of complexity and, by inference, of thinking.

Acheulian artefacts

From as early as 1.4 million years ago in Africa, and later in western parts of Asia as far east as India and in southern Europe, artefact assemblages have been found that not only have cores and flakes, but include large, shaped stone tools made to a pattern. These mark the beginnings of style: making things according to rules about what to make and how to make them. Being bound by rules, determined by a collective appreciation of what is right and proper, is what Glynn Isaac considered to mark the difference between proto-human and human behaviour. Style goes beyond the primary level of function, as it involves choice in the way different kinds of artefacts are made. Choice involves the mind: for this reason the making of bifaces is significant as a window on the mind of the ancients.

The large tools found in these artefact assemblages range in length from 100 to 200 mm or more. Collectively they are called bifaces because they are normally shaped by flaking on both faces. In plan view they tend to be pear-shaped and are broad relative to their thickness. Most bifaces are pointed and are classified as handaxes, but others

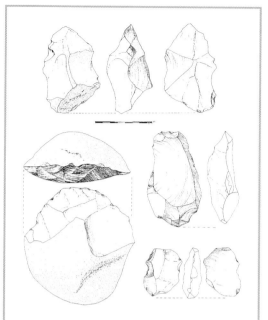

Figure 5.5: *Acheulian artefacts from Amanzi: cores (top and middle right), flaked cobble (bottom left) and flake (bottom right).*

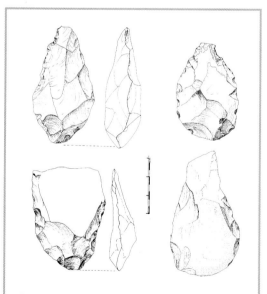

Figure 5.4: *Acheulian large bifaces: two examples of handaxes (top) and two examples of cleavers (bottom) from the Acheulian site of Amanzi Springs, near Uitenhage.*

have a wide cutting end and are termed cleavers. These bifaces are the *amandelklippe* (almond-shaped stones) that prospectors along the Vaal River in South Africa recognised as distinctive in the gravels which they were washing for diamonds. They are also the kind of artefacts Louis Péringuey collected from among the vines near Stellenbosch. The term 'Acheulian', from the site of St Acheul in France, has replaced the South African term 'Stellenbosch', originally proposed by Goodwin and Van Riet Lowe (1929) for this biface industry, to conform with what has now become an established term in international usage.

The habit of making bifaces persisted for more than a million years before they went out of fashion about 250 000 years ago in Africa. It was a habit shared by peoples on a continent-wide and even intercontinental scale. The bifaces made and used on the banks of the Vaal River have the same design, even though they are not made in the same raw material, as those found in Egypt and Morocco, southern Europe and India. Hallam Movius, the Harvard archaeologist who did much to stimulate an interest in Old World prehistory among American scholars, claimed that bifaces did not occur east of a north–south line that bisects India. Exploration of the Stone Age archaeology of the vast area of China has only progressed to a reconnaissance level and, although finds of rare bifaces have been claimed, it still has to be proved that Acheulian artefact-makers crossed the 'Movius line'. The distribution of bifaces shows that people over more than half the inhabited world shared, and passed on from generation to generation, the concept of a design for making these large stone tools.

Design types like handaxes and cleavers are called formal tools, to distinguish them typologically from the range of less standardised flakes and cores with which they are found in Acheulian assemblages. The formal biface component may make up less than 10 per cent of the artefacts in an Acheulian assemblage. The range of other less standardised artefacts may include some with clear edge damage, showing they were also used.

There are a number of interesting questions raised by Acheulian artefacts to which partial answers can be given. Why were bifaces made? Why did the design persist for such a long time? Why did bifaces have such a wide geographic spread? Bifaces were not ornaments and had a function as useful pieces of equipment. They are basically large and weighty pieces of shaped stone. There is no indication from the shaping that they were other than hand-held. Experiments at throwing them, using them as some sort of projectile, are unconvincing. Bifaces were shaped so as to produce continuous sharp edges and a point (a splayed point, in the case of cleavers). This suggests that they represent the best design for a hand-held large sharp tool. Its use in the hand rather than mounted on a handle limited the scope for any innovation and design changes.

Bifaces vary in finish: this has more to do with style than function. Making a biface requires initial shaping through the removal of a series of large flakes in sequence. The amount of further flaking required to produce a symmetrical finished product is variable even in the same assemblage. The whole process of making a biface, even one refined by much secondary shaping, would take a skilled knapper thirty minutes at most, a short time by any standard.

Most bifaces have an emphasis on the tip, while the sides, or laterals, receive various treatment. In older reports much was made of the so-called S-twist, the sinuous line of the laterals on some refined handaxes. This was thought to be linked to the innovation of using a soft wooden or bone hammer for removing the finishing flakes. Behind such classification lay the hope that archaeologists would be able to distinguish such evolutionary stages in biface manufacture and thereby obtain a relative dating for Acheulian sites. Bifaces, however, do not show strongly patterned trends in style of manufacture in either time or space. At best one can say that features like the S-twist and sinuous edges on bifaces, produced by numbers of flat invasive trimming flakes, indicate a later rather than an earlier Acheulian site.

The function of bifaces has been widely discussed in the archaeological literature. Inferences about function can be made from the edge damage that tools show and from what is associated with them. From the emphasis on the tip or, in the case of cleaver forms, the transverse cutting edge, and the general absence of heavy damage or utilisation on either the tip or the laterals, one can deduce that bifaces were used on soft, non-abrasive materials. This would rule out digging in the ground for roots or chopping at a hard material like wood. Of the many suggestions put forward, the most probable use was as a butchering tool, a heavy tool to get through the hide and sinew of an animal carcass. While a light-duty flake may do good service in cutting up an antelope, something heavier like a biface would be more appropriate for dismembering an elephant or hippopotamus. A butchering function is supported by the general association with animal remains where bone is preserved. There is experimental evidence for the effectiveness of large bifaces in butchery. Louis Leakey engaged in such exhibitions, and others who have followed by conducting more rigorous butchery experiments have provided ample confirmation (Schick & Toth 1993).

The dating of Acheulian sites is still relatively limited. Sites from the Cape to Morocco are assumed to cover broadly the same age range, while sites outside Africa probably date to the latter part of this range. This would be consistent with the expansion of handaxe-makers out of Africa to Eurasia.

We need to explain the wide distribution and

typological similarity of Acheulian artefacts wherever found. The explanation lies in what the biface-makers did for a living, the ecological niche that they occupied. There is an important clue in the setting of Acheulian sites. In southern Africa, where Acheulian sites are numerous, they occur normally in valley bottoms or wetlands. This indicates that Acheulian people had a preferred habitat: they were terrain specialists or, in technical terms, stenotopic as opposed to eurytopic. The fact that the riverine habitat is distributed in long narrow zones explains the continent-wide distribution achieved by Acheulian groups at the low density of population inferred for that time. This habitat is a relatively constant environment, buffered against seasonal changes, and productive of animal and plant foods. It is the favoured habitat of large herbivores, notably hippopotami, which as walking stores of fat would have been of particular importance. For Acheulian groups, occupying a narrow niche, there was no premium on innovation, and biface manufacture persisted unchanged for many millennia. Modern peoples, on the other hand, were able to range more widely in the landscape.

The task of the archaeologist has not been made easy by the biface-makers' preference for riverine camping sites. These are dynamic sedimentary environments where rivers cut and fill their beds. In such environments it is difficult to establish direct associations of artefacts with features and food remains, like the bones of particular animals. Acheulian sites are very ancient and as a rule are more often disturbed than younger Stone Age sites. Preservation of materials other than stone artefacts is normally limited. These considerations pose special problems for the researcher. All the same this million-year period of biface-making remains an important chapter in human history and is in need of more intensive research. The following case studies illustrate what evidence of these times the archaeologist can obtain in the field.

Case study: Vaal River

The valley of the Vaal River, where it flows past Windsorton, Pniel, Canteen Kopje at Barkly West and Schmidtsdrift to the junction with the Orange River near Douglas, is rich in Acheulian sites.

There are extensive beds of gravels: mining these in the diamond rush of the last century turned up unmistakable bifaces. One visitor commented that there were not only enough handaxes to fill a museum, but also enough to build the museum.

A detailed study of the artefacts in the Vaal River area was started by Van Riet Lowe and collaborators in 1935. The area was so large and artefacts, reworked by the river or uncovered by prospectors, so plentiful that there seemed no need to study the details of the stratigraphy by excavation. In the 1950s, when Revil Mason began a programme of excavation, it was shown that the artefacts lay on, rather than in, the gravels although they were sometimes covered by surface wash. In this ancient landscape the gravel bars had been formed long before the arrival of people, and from earliest times people living in the valley had mined the gravels for stone to make their artefacts.

There are impressive concentrations of artefacts at Canteen Kopje, a national monument, and at Pniel near Barkly West. One of these, known as Power's site after its discoverer, J.H. Power, has a rich concentration of handaxes and cleavers on the river bank. A meander in the river is eroding what was perhaps an Acheulian base camp, and many of the smaller artefacts have been winnowed out by the flow of the river. Sites away from the immediate course of the river are potentially more informative. In Acheulian times, there was a strong presence of people in the Vaal–Orange drainage basin, and sites are associated with pans and springs; there is even occupation in a rare cave, Wonderwerk Cave. This is a site museum open to the public.

The site of Doornlaagte, between Schmidtsdrift and Kimberley, was discovered by an observant bulldozer-driver working at a roadside quarry. The quarry was in calcrete, a naturally lime-cemented fossil soil that is found widely in the drier parts of the Northern Cape. The white of the powdery calcrete contrasted strongly with the artefacts, made of green lava, that appeared in abundance at a depth of 2 m. Prompt action by the National Monuments Council managed to preserve a 20 x 7 m area on the quarry floor for an archaeological study directed by Revil Mason.

At Doornlaagte the calcrete had developed in an ancient pan deposit. Pans are shallow seasonal lakes in hollows or depressions. They are formed

Figure 5.6: *Power's site on the Vaal River.*

by the combined action of the chemical weathering of *brak* spring waters breaking down the bedrock, and the scouring effect of wind blowing away the weathered products to create a depression. Pans are common in a broad strip from the Swaziland border to Namaqualand in rocks of Karoo age. They are associated with old drainage lines and dolerite dykes – impervious igneous rocks intruded into the lower Karoo sediments that force the salty, or *brak,* underground waters to the surface as springs. Dolerite (*ysterklip*) dykes, widespread in the Karoo, form long ridges and koppies of boulder-strewn shiny black rock. The presence of boulders of dolerite at Doornlaagte suggests that a dyke-controlled spring played an important role in the formation of this pan. Deepwater and shore-line deposits can be distinguished by the analysis of the sediments, as the shore-edge facies are coarser and sandier, like a beach.

The Acheulian artefacts occur in and on shore-edge deposits and are sandwiched between older and younger deeper-water sediments. The picture that can be pieced together is of people living on a gravel bar or beach ridge on the edge of a semi-permanent body of water. Under the present climatic regime, conditions are too arid for such a water body to exist but, as this and other episodes of full pans show, there have been wetter periods in the past.

The excavation exposed almost 2000 loosely packed artefacts on a sloping surface. Artefacts occur below this surface to a depth of some 300 millimetres. The total number of artefacts in the block of preserved deposit may be as many as ten times the number recorded on the surface. As only part of the deposit was saved from destruction, the numbers of artefacts discarded on the edge of this pan were in the tens of thousands. A relatively dense concentration like this can be described as a lag deposit. Some of the finer sediments, smaller flaking debris and all the organic material, plant and bone, have been lost through winnowing and decay. The larger artefacts have remained to mark the place. This number of artefacts may have accumulated over tens and hundreds of years. Current dating techniques do not have the precision to measure the time over which the site formed, and the site itself has yet to be adequately dated. Most of the Acheulian sites in the Vaal basin probably date between 1 million and 500 000 years; Doornlaagte may date to the younger part of this range.

The artefacts include a range of sizes of large bifaces, including classic handaxes and cleavers, and a number of very large flakes and the specially prepared cores from which these large flakes were struck. Called 'Victoria West cores' because they were first described from the Karoo town of that name, such cores were designed to produce flake blanks large enough to make bifaces. These cores allowed the artefact-maker to control the size and shape of the flake blank by removing preparatory flakes across the surface of the core and from the side of the core that was the striking platform.

This technique of preparing the core for the removal of blanks of predetermined size and shape is generally known as the Levallois technique. In the European Middle Palaeolithic of much younger dating, such techniques were used to produce standard flakes, though of smaller size. Van Riet Lowe described Victoria West cores as proto-Levallois cores, indicating they were a forerunner of the wider adoption of the prepared core or Levallois technique. The prepared core technique was an integral part of the African Acheulian: in Africa the presence or absence of the Levallois technique is not a marker for the distinction between what in Europe is known as the Lower and Middle Palaeolithic.

Mason interpreted the Doornlaagte site as a living floor. This implied that the site was a base camp. In the absence of faunal and plant remains there is no direct evidence of the range of these activities. That this was indeed a base camp is indicated by the localised concentration of artefacts in a context where transport has not been a factor. Given the number of artefacts included in the lag deposit, it was probably a place to which people frequently returned. We can only guess at the drawcard for their return – perhaps hippopotami wallowing in the waters were the reason why people came back to the site.

Case study: Elandsfontein

The Elandsfontein site is 10 km inland of the Langebaan Lagoon on the south-west coast of South Africa, north of Cape Town. It is significant for finds of Acheulian artefacts, a human skullcap and a diverse fauna.

The area is an impermanent dunefield, 1 x 2 km in extent. The sand substrate has been eroded by the wind into dunes; the dunes move up and down the area with the changing directions of dominant summer and winter winds. Wind is a powerful scouring agent and wind erosion continually exposes bones and artefacts in the swales between the dunes. Where erosion reaches the water table – the limit for wind erosion – standing pools of water form. It is around such water holes that animal and human activities have been concentrated in the past.

More than 100 000 fossil bones and several thousand artefacts have been collected from this extensive site and are stored in the South African Museum for study. The main fossil horizon, a zone about 1 m thick, is the source of most of these finds. The animal bones are from natural deaths, carnivore kills and hyena lairs; these have become buried at or near the water table by sand movement. As the relatively low frequency of artefacts

Figure 5.7: *Excavation in the sands at Elandsfontein.*

20 • Pointing a handaxe •

Putting a point on an Acheulian handaxe required knowledge of a set of rules. Goodwin described it as similar to sharpening a pencil with a blade, but how does one sharpen a pencil in stone? It takes five flake removals in a sequence. The first flake is struck from the upper surface towards the back of the piece. This provides the surface or platform for the removal of two flakes from either side across the ventral, or under, surface. These in turn provide the platforms for two further removals across the dorsal, or upper, surface. This sequence of removals blocks out the handaxe point; further flaking can shape the whole piece and remove any irregularities caused by the initial blocking-out. In the process the traces of the initial flaking sequence may be obliterated. Only by examining a large number of handaxes in varying stages of manufacture is it possible to follow the steps in pointing a handaxe. Learning a craft like handaxe-making occurs by observation rather than by explanation. For this reason we cannot assume that because rules were followed, spoken language, as we know it, was involved.

shows, human groups were present but theirs was a lesser role. This is confirmed by the study of marks on the bones. Richard Milo of Chicago has developed a technique, using a low-powered microscope, to distinguish between the tooth marks and gnawing of carnivores and the cut marks and impact fractures produced by human actions. Most bone damage at Elandsfontein is from carnivores.

From the species represented, the major part of the faunal collection is Middle Pleistocene in age (400 000 to 800 000 years). The fauna is dominated by modern genera but these genera are represented by extinct species. There are also genera that have become extinct: *Hipparion*, the three-toed horse, ancestral to the genus *Equus* to which modern one-toed horses like zebras and domesticated horses belong, survived into the Middle Pleistocene and is represented at Elandsfontein. The giant baboon, *Therapithecus oswaldi*, twice the size of the Cape Point baboons and related to the gelada baboon now restricted to Somalia, made its last appearance in southern Africa in the Middle Pleistocene. Also recorded from Elandsfontein are a short-necked giraffe with deer-like antlers, *Sivatherium*, particularly well represented in a 4.5 million-year-old Pliocene fauna from nearby Langebaanweg, and a sabre-toothed cat; these may be chance inclusions from an older fauna.

The diversity in the Middle Pleistocene fauna is most impressive. Historically, only the Cape hartebeest occurred in the plains around Malmesbury and Hopefield. In the Middle Pleistocene, however, as the faunal analyses most recently by Richard Klein and Kathy Cruz-Uribe (1991) have shown, there were as many as six members of the wildebeest–hartebeest tribe of antelopes, the alcelaphines, which are all dedicated grazers. There was also a niche for a browser like the kudu, a mixed feeder like the eland, and the larger herbivores, which included the extinct giant buffalo, *Pelorovis*, hippopotamus, the black and white rhinoceros, and elephant. Pigs, giraffids and carnivores were also present.

The challenge of Elandsfontein is to understand how and why the ecosystem has changed since Acheulian times. There are clues in the soils and in the animal remains that point to differences in vegetation and climate in the past.

Parts of the area are mantled by red-brown sands and there are upstanding ridges of rusty red-coloured cemented sands that snake across the site. Excavation has shown that the fossils and Acheulian artefacts occur beneath the red-brown horizon which formed as a soil after their deposition. The colour is due to the oxidation of iron, originally accumulated as iron humates from acids released by plants in a soil horizon at the water table. This soil, technically a podzol, seems to have formed in the sands under conditions of a higher water table and a cover of vegetation. Middle Stone Age artefacts apparently associated with this episode of soil formation suggest a dating in the Late Pleistocene, perhaps some 60 000 years ago.

The evidence for soil formation is significant in reconstructing the ecological setting in the past. Podzols are associated with acid sands. The vegetation at present surrounding the site, coastal fynbos, grows on nutrient-poor acid sands and has a low carrying capacity for animals. This vegetation, poor in grasses, would not support a diverse fauna, especially one rich in grazers, as in the Middle Pleistocene. Perhaps the best modern analogue for the vegetation of the Middle Pleistocene is the ribbon of strandveld, a thicket vegetation, growing on shelly alkaline sands along the coast today. In contrast to the fynbos it is capable of supporting a high animal biomass and possibly attracting herds of grazers seasonally. The basal sands at Elandsfontein, below the acid cover sands, are alkaline; thus an episode of deeper wind scouring in the past, to the depths at which the fossils occur, could have resulted in marked ecological changes.

The environment may have changed in other ways. Richard Klein has measured the sizes of the tooth rows of jackals and hyenas and related these measurements to body size. Body size in groups like carnivores correlates closely with mean annual temperature. Thus in cold glacial periods, body sizes tend to be larger and in warmer interglacials they tend to be smaller. The carnivores from Elandsfontein are about the same size as in the present in this area, suggesting that mean temperatures were the same as now. This would not rule out greater seasonal differences between summer and winter temperatures or differences in seasonal precipitation. As can be seen in the example of the Cango Valley, an increase in the summer rainfall component favours the spread of subtropical pioneer grass species: this may be the lesson to be learnt from the range of grazers in the Elandsfontein fauna.

In 1954 a significant find was made of the top of a human skull, not as a whole but in 60 pieces. The first fragment was found by an archaeological assistant, Keith Jolly, and recognised as human by Ronald Singer, a South African-trained anatomist who has had a long association with the University of Chicago and who initiated the investigation of

the Elandsfontein site. Singer immediately organised the search for the other pieces. The assembled pieces have become known as the Saldanha skull. Although not as massive as the Kabwe skull from Zambia, it represents archaic *Homo sapiens*.

From the Elandsfontein site researchers have collected artefacts as different as Acheulian hand-axes, rare Stillbay points found in the red-brown sands, and pieces of Khoekhoe pottery and some Dutch clay pipes on the surface. These finds show the attraction of water holes in this sandy environment. Not only was surface water scarce, but stone is completely absent and had to be imported. The raw materials of which the Acheulian bifaces were made are silcrete, for which the nearest source is Hopefield, and quartz porphyry, from a source near Saldanha. These sources are 10–30 km away. The presence of core-like blocks of raw material shows that some stone was imported for artefact-making on the site but the majority of artefacts may have been imported as finished products. Consistent with the Middle Pleistocene age of the main fossil fauna, the majority of the artefacts are typologically Acheulian.

Within the dunefield area, the most coherent concentration of Acheulian artefacts was excavated from below a remnant block of red-brown sands by Ronald Singer and his collaborator, John Wymer, an archaeologist well known for his Acheulian research in Britain. From the excavation and the wind-deflated margin of the red-brown sand remnant, the positions of some 130 artefacts and numbers of bones were plotted. The proportion of large bifaces – 49 handaxes and 1 cleaver –

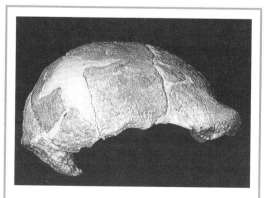

Figure 5.8: *The skull cap (calvarium) of the so-called Saldanha skull from Elandsfontein.*

is high for an Acheulian occurrence but would be expected if stone tools were imported. The hand-axes are in the smaller size range for such tools. They show a high degree of refinement, indicating that they were shaped by many flake removals, and in shape they are broad relative to their length, thin in cross-section and very similar to each other. This suggests they were made and used by the same pairs of hands and discarded at this place at the same time. Smaller refined handaxes found here are assumed to be characteristic of the later phases of the Acheulian.

Singer and Wymer (1968) have interpreted this occurrence as a kill site. None of the artefacts show sand blasting, which would have occurred if they had lain exposed on the surface between separate visits; their similarity in form is evidence that they represent a single, short-term visit to the location. However, we should not accept as obvious that it was a kill site, because the bones analysed by Richard Klein represent an assortment of body parts of different species rather than those of a particular animal. Bone is more susceptible to both physical and chemical attack and the bones at this location are in variable condition. Evidence from the marks of stone tools on the bone is mostly lacking. Instead, there is no direct association of the fauna with the artefacts at this location and other parts of the site. The fauna as a whole provides a comprehensive picture of the range of animal species that shared this habitat with the Acheulians. Although there would have been carcasses from carnivore kills to scavenge and a variety of antelope to hunt, people may have been there to get the fatty tissues of hippopotamus in the pools rather than concerning themselves with the lean meat of antelope.

The Earlier Stone Age: a perspective

When defined by Goodwin and Van Riet Lowe in 1929, the Earlier Stone Age comprised the Stellenbosch, Victoria West and Fauresmith industries. They saw these industries as representing the beginnings of Stone Age settlement of southern Africa. The term Stellenbosch has been replaced by Acheulian; Victoria West is now used to denote a technique to prepare cores so as to produce large flakes; and the Fauresmith, noted for small bifaces, is thought to be a late phase of the Acheulian. In 1929 it was not appreciated that for about 1 million years before Acheulian bifaces became the characteristic tool design, only cores and flakes of simpler Oldowan design were made. In the absence of any reliable dating techniques, it was inconceivable to men like Goodwin and Van Riet Lowe that Acheulian bifaces themselves had been made for a further million years. Since 1929 the dating revolution has radically changed our knowledge of the duration of the Earlier Stone Age.

People using Oldowan technology were living in South Africa as much as 2 million years ago. Oldowan artefacts may be associated with a habiline at Sterkfontein and *H. ergaster* at Swartkrans. It is the widespread occurrence of Acheulian bifaces after 1.5 million years ago that is striking: these are distinctive and easily recognised artefacts. In this chapter it has been argued that the Acheulian artefact-makers were terrain specialists (stenotopic), inhabiting valleys and wetlands. This narrow linear distribution explains why even with low population densities Acheulian groups are found from the Cape to Morocco.

The earliest Acheulian occurrences may be associated with *H. ergaster* but there are few fossils from Africa, apart from the Bodo skull, that date to between 1.4 million years and 600 000 years. The Bodo find is classified as an archaic *H. sapiens* and was associated with Acheulian artefacts. From these skeletal remains and from the size of flakes associated with Acheulian assemblages generally, we know that tool-makers were able to strike large flakes off hard materials like quartzite boulders. Some examples in the gravels of the Eerste River near Stellenbosch would have required remarkable strength and skill. We can therefore suggest that the Acheulian tool-makers were larger and more muscular than modern people.

The Hebrew University archaeologists Anna Belfer-Cohen and Naama Goren-Inbar have described the behaviour of Acheulian groups as near-modern, basing their description on the chain of operations followed in making bifaces. This shows an appreciation of geometry and form that is not too different from modern peoples. But it is the restricted habitat occupied by Acheulian groups that sets them apart from later, widely dispersed modern peoples of the Middle and Later Stone Ages. The implications of this distribution are discussed in the following chapters.

CHAPTER SIX

Emergence of modern people

The ape-men and the early true humans are remote in our ancestry. A more pressing question is, Where and when did our immediate ancestors emerge? Earlier in the twentieth century the conventional wisdom was that it may have been from some Neanderthal-like human, possibly in the Near East. In the 1920s and 1930s Dorothy Garrod excavated a number of important archaeological sites in what was then Palestine. In the Mount Carmel area, south of the town of Haifa, she excavated the caves of Skhul and Tabun with a team of labourers. To the eminent physical anthropologists Arthur Keith and Theodore McCown, the human remains that were recovered from among many thousands of artefacts seemed to represent a single variable population showing a mix of Neanderthal and modern characters. As these are adjacent caves and the deposits are of similar age it was logical to assume the inhabitants had belonged to the same population. Further research revealed that the Tabun remains are those of Neanderthals and are different from the early modern human remains at Skhul. It now appears that the Near East was once the boundary zone between the Neanderthals, adapted to cold climate, and the early moderns, adapted to warm climate, and their respective geographic ranges shifted with changing climates. This was a complication not foreseen by Keith and McCown. Different kinds of humans were sampled at these sites, not transitional forms between Neanderthals and modern people, as Keith and McCown had assumed.

In western Europe, both Neanderthals – the epitome of brutish cavemen in the popular imagination – and early moderns – called Cro-Magnons after a rock shelter in the foothills of the Pyrenees – were well known. However, in the layered French cave sequences the replacement of Neanderthals by Cro-Magnons appeared to be abrupt, too abrupt for Neanderthals to have evolved into Cro-Magnons in that part of the globe. For as along as the Keith and McCown interpretation was accepted, the Near East seemed to offer the solution to the problem of where the transition took place. It was assumed that the Near East was the centre of origin of modern humans and that they migrated to Europe and either exterminated or absorbed the Neanderthals. The hypothetical first meeting of the 'primitive' Neanderthals and 'advanced' Cro-Magnons has long fired the imagination of authors and film-makers.

As long as there were few human remains from outside Europe and the Near East to which even rough dates could be given, the Near Eastern centre for the origin of modern people went uncontested. The theory was weakened, however, when radiocarbon dating showed that modern people were present some 40 000 years ago at Niah Great Cave in Sarawak, the north-western portion of the island of Borneo, apparently as early as those in the Near East, and that modern people had reached far-away Australia more than 30 000 years ago. Even more puzzling were claims that in South Africa there were modern human remains dating to more than 100 000 years. All these provided indications that the emergence of modern humans was more complex than had been assumed.

It needed a new approach to encourage rethinking of the problem. In 1986 a paper published in Nature *on the patterning of varieties (polymorphisms) of nuclear (n) DNA in people from different geographical populations (Wainscoat et al. 1986) showed that humankind could be divided into two groups, African and non-African, and that the African group was ancestral. Another paper published in* Science *in the following year (Cann et al. 1987) reported the results of the study of mitochondrial (mt) DNA in different populations. One should note that mtDNA is inherited in the female line. This paper drew considerable press coverage because it stated in clear and catchy terms that all living humans are the descendants of an African 'Eve', a mother who lived some 200 000 years ago, somewhere in sub-Saharan Africa. These landmark papers stimulated teams of molecular biologists to look for evidence of our ancestry in different gene complexes and gave new purpose to physical anthropology and archaeology. The 'Eve' story has been recounted in a number of popular books by science journalists and she has appeared on the cover of* Time *magazine. Research specialists regularly convene meetings at learned societies to debate the question of modern human origins and consider evidence from all parts of the globe that might be relevant to their dispersal. This chapter gives a South African perspective on the emergence of our own kind of humanity. It also discusses the archaeology of the Middle Stone Age because the earliest-known modern human remains are from Middle Stone Age contexts in South Africa. [HJD]*

'Genetics means that now, at last, perceptions of human quality need not depend on what is on the surface. For the first time it is possible to form an impartial view of just how different races might be. The answer is clear. The biological differences among them are small and the evidence for the mental superiority of one or the other so flimsy, confused and full of intellectual dishonesty as to be scarcely worth considering' (Jones 1996).

Unity of living humans

All living humans are members of one single variable (polytypic) 'rainbow' species, *Homo sapiens*. Different languages are spoken, different beliefs held and different customs practised, but mates from any culture or region can produce fertile children – the hallmark of a species. With the wide geographical distribution of humankind, local populations have become relatively isolated and regional differences have developed through natural selection. Peoples living in regions of the hot savanna climates tend to have a tall, slender build, as this biotype aids dissipation of heat, while those living in high latitudes tend to have stout bodies and short arms and legs because their biotype conserves body heat. In the same way the melanin of darker skins in the tropics gives better protection against the sun's ultraviolet rays, a cause of

melanoma or skin cancer that can be fatal. Selection for lighter, more transparent skins in the cooler regions may aid in the synthesis of vitamin D, but the reasons are likely to be more complex and are not fully understood. While body build, skin colour, hair form and facial features are expressions of small biological differences, in general all living humans are remarkably alike.

The reason is that modern people are members of a geologically recent species, *H. sapiens,* and their dispersal is even more recent. With the spread of agriculture, the development of trade, the growth of cities and the invention of means for long-distance travel within the last 10 000 years only, the world has become crowded with people and their numbers are doubling each generation.

The biological unity of humankind is encoded in our bones and soft tissues, in our genes and in the way we think and act. This unity is not generally appreciated and it makes nonsense of perceived differences of race and ethnicity, the point made by Steve Jones in the quote at the head of this chapter.

Fossil evidence for the emergence of modern humans

Finds of the oldest fossils and artefacts show that Africa was the evolutionary centre for the emergence of the genus *Homo*. What is currently being debated is whether Africa continued to be the centre of human evolution and was the continent where modern people like ourselves, *H. sapiens*, evolved. But many scientists, including Colin Groves and his colleague Marta Lahr of the University of São Paulo in Brazil, make the point that it is only in Africa that a series of fossils that link *H. ergaster / H. erectus* to modern humans has been found. This is strong reason to associate Africa with the emergence of modern humans.

The fossils that form this series would include those informally termed early archaic and late archaic *H. sapiens*. Gunter Bräuer of the University of Hamburg (Bräuer *et al.* 1997) dates the transition from early archaic *H. sapiens* or *H. heidelbergensis* to late archaic *H. sapiens* at 350 000–250 000 years ago. The late archaic group includes specimens from North and East Africa, and the Cave of Hearths in the Makapan Valley near Pietersburg and the Florisbad hot-water spring deposit, 40 km north of Bloemfontein, in South Africa. The Florisbad skull, which may be as old as 250 000 years (Grün *et al.* 1996), was formally named *H. helmei* in 1935 by T.F. Dreyer, a zoologist and a pioneer South African palaeoanthropologist. The specimen shows the combination of archaic and modern characteristics that typifies this group of fossils as a whole. *H. helmei* is a possible scientific name for the late archaic group if together they merit recognition as a separate species of *Homo*. In a recent discussion of the evolution of modern humans Rob Foley, the biological anthropologist from Cambridge, and Marta Lahr (Foley & Lahr 1997) see *H. helmei* as the immediate ancestor of modern humans in Africa and, more controversially, of the Neanderthals of Europe and the Near East.

The Neanderthals are of particular interest because they are so well represented in the fossil record in Europe and because so much has been

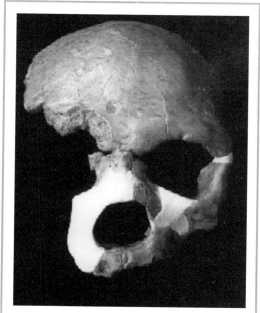

Figure 6.1: *The Clarke reconstruction of the Florisbad cranium* (H. helmei). *Note the impression of a hyena canine on the forehead.*

written about them. *In Search of the Neanderthals: Solving the Puzzle of Human Origins* by Chris Stringer and Clive Gamble (1993), *The Neandertals: Changing the Image of Mankind* by Erik Trinkhaus and Pat Shipman (1993) and *The Last Neanderthal: The Rise, Success, and Mysterious Extinction of our Closest Human Relatives* by Ian Tattersall (1995) are among the well-informed and readable accounts of the Neanderthals. *The Neanderthal Legacy* by Paul Mellars (1996) is an authoritative account of their archaeology. Since their discovery in the last century in Europe, the Neanderthals have been variously classified as a different species, *H. neanderthalensis*, and as a separate subspecies, *H. sapiens neanderthalensis*. In the early years of this century the French anatomist Marcellin Boule undertook a detailed anatomical study of the La Chapelle-aux-Saints skeleton, which was to prove very influential. Boule presented the Neanderthals as an overly primitive form of humankind; this became the stereotype for the brutish caveman in the popular imagination. Later researchers have been able to correct the bias in Boule's research. We now understand the

Neanderthals as close relatives of modern people but different from them. Views have been divided on whether Neanderthals contributed to our genes or became extinct without issue. A recently announced breakthrough has been the extraction of Neanderthal mtDNA from the arm bone of the 30 000 year-old skeleton found in 1856 – the original Neanderthal specimen – by a University of Munich team of researchers led by Svante Pääbo. Differences in the Neanderthal mtDNA sequence from that of all modern humans indicate that interbreeding was improbable and that Neanderthals diverged from the common ancestor before the emergence of modern humans.

Among the marks that distinguish the Neanderthals from modern humans are features of the back of the skull, a ridge (occipital bun) and hollow (suprainic depression), features of the ear and nose regions (they had particularly large noses) as well as characteristic brow ridges, and lack of a chin. They were very strong-muscled, stocky people whose body form indicates a strenuous life in the cold and dry environments of Ice Age Europe. *H. neanderthalensis,* with a brain capacity as large as or larger than that of modern humans, appears to have suffered a wave-like extinction initiated· about 40 000 years ago; the last survivors persisted in southern Spain until 27 000 years ago (Tattersall 1995).

Apparently contemporary with modern humans in Africa and Neanderthals in Europe were late representatives of *H. erectus* in parts of Asia. The main finds, 15 human crania and a few other body parts, come from a geomorphologically young, fossil-rich terrace of the Solo River at Ngandong in central Java. This is the same area where the original but much older *H. erectus* specimens were found. The crania are relatively large-brained, overlapping in range with modern humans, but they retain a *H. erectus* morphology. These finds (also known as *H. soloensis*) have proved difficult to date, partly because the associated fauna has not been adequately analysed. To obtain a more precise estimate of the age of the specimens, Carl Swisher and his team (Swisher *et al.* 1996) have used ESR and uranium disequilibrium dating on the teeth from a small faunal sample excavated from the same bone-rich terrace deposit that yielded the human crania. The results indicate an age of 50 000 years or younger, well within the time range of Neanderthals and modern humans elsewhere. The implication is that until recently very different kinds of humans lived in parts of the world, but now there is only one.

Most living populations have lost the robust architecture of the skull and limbs of early modern humans. Changes in diet and lifeways have reduced the need for heavy chewing, as reflected in the skull, and for strenuous activities, which required stout limb bones. However, early modern humans can be linked to living humans in the high vault to the skull, the retraction of the face under the brain case, and the presence of a chin. Among the South African sites (Figure 6.3) that have yielded early anatomically modern human remains dating to 120 000 years and younger are Klasies River main site, Border Cave, Die Kelders Cave 1, Blombos Cave and Equus Cave. A further site at Hoedjiespunt has produced remains that may relate to this group. Other find sites of early modern remains in sub-Saharan Africa are Mumba Cave in Tanzania, the Omo River deposits north of Lake Turkana, and Diré-Dawa Cave in Ethiopia. Of comparable antiquity, dated to 90 000 years, are the very complete finds of early modern human remains from the caves of Qafzeh and Skhul in Israel. Ofer Bar-Yosef, a Harvard-based archaeologist working in Israel, has argued that early modern people in the Near East were replaced by Neanderthals some 75 000 years ago, with the Neanderthals in turn being replaced by later modern people 45 000 years ago. This picture of one population replacing another is understandable if the geographical range of the cold-adapted Neanderthals, centred on Europe, expanded and contracted with the shifts in climatic zones during the Last Glacial period. Under the warmer climatic conditions of the early Late Pleistocene, African faunas expanded into the Near East and, with them, as the sites of Skhul and Qafzeh show, so did early modern humans.

The modern human origins debate

The debate on the emergence of modern humans has polarised around two competing hypotheses. The hypothesis that enjoys the majority support, and the one preferred here, is that of the single centre of origin. In variant forms it is also known as the 'African Eve', the 'Garden of Eden', the 'Out of Africa 2' and the 'Recent African Origins' hypothesis, each with slightly different predictions. The last hypothesis, for example, which has amongst its prominent advocates Gunter Bräuer and Chris Stringer of the Natural History Museum in London, holds that all living people are descended from a population that had its centre of origin in Africa and adjacent areas. This implies that early modern people everywhere share an African skeletal morphology. Dispersal of the early modern ancestors out of the centre resulted in the replacement or assimilation of archaic peoples elsewhere. As a consequence of the movement out of Africa, all parts of the Old World and the New Worlds of Australia and the Americas became populated. The recent African origin of modern peoples carries the further implication that geographical or racial differences cannot be traced back to archaic kinds of humans.

The second hypothesis, the multi-regional hypothesis, appeals to an evolutionary process known as anagenesis, a term that means that evolutionary change took place within a single lineage without branching into separate species. This hypothesis stresses continuity in evolution in the many regions to which humans dispersed after leaving their African homeland a million or more years ago. What has allowed the regional populations to evolve together is gene flow, not through large-scale migrations, but through people meeting and interbreeding. This implies that early humans like *H. erectus* were ancient forms of *H. sapiens* and that as a consequence of gene flow, modern humans have had many ancestors but no single centre of origin. In direct contrast, the single centre of origin hypothesis appeals to the evolutionary process known as cladogenesis or branching and holds that *H. sapiens* is a recently evolved and the only surviving branch of humankind.

The multi-regional or polycentric concept was proposed in the 1940s by the anatomist Frans Weidenreich, who had been responsible for the study of the Chinese *H. erectus* fossils from the caves at Zhoukoudian near Beijing. His particular interest (Trinkhaus & Shipman 1993) was in explaining the place of the Chinese *H. erectus* fossils in the ancestry of the Mongolian (Chinese) group or race. Weidenreich considered that the long separation of the major regional populations

which he recognised – the Australian, Mongolian, African and Eurasian groups – could be traced in the anatomical characters of the fossils from those regions. Biological connections between the regional populations – the flow of genes – enabled parallel evolution from the archaic to modern forms to occur in all regions.

Weidenreich's ideas have been taken up and extended by a later generation of researchers in their formulation of the multi-regional hypothesis. The hypothesis has been seen by some as having racist overtones but this is vigorously disputed (Wolpoff & Caspari 1996). There are, however, reservations among other anatomists and geneticists, who doubt that regional continuities can be traced in specific anatomical characters or that gene flow between small, widespread populations in the Pleistocene would have balanced the tendency for populations to become isolated and to diverge.

Genetic evidence for modern human origins

While human fossils are, and always will be, rare chance finds, the some 40 000 genes of living humans are potentially a considerable source of information on the history of our species. Advances in analytical techniques have made it possible to make comparisons between individuals not only in terms of conventional genetic markers like blood groups but also through sequencing or decoding the chemical composition of lengths of DNA. Much research has focused on the patterns of variation in mtDNA in different geographical populations because, among other advantages, mtDNA is easy to isolate. Studies of nDNA from other parts of the human genome, like the Y chromosome, which determines the male sex, are developing in importance.

The initial mtDNA studies, like those of Alan Wilson and his students Rebecca Cann and Mark Stoneking (Cann *et al.* 1987), introduced the concept of an 'African Eve', and carried strong predictions (Stoneking 1993):

• All mtDNA in living populations can be traced back to a single ancestor, a woman, because mtDNA is inherited in the female line. This woman, dubbed the lucky mother, was not the only person alive but one in a population whose

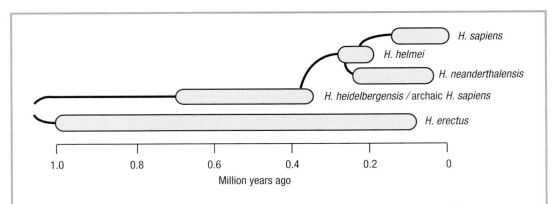

Figure 6.2: *One of several possible interpretations of the fossil record. Archaic* H. sapiens *is shown as ancestral to* H. helmei, *which is in turn ancestral to* H. sapiens *(modern humans). The late survival of* H. erectus *and* H. neanderthalensis *is indicated and as recently as 50 000 years ago there were three contemporary human species.*

mtDNA did not become extinct. She would have been the mtDNA ancestor and other genes would have had other ancestors. As diversity or variety develops through time as a product of mutation, the mtDNA ancestor is the starting point, or point of coalescence, from which the diversity in contemporary populations derives.

• The mtDNA ancestor lived in Africa. The source of new variation in mtDNA is mutation, and the number of differences in two mtDNA types due to mutation reflects how recently the individuals shared a common ancestor. Constructing an ancestor–descendant, or phylogenetic tree from the geographic distribution of mtDNA types produces a basic tree with two branches. One branch includes only types found in individuals of African descent and the other branch includes individuals of African and non-African descent. This pattern has been explained by assuming an African ancestry for all mtDNA. Questions have been raised, for it cannot be shown statistically at a confidence level better than 1 chance in 20 that the ancestor was non-African. However, this criticism has more to do with the methods available to construct trees from the mtDNA data than with the ancestry. An African mtDNA ancestor remains the probable explanation because African populations show more mtDNA diversity and more divergent mtDNA lineages than populations elsewhere.

• The mtDNA ancestor lived about 200 000

years ago. This figure is calculated from measures of the amount by which human mtDNA sequences have diverged, and from estimates of the rate of divergence through mutation. Statistical errors associated with these calculations give a 95 per cent confidence that the date lies between 500 000 and 50 000 years ago.

While the mtDNA data may not pinpoint the geographic centre of origin of modern humans to the satisfaction of all critics, they can be used to provide interesting information on past population history. This approach has been developed by Henry Harpending and his colleagues from the Pennsylvania State University, Stephen Sherry and Mark Stoneking, and Alan Rogers from the University of Utah. They point out that projecting the modern mtDNA diversity back in time to the point of coalescence, at about 200 000 years ago, does not mark the time when a new population or species arose. Rather, it tells us that at that time the effective ancestral population – the number of reproductive females – was between 1000 and 10 000: a very small population. This is a point used to argue against the multi-regional hypothesis on the ground that such a small population distributed between Cape Town and Beijing would have been spread too thinly to maintain the significant gene flow demanded by the multi-regional hypothesis. These researchers have used non-equilibrium population genetics theory to propose two models – both forms of the 'African Eve' or

'Garden of Eden' hypothesis (Harpending *et al.* 1993; Rogers & Jorde 1995). These are the strong and the weak 'Garden of Eden' models, and it is the weak form that they favour.

Both models accept as the starting point that modern humans originated in a centre of origin within a small sub-population. The strong model proposes that dispersion out of this centre was accompanied by expansion (increase in population). By contrast, the weak model proposes that modern humans spread slowly from the centre of origin and that population expansion occurred some tens of thousands of years after the daughter populations had separated. The timescale for the separation of the main continental or daughter populations would be some 100 000 years ago, while subsequent expansion in all continental regions (in terms of the weak model) was initiated about 60 000 years ago. The weak model leaves open the possibility that population expansion occurred earlier in Africa. A very significant conclusion to follow from these genetic studies is that populations everywhere underwent a massive expansion in the Late Pleistocene, long prior to the advent of agriculture. Supporters of the single centre of origin hypothesis would accept that there were numbers of movements of people out of Africa and that reverse movements of people into Africa cannot be excluded. Genetic studies are well suited to unravelling some of these details as research progresses.

The Khoisan are a regionally distinctive population largely restricted to southern Africa. Southern Africa was in times past the southernmost part of the inhabited world and thus a region where a relatively isolated population might be expected. This makes the Khoisan genotype of particular interest. Their ancestors have been resident in the subcontinent for tens of thousands of years and through interbreeding their genes are represented in all South African peoples. The University of the Witwatersrand geneticists Trefor Jenkins and Himla Soodyall have begun an investigation of the history of southern African populations using newer analytical techniques available to map the chemical sequences in lengths of mtDNA. Their initial results indicate that the major groupings – the Khoisan, Negroid and Pygmy populations – have had different evolutionary histories and their separation times are estimated to be of the order of

150 000 years. The greatest difference is found between the Khoisan and Pygmy populations and their separation is the most ancient. The start of the subsequent expansion of these major population groupings is estimated at some 90 000 years for the Negroids and Pygmies and at some 60 000 years for the Khoisan. For the start of the Khoisan expansion this dating is not consistent with the archaeological evidence, discussed in Chapter 2, which suggests that population expansions occurred somewhat earlier and again in the last 20 000 years. San, Khoekhoe and other ethnically differentiated groups in southern Africa carry in their genes a history that can be unravelled through genetic studies, and this must become a priority for future research.

The archaeological evidence for the emergence of modern humans

The Acheulian industries, with their characteristic bifaces, handaxes and cleavers, were replaced by flake industries about 250 000 years ago throughout Africa. Given the unevenness of the archaeological evidence and difficulties of dating very old sites, the nature of the technological transition is still not well understood. It is assumed that the most recent phase of the Acheulian industry is represented in South Africa by sites labelled Fauresmith by Goodwin and Van Riet Lowe and best known from the Vaal–Orange drainage basin. One site, Rooidam near Kimberley, excavated by Gerhard Fock, provides a minimum age of 200 000 years. The Fauresmith artefact assemblages are

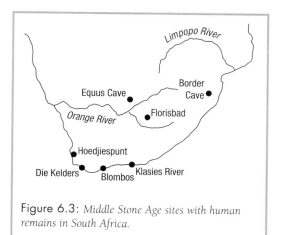

Figure 6.3: *Middle Stone Age sites with human remains in South Africa.*

characterised by small bifaces and flakes made from prepared cores, not as blanks for bifaces but as usable pieces in themselves. The Fauresmith may signal the replacement of the long Acheulian tradition of making bifaces by a Middle Stone Age flake technology.

Acheulian bifacial tools were hand-held and the only leverage was provided by the arm. Middle Stone Age flakes attached to a handle acting as a lever represented a significant technical advance. Lighter, more transportable flake toolkits would have been flexible in use. Judging from the shift of the focus of settlement from the confinement of the valleys in Acheulian times to the wider landscape in the Middle Stone Age there is an indication that technological change accompanied significant economic and social changes. These are discussed later in this chapter.

'Middle Stone Age' is a term introduced in 1929, as a South African equivalent of the European Middle Palaeolithic (middle Old Stone Age) or Mousterian industry. Although use of the term Middle Stone Age has been extended to the whole of sub-Saharan Africa, equivalent industries in North Africa, the Near East and Europe are categor-ised by the European terms, Middle Palaeolithic or Mousterian. But it is artificial to accept a divide at the Sahara, and both the Middle Stone Age and Middle Palaeolithic represent the widespread adoption of flake and prepared core technology. Middle Palaeolithic sites are to be found from Afghanistan to France and have equivalents throughout Africa. It is not known whether the oldest sites are in Africa or in Eurasia. The principle of preparing cores was an established part of the southern and eastern African Acheulian and, as this principle is basic to Middle Palaeolithic technology, the beginnings may have been in Africa. Neanderthals and early modern humans shared this technology, and the technology is presumed to be older than their separation. Bar-Yosef suggests that differences in Neanderthal and early modern human lifestyles and in the use of artefacts were more significant than similarities in the kinds of artefacts made.

In their original description of the Middle Stone Age in South Africa in 1929, Goodwin and Van Riet Lowe assumed that it was younger than and derived from the Mousterian of Europe. They also assumed that the Middle Stone Age had a duration

21 • Caves as archives •

Caves were used as home bases when conveniently located. The reason why caves are important to the archaeologist is that every group of people who have lived in a cave, even for a brief time, have left behind a trace of their visit. The traces of many visits pile up one on top of the other as a succession of layers. These layers are like the pages of a visitors' book, an archive or history of who was there, when they were there and what they did. The bindings of the book are the confines of the cave, keeping the traces of successive visits together. The bottom-most layer is page 1 and the last page is still being written. Page numbers are the radiocarbon and other dates obtained for the layers. In this analogy the contents of the layers, the artefacts, plant and animal food waste, and features like hearths and sleeping hollows, are the words that have to be read by the archaeologist. Decoding the message in these words is a lengthy task, only possible for a team of specialists. Information has to be teased from the strata using geological techniques, while plant and animal remains can provide important botanical and zoological data once sorted and identified. Archaeological excavation yields a diverse range of information, none of which can be ignored. Because the act of excavation separates the words and pages in the archive, the archaeologist must record them meticulously. Excavation is a destructive process that cannot be repeated and is only justified when there is a significant theoretical problem to research. Caves as archives are a priority for conservation.

of a few thousand years rather than a few hundred thousand years, as is now known from developments in chronometric dating techniques. While Goodwin and Van Riet Lowe assumed that Middle Stone Age sites fell within a short time range, the variability in Middle Stone Age artefact assemblages was believed to relate to geographical and regional environmental factors. They proposed and named a number of Middle Stone Age 'industries' and, at a more provisional level, 'variations'. This is the source of names or terms like Pietersburg, Mossel Bay and Stillbay 'industries' and Howiesons Poort 'variation', which are found in the older literature on the Middle Stone Age. Some of these terms are still used as convenient labels but have taken on different meanings. But the kind of variability in the South African Middle Stone Age that Goodwin and Van Riet Lowe perceptively recognised can be better explained by changes in time rather than geographical space. South Africa is too small a geographic area to show marked regional variation. However, Desmond Clark of the University of California has long argued that there are regional differences in the Middle Stone Age artefact traditions, though on a larger geographic scale, as between southern, eastern, central and northern Africa. This is in marked contrast to the continent-wide uniformity of the Acheulian. The subcontinental pattern of differentiation in the Middle Stone Age, recognised by Clark, may relate to the emergence of genetically and, possibly, linguistically distinct populations.

Advances in dating techniques have been fundamental to the reinterpretation of the Middle Stone Age in sub-Saharan Africa. Investigations in the Lake Baringo area of northern Kenya, led by Sally McBrearty of the University of Connecticut, indicate that standardised Middle Stone Age flake blades were being made some 250 000 years ago. Larry Barham (Barham & Smart 1996) of the University of Bristol, who is directing a programme of research on modern human origins in Zambia, has obtained a uranium disequilibrium dating of 230 000 years on the cave travertine layer containing Middle Stone Age artefacts at the Leopards Kopje site. These are among the growing number of age determinations for the African Middle Stone Age that fall within the Middle Pleistocene. However, it is from the beginning of the Late Pleistocene (125 000 years ago) that the

22 • Prepared core technique •

A flake struck from the edge of a block of stone serving as a core will be irregular in shape. The size and shape of any flake can be controlled by first 'preparing' the core. This is done by removing a number of waste flakes to shape the core and trimming flakes to prepare the edge or platform at which the final blow will be directed. The products of prepared cores are standardised flake blanks. Much as Victoria West cores were designed to produce very large flake blanks for making handaxes and cleavers, so in the Middle Stone Age prepared cores were set up to produce flake blanks mostly in the 40–100 mm range. These Middle Stone Age flake blanks may carry as many as four negative scars of trimming flakes, called facets, removed in shaping the striking platform so that the point of impact was restricted. The care taken in preparation made it possible to produce regular parallel-sided flake blades and convergent-sided pointed flakes as required. These were ready-to-use artefacts, which for most functions did not require further shaping by retouch. There is considerable variation in the ways cores were prepared, depending on the form of the raw material, its hardness and the choice of the artefact-maker. In Europe, where flint nodules were the usual raw material, cores were commonly prepared by what is called the Levallois technique. Core preparation using the classic Levallois technique is uncommon in the Middle Stone Age of South Africa.

Middle Stone Age record from southern Africa is particularly rich. There are a number of important dated sites and here the associations are with modern humans.

Middle Stone Age technology continued to be used through much of the Late Pleistocene. The Boomplaas Cave deposit shows that the Middle Stone Age ended between 32 000 and 21 000 years ago. The Apollo 11 site in Namibia, excavated by Erich Wendt and discussed in the next chapter, narrows the range further, to between 27 000 years and 20 000 years. The Strathalan B site, in the foothills of the Drakensberg near Elliot, is a small dry cave perched in a rock face. Here the preservation of plant remains is exceptional and the excavator, Hermanus Opperman of the University of Fort Hare, has obtained a number of radiocarbon dates for Middle Stone Age occupation on materials like grasses as well as charcoal from longer-lived woody plants. These age determinations fall between 22 000 and 24 000 years ago, making this the youngest well-dated Middle Stone Age site. These sites have provided the primary evidence for dating the end of the Middle Stone Age to 22 000 years ago. In many, if not all, parts of sub-Saharan Africa the Middle Stone Age terminated at this time.

Few caves were occupied in Acheulian times in South Africa. Wonderwerk Cave in the Northern Cape, the Cave of Hearths in the Makapan Valley north of Pietersburg and near the australopithecine site of Makapansgat Limeworks, and Montagu Cave in the Western Cape are the few known examples. This is in contrast to the large number of caves and rock shelters occupied later. Because caves and rock shelters were often occupied, information on the Middle and Later Stone Ages is much more accessible to archaeologists (Box 21).

What characterises the Middle Stone Age?

The Middle Stone Age seemed an obvious division of the Stone Age for Goodwin and Van Riet Lowe.

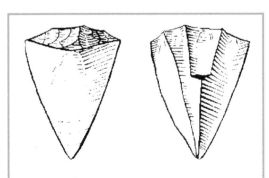

Figure 6.4: *Convergent flaking and faceting of the platform in the Middle Stone Age. (From Goodwin & Van Riet Lowe 1929)*

Goodwin, who wrote the relevant section in their 1929 publication, was aware that Middle Stone Age artefacts occurred in distinct layers below those of the Later Stone Age in stratified cave sequences and were therefore older. He termed the Middle Stone Age a flake industry, meaning it lacked the large handaxes and cleavers characteristic of the Earlier Stone Age, the oldest stage. What, then, characterises the Middle Stone Age?

• Flake blanks in the 40–100 mm size range struck from prepared cores. The proportion of these blanks shows secondary trimming is rare.

• The striking platforms of the flakes reveal one or more facets, indicating the preparation of the platform before flake removal (the prepared core technique).

• Flakes show what Revil Mason termed dorsal preparation – one or more ridges or arises down the length of the flake – as a result of previous flake removals from the core.

• Flakes with convergent sides (laterals) and a pointed shape, and flakes with parallel laterals and a rectangular or quadrilateral shape: these can be termed points and flake blades respectively. Other flakes in Middle Stone Age assemblages are irregular in form.

• Rare pointed flake blanks that show flat invasive flaking over one (unifacial) or both (bifacial) surfaces, and possible removal of the bulb of percussion or other treatment of the base of the point to facilitate hafting on a handle. Points that have been shaped by secondary trimming in this way are design types, and their styles vary through time.

• Relatively rare flake blanks with one or more notches along the laterals. Where multiple notches occur along an edge, the term 'denticulate' (toothed) is sometimes used to describe the piece. Notching can be equated with damage from use on hard materials like wood.

• Rare flakes with steep trimming or retouch on the side or end. Such retouch is conventionally described as scraper retouch.

• Blade blanks shaped by steep retouch or backing to blunt one side, like the blunting on a knife. These are mainly restricted to the Howiesons Poort phase of the Middle Stone Age (80 000 to 70 000 years).

• Few reported associations of grindstones, wood and bone artefacts, and personal ornaments like beads. Such items may be rare because of fac-

23

• What is a blade? •

A blade is defined as a flake that is more than twice as long as it is wide. However, a distinction can be made between flake blades – parallel-sided flakes made by direct percussion – and 'true' blades made by indirect percussion. This distinction has been seen as very important in European archaeology. Flake blades struck from prepared cores occur in the Middle Palaeolithic Mousterian industries, associated with Neanderthals, and true blades, struck from cores shaped like an inverted pyramid using a bone punch, are distinctive of the Upper Palaeolithic industries, associated with Cro-Magnons – modern people. The technological distinction is less useful in the South African context where blade technology, different from that of the Upper Palaeolithic, was used in the Middle and Later Stone Ages, and modern humans, not Neanderthals, made the Middle and Later Stone Age artefacts.

tors of preservation or for cultural reasons. Researchers are cautious about accepting evidence of associations that cannot be confirmed in repeated observations.

• General use of red ochre, a natural pigment. The colour is universally of symbolic significance.

• Frequent circular hearths (300 mm in diameter) attesting to the ability to make fire.

• A hunting and gathering lifeway, as associated animal and plant remains attest.

• Association with anatomically modern human remains but without evidence for defined burial practices.

The Middle Stone Age artefact sequence

Most Middle Stone Age occurrences are too old to date by radiocarbon. But there is still much progress to be made in dating sites by new methods. Moreover, the superimposed layers of cave sequences provide good relative dating for artefact changes through time.

In view of the similarity of standard flake blanks in the Middle Stone Age coupled with the low frequency of retouched pieces, changes in time are more obvious in the variation in size of the flakes than in the introduction of new types of formal shaped tools. Flake blanks tend to reduce in mean size to a low in the Howiesons Poort phase in the middle of the sequence, and thereafter they again increase in size. The typologically distinctive backed tools in the Howiesons Poort were made on thin blade blanks; this is associated with a reduced mean size.

The basic typological description of the Middle Stone Age sequence has been provided by John Wymer, who excavated at the Klasies River sites for Ronald Singer over two long seasons in 1967–8. At Klasies River he was able to show that the Howiesons Poort artefacts (Figure 6.5) were stratified between what he termed the MSA I and II and the MSA III and IV. Other researchers have adopted and modified this numbering of phases in the Middle Stone Age sequence. These phases recognise the general similarity and the continuity, rather than discrete changes in the style of making artefacts, in the Middle Stone Age sequence. In the modified version proposed by Tom Volman of Cornell University, for example, the MSA 1 includes samples, from sites like Skildegat (Peers Cave, Fish Hoek) on the Cape Peninsula, of large flake blades, cruder and older than those from the base of the Klasies River sequence. He then grouped Wymer's MSA I and II into an MSA 2a and 2b, followed by the Howiesons Poort and later post-Howiesons Poort MSA 3 and 4 phases.

Once it was appreciated that the Howiesons Poort was a middle phase of the Middle Stone Age sequence and that it was of the same dating (centred on 70 000 years ago) throughout southern Africa, it could be used as a marker horizon to correlate between sites. At some sites like the Cave of Hearths and in Richard Klein's excavation of Nelson Bay Cave on Robberg peninsula, the Howiesons Poort is the top Middle Stone Age level. Other sites

24 • Direct and indirect percussion •

The flake can be struck by direct percussion, in which the hammer strikes the core to release the flake. Hammers are usually of 'hard' stone but bone and wood 'soft' hammers were also used. Most Middle and Later Stone Age flake blanks were produced by direct percussion. The difference is that in the Middle Stone Age prepared cores were used whereas in the Later Stone Age cores were not prepared in the same regular way. Indirect percussion uses a punch so that the force of the blow is transmitted through the punch to a small target area on the core. This is a specialised technique that can be adapted to produce thin blade blanks. Extensive use was made of indirect percussion to make blade blanks in the Howiesons Poort phase of the Middle Stone Age and in the Robberg phase of the Later Stone Age.

like Border Cave, excavated by Peter Beaumont, Rose Cottage Cave near Ladybrand, which is being excavated by Lyn Wadley of the University of the Witwatersrand, and Klasies River main site, show human occupation before, during and after the Howiesons Poort. Still others, like Boomplaas Cave, excavated by H.J. Deacon, were occupied during and after Howiesons Poort times.

There are Howiesons Poort horizons in cave sequences in sites like the Matopo Hills of Zimbabwe and in sequences like Apollo 11 in Namibia. However, no Howiesons Poort occurrences have been reported from Zambia. In central Tanzania at the site of Mumba, near Lake Eyasi, Mike Mehlman has reported an industry of similar age to the Howiesons Poort, which also includes backed tools of the same design and size. This distribution, south of the Zambezi, with an outlier in central Tanzania, is the same disjunct geographical pattern shown by present-day click-language speakers and Later Stone Age naturalistic rock art. It will require research on a continental scale to begin to understand if and why distribution patterns like these are linked. As a relatively short-

lived (10 000–15 000 year), typologically distinctive horizon in the Middle Stone Age, the Howiesons Poort is of considerable interest.

Middle Stone Age lifeways

The distribution of Middle Stone Age artefacts in the landscape suggests that settlement was widespread. Frequently the same shelters were occupied, as in Later Stone Age times. This indicates that group sizes and within-group kin relations were the same as those in the Later Stone Age and among present-day hunter-gatherers.

In the Middle Stone Age, sites were occupied in the mountain uplands as well as lowlands. This gave the occupants wider access to natural fields of edible plants and other resources. In the latitudes of southern Africa, plant rather than animal food would have contributed the bulk of the diet. In most sites plant residues have long since decayed but traces may be evident in the carbonised surrounds of hearths. At the Strathalan B site in the Drakensberg, dry conditions have preserved grass bedding heaps around the wall and central hearths and activity areas at the front of the cave. Here the University of Fort Hare researchers Hermanus Opperman and Bea Heydenrych were able to recover identifiable corms of geophytes like *Watsonia* of the Iris family. Geophytes are a class of plants in which the new bud forms underground, and they have potato-like corms or bulbs, which are carbohydrate-rich food stores. They were an important food source in Middle and Later Stone Age times. Geophytes proliferate in the plant succession immediately after fire. The underground corm is protected from the heat of the fire; the release of nutrients from the ash stimulates flowering and division of the corm. A study we carried out on a natural field of *Watsonia* at the Jonkershoek Nature Reserve near Stellenbosch showed that some 40 per cent of the estimated million plants in this field flowered after fire, as opposed to 5 per cent in a non-fire year. As each plant that produces an inflorescence, or flower, vegetatively divides to produce two new corms, this represents a substantial increase apart from any new plants growing from seed. To be productive as food resources, geophytes need to be fire-managed. Farming with fire can be inferred for both the Middle and Later Stone Ages and it is practised by contemporary hunter-gatherers.

There is direct archaeological evidence for the harvesting of tree fruits in the more northern savanna habitats of South Africa extending into Zimbabwe. Ina Plug of the Transvaal Museum, who studied the Bushman Rock Shelter in Mpumalanga, was able to show that the marula (*Sclerocarya birrea*) occurred through much of the long Middle Stone Age sequence there. The maru-la endocarp, or shell, is traditionally roasted to remove the edible embryos (nut-meat); in the roasting process some endocarps become carbonised, increasing the probability of preservation. Extracting embryos is the kind of task carried out at home by older women in present-day African societies in the area because it requires a certain skill and patience. In the Middle Stone Age it was a similar home-based activity. Though marula remains are archaeologically very visible because the endocarps needed processing, other tree fruits more rarely recorded in deposits would have had as much importance in the savanna habitats.

While plants were the dietary staples in the Middle Stone Age, hunting was also important. Hunting provided an essential high-protein supplement to a plant diet rich in carbohydrate. As African bovids are notoriously lean, this places a limit on the amount of meat that can be eaten without suffering from protein poisoning. However, as bone preserves better than plant tissue, there is more direct evidence for the use of animal foods in coastal and inland areas.

In the Middle Stone Age there occurs the first evidence for the systematic use of marine foods. The Cape coastal sites have been well studied; they show seals, penguins and shellfish were eaten. Fishing, however, was not practised – the necessary technology may have been lacking.

There is evidence for the active hunting of all sizes of bovids (Bovidae is the family that includes antelope and buffalo). Signs of active hunting, as opposed to scavenging (Milo 1998), are to be found in the butchering of whole or near-whole animals on site; this is evident in the body parts represented and in cut marks and other damage on the bones. Hunting does not rule out opportunistic scavenging. It is very probable that seals were scavenged rather than hunted. With control of fire there was the possibility of driving even large carnivores off their kills.

Richard Klein has devoted many years to the study of Middle and Later Stone Age faunas from archaeological sites in South Africa. He characterises hunting in the Middle Stone Age as focused on the more docile rather than dangerous game. In a recent paper he and Kathy Cruz-Uribe of the Northern Arizona University argue that although buffalo may have been more common than eland in the environment, there are many more prime adults of eland in samples analysed from the Middle Stone Age layers at Klasies River main site and Die Kelders Cave 1. Klein has suggested that eland may have been hunted by being driven over coastal cliffs at these locations, as they are readily herded. In Klein's analyses the more dangerous game like the Cape buffalo and the extinct giant buffalo, *Pelorovis*, are represented by young or very old individuals, which would have been easier to obtain than confronting aggressive prime adults. In Klein's view, Middle Stone Age people did not use the animal resources in their environment as effectively as Later Stone Age people because in the Middle Stone Age the people were neurologically (mentally) different. There are, however, other possible explanations – for example, demographic, ecological and technological reasons – why in the

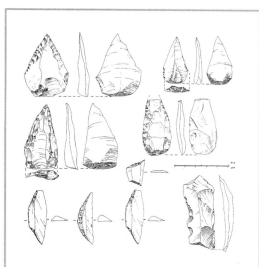

Figure 6.5: *Artefacts from the Howiesons Poort name site near Grahamstown: unifacial and bifacial points (top and middle rows), two segments (bottom left) and two trapezes (bottom centre), and a notched blade (bottom right).*

• Craft specialisation in the Middle Stone Age •

As a tribute to the pioneer collector C.H.T.D. Heese, a schoolmaster from the small southern Cape town of Riversdale, Goodwin chose the name 'Still Bay industry' for one of the 'variations' of the Middle Stone Age. Heese's collections came from eroded sands on a hill overlooking the resort of Stillbay on the coast immediately south of Riversdale. The kind of artefact that became associated with the Stillbay (the modern form of the name is used here) was the leaf-shaped bifacial point. Perhaps the finest craftsmanship is shown in the example that Heese picked up at the nearby Blombos school. This is a long symmetrical leaf-shaped point, thin in cross-section: the whole surface has been worked by fine flaking. This fine flaking, sometimes called fishscale flaking, can be reproduced by pressing rather than knocking off little trimming flakes. The skill lies in reducing the thickness with techniques like pressure flaking, without reducing the width of the piece. Artefacts like the Blombos point are evidence of craftsmanship.

Stillbay-like points occur widely in Middle Stone Age industries in sub-Saharan Africa and appear more common in regions other than South Africa. This may be a clue to a functional association with hunting by spear because regions to the north are richer in large mammal species. Very fine examples like the Blombos point would not have made better weapons but they may have given the owner higher status as a hunter. Style is more about looking successful than being successful.

The low incidence of Stillbay points at larger habitation sites, from as early as 90 000 or more years ago, and their relatively high incidence at two known small sites, suggest that these were places where the craft was practised. Craft specialisation and, by extension, trading were among the behaviours shown in the Middle Stone Age. In the 1930s two schoolboys decided to investigate the small Tunnel Cave in the Muizenberg Mountains above Fish Hoek near Cape Town. They found a cache of finely worked bifacial points. More recently, Chris Henshilwood and Judy Sealy of the University of Cape Town have found numbers of Stillbay points, associated with ochre, bone points and stone scrapers (for making clothing) and food remains, stratified above a MSA II ('Mossel Bay') layer in a small cave on the coast at Blombos. Are these places where craft specialists lived and traded their goods? Among modern people reciprocal trading is universal.

Middle Stone Age there was a lower intensity in the use of resources – reasons that do not assume differences in intelligence.

Questions of cognition and behaviour

Cognition refers to ways of thinking, or how the mind operates. Behaviour represents the way our cognitive abilities are used in particular circumstances. The usual archaeological criteria taken to indicate the appearance of modern cognition are the behaviours that distinguish the anatomically modern Upper Palaeolithic Cro-Magnon people from the Mousterian Neanderthalers. The Upper Palaeolithic is characterised by the presence of art and personal ornaments, blade and burin stone technology, and the making of bone artefacts; these indicators or markers are not found at Mousterian sites. The Upper Palaeolithic, dating from about 40 000 years ago, is a regional phenomenon restricted to Europe and the Near East. It represents a period of intensification in the use of food resources under particular favourable glacial climates, and the innovative use of specialised equipment for hunting and fishing. The large number of archaeological sites of this period indicates significant population densities. As population densities rise there is more need to identify individuals and groups: this explains the occurrence of bone and shell ornaments, art and elaborate artefacts used as symbols in social signalling. All people in the world use symbols – a flag, a style of dress or objects like a motor car – to communicate their social position. The Upper Palaeolithic Cro-Magnons made use of symbols, but their Neanderthal cousins did not.

Once human populations left the safety of the valleys and began to occupy entire landscapes, regional differences emerged. One should expect that in regions as different in climate and resources as Eurasia and Africa, different cultural and population histories would be recorded. Indeed, the Upper Palaeolithic was not a universal stage in human history: in sub-Saharan Africa there was no phenomenon like the Upper Palaeolithic. There were not the same conditions of predictable, seasonally abundant food resources needed to encourage particular technological innovations and permit population increase. Indeed, at the time when populations were expanding in Eurasia, they appear to have been contracting after an even

earlier expansion in Africa. Thus the usual Upper Palaeolithic indicators for the appearance of modern cognition have no relevance for the archaeological record in Africa. Another important difference is that anatomically modern people were present in Africa in the Middle Stone Age, tens of thousands of years before their appearance in the Upper Palaeolithic in Europe.

If the Middle Stone Age is associated with anatomically modern people, then the question arises, Were these people modern in their way of thinking or, as Klein argues on economic grounds, modern in body but not in mind? It is a logical assumption that mental or cognitive abilities would have been set at the time of speciation, and early anatomically modern Middle Stone Age people 100 000 and more years ago should have had the capacity for modern behaviour. If we take into account appropriate criteria, and not those that separate Neanderthals and Cro-Magnons, the indications are that Middle Stone Age people did think like us. On this reckoning the criteria for recognising modern cognition in a southern

---

26 • Howiesons Poort technology •

Control over the flaking products in stone tool-making is well evidenced in the Howiesons Poort. Long, thin blanks, properly called blades, were produced by the use of a punch technique. This can be inferred from the area of the platforms, a few millimetres wide and long, presenting a target too small to strike other than with a punch. Further indicators of the use of a punch technique are an overhang or lip on the platform and a bulb of percussion that is diffuse. Sarah Wurz (Deacon, H. J. & Wurz 1996) has made a detailed study of the platforms on Howiesons Poort blade blanks: these are set at an angle to the length of the piece, showing the punch flexed when struck. An elastic punch, made of wood rather than bone, would have the effect of 'flicking' off the blade as the forces of the blow were released and ran through the core material. It is only in the Robberg industry of the Later

Stone Age that there is again extensive use made of indirect percussion or punch technology, but then to produce micro-bladelets (<25 mm).

The Howiesons Poort blades had a special purpose. They were the blanks for making segment- and trapeze-shaped tools, about 40 mm in length (Figure 6.5). The shape was obtained by steep retouch or backing, so as to blunt one side, as on the back of a penknife blade. The shape differences have no functional significance. These backed tools all have a mean size of 40 mm; the regularised shape and size is simply to facilitate hafting. Identically shaped but smaller (12–16 mm) backed tools are found in the Later Stone Age Wilton industry (discussed in the next chapter) and are thought to have been armatures for arrows. A probable function for the larger Howiesons Poort backed tools was in arming spears.

African context would be those behaviours that link Middle and Later Stone Age and contemporary hunter-gatherers. These criteria would include the following:

• Family foraging groups. The evidence is in the occurrence of small circular hearths that are associated with food waste. These are domestic hearths and they are universally 'owned' by a woman with a family.

• Strong kinship ties allowing foraging groups to split up and disperse at some times, and at other times to come together and form larger aggregations. The evidence is indirect but is indicated in the dispersal of sites in the landscape. The earlier peoples who made the Acheulian artefacts, by contrast, were habitat specialists and lacked this ability to disperse.

• Active hunting, as evidenced in the faunal remains.

• Ability to manage plant food resources with fire, as indicated in the collection of geophytes.

• Capacity to communicate by the use of symbols. The prime evidence is in the use of red ochre. Throughout Africa, a triad of colours, red, white and black, serve as colour symbols. Red symbolis-es blood and life and is featured in rites of passage like birth, initiation into adulthood, marriage, and death and burial.

• Reciprocal exchange of artefacts. The primary evidence is in the selection of exotic raw materials for making artefacts, like the Howiesons Poort backed tools in the Middle Stone Age. Gift exchanges are very important in maintaining interpersonal relations among contemporary hunter-gatherers, and Lyn Wadley has argued that they were equally important in the Later Stone Age. Craft specialisation in the manufacturing of Still-bay points in the Middle Stone Age also suggests a high antiquity for reciprocal agreements.

Case study: Klasies River

The Klasies River (Singer & Wymer 1982) is a small stream that flows into the sea on the Tsitsikamma coast between Cape St Francis and Plettenberg Bay. A number of caves have been cut into the cliff face at 6 m and 18 m above sea level in a kilometre-long section of coast near the river mouth. At the Klasies River main site there is a natural amphitheatre formed by the cliff in which

Figure 6.6: *Klasies River main site.*

cave openings are found. In the shelter of the cliff and spilling into the caves, some 20 m of layered archaeological deposits have built up over thousands of years. A fossil dune, originally composed of shelly sand, blankets the cliff above the main site; this dune is the source of lime-rich waters that have flowed over the cliff face, cementing the deposits and forming stalagmites in the caves. This has helped to preserve the deposits and the bones they contain.

At the beginning of the Late Pleistocene (125 000 years ago), sea levels were as high as or slightly higher than the present. The sea washed into the floor of the lower caves, cleaning them out; then, as the sea level dropped and a protecting dune formed at the back of the beach, deposits began to accumulate. The deposits are sands from the beach and the fossil dune, and materials brought in by people living there. People left behind the remains of the shellfish they gathered off the rocks, the bones of various species of antelope they hunted, and the bones of dead seals and penguins they might have picked up along the coast. Seals still sometimes wash up on the beach and would have been an important source of fat. People also collected plant food (Deacon, H.J. 1993), which is now represented only by burnt layers surrounding their cooking hearths. Beach cobbles provided plentiful raw material for making stone artefacts.

The debris left by people camping here forms distinct layers separated by sands: this shows there were many visits of several weeks rather than extended stays for longer periods. Hunter-gatherers cannot afford to stay too long in one place because they deplete the local food stocks. From the evidence of hyena coprolites (dung) and leopard bones, we know that large carnivores used the caves for dens too, as did porcupines and genet cats. The cliff face was a roost for owls and sea birds like cormorants; from their perches the bones of the mice and fish they caught dropped into the deposit as well. These varied contents of the layers make the site a treasure house of information for the archaeologist to piece together.

Most of the layers are too old to date by radiocarbon, and other dating techniques have had to be used. From oxygen isotope measurements on the opercula (trapdoors) of the sea snail, *Turbo sarmaticus* (alikreukel), uranium disequilibrium dating of stalagmites, electron spin resonance dating

Figure 6.7: *Frontal bone from the SAS member at Klasies River (90 000 years old) showing modern features like a vertical forehead and the absence of brow ridges. A scar made when the bone was torn apart while still fresh is visible at the top right adjacent to cut marks – evidence for interpersonal violence.*

of the tooth enamel of antelope, and the amino acid dating of bone and shell (see Chapter 2), it has been shown that the deposits accumulated mainly between 120 000 and 60 000 years ago. In this time, sea levels rose and fell several times but always remained below those of the Holocene, the last 10 000 years. The offshore profile of the coast is steep; and even when sea levels were low, the coast was near enough for the site to be a base for collecting sea foods.

Apart from being possibly the oldest-known sea-food 'restaurant', the Klasies River main site has special importance as the find site of the remains of early modern human fossils. In 1967 and 1968 Ronald Singer and John Wymer mounted an extensive excavation of the site and recovered a number of fragmentary human fossils, mainly jaws and teeth and cranial pieces (Rightmire & Deacon 1991). These are mostly from an horizon now dated to 90 000 years ago; subsequent excavations have produced further remains dating between 110 000 and 120 000 years ago. It was on the basis of the initial finds that a claim was made that morphologically modern humans were living in southern Africa at a time when Neanderthals were roaming Europe.

Peter Beaumont made similar claims for the evidence from an important site on the KwaZulu–Natal–Swaziland border, appropriately named Border Cave. Here human remains, which includ-

Figure 6.8: *Burnt maxillary fragment of a young male from the base of the Klasies River deposit dating to 120 000 years. The remains from this level are modern in morphology and are some of the oldest remains of modern humans yet found.*

ed a complete skull, had been recovered some decades earlier when a local farmer dug out part of the deposits to use as fertiliser. Because the associated artefacts were like those from Klasies River, Beaumont reasoned the Border Cave deposits must be equally old. These claims were contrary to the idea then accepted that modern humans had their origins in the Near East a scant 35 000 years ago, but they only gained wider acceptance when genetic evidence also pointed to the emergence of modern humans in sub-Saharan Africa.

Although fragmentary, the human remains from Klasies River and Border Cave are those of individuals of short stature, with marked sexual dimorphism. The shape of the forehead, the lack of brow ridges, the form of the chin and tooth size are some of the features that indicate this was an early modern population.

The Klasies River human remains are not from conventional burials and they are not fragmentary because of any natural disturbance in the site. Some pieces have been charred in the fire and some show impact fractures and cut marks. One fragment, a piece of face or frontal, has cut marks on the forehead and a place where the bone had torn rather than broken while still fresh. In the sample of jaws, many of the front teeth are missing while the cheek teeth protected by the masseter, or chewing muscle, are still in place. Most of the

pieces are from the cranium and only a few other body parts have been recovered. The human remains are of interest not only for their modern morphology but also for their taphonomy – how they got into the deposit.

Excavating a square metre into the oldest layer in the Klasies River site produced two fragments of upper jawbone from a shell heap or midden – a rubbish dump, in modern terms. The larger fragment is part of the right side of the jaw and palate. It is of a young individual because the upper jaw and the lower jaw are really two bones that fuse together with age, and the specimen had broken at the junction, so the jaw had not completely fused. There are no teeth in this fire-blackened piece but the root of the eye-tooth or canine is present. An X-ray shows this root to be fully formed. From this and other evidence the age at death is estimated at about 10 or 12 years. Although young, this was a robust person, a male. The other piece was found protected under a discarded limpet shell. It has a single worn cheek (molar) tooth in place. The jagged breaks of the piece are well preserved because it lay under the shell. This tooth is from an adult, and the tooth wear, the tooth size and the bone around it point to a mature, even elderly, female. These are fragments belonging to two individuals of different sexes and ages. One was burnt almost to a cinder and the other, not visibly burnt, was smashed out of the jaw. Both were thrown out with the kitchen garbage at about the same time because they landed up in the same heap. Most of the other human remains from the site come from a younger horizon and accumulated over an equally short period.

Tim White of the University of California, at Berkeley, who studies early hominids in Ethiopia, has been able to point to breakage patterns and marks on the human remains from Klasies River that are consistent with cannibalism. Having also investigated the evidence for cannibalism among a Native American group called the Anasazi, who lived in the south-west United States about 1000 years ago, he posed the question whether there were cannibals living at the Klasies River sites.

Some peoples are known to practise secondary burial rituals. The graves are dug up and the human remains are treated in some way, before being disposed of a second time, often not in the ground. Some similar ritual cannot be ruled out on the evidence from Klasies River. However, episodic cannibalism would be a more convincing explanation for the occurrence of the human remains in discrete horizons rather than dispersed through the layers of the site. The strongest evidence for dietary cannibalism is the paucity of limb bone fragments. White has been able to show in the Anasazi example that these were treated in the same way as the bones of other animals and were broken open for marrow. Dietary cannibalism may seem unlikely in what we perceive as a rich coastal habitat but these episodes might represent extreme events. All cannibalism has a ritual component and the main site in its size would have been a powerful place, a place of gathering and a place where ritual observances were carried out. One may speculate that such extreme events could have been inspired by ritual rather than hunger. The evidence points to interpersonal violence. But the victims and the perpetrators are long gone. All the same, Klasies River provides a good example of the questions that taphonomy, the study of how bones

accumulated where they do, tries to answer.

At Klasies River hundreds of thousands of stone artefacts were used and thrown away during the many occupations that took place in the shelter of the cliff. These artefacts are irregular flakes, long flake blades and cores. The artefact-makers were very competent at producing standard shapes, and rarely are the edges secondarily trimmed. Though the flake blades at the bottom of the sequence are long and heavier than in the overlying layers, they show little change.

The exception is in the Howiesons Poort layers dating to about 70 000 years ago. Here one finds an increase in the use of a fine-grained stone called silcrete, a kind of fossil soil, in addition to the local rock. Silcrete was mostly used to make backed tools on very thin blades, which were thought to be parts of projectiles, spears rather than arrows. The use of silcrete, probably from sources in the Longkloof 20 km or more away, only makes sense if more than function was involved. For the same tools can be and were made in the local quartzite

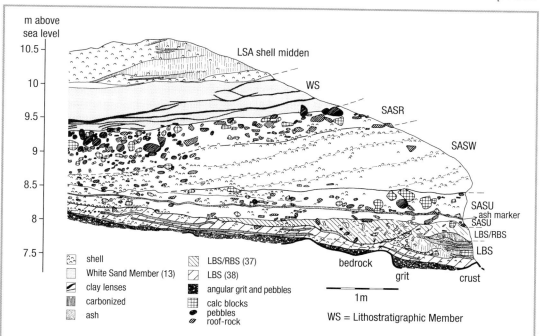

Figure 6.9: *Details of the stratigraphy in cave 1 at the Klasies River main site. In this section of the deposit a Later Stone Age midden overlies white sands of the WS (MSA IV) member and rubble (SASR) and sands (SASW) of the SAS member, all representing sediments washed into the cave. The main finds of human remains in cave 1 are associated with the SASU and the LBS members; when these deposits were accumulating, people were able to live in cave 1, as shown by the hearths they made.*

27 • Cannibalism •

Cannibalism can take many forms and one form, medicine murder, is still practised in South Africa. Medicine murders are ritual killings with a particular part of the victim used in making a potion to ward off some evil. There are caves marked on maps in Lesotho that, according to tradition, were occupied by cannibals during the troubled times in the first half of the nineteenth century. As the European farming frontier advanced inland, new tribal alliances were forged to face this threat; this in turn led to widespread raiding and conflict. People disappeared and were probably taken captive as slaves, but the possibility cannot be ruled out that there were also incidences of cannibalism under conditions of extreme stress when residents ate their captives in an effort to stay alive. Such cases may qualify as dietary cannibalism.

The accounts of cannibalism were recorded by missionaries, who relied on stories told to them. Checking these stories is a task for the archaeologist. One story of a cannibal kraal near Clarens in the Free State did not stand up to scrutiny. Clay structures where the cannibals were supposed to have lived turned out to be the bases of clay grain bins. These stores of grain hidden in the hills would have been reserve supplies against raiding and probably date to the right period, but provide no evidence for cannibalism.

stone, but the silcrete and the rarer examples of other exotic stone are finer-grained, superior in flaking quality and attractively coloured. One can explain the added value given to what was probably hunting equipment, used exclusively by men, if the men exchanged the equipment among themselves. Reciprocal exchanges of arrows (as discussed in the next chapter) are a feature of male society in present-day hunter communities and may have a long history.

The Howiesons Poort phase lasted perhaps 10 000 –15 000 years. In the layers overlying the Howiesons Poort at main site, the making of backed tools, a technological innovation, was discontinued in a seeming reversal of progress. This is understandable if Howiesons Poort backed tools were not only functional items but also had symbolic value, for example in gift exchanges. If exchange obligations were met in other ways, backed tools would have gone out of fashion and become redundant.

To the excavator, trowel and brush in hand, the most impressive feature of main site is the way the deposits have built up – the site formation processes involved. People were continually bringing in plant foods, preparing them around the domestic hearth, and then cooking food on the hearth. Keeping the home tidy meant that the bones and shells from meals were discarded on a rubbish pile while the plant food debris carpeted the domestic area. Inevitably plant debris that was not noxious accumulated around the hearth, was trampled under foot, partly buried, set alight, smouldered and was carbonised. This shows up in the deposit as the carbonised surround to a hearth, which may be several square metres in extent. In the course of time in a damp deposit, the plant materials decay to soil humus but carbonisation preserves a trace of them. Together, these hearths, the carbonised and brown humic soils, the artefacts associated with them, and the middens of shell and bone are what was left behind after a group of hunter-gatherers moved on.

Through this process and through repeated episodes of occupation, the 20 m of deposits accumulated at the main site. In the same way the sites of San hunter-gatherers in this area, dating to the last few thousand years, built up. As site formation reflects the social organisation and rules of group behaviour, it would seem that these rules have not changed in the last 100 000 or more years. This is some of the strongest evidence that the Middle Stone Age groups at Klasies River were modern in mind and body. They were probably the direct ancestors of the Later Stone Age peoples discussed in the following chapters.

CHAPTER SEVEN

Innovation and the Later Stone Age

'But how do you know where to dig?' is like asking 'But how do you know where to set up a business?' It is an educated guess.

Excavations are never done on the spur of the moment. They need to be carefully planned, funding has to be secured, and permits and permissions have to be obtained. Archaeologists excavate to test hypotheses and answer specific questions. First, a survey of possible sites is made and those most likely to have the kinds of deposits that will answer these questions are selected. Sometimes the guess does not pay off. Sometimes the payoff is even greater than expected. There is always an element of luck.

In the early 1970s we were looking for an inland site in the southern Cape with a Later Stone Age sequence comparable to that from the coastal and Eastern Cape sites. At Melkhoutboom in the late 1960s Hilary had found a small sample of early Later Stone Age artefacts that did not fit into the sequence described by Goodwin and Van Riet Lowe. Subsequently, Richard Klein had found a much larger sample of the same industry at Nelson Bay Cave and had called it the Robberg. We wanted to know how widespread the Robberg industry was and what it was derived from. To answer these questions we needed a cave or rock shelter with good conditions for bone preservation that had been occupied during the change from the Middle to the Later Stone Age between 30 000 and 20 000 years ago. As Nelson Bay Cave and Melkhoutboom had not been occupied in this time range, we did not know whether the change correlated with different hunting preferences or different lifestyles.

Hilary began looking in the vicinity of the Cango Caves. Limestone formations are more likely to preserve bone, and perhaps even plant materials, in layers older than 10 000 years than caves in the acid rocks of the Cape Fold mountains. There had been archaeological excavations at Cango in the 1930s, but the development of the caves for tourism since then had partly destroyed the archaeological deposits. We made several trips to the area, assisted by members of the Speleological Society. They had mapped several of the limestone caverns, but in the end we selected a large open shelter on the farm Boomplaas in the Cango Valley that had been shown to us by a local farmer, Abrie (Abraham) Botha. As it is always difficult to estimate how deep the deposits will be, we laid bets during the first excavation season in January 1974. As we went down and down, excitement mounted, though by then we could not change our guesses. All 15 of us underestimated, but Hilary's guess of 2.6 metres was closest to the actual depth of 4.3 metres. There was a full sequence of occupation horizons. At the top was the most recent Stone Age, when the cave was used as a sheep kraal by Khoekhoe herders. Below this was the classic Later Stone Age, followed by the Middle–Later Stone Age transition, and finally, at the base, the Howiesons Poort phase of the Middle Stone Age. Hearths, artefacts and bone were preserved all the way down to 80 000 years ago. The investigations took ten years to complete, involving many students and considerable effort, time and expense.

   Later Stone Age deposits are more likely than others to deliver the unexpected things, like chance finds that are of intrinsic interest, but do not necessarily answer the big questions. Earlier Stone Age sites are pretty predictable as far as artefacts are concerned and, even when there is bone and shell preserved, one has to work hard to extract something unusual from Middle Stone Age sites. But better preservation in the Later Stone Age means you can be lucky beyond testing the hypothesis that encouraged you to go there in the first place. Many of these chance finds were made in the early part of the twentieth century when recording methods left much to be desired. Painted stones, arrows and stone tools mounted in mastic handles were left in museums without enough information to date them, or remained in private hands and were lost to science altogether.

   Some of the most exciting finds Hilary made at Boomplaas could not be taken away. They included 'features' in the deposits where storage pits had been dug, lined and filled but never emptied; a massive charcoal pit that had been made, perhaps to dry meat; and a small cache of bladelets that had been left in a little heap more than 12 000 years ago. They would not have been recognised for what they were if the excavators had not been trained to recognise them. [JD]

This chapter describes the characteristics and sequence of the technological aspects – the tools or artefacts – of the Later Stone Age in South Africa. It then summarises the sequence of events at several key sites in the southern and Eastern Cape as an example of the kind of information archaeologists can obtain from sites that have been occupied over long periods. We have chosen this region partly because we know it best, but also because it is one of the few in southern Africa where both good preservation of bone and plant materials and an unbroken sequence through the Later Stone Age are most frequently found together. Inevitably, the interpretation of this information has changed over the past 80 years. As in history, there is no single 'truth' about the past, but the wealth of archaeological research in the southern and Eastern Cape makes this a good place to start, and we fully expect future research to modify the conclusions.

What characterises the Later Stone Age?

The change from the Middle Stone Age to the Later Stone Age took place in most parts of southern Africa little more than about 20 000 years ago. It is marked by a series of technological innovations or new tools that, initially at least, were used to do much the same jobs as had been done before, but in a different way. Their introduction was associated with changes in the nature of hunter-gatherer material culture.

   More importantly for our understanding of this period, some of these tools were still being made by Khoisan people in South Africa at the time of European contact. For the first time we have eye-witness accounts of what they were used for, both literally and symbolically. It is these ethnographic

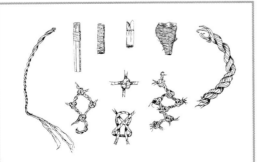

Figure 7.1: *Later Stone Age string and netting made of vegetable fibre with details of the knotting used; a stone flake wrapped with fibre; the nocked end of an arrow; and two pieces of reed with grass binding. All come from Melkhoutboom.*

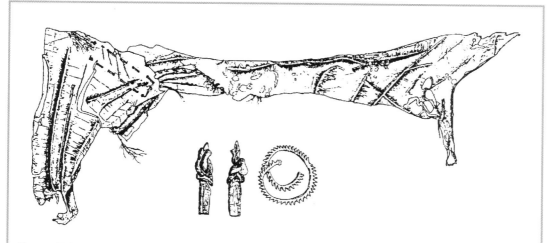

Figure 7.2: *Leather items from Melkhoutboom. The long sewn piece is part of a man's loin cloth and the smaller items are decorative pieces.*

accounts that help us to piece together a history of the Khoisan and their ancestors.

The innovations associated with the Later Stone Age 'package' of tools include:

• rock art (both paintings and engravings)

• painted and engraved stones (a few of the former were found with the final MSA at Apollo 11)

• deliberate burial of the dead in formal graves

• smaller stone tools, so small that the formal tools less than 25 mm long are called microliths (sometimes found in the final Middle Stone Age)

• preservation of organic materials like string (Figure 7.1), leather (Figures 7.2 and 7.3) and wood (Figure 7.4)

• bows and arrows

• bored stones as digging-stick weights

• grooved stones

• stone tools fixed to handles with mastic (one was found in the final Middle Stone Age at Apollo 11) (Figure 7.4)

• decorative items like beads and pendants of shell and ostrich eggshell (a few found in Middle Stone Age contexts) and bone tools with engraved decoration (Figure 7.4)

• decorated ostrich eggshell flasks (some fragments were found with the Howiesons Poort at Diepkloof)

• tortoiseshell bowls

• polished bone tools such as eyed needles, awls, linkshafts and arrowheads (a few polished

bone points have been found with the Middle Stone Age at Blombos and one at Klasies River)

• fishing equipment such as hooks, gorges and sinkers

• earthenware pottery (within the last 2000 years).

We cannot pinpoint the place or time of origin of all innovations. Some are found with well-preserved Middle Stone Age assemblages, while others became common only in Later Stone Age assemblages in the Holocene (the last 10 000 years). Microlithic stone tools were very widespread and were made in the period known as the Epipalaeolithic in Europe as well as in India and Australia. They are also found in Africa from about 20 000 years ago, from as far afield as the Ibero-Maurusian industries of the Maghreb in Algeria and Morocco to Later Stone Age sites further south. The characteristic early Later Stone Age 'package' of tools has been described at Porc Epic cave in Somalia, Lukenya Hill in Kenya, Nachikufu in Zambia, Matupi in Zaire, the Matopos in Zimbabwe, Apollo 11 in Namibia, and several sites in South Africa and Lesotho.

The Later Stone Age includes all assemblages dating within the last 20 000 years, when tool-makers were using essentially similar techniques to flake stone or polish bone. By using this kind of classification (see Box 28), we imply that there was both technological unity in the way that tools were

0   30
mm

Figure 7.3: *A bundle of leather bound with string from Faraoskop Rock Shelter east of Elands Bay in the Western Cape. It was found at a level dated to between 2000 and 2500 years ago (Manhire 1993). The bundle was X-rayed but showed only compressed folds of leather inside.*

made, and functional unity in that similar tasks were done in similar ways with similar tools, regardless of who the people were and where they lived.

The major difference between the Middle and Later Stone Ages lies in the preferred technique of stone tool-making. Whereas the Middle Stone Age tool-makers made mostly triangular flakes or large flake blades that were often used without further retouch, Later Stone Age people were more likely to make microlithic tools. They tended to shape stone flakes and bladelets by secondary retouch into a variety of small formal tools that were hafted onto handles with mastic.

At another level of abstraction, the complexes or traditions that are subdivisions of the Later Stone Age have been named after type sites where they were first found and described. They are the Robberg, Oakhurst (or Albany), Wilton, Interior Wilton (also called Post-Wilton) and Smithfield. Each of these subdivisions groups together assemblages in which the frequency, size and style of certain formal tools, as well as the raw materials selected and the shape of the flake blanks, are broadly similar. The frequency of formal tools differs from place to place depending on the tasks that were done there. The stylistic features that distinguish Robberg, Oakhurst or Albany, Wilton, Interior Wilton or Post-Wilton, and Smithfield from each other are recognised in much the same way as one makes an educated guess about the time period in which a house was built or an oil painting was done. Each represents the way in which people living in a region over a period of time preferred to make their stone tools or design their homes. It does not necessarily mean they spoke the same language or shared other cultural traits.

The notion that technological change will occur as an 'evolutionary' phenomenon has been suggested not only for the Stone Age (Clarke 1968; Deacon, J. 1972; Beaumont 1978; Spratt 1982), but also for modern times. The form and range of artefacts change through time as their efficiency and usefulness grow and decline. Change in technology is assumed to improve the efficiency of tools by reducing the cost (or input) and improving the capability (or output). But technological change need not be progressive or evolutionary. It can occur simply because one group of people will prefer to make tools one way and their neighbours will prefer to make them another way.

Change occurs both in the size and shape of tools and in their frequency. The miniaturisation of many artefacts through time provides an example of how change operates in the size dimension (think of the camera, portable radio or computer as well as changes in the size of stone tools from the Earlier to the Middle and Later Stone Ages). The introduction and subsequent phasing out of artefacts – such as the quill pen, donkey cart or tinderbox – provide an example of change in frequency, which can be seen also in the Stone Age in the relative frequency of specialised tools like segments and scrapers. The phasing out of the quill pen did not mean that people stopped writing, any more than the absence of stone scrapers means that people stopped making leather clothing.

The way in which archaeologists have analysed the remains of Later Stone Age hunter-gatherer camps and artefacts is, of course, very different from the way in which the hunter-gatherers themselves would have done the job. People using stone tools in New Guinea who were interviewed by Peter White and David Thomas (1972), for example, were not as concerned as the archaeologists were with style and function, and pointed out that some artefacts in fact were multi-functional. They spoke, too, of the social meanings of the artefacts they made and of the rules regarding their use and the reasons for their discard.

In 1995, Steve Brandt interviewed leather workers in Ethiopia who were still making stone tools to scrape and prepare leather. Each group had its own preferred way of making and mounting the stone scrapers, which distinguished it from the style of another. These observations confirmed that people with a strong group identity make similar tools. However, unless we know something about the meanings that a particular group attach to a particular tool, it is not possible to discern which characteristics are stylistic markers and which are not, nor determine which characteristics are considered

to be stylistic rather than functional.

In many ways archaeologists work in the dark when they analyse stone artefacts. The challenge lies in finding innovative methods to unlock the reasons that may explain why the Stone Age toolmakers did what they did. Many of these reasons were probably quite mundane but, thousands of years later, they continue to lure archaeologists into offering both sensible and outrageous explanations.

A technological history of the Later Stone Age

Initially, the pioneering classification scheme of Goodwin and Van Riet Lowe in 1929 placed the Later Stone Age at the most recent end of the Stone Age sequence. Without the benefit of radiocarbon dating, two major Later Stone Age complexes, the Smithfield and the Wilton, were described as geographically distinct, with different origins and, in the case of the Smithfield C and Wilton, at least partly contemporary.

The Smithfield A, B and C were named after a series of open sites in the Smithfield district of the Free State described by Van Riet Lowe (1929, 1936; Goodwin 1930). The Smithfield was later

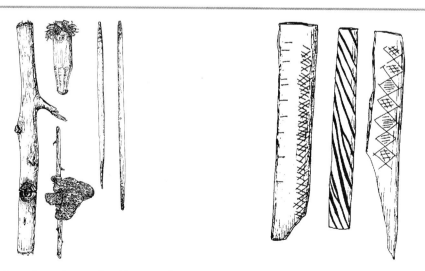

Figure 7.4: *Later Stone Age wood and bone artefacts. Left: On the left is a stick that was used for fire-making. At the top, centre, is a wooden peg and below it is a stick with a lump of mastic. On the right are two fire-hardened wooden points (all from Melkhoutboom). Right: Three decorated bone artefacts, possibly handles for mounted tools, from Nelson Bay Cave (after Inskeep 1987).*

• How stone artefact assemblages are analysed •

An essentially similar method of stone tool analysis is used by all archaeologists for the Later Stone Age. Because we have so little detailed evidence directly from southern African hunter-gatherers on the ways in which stone tools were made and used, the method of analysis tries to reconstruct the stages of tool manufacture. The theory on which the method is based is that the choices made by the tool-maker in the 'chain of operation' from natural rock to artefact can be recognised in the following stages:

• selection and collection of pieces of rock suitable for tool-making (raw material), called chunks or cores

• production of flakes or blades (blanks) by flaking the core

• immediate use of suitable blanks as informal tools

• retouch of other blanks to produce formal tools that are made to a standardised pattern (usually so they will fit into composite tools)

• re-trimming the tool when the edge has dulled

• discarding the tool when there is no further use for it.

The archaeologist examines each piece of stone and asks a series of questions.

1. Has it been deliberately flaked? If it has not, and is of a raw material different from the rock-shelter wall and roof, it is called a manuport and was probably brought into the site by someone who wanted it for raw material but decided not to use it after all. It may also be a fragment of ochre or specularite used for pigment, or a quartz crystal or other stone required for a special purpose. If the stone is not flaked, but is a naturally shaped stone that has been used as a hammerstone or grindstone, it is classified in the category of utilised pieces.

2. If it has been flaked, is it a core or a flake, i.e. can you see a negative or a positive bulb of percussion on the flake scar? If you can see neither because it has broken during the flaking process, it is classified as a chunk.

3. If it is a core, can you see the negative scars of more than two flakes that have been taken off it? If so, it is classified as a core. If not, it is classified as a chunk.

4. If it is a flake with a bulb of percussion, what shape is the flake? Does it show signs of having been used, or has it been flaked or retouched again after it was struck from the core? If it has not been retouched, it is called a waste flake or unretouched flake. If it has been used casually so that the margins of the flake have been lightly damaged it is classified as a utilised flake, and if it has been retouched it is called a formal tool.

5. If it is a formal tool, what kind of retouch has been used and what shape is the artefact? The range of formal tools is not great, and most will fall into three or four classes. If retouch is steep around a convex edge, it is most likely a scraper used for preparing skins for leather-working. If retouch is uneven and steep along a straight or concave edge, it is most likely an adze used for woodworking. If it is a bladelet and has steep regular retouch along one or more margin opposite a sharp cutting edge, it is likely to be a backed bladelet or segment used for a knife or arrowhead. If it is small and rod-like with steep retouch all around a blunt point, it is probably a borer used for making holes in ostrich eggshell beads.

All the artefacts recovered from an archaeological excavation are kept in separate packets according to the square and level in which they were found. The analysis records how many artefacts in each category and class are in the packet. The numbers are then counted for all the squares in each level.

After this basic classification is completed, tables are compiled with the numbers and percentage frequencies of artefacts in the Waste, Utilised and Formal Tool categories. In the majority of assemblages the waste category will include over 90 per cent of the artefacts. Only occasionally will utilised pieces be more common than 6 or 7 per cent. Formal tool classes rarely account for more than 4 or 5 per cent, and are more commonly less than 1 per cent. These figures are helpful for a quick assessment of the type of assemblage that is being studied so that comparisons can be made between different levels at the same site and between one site and another.

More detailed analyses can also be done. Measurements of unretouched flakes, for example, will reflect whether the tool-makers were trying to make blade-shaped or square flakes, whether certain kinds of rocks were selected for particular shapes, and what degree of standardisation was achieved in flake production. Formal tool sizes vary; here again the patterning between levels and sites can be quantified. Raw material frequencies reveal interesting behaviour patterns, as some rocks are common in the landscape and are easy to collect, whereas others are rarer and were collected or even traded for their special properties.

expanded to include Smithfield N and P as well. Each had a distinctive type of stone tool. Smithfield A had large scrapers (longer than 30 mm) for leather-working that were mostly round or rectangular. Smithfield B leather-working scrapers were long and narrow. Smithfield C scrapers were small and were mounted onto handles. Smithfield N scrapers were concave and were probably woodworking tools. Smithfield P scrapers had straight sides and steep retouch and were probably also used more for woodworking than for leather. Some variants were distinct geographically, as Smithfield N was found in Natal and Smithfield P was found in Pondoland. The Smithfield was not found north of the Limpopo River. Both the Smithfield B and C were associated with backed bladelets used as inserts for arrows and cutting tools, but not with large numbers of segments.

The term Smithfield (without an accompanying letter) is used today only for assemblages with backed bladelets and long end-scrapers at the end of the sequence in the Karoo (Sampson 1988),

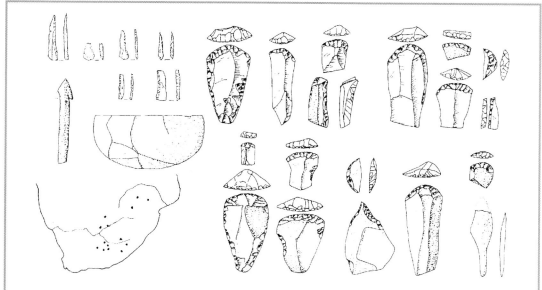

Figure 7.5: Distribution and artefacts typical of the Smithfield. Note the iron arrowhead (bottom right), the long end-scrapers, the backed bladelets (top left), the bone arrowhead (left) and grass-tempered pot.

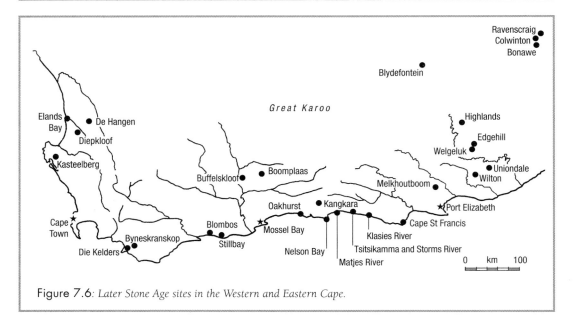

Figure 7.6: *Later Stone Age sites in the Western and Eastern Cape.*

dating to within the last 1000 years (Figure 7.5). It replaces the term Smithfield B. The terms Smithfield A and C have fallen away, being replaced by the Oakhurst Complex and the Interior Wilton or Post-Wilton respectively.

Preceding and contemporary with the Smithfield, as now defined, are assemblages that some researchers have described as macrolithic ('large stone') or informal. They are difficult to classify because they have very few formal tools. They are characterised by large untrimmed flakes, they tend to date within the last 3000 years, and have not been formally named (Deacon, J. 1984a&b). Although Sampson (1974) tentatively grouped those along the coast into a Strandloper industry, this term has not been widely used. Those with pottery have been linked to the Khoekhoe herders, but those that predate the introduction of pottery and sheep obviously cannot be. It may be more appropriate to see them as an activity variant. For example, a small group of men without their families may have made them while staying overnight on a hunting trip, or may have habitually used the site for such trips. Alternatively, the informal stone tools could have been made by people who were using other raw materials such as bone, wood or metal for formal tools.

The term Wilton, named after two rock shelters on a farm near Alicedale in the Albany district of the Eastern Cape (Figure 7.6) which were excavated by Hewitt (1921), was used to refer to assemblages with a high incidence of backed bladelets and especially of segments or 'crescents'. Wilton assemblages occur in Zimbabwe, Botswana and Namibia as well as South Africa, but not in the dry interior. Today the term is applied to both mid- and late Holocene microlithic assemblages. The mid-Holocene Wilton or Classic Wilton dates approximately between 8000 or 7500 and 4500 years ago. Late Holocene assemblages with fewer segments, dating within the last 4500 years ago, would previously have been called Smithfield C. Now they are variously referred to as Interior (or Inland) Wilton, Late Wilton, Post-Wilton or Post-Climax Wilton.

Wilton assemblages also include a wide range of microliths such as borers, small scrapers (less than 25 mm long) made on snapped flakes and blades (Figure 7.7), so-called double-scrapers or double segments that are oval with steep retouch along both margins, ornaments and polished bone tools.

By the end of the 1960s, the Wilton name site (Deacon, H.J. 1972; Deacon, J. 1972, 1974) and several new sites in the Smithfield region (Sampson 1974) had been excavated and dated. It was apparent that what Goodwin and Van Riet Lowe had described as contemporary regional cultures – the Wilton and Smithfield C – were in fact parts of a time sequence. This sequence began with the Smithfield A and was succeeded by the Wilton, Smithfield C and Smithfield B. The earliest stage, formerly the Smithfield A, is now known as the Oakhurst Complex (Sampson 1974); this incorporates several regional variants or industries.

The Oakhurst Complex is named after a farm near Wilderness in the southern Cape where Goodwin excavated a rock shelter in the 1930s. The Oakhurst Complex dates to the early Holocene – between about 12 000 and 8000 or 7500 years ago. It is characterised by round, end- and D-shaped scrapers, so-called duckbill scrapers, which have parallel sides and splay out at the working end; a wide range of polished bone tools; and few or no microliths (Figure 7.8). In some sequences it is also distinguished by the use of coarser-grained raw materials than in the assemblages below or above it. However, where fine-grained raw materials are used, the size range of the scrapers is larger than the overlying ones but is seldom greater than 30 mm. The Oakhurst was named by Garth Sampson (1974) and encompasses regional variations such as the Albany industry in the southern Cape (Klein 1974; Deacon, H.J. 1976; Deacon, J. 1978, 1984a&b) and the

Lockshoek industry in the Karoo (Sampson 1974; Bousman 1991).

By the mid-1970s an additional piece of the puzzle had been described and dated. Artefact assemblages older than the Oakhurst (Smithfield A) were found and were named the Robberg industry after the Robberg peninsula at Plettenberg Bay. The Robberg is the earliest technological expression of the Later Stone Age. In the southern Cape it dates to the end of the Late Pleistocene, between about 22 000 and 12 000 years ago. It is characterised by a few backed tools, a few scrapers of variable size, and significant numbers of un-retouched microlithic bladelets struck from distinctive cores (Figure 7.9) (Klein 1974; Deacon, H.J. 1976, 1979; Deacon, J. 1978, 1984a&b). It has since been found in the Free State (Wadley 1996b), Lesotho (Mitchell 1995) and further afield.

Case study of Nelson Bay Cave and Boomplaas

At least 30 rock shelters that were occupied by Later Stone Age people have been excavated in the southern and Eastern Cape. They provide as complete a record of technological change as is

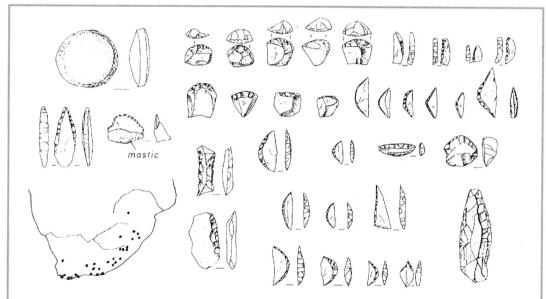

Figure 7.7: Distribution and characteristic artefacts of the Wilton. Note the variety of segments, small scrapers and the milled-edge pebble (top left).

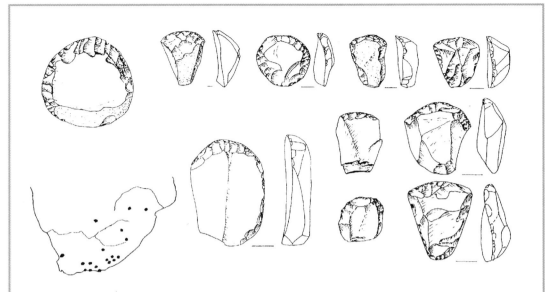

Figure 7.8: *Distribution and characteristic artefacts of the Oakhurst Complex, including the Albany industry.*

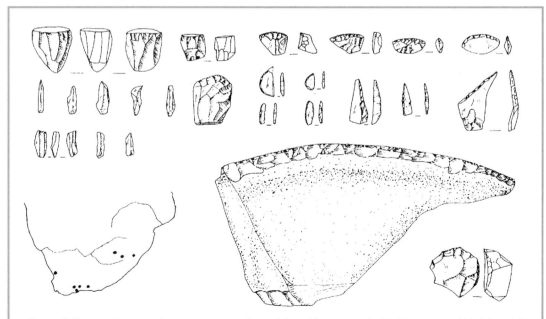

Figure 7.9: *Distribution and characteristic artefacts of the Robberg. Note the bladelet cores and bladelets (left), the large and small scrapers, and backed tools.*

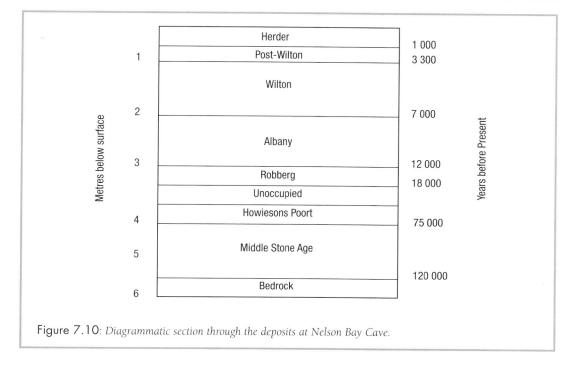

Metres below surface		Years before Present
	Herder	1 000
1	Post-Wilton	3 300
	Wilton	
2		7 000
	Albany	
3		12 000
	Robberg	18 000
	Unoccupied	
	Howiesons Poort	
4		75 000
5	Middle Stone Age	
		120 000
	Bedrock	
6		

Figure 7.10: *Diagrammatic section through the deposits at Nelson Bay Cave.*

available anywhere else in southern Africa. They are commonly cited as an example of the range of techniques used to describe and interpret the Later Stone Age. Similar Later Stone Age regional studies have been done in the Western Cape (Schweitzer & Wilson 1982; Parkington 1987; Jerardino 1996), Northern Cape (Humphreys & Thackeray 1983; Beaumont & Vogel 1989), Eastern Cape (Deacon, H.J. 1976; Opperman 1987; Leslie 1989; Hall 1990), KwaZulu–Natal (Mazel 1989b), the Free State (Wadley 1996b), the Magaliesberg (Wadley 1987) and the Waterberg (Van der Ryst 1996).

Two sites cover the sequence from the Late Pleistocene through the Holocene especially well: Nelson Bay Cave on the coast near Plettenberg Bay, excavated by Richard Klein and Ray Inskeep, and Boomplaas Cave (Figure 7.11) in the Cango Valley about 80 km inland, excavated by H.J. Deacon. Although both sequences have Middle Stone Age occupation horizons at the base, we focus here on the 22 000-year time period of the Later Stone Age. This includes the Last Glacial Maximum (18 000 years ago) when global temperatures were colder than at any other time over the past 120 000 years. It also encompasses the Present Interglacial (10 000

years ago to the present) when temperatures rose and reached a peak during the mid-Holocene about 5000 years ago.

The two sequences make it possible to track the timing and nature of change not only in the artefacts that people made, but in diverse ecosystem indicators. These indicators include oxygen isotopes in a stalagmite that reflect temperature; the size and range of small mammals caught and eaten by owls; the larger mammals hunted by people; the range of woody plants selected for firewood by the cave inhabitants; pollen blown into Boomplaas Cave by the wind; and fish and shellfish remains brought into Nelson Bay Cave, which can be correlated with changes in ocean temperatures and sea levels, and therefore with global climatic changes.

The sequence can be conveniently described in five stages.

22 000–12 000 BP. The stone artefacts from units dated within this time range at Nelson Bay Cave and Boomplaas are typical of the Robberg industry. The numbers of stone artefacts from the Robberg levels at Boomplaas are larger (92 000) and the number of artefacts per bucket of deposit excavated is much higher (133) than at any other time in the sequence. These figures partly reflect the original choice of raw material, and in particular the choice of quartz, as the flaking technique generated large numbers of small quartz chips. The most characteristic feature of the Robberg assemblages, though, is the relatively high incidence of small bladelets (about 16 mm long) struck from small pyramid-shaped cores. The fact that bladelets often occur clustered together in a small patch seems to indicate either that they were kept together – perhaps in a small bag – or that the flaking technique generated a lot of bladelets that were left where they fell. One possibility is suggested by Peter White's observation of people in New Guinea binding their cores with twine and then tapping the striking platform. The binding encourages the force to extend downwards and bladelets are pro-

duced. When the knapper has finished his task, he unwinds the twine and selects the bladelets required, leaving the rest in a heap.

By contrast, the incidence of formal tools in the Robberg units is the lowest in the sequence at both sites (0.02 per bucket at Nelson Bay and 0.15 at Boomplaas). Where formal tools are present, they include a full range of scrapers and backed bladelets but the size and shape are not as standardised as in the Albany and Wilton.

The non-stone tools associated with the Robberg include polished bone points, bone and ostrich eggshell beads, and tortoiseshell bowls or containers. They show a fine degree of workmanship but occur in small numbers relative to later levels. Fragments of ostrich eggshell flasks with

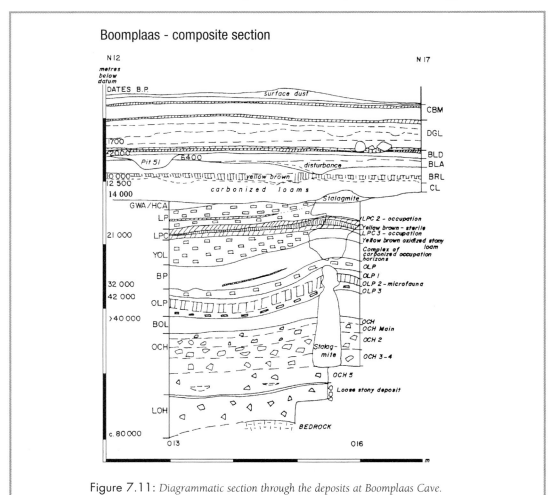

Figure 7.11: *Diagrammatic section through the deposits at Boomplaas Cave.*

29 • Summary of the Later Stone Age sequence •

- **22 000–12 000 BP:** Bladelets, including a few segments and backed bladelets, and characteristic bladelet cores, with a small range of scrapers in an otherwise informal assemblage (Robberg).
- **12 000–8 000 BP:** Stone artefacts with large scrapers and large adzes, very few backed tools but a variety of polished bone tools (Oakhurst Complex encompassing the Lockshoek and Albany industries).
- **8000–4000 BP:** Stone artefacts with small scrapers, relatively high numbers and a wide variety of backed tools and segments, and ornaments and polished bone tools (Wilton).
- **4000–2000 BP:** Two kinds of assemblage may be found, both without pottery:

(a) with few formal tools; or (b) with small scrapers and backed tools, but relatively small numbers of segments (Interior Wilton or Post-Wilton).
- **2000–100 BP:** Two kinds of assemblages may be found, with or without pottery: (a) with informal stone artefacts on coarse-grained rocks made by, or contemporary with, Khoekhoe stock farmers; or (b) with pottery and stone tools on fine-grained rocks such as indurated shale, chalcedony, quartz or silcrete, which may have long scrapers with backed bladelets (Smithfield) or small scrapers with some backed bladelets but rare segments (Interior Wilton or Post-Wilton). Adzes tend to be more common in these assemblages than in the preceding time period.

---

engraved patterns on them and traces of ochre indicate an interest in decorative art at this time.

Richard Klein's analysis of the faunal remains from the two sites shows how climatic conditions influenced the range of land mammals available to the cave inhabitants. The soils on the land exposed to the south of the present coastline during the Last Glacial Maximum, between 22 000 and 12 000 years ago, were favourable for grassland. The animals found there were therefore mainly grazers and included two species that are now extinct and that were larger than their present-day counterparts, the giant buffalo (*Pelorovis antiquus*) and a giant hartebeest (*Megalotragus priscus*). In addition, an extinct giant horse or zebra (*Equus capensis*) is known from Boomplaas and other sites of similar age in the region. It is widely assumed that these animals became extinct through the combined pressure of climatic and vegetation change and more effective hunting practices. Similar extinctions of large mammals at this time are known worldwide and, as with the Later Stone Age, often coincided with the introduction of the bow and arrow. Whatever the reason, these species are not, however, found in any deposits younger than 10 000 years.

Both Nelson Bay Cave and Boomplaas were occupied by owls at times when people were not living there. The bones of the small animals eaten by the owls have become incorporated into the deposits and have been studied by Margaret Avery. As a general principle, not only does the range of species change when climatic conditions are colder or warmer, but the average size of animals of certain species will also change with mean annual temperature changes. By applying these principles to the archaeological samples, Avery has demonstrated from the Boomplaas sequence in particular that the rats, mice and shrews eaten by owls were more sensitive to temperature changes than the larger mammals eaten by people. The shift from the range of species typical of glacial conditions to the range typical of interglacial conditions occurred at about 14 000 years ago, 2000 years earlier amongst the small mammal population than amongst the larger mammals (Figure 7.12). It coincided with independent evidence of temperature changes recorded in the Cango stalagmite (described in Chapter 2) and with changes in the woody plants used for firewood. Anton Scholtz has identified these woods from fragments of charcoal in hearths at Boomplaas. There is a dramatic increase in charcoal from *Olea* sp. (wild olive) and

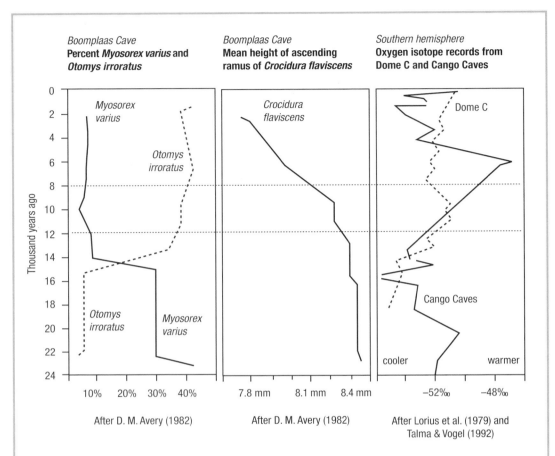

Figure 7.12: *Comparison of changes in the relative frequency at Boomplaas Cave of vlei rats* (Otomys irroratus) *and forest shrews* (Myosorex varius) *caught by owls, in the size of the red musk shrew* (Crocidura flaviscens), *and in temperature as recorded in the oxygen isotopes of the Cango Caves stalagmite and the Dome C ice core in Antarctica.*

Rhus sp. trees after 14 000 years ago (Figure 7.13).

12 000–8000 BP. This time period is characterised by the Albany industry. Raw materials were selected for large flakes and scrapers. At Nelson Bay Cave more than 90 per cent of the Albany artefacts are made of quartzite. At Boomplaas, though quartz is the dominant raw material throughout the Later Stone Age, there are more quartzite artefacts during the Albany than at any other time in the sequence. At both sites the incidence of polished bone tools is higher during the Albany than at any other time, but the frequency of formal stone tools is intermediate between the Robberg and the Wilton.

The hunting pattern during the Albany is also transitional (Figure 7.14). At about 10 000 years ago the ratio between grazing and browsing antelope at Nelson Bay Cave and Boomplaas was about even, and the size range was intermediate between the Robberg and the Wilton. The small mammals eaten by owls are essentially interglacial in character and the woody plants are well represented.

The shellfish at Nelson Bay Cave include species like the black mussel, *Choromytilus meridionalis*, which today is most common in the colder waters of the west coast. Fish were caught, possibly on lines with the double-pointed polished bone tools, or fish gorges, found in these levels (Figure 7.15).

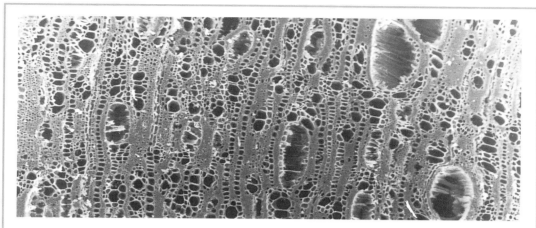

Figure 7.13: *Scanning electron microscope photograph (x 50) of a section through a fragment of Olea sp. charcoal from Boomplaas Cave.*

8000–4000 BP. There is only one occupation horizon in this time range at Boomplaas and it is dated to 6400 BP. The Wilton sequence at Nelson Bay Cave is more complete and fits in well with the larger samples from the Wilton name site, and from Melkhoutboom and other sites in the Eastern Cape. The density of stone tools is higher than in the Albany and the incidence of formal tools, especially small scrapers and segments and other backed bladelets, is the highest in the sequence. Fine-grained raw materials were commonly selected. Bone tools are found and there are lots of ornaments like ostrich eggshell beads and pendants. A painted stone was found in the unit dated to 6400 BP at Boomplaas: it is one of the oldest securely dated paintings in South Africa (Figure 7.16). Two oval pits about 1 x 2 m in size and filled with charcoal were found in this same level and were possibly used for drying meat to make biltong.

All evidence globally points to this period as being the warmest since the Last Interglacial ended 120 000 years ago. The charcoals are from the wood of bushes rather than large trees, suggesting that conditions may have been dry as well as hot.

Richard Klein's analysis of the bones of mammals hunted by the people living at Boomplaas and Nelson Bay shows an increasing tendency to rely on smaller browsing antelope such as the bushbuck, grysbok and steenbok and the extinct bloubok. These animals commonly live in pairs and are territorial, and so do not migrate in large herds. They feed in the early morning and evening rather than during the day: they are thus more easily caught in traps than by bow and arrow.

4000–2000 BP. At Nelson Bay Cave, Ray Inskeep recognised a significant difference between the assemblages older than about 3200 years ago and those that are younger. The older ones were clearly part of the Wilton tradition, with segments and other formal tools made in a variety of raw materials, but the younger ones were more informal and dominated by quartzite. Those dating between 4000 and 2000 BP included several tanged points prepared for hafting, small pebbles with a groove around the middle that weighed less than 2 g and were probably used for sinkers, smoothed flat shale artefacts sometimes called palettes, and a wide variety of polished bone tools.

The food remains at Nelson Bay Cave included large numbers of fish and shellfish. The most common mammals were seals and hyraxes (dassies) but there were also small numbers of small to medium browsing antelope and only a few larger animals like Cape buffalo. The cave inhabitants seem to have been focusing more on food sources in the immediate vicinity of the site.

2000–200 BP. The artefacts from the uppermost levels at Boomplaas differ from those at Nelson Bay Cave. Boomplaas is an example of a site where pottery and sheep are associated with a continuation of the Wilton tradition; this has small scrapers and backed tools in fine-grained raw

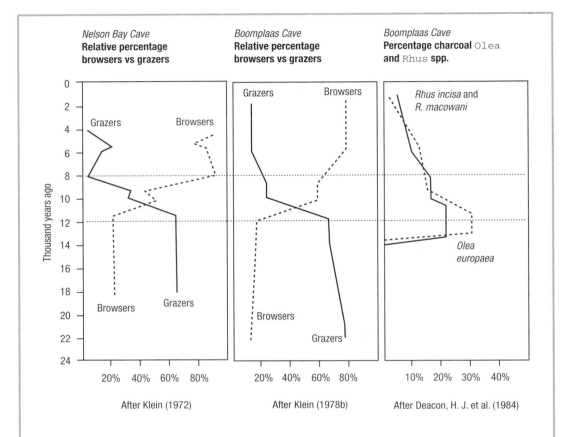

Figure 7.14: *Comparison of changes in the relative frequency of grazers and browsers in the mammal fauna at Boomplaas and Nelson Bay, and woody plants identified from charcoals at Boomplaas Cave over the past 20 000 years.*

materials but few segments. There are also rare finds of stone tools mounted in mastic as well as of bone tools, ostrich eggshell and shell beads and pendants and, more rarely, painted stones (Figure 7.16). In the upper levels at Boomplaas there are over 40 small pits dug into the deposits to store fruits. With the exception of the storage pits, all these latter items have also been found at Nelson Bay Cave or at other sites on the Robberg peninsula. The stone artefacts at Nelson Bay Cave are, however, large with few formal tools.

The earliest pottery at Boomplaas dates to about 1800 years ago and at Nelson Bay Cave to a few hundred years later. At first the sherds are thin and well fired, but in the upper levels they tend to be coarser. The faunal and shellfish remains from the

uppermost levels at Nelson Bay Cave are not very different from those from the period 4000–2000 BP, but sheep were introduced at least by 1100 BP. At Boomplaas, the small to medium antelope were almost entirely replaced by sheep. An analysis of the sheep bones by Angela von den Driesch shows that the herders who were living in the cave were slaughtering younger animals for lamb rather than older ones for mutton.

In summary, the different environmental settings of Boomplaas and Nelson Bay Cave offered very different food and raw material resources, yet the range of artefacts and the timing of changes in hunting patterns and technology are almost identical in the two sequences. This suggests that stone artefacts are not a good reflection of environment

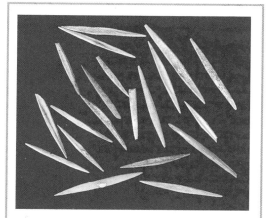

Figure 7.15: *Polished bone fish gorges from Nelson Bay Cave. The longest is about 35 mm.*

or ecology in the vicinity of a site. Toolkits were adapted for social rather than environmental reasons. Although the food remains indicate what was available in the vicinity of the site, the artefacts do not. At times Later Stone Age people went to a lot of trouble to import fine-grained stone from afar for their artefacts and they regularly changed the range and size of their tools.

Climatic changes that affected the range of animals available for hunting were evident at both sites at about the same time (Figure 7.14), but the range of microfauna taken by owls changed earlier (Figure 7.12). Either small mammals were less adaptable and changed more rapidly in concert with warmer conditions than did the larger mammals hunted by people, or the people were slow to

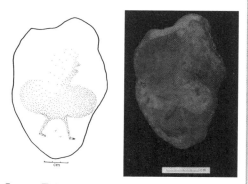

Figure 7.16: *One of the painted stones from Boomplaas dated to about 2000 BP.*

change their hunting preferences. In the latter case, this may have led to the extinction of certain larger species when they became vulnerable to predation at the end of the Pleistocene.

Wilton and related sites

Wilton, re-excavated in 1966–7, provided an important key to the Holocene artefact sequence. We excavated there because it was the name site of the Wilton Complex and more precise descriptions of the stratigraphy and artefacts were needed for accurate classification. Brian Fagan (1960) and Carmel Schrire (1962) had tried to make sense of the artefact sequence from Oakhurst near Wilderness in the southern Cape, but this was a tall order without re-excavating the site. Comparative information from new excavations at Wilton was therefore needed.

When Wilton was first excavated by Hewitt in the 1920s, radiocarbon dating had not been developed and so samples were needed for dating too. Although the Matjes River Rock Shelter on the coast east of Plettenberg Bay was the first Holocene sequence in South Africa to be dated by radiocarbon (in the 1950s), the small size of that artefact sample and the lack of well-controlled excavations made the dates difficult to interpret (Louw 1960).

At Wilton the layers of occupation deposit were carefully separated so that the artefacts could be divided into a series of time slices. Scrapers were the most common formal tool that was found. Because classification into the Smithfield–Wilton scheme was determined by scraper shape and size, a series of measurements was taken to describe changes in scraper dimensions. Changes were also measured in the relative frequency of segments and other backed bladelets.

At the base of the sequence was an early Holocene assemblage, dating to about 8000 years ago, which had large scrapers and very few other formal tools. In the middle were layers with small scrapers and increasing numbers of segments in the mid-Holocene that peaked around 6000 BP. Segment numbers tailed off after 4000 BP. At the top of the deposit was a late Holocene assemblage with large scrapers and backed bladelets, but few segments (Deacon, J. 1972).

A similar pattern to that from Wilton was found in the sequence from Melkhoutboom in the

Suurberg north of Port Elizabeth. At the base of the Melkhoutboom sequence dating to *c.* 15 000 BP was the first small sample of what was later called the Robberg industry. From *c.* 7300 to 3000 BP the stone tools of the mid-Holocene Wilton had accumulated in four densely packed occupation horizons with more than 42 000 stone artefacts and a variety of well-preserved plant remains.

The dry conditions in Melkhoutboom Cave (Figure 7.18) prevented the decay not only of the residues of plant foods but also of wooden tools. They included pegs, fire drills, parts of reed arrow shafts, a lump of mastic on a stick and mastic traces on hafted tools, a flake bound with *Boophane disticha* bulbar leaves (see Figure 7.1), and netting, string and fragments of sewn leather clothing. Some of these were more than 6000 years old.

The presence of sea and estuarine shells indicated trade with coastal people or movement between the mountains and the coast, about 50 km away. In the upper layers, the replacement of rare marine shells with freshwater mussels suggested a change in this pattern of trade or seasonal movement. The increased exploitation of *Cafferia caffer* freshwater mussels after about 3000 years ago has also been seen at several other sites in the Eastern Cape. Examples are Mary Leslie's excavations at Uniondale Rock Shelter and Simon Hall's research at Edgehill and Welgeluk in the Koonap Valley, all east of Grahamstown. At Uniondale, however, trade with the coast was still evident as marine sand mussel shells, *Donax serra*, were still being brought in as artefacts (Figure 7.19).

Combined with evidence from other food remains in the Koonap Valley, such as fish and plant foods, Simon Hall interpreted this trend as an indication that population density was increasing, band territories were becoming smaller, and people were focusing more and more on foods and raw materials near at hand. Significantly, this trend was well under way before herders came to the Eastern Cape.

Figure 7.17: *Wilton Large Rock Shelter in the early 1920s. (Photo: J. Hewitt)*

The concept of intensification assumes that people who are under stress from the environment or from population increase will try to alleviate their problems by working harder, by intensifying their search for food. They may turn to foods they may not have eaten before, they may increase the frequency of hunting expeditions, they may improve their toolkit to increase productivity, or – in the case of many societies in the last 10 000 years – they may domesticate plants or animals.

H.J. Deacon, whose analysis of radiocarbon dates for the Eastern Cape suggested that the change towards an increased exploitation of fresh-water shellfish and small ground game began about 3000 years ago, thought it may have been precipitated by the influx of Khoekhoe herders. Some years later and with the benefit of a larger sample of excavated sequences and radiocarbon dates, Mary Leslie and Simon Hall's data from Uniondale, Welgeluk and Edgehill showed that the change occurred well over 1000 years before the introduction of pottery and domesticated stock. It can be related to the increase in rainfall that has been documented in several regions between 3000 and 2000 years ago.

The same pattern of change towards intensifica-tion up to 1000 years before the introduction of herding can be seen in analyses of faunal remains from sites in other regions too. It has been des-cribed in sites in the Karoo around Blydefontein excavated by Britt Bousman and Garth Sampson, in the Thukela Valley of KwaZulu-Natal excavated by Aron Mazel, and on the west and southern coasts of the Western Cape described by Richard Klein, Kathy Cruz-Uribe and Antonieta Jerardino.

Comparisons

When the artefact sequence from the Wilton name site and other sites within 50–80 km of the coast is compared with sequences from sites inland, there are some interesting differences. Both start in the early Holocene with assemblages that have large scrapers and few other formal tools. However, at sites in the interior the mid-Holocene Wilton part of the sequence, with high frequencies of segments, is seldom represented and many sites have a gap in occupation between about 8000 and 5000 years ago, which lasted several thousand years. Thereafter, within the last 4500 years at

Figure 7.18: *Section through the deposits at Melkhoutboom. The layers with preserved plant materials can be clearly seen between the ash from hearths.*

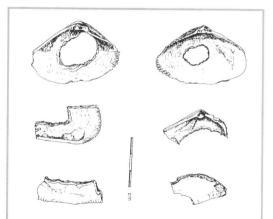

Figure 7.19: *Shells of the white mussel,* Donax serra, *found at Melkhoutboom, about 50 km from the coast. They have been used for some purpose as the edges are damaged and some have holes in them. Shells utilised in the same way are also found at coastal sites.*

inland sites, the Interior Wilton, with small scrapers and a few backed tools, is succeeded by the Smithfield with long end-scrapers and backed bladelets. Pottery and, later, glass trade beads are found at the top, associated with the Smithfield.

A comparison between an inland site at Highlands Rock Shelter, near Fish River, north of Cradock in the Karoo, and Melkhoutboom, which is within 80 km of the coast, shows that although the hunting and gathering pattern throughout both sequences was essentially similar, the artefacts are not. The stone tools are initially both functionally and stylistically similar up to about 4500 years ago. Thereafter, although they remain functionally similar, the Highlands industry becomes less Wilton-like through time until in the upper levels it is distinctively Smithfield in character and very different from the final phase of the Later Stone Age at Wilton and other coastal sites.

The scenario used to explain these change has both environmental and social overtones. H.J. Deacon (1972, 1976) suggested that global climatic changes caused prolonged hot and dry conditions in the Karoo between about 7500 and 4500 years ago, leading to a dramatic decrease in the carrying capacity of the land. People in the arid interior were unable to live there for sustained periods. When they moved to better-watered areas within about 80 km of the southern and eastern coast and in the foothills of the Drakensberg and other mountain ranges, population density decreased. Their tool-making tradition, which we now call the Wilton, is therefore more commonly found in areas with higher rainfall. When conditions improved, groups of people began expanding their range back into the Karoo and other inland regions.

Britt Bousman has analysed a range of environmental indicators, spanning the last 10 000–14 000 years, based on Later Stone Age occupation horizons from rock shelters and open sites near the town of Colesberg in the Karoo. These have enabled him to draw a number of threads of evidence together and to suggest links between the availability of basic foodstuffs and the density of human settlement. Using key climatic and environmental indicators, he noticed several general correlations between climate and resources that affect response to risk, range and technology amongst non-agricultural people worldwide. For example, when populations change their ways,

from obtaining their food mainly in a few large parcels, such as large antelope or other game animals, to collecting mainly small parcels of food like plant foods, rats and mice, fish, shellfish and insects, the change in diet often coincides with an increase in the number of people in the area. When this happens, there is a tendency for these people to be less mobile. Family groups have smaller and better-defined territories and do not move around as frequently as they would do if they were big-game hunters. This kind of model is climate-driven. It highlights carrying capacity and population density as the factors that had most influence on what people did. It therefore has the power to explain the distribution of sites through time and space, but it does not explain why people in one region made their stone tools differently from people in another region.

Interpreting functional change

Some of the variability in the kinds of stone artefacts found at sites of similar age may be the result of functional differences – in other words, different things were done at different places.

From the early 1970s, John Parkington (1972, 1980) developed a hypothesis of seasonal mobility for the Western Cape that applied some of the principles governing seasonal movements of hunter-gatherers in the Kalahari. He suggested that over the past 10 000 years the hunter-gatherers along the west coast north of Cape Town tended to live in winter on the coast where seals and shellfish were plentiful, and inland in the Cape Fold mountains in summer when plant foods were most abundant there.

To support the seasonal mobility hypothesis Aron Mazel designed research into the relative frequency of formal tools in Later Stone Age sites in the Western Cape. He reasoned that the higher frequency of adzes at inland mountain sites was the result of summer occupation, when women were concentrating their efforts on digging up underground plant foods like corms and bulbs. They therefore had to spend more time keeping their digging sticks in shape than at other seasons of the year. As adzes are probably woodworking tools, they would be expected to be more common in such circumstances (Mazel & Parkington 1981).

By contrast, open sites in the sandveld between the mountains and the coast tended to have the

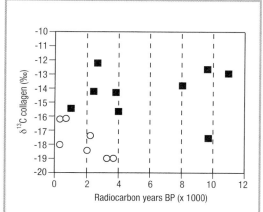

Figure 7.20: *Carbon isotope ratios in Later Stone Age human skeletons in the Western Cape. The squares represent skeletons buried at or near to the coast and the circles are skeletons buried inland in the valley of the Olifants River and in the mountains of the Cape Fold belt over the last 12 000 years. With one exception, the results indicate that Later Stone Age people living along the coast ate sea foods (^{13}C between -16 and -20) whereas those living inland did not (^{13}C between -12 and -16). (Diagram courtesy of J. Sealy)*

Because the absence of seasonally available foods in archaeological deposits could not prove that people were not living at the site at times of the year when these foods were unavailable, the evidence seemed clear. It was only after Judith Sealy had completed the analysis of carbon isotope ratios in human skeletons buried inland and on the coast over the past 10 000 years (Sealy & Van der Merwe 1986) that doubt was cast on these conclusions. The reconstruction of the life-long diet of a small sample of individuals shows that they, at least, had not alternated on an annual basis between the mountains and the sea, but had remained in one zone or the other (Figure 7.20).

What do the changes signify?

We can conclude from this summary of the Later Stone Age sequence that changes in the type and style of stone were broadly contemporary throughout South Africa and that sometimes they coincided with changes in subsistence. But there is no logical connection between particular tools and particular subsistence strategies. This suggests that formal tools like scrapers and backed bladelets are not directly linked to what people ate and the way they obtained their meat and vegetables. Scrapers prepare skins for clothing and backed bladelets and segments are cutting tools, some of which may have been mounted as arrowheads. The absence of backed bladelets in Albany assemblages has no correlation with the number of game animals hunted. Skins could be prepared with either large or small scrapers. Opting for large scrapers rather than small ones throughout South Africa between 12 000 and 8000 years ago seems therefore to have been a stylistic preference adopted for social reasons that are not yet fully understood.

Information on subsistence is to be found instead in the faunal and floral remains and in the distribution of sites in the landscape, the dating of occupations within these sites, and the density of artefacts that are indicators of group size, social organisation and population density. The next chapter explores factors other than food that influenced people of the Later Stone Age.

highest frequencies of scrapers and backed tools. This was interpreted as evidence for occupation of these sites at times of the year when hunting was important, between summer and winter. On the coast, the numbers of formal tools were consistently low: this was interpreted as confirmation of a pattern of winter exploitation of seals and shellfish, which did not require high frequencies of formal stone tools.

This functional explanation did not take into account the age of the assemblages, because many of them were open sites that could not be dated. With better dating from rock shelters in the area, we now know that assemblages with high frequencies of segments almost certainly date between about 8000 and 4000 years ago, while those with high frequencies of adzes are more likely to be less than 4000 years old. Age would therefore account for some of the variability Mazel described in the open sites.

CHAPTER EIGHT

The Later Stone Age as Khoisan history

Stone Age archaeologists often fantasise about travelling back in a time machine to observe the people who lived in the site they are excavating. The next best thing is ethnoarchaeology, even if all you can do is read about what other people have done. You also learn a lot by trying your hand at making stone artefacts, cooking for 30 students over an open fire, lying awake in a leaky tent through a stormy night, and gathering your food from the veld.

Hilary's excavations at Melkhoutboom and Boomplaas showed how important underground plant foods were in the Later Stone Age. We dug up watsonias in our garden and saw how the corm changed with the seasons. We passed some through the bars of a cage at the zoo and watched as the baboon gently plucked off the inedible bits and popped the white flesh into his mouth. Then we ate them ourselves, roasting them first over the fire in our lounge. Eating shellfish off the rocks was even easier. And you really can skin an animal with a stone flake or two.

This knowledge came in handy in 1979 when the Southern African Association of Archaeologists held their biennial conference in Cape Town, with a symposium on the Middle Stone Age at Stellenbosch afterwards. John Parkington challenged Janette to organise an indigenous dinner of hunted and gathered foods. It took five months to get the ingredients together on 5 July at the Coetzenburg Hotel. The menu was printed with a description of each item, together with references from the botanical, ethnographic and historical literature.

A huge fire blazed in the hearth at the hotel. When the guests arrived they cracked their own mongongo and marula nuts with hammerstones gathered from the bed of the Eerste River. All the photographs show heads bent low over the ground and bums in the air. The tables were set with bowls of dried mopane worms (there were lots of leftovers), wild figs and a tortoise liver paté. The next course was a seafood soup with a variety of crustacea, shellfish and fish (caught by Cedric Poggenpoel). Then came roast porcupine provided by the local Nature Conservation officer and skinned by James Brink, stewed buffalo from the Kruger National Park, gemsbok fillet from the Kalahari, ostrich meat and ostrich egg from Oudtshoorn, and roasted springbok and guinea fowl from the local butcher, who proved very helpful. Watsonia corms were roasted on the fire, and there were bowls of waterblommetjies from the Western Cape, millet and sorghum from Natal, beans from Botswana, and wild spinach that had been collected in the vineyards. Erich Wendt had brought !nara and tsamma melons and dried !nara flesh and seeds from Namibia. There was also comb honey and jelly from numnum fruits that had ripened all over the Stellenbosch campus months before.

It was a night to remember – if only because so many extras arrived that the hotel demanded more money, the wine ran out, and expenditure exceeded income. So much for Stone Age economics. [JD]

Genetic and linguistic studies together confirm that twentieth-century peoples often referred to collectively as the Khoisan are the aboriginal inhabitants of southern Africa. Khoisan history is therefore closely connected with the history of the people of the Later Stone Age. As we have seen from the previous chapter, the time depth of San art, tools and other remains of the hunter-gatherer lifestyle extends as far back as 20 000 years ago but their social structure is most clearly traceable during the Holocene, the last 10 000 years. The herder way of life associated with people who spoke Khoe languages extends back about 2000 years in South Africa.

We can summarise the major events in the history of the Later Stone Age San hunter-gatherers and, later, the Khoekhoe herders, which have been traced archaeologically, as follows:

• elaboration of art and other indicators of complex belief systems;

• introduction of specialised Later Stone Age technology;

• noticeable increases in population density from about 14 000 years ago, and most significantly in the last 4000 years;

• the adoption of a herding economy by Khoe-speakers about 2000 years ago;

• trade and interaction with metal-working agriculturists of the Early Iron Age after 2000 years ago; and

• loss of Khoisan control over their land in the wake of European colonisation.

This chapter focuses on the archaeology and ethnography of the Later Stone Age as it applies to the San hunter-gatherers and their ancestors. The next chapter looks more closely at the archaeology of the Khoekhoe herders.

Khoisan, Khoekhoen and San

There is much confusion over the words used to describe the indigenous people of South Africa. The confusion has been caused partly by the absence of words in their own vocabularies to describe hunter-gatherer and herding groups larger than linguistic units. Equally problematic was the unrealistic European belief that there ought to be a generic word to describe all the people who lived by hunting, gathering and herding in the region prior to colonisation. As Michael Wilson

(1986) so aptly noted, we may have difficulty even today in finding a word to describe ourselves if asked by the proverbial 'man from Mars' who we are. In contrast to Martians – if indeed there are any – we are *Homo sapiens sapiens*, we are people or citizens of the world, but on progressively smaller scales we are also people of the southern hemisphere, Africans, South Africans, and members of communities in various provinces, cities, towns or farm districts. Or we may class ourselves as men or women, Xhosa-, English- or Afrikaans-speakers, politicians or farmers, and so on.

For several hundred years the European colonists used variations on the words 'Bushmen' and 'Hottentots' when referring respectively to the hunter-gatherers and herders of southern Africa. The word 'Hottentot' is said to have been derived from a word sung by Cape Khoekhoen during a dance. Although at first it was applied to all the indigenous people at the Cape by European writers, by the mid-nineteenth century it was more often used only for herders. Unfortunately, the words Bushman and Hottentot have been increasingly misused and have become derogatory. Individuals quite rightly object to being called a 'Boesman' or a 'Hotnot' because it implies that they are uneducated and almost subhuman. Any word we select to describe all the indigenous people in South Africa will therefore be artificial. Some archaeologists and anthropologists prefer to use the economic terms 'hunter-gatherer' and 'herder' instead, but even these are problematic.

The word 'Khoisan' was coined in 1928 by Leonhard Schultze as a collective term for the indigenous hunter-gatherer and herding peoples, whom he regarded as being biologically similar. He combined 'Khoi' or Koï (which is now spelled Khoe), the common-gender singular word for 'person' in the Nama and Korana languages, with 'San', which was the word (common gender, plural) that the Nama used to describe their hunter-gatherer neighbours. Directly translated, San means 'forager' (sa) – 'people' (-n) but, like 'Bushmen', has unfortunately taken on the connotation of 'rascals' or 'vagabonds'. It is pronounced with a long *a*, 'Saan'. Literally, then, the word Khoisan is a grammatical mistake meaning 'person-forager-people'; nevertheless it has become a generic term for most of the hunter-gatherers and herders in southern Africa. We use it in this book as a convenient shorthand label but acknowledge that it masks a great deal of variability and was never used by the indigenous people themselves.

The word 'Khoekhoen' is the common-gender plural of 'Khoe' in Nama and Korana and means more than one person, or 'people'. Without the *n* at the end it can be used as an adjective, such as in 'Khoekhoe pottery'. To complicate matters, 'khoeb' means one man, 'khoes' means one woman, 'khoera' means two women and 'khoeti' means three or more women. Sometimes more romantically translated as 'men of men', Khoikhoi – the older spelling of Khoekhoe – has been widely used in school textbooks and other popular literature. We have even seen it misspelled as 'Koi', which turns people into Japanese goldfish.

In his diary, Jan van Riebeeck used the word 'Quena' instead of 'Khoekhoen'. Both words are the common-gender plural, meaning 'people', but Quena was the equivalent in the language used by herders living in the vicinity of present-day Cape Town, such as the Goringhaiqua and Cochoqua. Although spelled differently, the pronunciation of the words for person, 'que' and 'khoe', is essentially similar. The south-western Khoe languages, which were never recorded in any detail, had different suffixes from those used in Nama. Instead of doubling the word to make a common-gender plural, the suffix '-na' was added. By contrast, most of the tribal names that Van Riebeeck recorded for the Khoekhoen, such as Goringhaiqua, Guriqua and Attaqua, have the male plural suffix '-qua' which means 'men', and are therefore equivalent to the usage in English of a word like Englishmen.

Van Riebeeck used the name 'Sonqua' or 'Soaqua' (masculine, plural) for the hunter-gatherers and other people without domesticated animals in the Western Cape. Some historians say that, translated, it means 'Bush-people' from 'soa-' meaning 'bush' and '-qua' meaning 'men', but others disagree and refer to Van Riebeeck's translation of the word as robbers and stock thieves and to the Nama word 'Sa' for forager.

The choice of 'correct' words to describe the indigenous hunter-gatherers and herders is therefore fraught with problems. Like the ideas and information that history and archaeology produce, the usage will no doubt be changed in the years to come as perceptions alter and new information becomes available.

Archaeology as history

Historical accounts are usually based on a sequence of events that took place and on the motives and actions of the people involved. Archaeological sequences are different. They do not describe events in the same way as historical accounts because archaeological methods are ill equipped to isolate and therefore to recognise individual people, actions and events. Instead, archaeologists design research programmes to answer questions about the behaviour patterns of people in general in the past.

But we cannot make sense of these patterns without some clues about what they meant to the people who created them. We cannot work in a theoretical vacuum assuming that because we do things in a certain way, Stone Age people would have done them in the same way too. For the Later Stone Age, some clues can be found in what is commonly referred to as 'the ethnographic record', the observations of anthropologists, ethnographers, ethno-archaeologists and other specialists who have recorded their impressions of the lifestyles of societies different from their own. Caution is advisable, though. As many archaeologists have pointed out, it is unrealistic to suppose that the hunting and gathering habits of Later Stone Age people remained unchanged for 20 000 years.

The best source of information from which to construct an archaeological history of the San and Khoekhoen is drawn from Khoisan ethnography. We have felt comfortable about doing this because Khoisan people were until recently still using artefacts like bows and arrows and ostrich eggshell beads, and their economy was still largely based on hunting and gathering. More significantly, there is good ethnographic information about the belief system of nineteenth- and twentieth-century San, which gives us an insight into their lifestyle and especially their rock art, of a kind that is not available for earlier stages of the Stone Age.

But although there is also widespread similarity in the technology at Later Stone Age sites in many parts of Africa, we do not imply that Khoisan people were the makers of Later Stone Age artefacts wherever these occur. People with this technology did not necessarily have the same beliefs, speak the same language, eat the same foods or have the same social structure. The boundaries between different cultural traits do not always coincide. For this reason ethnography must be used with caution.

Distribution of San in colonial times

We have only patchy historical records on the distribution, society and economy of San hunter-gatherers in South Africa, because at the time of European contact few colonists wrote about their encounters with them. The policy was to exterminate the San, who were regarded as thieves and robbers when they defended their rights to their water resources and land. There was little room for ethnography.

Contrary to popular belief, the San did not move to the mountains and deserts to escape colonial domination. Those close to colonial settlements were either killed or taken into service; their descendants still form the core of the rural population. San living in more inaccessible mountainous regions, particularly the Drakensberg, or in areas like the Northern Cape which were at least initially unfavourable for farming until wind pumps assured a secure water supply, managed to hold out against the colonial onslaught a little longer.

In South Africa, all the languages recorded as having been spoken by San hunter-gatherers have been placed by linguists into the !Kwi group, one of several groups within the family of Southern Bushman languages, which included the whole of South Africa and extended into southern Botswana (Figure 8.1). !Kwi (Bushman) languages were recorded in the Northern Cape (/Xam, #Khomani, /'Auni and //Ng!'e), the Free State (//Kx'au and //Ku//e), Lesotho (Seroa), Transkei (!Ga!ne) and southern Mpumalanga (//Xegwi from Lake Chrissie). Of these, /Xam was probably the first to become extinct although it is the best and most thoroughly recorded of all. By the 1980s there were only a few speakers of #Khomani and /'Auni left and they are unlikely to survive long into the next century (Traill 1996:64). The map summarises what linguists like Otto Köhler, Ernst Westphal and Tony Traill have been able to piece together from a wide variety of sources.

Even this rather sketchy information on the structure and distribution of the !Kwi group of languages in South Africa highlights their diversity and small geographical range. Although they are

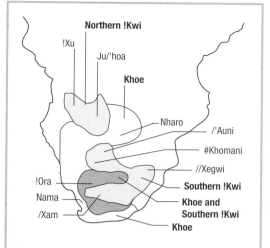

Figure 8.1: *Diagrammatic representation of the distribution of Khoisan language groups (bold) and languages. (After Traill 1995)*

grouped into one language family, partly for the sake of convenience, not all the languages in this family were understood by all San hunter-gatherers and not all were linguistically related. The differences between some of the !Kwi languages are so great that some neighbouring groups were not able to understand one another unless individuals were bilingual. This is in sharp contrast to the siNtu (Bantu) and Khoe languages, which are more clearly related to each other and are distributed over a much larger area as a result of the relatively recent migration of herders and agriculturists into South Africa within the last 2000 years.

The diversity of the !Kwi languages reflects both their long history in South Africa and the small scale of hunter-gatherer territorial ranges. San groups and their Later Stone Age ancestors retained their identity in relation to neighbouring groups, although individuals could move around quite freely and often did so. The variety of languages is no more complicated than it is in Europe, for example, where a community may be clearly recognisable as Italian or French, yet individuals from these communities are free to visit, join and even marry people who speak a language different from their own.

There are complex reasons why small-scale societies that consist of kin-related bands held

Figure 8.2: *#Khomani children at Kagga Kamma in the western Cape play with Lego. They are fully integrated into the twentieth century, despite the fact that they and their parents are marketed as 'Bushmen', as a tourist attraction. (Photo: J. Deacon)*

together by their language retain their identity over long periods of time. One of these is what Yi-Fu Tuan (1974) has called 'topophilia', the affective bond between a people and the landscape in which they live that extends into a desire to stress the individuality of the group. The power of the bond that developed between the San and their surroundings is obvious from remarks they made about the land they regarded as their own. It is also evident in their distress at losing rights to their land and being moved from one place to another in colonial times. The rich folklore surrounding features in the landscape underscores this. Such a bond is especially necessary for hunter-gatherers, who are dependent on natural resources and need to conserve them, but it is also present in many settled communities too. Judith Sealy's reconstruction of the diets of Later Stone Age people in the Western and southern Cape and Garth Sampson's (1988) analysis of hunter-gatherer pottery in the Seacow Valley have shown that some people probably spent their entire lives in relatively small territories. We can therefore speculate that topophilia was a significant force in their lives.

San ethnography and the Later Stone Age

Most of the ethnographic information we have about the way in which hunter-gatherer communities in southern Africa lived comes from a series of studies in Botswana and Namibia conducted between the 1950s and the 1980s by researchers from Europe, Japan, North America and South Africa. They introduced a different perspective from that of the early European travellers, naturalists and big-game hunters who had seen the San as a curiosity of nature, only marginally more civilised than baboons. These perceptions are well illustrated in several of the papers in the book *Miscast* edited by Pippa Skotnes and published in 1996. Instead of describing in an anecdotal way chance encounters with San during a trek across South Africa, the twentieth-century researchers lived with San groups for months and even years at a stretch. They learned the language of their subjects and made detailed notes, films, audio tapes and photographic records.

Such close contact between Western-style

researchers and San led to a new respect for the indigenous people of southern Africa, as is evident from books like Lorna Marshall's *The !Kung of Nyae Nyae*, Elizabeth Marshall Thomas's *The Harmless People*, Megan Biesele's *Women Like Meat* and Richard Katz's *Boiling Energy*, and from research results published by Richard Lee, Nancy Howell, Marjorie Shostak, John Yellen, Phillip Tobias, George Silberbauer, Mathias Guenther, Jiro Tanaka, Alan Barnard, H.P. Steyn and others. The results of the seminal *Man the Hunter* conference, edited by Richard Lee and Irven Devore, was followed by *Kalahari Hunter-Gatherers* a few years later. All these were a welcome contrast to the more romanticised accounts typified by Sir Laurens van der Post's *Lost World of the Kalahari* and movies like *The Gods Must be Crazy*. Films, particularly those by the Marshall family, allowed the world to know individual San by name and to see almost at first hand how a giraffe could be hunted apparently without a gun and how a hunter-gatherer family could live apparently without great effort on a diet of mongongo nuts.

But how accurate were these accounts? Did they give a true reflection of the lifestyle of the Dobe !Kung or Nharo? Or were the films artificially contrived to increase public interest? Changing circumstances of both the San and the researchers led in the late 1980s and 1990s to what has been dubbed the Great Kalahari Debate. Many articles and books, such as *Land Filled with Flies* by Ed Wilmsen and *The Bushman Myth* by Robert Gordon, fuelled the debate. The gist of the argument is that the people whose lifestyle supposedly typified that of Later Stone Age hunter-gatherers of the past 20 000 years or more had not lived in isolation. They had, it was argued, been greatly influenced for at least 1000 years, and probably longer, by regular and sustained contact with Iron Age agriculturists and, later, European farmers and traders. Cattle rearing and trading, it was reasoned, had been a vital part of the economy of the San. At issue, then, was whether inferences derived from studies of the lifestyle of the twentieth-century San could be used to interpret Later Stone Age and even older human behaviour.

According to the 'revisionists', the earlier or 'traditionalist' researchers deliberately focused on those aspects of San lifestyle that stressed isolation from the outside world and perpetuated old stereotypes. In so doing they created a one-sided account of the hunting and gathering aspect of San economy and downplayed the incidence of violence and poverty. As Alan Barnard notes, the current situation of the San as a poor underclass in a much larger social system must by definition be very different from what it was more than 2000 years ago, when theirs was the only economy being practised in southern Africa.

In contrast to the twentieth-century ethnographies of San in Namibia and Botswana, the most detailed descriptions we have in South Africa on the technology, economy and beliefs of the San are from a small group of /Xam San. Four /Xam men and one woman from the area in the vicinity of present-day Brandvlei, Kenhardt and Vanwyksvlei in the Northern Cape were interviewed in the 1870s. The /Xam regarded themselves as 'Bushmen' with a strong hunting and gathering tradition. At the time the interviews took place, though, they had already been acculturated to some extent by farmers of European descent who had moved onto the land the /Xam had formerly occupied and had given the /Xam casual employment from time to time.

Figure 8.3: *Prison photograph of //Kabbo, the oldest of the /Xam San informants interviewed by W.H.I. Bleek and Lucy Lloyd in Cape Town in the 1870s. (After Bleek & Lloyd 1911)*

Figure 8.4: *Dr Lucy Lloyd, who was the first woman to receive an honorary doctorate at a South African university, spent most of her life learning and writing about the /Xam and their language. (Photo courtesy of Dr K.M.F. Scott)*

The four men, //Kabbo (Oud Jantje Tooren), /Han#kass'o (Jantje), Dia!kwain (David Hoesaar) and #Kasin (Klaas Katkop), were arrested in 1869 for stock theft and culpable homicide and were sentenced to terms of imprisonment in the Break-water Prison in Cape Town. While they were there, a German linguist, Dr Wilhelm H.I. Bleek, heard of them and conducted interviews to ascertain whether any of the prisoners could speak a Bushman language. A young man named /A!kunta spent a short while with Bleek, but //Kabbo, /Han#kass'o and Dia!kwain were identified as the most fluent, and arrangements were made for them to live at the Bleek home in Mowbray, Cape Town, at the end of their prison terms. While Dia!kwain was there he was joined for a few months by his sister !Kweiten-ta-//ken, her husband #Kasin and their small children.

Bleek and his wife's sister, Lucy Lloyd (Figure 8.4), slowly learned the language and devised symbols for the many clicks in /Xam. Lucy Lloyd was unmarried and lived with the Bleek family. After Dr Bleek died in 1875, she carried on the

work of interviewing /Xam and Korana informants for another nine years. She was the first woman to be awarded an honorary doctorate by the University of Cape Town in 1911 in recognition of her work on San languages. Bleek and Lloyd filled over 11 000 quarto-sized pages in more than 130 notebooks with verbatim testimony in /Xam; these were later translated into English. Some of the records were published by Lucy Lloyd as *Specimens of Bushman Folklore* in 1911 and in a series of articles edited many years later by Bleek's daughter, Dorothea Bleek, for the journal *Bantu Studies* in the 1930s.

Using San ethnography

One of the most poignant aspects of the Bleek and Lloyd records, and of collections of folklore from Nharo informants published by Mathias Guenther and Ju/'hoan informants published by Megan Biesele, is the strength and resilience of San beliefs in the face of major changes in economy and lifestyle. Just as Christianity, Buddhism and Islam have survived almost 2000 years of technological advancement at a scale and pace unprecedented in human history, so San religion has retained its core despite modern modifications.

It cannot be assumed that 5000 or 10 000 years ago Later Stone Age people in South Africa had the same lifestyle, beliefs and social organisation as the Dobe !Kung or Nharo in Botswana in the 1960s and 1970s. We are also conscious of the problems in referring to 'the San' as a homogeneous group of people when we know that there were differences between groups and changes through time. Yet even though there is no invariable correlation between physical type, language and material culture, we can demonstrate that there was greater similarity in the style and range of rock art and stone tools made by the Later Stone Age hunter-gatherers in southern Africa south of the Zambezi than there was between them and people living to the north. Within the subcontinent there must have been an effective network of information exchange and a common belief system. Even though only a remnant population of southern African hunter-gatherers was still living in the region in the nineteenth century, there are enough clues to justify linking some of the details of their lifeway, known to us from written records, to their

Later Stone Age ancestors.

Ethnography can enrich the results of archaeological research. When ethnographic analogy is used, one can better understand the general principles, if not the details, of how hunter-gatherers thrived without farmers (and anthropologists) as neighbours, and then developed ways of both challenging and co-operating with them.

It is ethnographic principles that we use below with the evidence from archaeology to construct a generalised, and sometimes speculative, picture of how pre-agricultural societies operated in the subcontinent in the last 20 000 years. We present at the same time a range of views to show that there is no single 'truth' in either archaeological or historical interpretation. One needs to be aware, too, that the highs and lows of human endeavour – the passions aroused by love, hate, envy, greed, hunger and creativity – were as common in the Stone Age as they are today, but are not easy to identify by archaeological methods. In distinguishing between an explanation that is valid and another that is not, one has to check assumptions and test them in a variety of situations so as to filter out general trends from unusual events. This should keep us busy for some time to come.

To avoid unnecessary repetition, we refer to the twentieth-century San ethnography from the Kalahari in the present tense. This is to distinguish these generalisations from those derived from South African records of the nineteenth-century /Xam, earlier European travellers and Later Stone Age hunter-gatherer archaeology, all of which are referred to in the past tense.

Social life

Later Stone Age people and their descendants, who have come to be called the San, lived throughout South Africa. There are Later Stone Age sites and artefacts to be found in the coolest mountains of Lesotho, in the driest corners of the Karoo, and in the hottest and wettest subtropical environments of KwaZulu-Natal and the Northern Province. Yet, as in the Middle Stone Age, occupation was not continuous in all regions throughout the 20 000-year history of the Later Stone Age, particularly where surface water was unavailable during times of lower rainfall. This variability meant that some regions, such as the southern

Cape, were favoured and sustained a viable population throughout the Holocene, whereas more marginal environments, like the Waterberg and parts of the Karoo, were occupied only sporadically.

The San adjust to the availability of resources like water and plant foods by altering their band size both seasonally and according to environmental conditions. In the Western Cape and Northern Cape, travellers in the seventeenth and eighteenth centuries reported bands of between 12 and 40 people, but in the Eastern Cape in the nineteenth century some bands had as many as 120 and 200 people (Steyn 1990:71). In the Kalahari, most people live in nuclear family bands with between 12 and 25 people, consisting of a married couple with their children, a brother or sister, cousin or friend of the couple with their married partner and children, and several grandparents or elderly relatives. They are therefore essentially kin-related groups, which own rights to the resources within a defined territory. Although the individuals may not remain in the same band throughout their lifetime, the size of the band and the territory they occupy are fairly stable. Depending on the food resources in the environment concerned, bands that form part of the same extended family (brothers, sisters, cousins, in-laws) come together regularly or irregularly at certain seasons of the year or during times of plenty.

Each language group has a defined territory in the Kalahari, and within this territory each band has a series of water sources that it regards as its own. Anyone may use these resources, but it is expected that invitations will be extended or permission requested before they do so. The territory of each band is handed down in an informal way from father to son or other relative. In this way families will bond with a particular landscape and build up myths and legends about the features in it. Mathias Guenther (1986:172–3) records that if a Nharo band faces a crisis in a drought year, the band may move as a unit to a permanent water source and ask permission of its owners to spend the winter there. They may be joined by other bands. Over time loose ties develop amongst the people in this 'band alliance', which will lead to and be strengthened by visiting, intermarriage and meeting together for the performance of rituals such as initiation ceremonies and trance dances.

The G/wi in Botswana tend to live in larger

Figure 8.5: *A Nharo man and his dog return home after a successful hunt. (Photo: H.P. Steyn)*

groups in summer when there is standing water available, melons are in season and larger animals are hunted, but in winter, when surface water is scarce, band size is smaller. This contrasts with the Dobe !Kung, who live in smaller bands in the summer when mongongo nuts and fruits are in good supply, but they come together in larger groups in the winter.

Alan Barnard suggests that these patterns reflect a correlation between the availability of water and the degree to which band organisation in a territory is 'nucleated'. Where there is less water, people will stick together in their bands to protect and manage their water resources, whereas if there is a lot of water the bands are less nucleated and people move around more freely. This reveals a complex interplay of environmental and social factors that will vary even within one apparently homogeneous environmental zone such as the Kalahari.

The division of labour amongst the San is typical of almost all hunter-gatherer communities worldwide. Women are responsible for the daily task of gathering plant foods and small animals like tortoises and insects, whereas men are responsible for hunting. Apart from this division, San society is egalitarian and everyone has an equal say in the decisions made by the band. There are no formal 'chiefs' although elderly men and women, especially if they are healers or rain-makers, do enjoy some stature in the community. The role of these medicine people, or shamans, is discussed in more detail in the next chapter.

San gender relations – the ways men and women interact with each other at both a practical and symbolic level – are more deeply embedded in their social life than the simple division of labour suggests. Structuralism, which was developed comprehensively in anthropological theory by Claude Lévi-Strauss, accepts the notion that all human beings structure their lives, beliefs and thoughts in terms of binary oppositions such as good–evil, beautiful–ugly or day–night. These oppositions are often most clearly discernible in their ideology and folklore. San folklore is no exception. Megan Biesele (1993) summarises this notion neatly in the title of her book *Women Like Meat*, which has a clever double meaning. Not only do Ju/'hoan women enjoy eating meat, but men think of women symbolically as meat to be pursued as prey.

Biesele's (1993) analysis of Ju/'hoan folklore reveals that 'women are connected in the stories with both the central spring of creation and with the origin of water'. Men, on the other hand, 'are associated with a central fire of creation and with the origin of fire'. Both fire and water are needed to keep people alive, and both men and women are necessary for the continuation of society. These metaphors are carried through in a variety of further oppositions. Women are 'cool' and men are 'hot', so at certain times a woman should not touch a man's 'hot' bow and arrows or she will 'cool' them and make them less effective. This provides a conceptual justification of the division of labour whereby women are gatherers of plant foods while men are the hunters of meat.

An important feature of social relationships in the Kalahari is the practice of sharing and of formalised gift exchange known as *hxaro* by the Ju/'hoansi (or !Kung) and *//ai* by the Nharo. Although it was not explicitly mentioned, remarks made by Bleek and Lloyd's /Xam San informants indicate that this practice was important in /Xam social relations too. Biesele (1993:42) has drawn attention to the fact that all hunting and gathering societies are alike in this respect because sharing and the exchange of information, food and goods along agreed-upon lines are essential for their continuation. For this reason they are constantly reinforced not only through actions but also through folklore and narrative, which provide 'a kind of scaffolding upon which explicit information about resources can be vividly and memorably hung'. Stories and storytelling therefore play a vital role in structuring hunter-gatherer subsistence activities and survival by detailing what is or is not acceptable and profitable behaviour.

First described by Lorna Marshall, the details of the !Kung *hxaro* networking system have been carefully investigated by, amongst others, Elizabeth Cashdan and Polly Wiessner, who call it a form of insurance. An average young man or woman will have between ten and sixteen *hxaro* partners, comprising friends as well as close and distant relatives living within a radius of 100 km or more. By giving a gift to a *hxaro* partner, the giver can expect to receive one in exchange or to ask for something in exchange if she or he is in need – for example, rights to gather plant foods or collect water. The gifts do not necessarily have to

Figure 8.6: *San women with weighted digging sticks and collecting bags depicted in a rock painting in KwaZulu-Natal. (After Vinnicombe 1976:276)*

be of the same value, and the period within which the exchange takes place can be either long or short but is never immediate because this would imply that the relationship is ended. As Alan Barnard (1992:141) says, 'the delay keeps it alive'. Exchange between !Kung and other language groups is also well developed, and finds of seashells at Later Stone Age sites far inland suggest that trade in such items, and possibly gift exchange as well, have a long history.

Archaeological evidence for gift exchange?

Lyn Wadley (1989) has used San ethnography on gift exchanges and seasonal movements to help explain the differences observed between the broadly contemporary Later Stone Age artefact sequences in Jubilee Shelter and Cave James in the Magaliesberg in North-West Province. Kinship, as the dominant social relationship, is reflected in the regular aggregation (living together) and dispersal (living apart) of extended family groups. Aggregation is a public phase of band life in which kin-related households come together to socialise, make and exchange gifts, and arrange marriages, initiation, curing dances and other rituals. Dispersal, on the other hand, is a private phase in which the extended family bands live away from each other and focus largely on subsistence tasks.

Certain activities are kept to a minimum, among them ritual, travelling, manufacturing and subsistence activities, which require more people than usually live in a band. Social rules are also relaxed so that men may help women with food and wood gathering even though these jobs are considered to be the preserve of women.

The archaeological question is whether aggregation and dispersal can be identified in the artefacts and arrangement of camp sites. Jubilee Shelter has evidence for regular occupation and radiocarbon dates for almost every millennium over the past 8000 years. Evidence for public behaviour and an aggregation site can be found in a wide range of stone tools made in different raw materials, ostrich eggshell beads and other ornaments, and tools that could be used for gift exchange. On the other hand, Cave James and other small shelters in the vicinity have not been as regularly occupied, have fewer formal stone tools, and do not include items like beads used for gift exchange amongst twentieth-century San. Wadley (1987) has interpreted them as private or dispersal sites.

Differences in the food remains at the two sites have also been linked to seasonal aggregation and dispersal. There is a wide range of large and small mammal bones and seeds of only winter fruits in Jubilee, contrasting with finds at Cave James of bird, rodent and small bovid bones with seeds of summer fruits.

If these correlations are valid, can we assume that changes through time in stone artefact frequencies from, say, the Oakhurst to the Wilton can be interpreted by using the same ethnographic analogy? Earlier researchers regarded the wide range of raw materials and formal stone tools, ornaments, burials and portable art in the Wilton as a cultural 'florescence' in contrast to the Oakhurst. Wadley, however, notes the absence of Wilton assemblages in the dry interior and speculates that the Wilton reflects a time of hardship. The struggle for survival and competition for resources forced people to migrate from the dry interior to better-watered areas that were already occupied by other groups. The need to establish new networks and alliances, she suggests, would have led in turn to intensification of gift exchange and the use of specialised artefacts to make the best of scarce resources.

Later Stone Age graves

Only during the last 10 000 years is there consistent evidence for deliberate burial of the dead by Stone Age people in South Africa. Even then, in the period between 10 000 and 2000 years ago, the practice was largely confined to open-site shell middens along the coast and to rock shelters along the Western Cape and Eastern Cape coast and in the Cape Fold mountains. Some of these rock shelters were used repeatedly as burial places, especially in the millennia between 8000 and 4000 BP. Several of those excavated contained the remains of between 10 and 50 individuals.

Strangely, there are remarkably few reports of formal hunter-gatherer burials in caves in the interior of South Africa. Burials in the open in the interior, either in antbear holes, or in graves with no surface marking or those covered by stone cairns, tend to date within the last 1000 years. A significant number of these have been linked to Khoekhoe herders along the Orange River. Part of the reason for the low incidence of graves in the interior may be due to the acid soils, which do not preserve bone beyond one or two thousand years, or it may simply reflect the fact that most people were not formally buried.

The ethnographic burial customs summarised by Schapera (1930) and elaborated by the research of Alan Morris (1992) along the Orange River suggest that although there was some variation, hunter-gatherer graves tended to be relatively shallow. Twentieth-century !Kung customs summarised by Polly Wiessner, and a wider range of San customs summarised by Lyn Wadley (1996a), indicate that funerals are not elaborate rituals and serve only to say farewell to the departed spirit. This allows for wide variety both in the kind of grave that is dug and in the range of goods placed in the grave with the body. Much more energy may be spent on trance healing just prior to death than on the burial. Where nineteenth-century beliefs about death and the afterlife have been recorded, as from the /Xam informants, it appears that the spirits of the dead were believed to have remained in the landscape and could be called upon for assistance with rain-making and controlling the game.

According to archaeological evidence, the body was usually placed on its side with the arms and legs bent so that the knees and hands were under the chin. Sometimes the body was seated vertically in the grave shaft. In contrast to the simple burial practices that have been recorded ethnographically amongst the Khoisan (Schapera 1930), Later Stone Age burials are often elaborately decorated. Ground ochre was sometimes placed in or over the

Figure 8.7: *Burial shaft seen in section at Melkhoutboom. Note the large stones placed on top of the body. The top of the shaft was covered with a layer of powdered red ochre.*

Figure 8.8: *Shell pendants and beads from various sites in the Western Cape are typical of those often found with burials.*

grave shaft, the body was decorated with ostrich eggshell beads and shell beads and pendants, and in some instances artefacts, shells or animal bones were placed in the grave as well. Eight burials from Oakhurst Cave near Wilderness were especially elaborate: some contained not only ornaments, but whole ostrich eggshell flasks, quartz crystals, tortoiseshell containers, bone and ivory arrow points, bored stones and shale palettes (Wadley 1996a). In certain instances, for example at rock shelters on the Robberg peninsula, the top of the grave shaft was covered with large stones, and on rare occasions a grave stone was painted or ochre-stained.

Simon Hall and Johan Binneman (1987), in a review of some Eastern Cape rock-shelter burials, noticed that the bodies of infants and children dating within the last 5000 years were more elaborately decorated than those of adults. Although there is no direct ethnographic evidence from southern Africa, they suggest that this anomaly may relate to a well-developed gift exchange system in which the children concerned had been too young to be formally involved in the gift exchange network. The gifts with which they were buried therefore symbolised for their families the potential that death had made them unable to achieve. Adult possessions, in contrast, would have been passed on to gift exchange partners and to the younger generation.

Burial practices have clearly changed over time and show regional variation as well. In a review of the evidence from over 500 Later Stone Age burials throughout South Africa, Ray Inskeep (1986) pointed out that almost half came from the southern Cape. Where they could be dated, 10 per cent of those buried with ornaments such as beads and pendants were associated with the Albany industry dating to between 12 000 and 8000 years ago. The highest number, 64 per cent, were associated with the Wilton between about 8000 and 4000 years ago, and 28 per cent were associated with the Post-Wilton, mainly between about 4000 and 2000 years ago. In contrast, 40 per cent of the Albany, 28 per cent of the Wilton and 14 per cent of the Post-Wilton graves were associated with ochre.

Hall and Binneman were intrigued by the dating of the more elaborate burials to the time period of population growth at the end of the Wilton in the Eastern Cape, where painted stones and other unusual objects have also been found. Their interpretation is that elaborate burial is an indicator of intensified ritual behaviour, which was in turn the result of social stress. Too many people living in a region with limited carrying capacity may have given rise to competition for territorial control over resources such as food and water, and maybe even rock shelters.

Women's work

People eat plants that store food reserves. These include underground roots, rhizomes, bulbs, corms and tubers, which are all known as geophytes; above-ground storage organs like seeds, fruits, berries, nuts, stems and leaves; and runners that grow along the ground (like melons and cucumbers), which are known as cucurbits. Generally speaking, the geophytes are more common in plant communities with fewer trees, like the fynbos and grassland. Above-ground foods are most common in savanna habitats, and the cucurbits are most common in arid and desert regions.

As the gatherers of plant and other foods, women provide the bulk of the staple diet of most hunter-gatherers. It is indeed ironic that more credit and prestige is given to the less successful 'man the hunter' than to 'woman the gatherer'. The pioneering survey by the botanist Story (1964) of the vegetable foods used by San groups primarily in Botswana in the 1950s showed clearly that plants provide a greater proportion of the diet than does meat. But because plant foods provide mainly car-bohydrates and are more seasonal than game, hunting is still necessary to provide protein and fat and to fill in during periods when plant staples are scarce.

There is more to understanding plant food gathering than calories and seasonal abundance. George Silberbauer's research among the G/wi highlights the way their belief system justifies the difference in importance allocated to plant foods and meat. They believe that because plants have no power of locomotion, they do not feel pain or pleasure and have neither will nor intelligence. By contrast, San have what Mathias Guenther calls 'a common sense of purpose' with animals, that leads to 'a deeply rooted participation mystique ... which ... renders personal and moral the man–animal relationship'. For this reason, 'except-ing the ripening of a prolific growth of tsamma melons, plants have none of the emotive signifi-cance of game animals but are discussed and dealt with as a routine necessity of life ... [T]he fact that plant foods are not exchanged as gifts and thus have less social significance than meat, perhaps explains why food plants are regarded with gener-al emotional neutrality.'

Nevertheless, as plants are regarded as the prop-erty of the deity N!adima, they may not be destroyed wantonly any more than animals can be. The G/wi are conscious of the need to conserve plant foods and avoid stripping an area, preferring to move camp to another patch of plant food rather than taking everything that is available.

Certain medicinal plants, however, are treated with considerable respect. //Kabbo told Lucy Lloyd about the plant he called *so-/oa* or *//kar-rukan//karrukan*, which was used for healing wounds and as a charm. When men wanted to hunt they would make cuts on their faces and rub burnt *so-/oa* into the cuts to blacken them; or when men had been fighting, one might revive the other with *so-/oa*. 'He rubs himself under the arms, where he has rubbed the medicine before going to fight, and then rubs the sick man's face with per-spiration and the scent of the plant together. Afterwards he cuts the man's chest and back and rubs the *so-/oa* into the cuts; and then afterwards gives the patient the piece of *so-/oa* that he had doctored him with, having more in his own pos-session' (Bleek 1936:149).

Figure 8.9: *Part of a digging stick and plant remains at Strathalan Cave A dating to about 2500 years ago. (Photo: H. Opperman)*

Careful rules were followed in collecting *so-/oa* to ensure that the supply was not used up. 'Having broken the long pieces of root or stem, which were in the ground, into bits about a foot long, they put them into an old bag; they leave the green part which was above behind, having planted some of it (the top with a bit of stem to it) back in the hole that they took the roots out of, so that it may grow again' (Bleek 1936:150).

Not surprisingly, women gatherers are very knowledgeable about the plants in their environ-ment and exploit them not only for food but for medicinal purposes as well. Yet of the 105 plant species used regularly by the Dobe !Kung, Richard Lee notes that only 14 are staples although they provide almost 75 per cent of the calories in the plant food diet. Silberbauer's study of the G/wi, who live in a drier area and do not rely on mon-gongo nuts as much as the Dobe !Kung, reported that only 13 plant food species are used as staples. A similar pattern prevailed in the past, even though the details differed, because the range of plant food remains in archaeological sites is similarly small.

The archaeological samples from Holocene sites in Mpumalanga, Northern Province, Gauteng and KwaZulu-Natal have the remains of seeds, nuts and husks of fruits like the marula; sometimes, as at Kruger Cave in the Magaliesberg (Mason 1988b), a few *Hypoxis* corms may also occur. In the Western and Eastern Cape the remains of geophytes like *Watsonia* sp., *Gladiolus* sp., *Hypoxis*

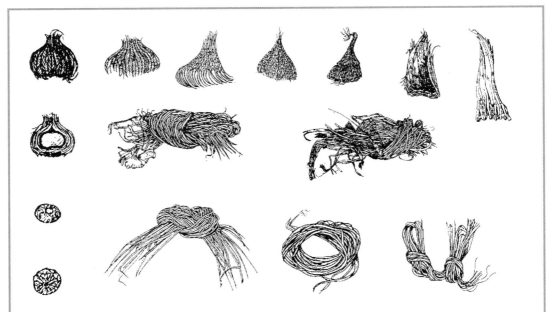

Figure 8.10: *Plant food remains from Melkhoutboom. The drawings illustrate the range of corms represented and the way in which the leaves were tied together by the person who collected them.*

sp. and *Cyperus usitatus* predominate. Western Cape sites like De Hangen and Steenbokfontein, and Eastern Cape sites like Melkhoutboom and Scott's Cave, have a superabundance of corm remains. Strathalan Caves A and B, excavated by Manie Opperman in the foothills of the Drakensberg in the Eastern Cape, have preserved

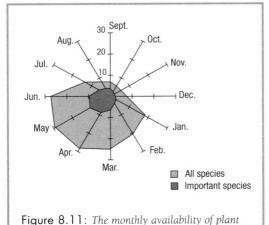

Figure 8.11: *The monthly availability of plant foods used by the /Gwi in Botswana. (From data collected by George Silberbauer)*

plant remains to a remarkable degree (Figure 8.9). They have the same range of plant foods preserved in association with Later Stone Age debris of the last 9000–300 years as that with Middle Stone Age artefacts dating to between 29 000 and 23 000 years ago.

As H.J. Deacon has detailed in the book *Where Hunters Gathered*, most plant foods are only available or edible in certain seasons of the year. Thus their presence in archaeological deposits gives some indication of the time of year that the site was occupied. In a modern example, Figure 8.11 illustrates the changing rhythm of plant food collecting by the G/wi in a typical year. A similar rhythm can be expected in the Western Cape and Eastern Cape, where geophyte abundance was predictable mainly in spring and summer. The geophytes are known as *uintjies* (little onions) locally and are mentioned in a number of the journals of early European travellers as being eaten by Khoisan people during the time of year known as *uintjiestyd*, or 'onion time'. Analysis of the range of geophytes represented at Melkhoutboom (Figure 8.10), for example, shows that the site was occupied at least between September and December from *c.* 7000 to 3000 years ago, and in the upper-most levels in summer and autumn.

At Boomplaas Cave in the Cango Valley, remains of underground plant foods were not abundant. A survey in the 1970s of the vegetation showed that edible plants are uncommon in the vicinity: Later Stone Age people probably did not stay here for extended periods. At about 2000 years ago, how-ever, they used the cave to store the seeds of *Pappea capensis.* The fruits are edible and the seeds are rich in an oil that was used by indigenous people for cosmetic purposes. Small pits were dug in the floor of the cave both at Boomplaas and at Melkhoutboom. They were lined with alternating layers of grass and the papery bulbar leaves of the poisonous onion-like bulb *Boophane disticha,* which presumably acted like an insecticide to pro-tect the fruits from ants and other insects.

Pits such as these represent the only archaeolog-ical evidence for artificial storage of vegetable prod-ucts. Because geophytes are easily available if one knows where the patches are to be found, there seems to have been no motivation for Later Stone Age people to lay in stocks for lean times. Instead,

they ensured that there would be a good crop by managing geophyte growth with fire, as we have discussed in Chapter 6. This proved to be at least as efficient as planting and harvesting in formal fields, as agriculturists did for grain crops, and it enabled hunter-gatherers to reap the same kind of benefits as their farming neighbours enjoyed.

Most archaeological sites preserve no plant food remains because the soil conditions are too moist and they rot away. Carbonised deposits, as dis-cussed in Chapter 6, may be all that remains. The absence of plant food residues does not therefore indicate that plants were not eaten. Some researchers have argued that an increase in plant food remains in deposits dating within the last 4000–5000 years reflects a change in collecting practices. However, as Michael Wells was able to show at Scott's Cave, plants are less well preserved in the lower layers than they are in the more recent ones. Despite the lack of preservation at archaeo-logical sites, the ethnographic evidence indicates unequivocally that the gathering of plant food was the most important economic activity throughout the Later Stone Age.

Figure 8.12: *The upper levels of Boomplaas Cave dating to about 2000 years ago, showing the distribution of storage pits and stone-lined hearths.*

Gathering of ground game and insects

According to the archaeological evidence, as Later Stone Age populations increased within the last 4000 years, more use was made of small animals like birds and their eggs, dassies, rats, mice, hares, frogs, tortoises, lizards and similar-sized creatures in the diet. If ethnographic observations are anything to go by, many of these animals would have been collected not only by women on gathering trips, but also by men and children.

A meticulous study by Richard Klein and Kathy Cruz-Uribe has given some insight into the effect that the collection of small animals had on resources during the Later Stone Age. They measured the size of individual tortoises from Byneskranskop Cave and the nearby Die Kelders Cave in the south-western Cape. Their results showed that over the past 12 000 years there was a gradual reduction in the average size of *Chersina angulata* tortoises collected and eaten by Later Stone Age inhabitants of the sites. They concluded that the most likely reason for this reduction in size was that an increase in human population density had caused people to 'farm down' the tortoises in the area by selecting the largest (and oldest) tortoises until there were only smaller ones left.

Ostrich eggs were eaten and the shells provided useful flasks for storing water. Several water flasks were often buried together, to be retrieved when they were needed. Each one was sealed with a grass or clay plug. Flasks like these are dug up accidentally from time to time by farmers or in the course of road building or laying of pipes. A number have been found filled with ochre and specularite and there are ethnographic and archaeological examples of decorated ones. Some of the oldest fragments of decorated ostrich eggshell in Later Stone Age contexts come from Melkhoutboom and Boomplaas in levels dated to between 14 000 and 15 000 years old, including a fragment of a flask aperture. These are identical to designs used in the Kalahari in the twentieth century.

Insects also provide a significant source of food for hunter-gatherers although the archaeological remains are mainly lumps of termite mound brought into sites like Melkhoutboom and De Hangen. Locusts were a favourite food of the /Xam San in the Northern Cape and Karoo. They occur in large swarms after rain and are easily collected and then roasted. The Dutch traveller Wikar (Mossop 1935) saw San waiting for locusts to settle on a bush at night and then setting fire to it, collecting the roasted locusts the next morning.

A glimpse into the complex folklore of food is provided in the following extract from testimony given by /Han#kass'o in an interview with Lucy Lloyd in 1878 (Bleek 1933:301). 'Bushmen do not kill frogs, because the rain does not fall if we kill frogs. A drought comes if we have killed frogs ... Then it is that the Bushmen grow lean ... and the springbok are not there, and the locusts are not there. Then the locusts vanish, the Springbok also vanish. The Bushmen eat gambro (a sort of melon) ... The gambro also dries. Then gambro poisons us, we are intoxicated by it. Gambro harms some people, therefore we take out the skin of the porcupine's tail, for we want to have it out in order to smell it, then the gambro will not injure us. Drought is that which makes the country grow white, the bushes dry up in the drought. When the rain falls like this (a Cape winter), food will be plentiful, then people say, the rain falls bringing plenty, and people are not careful of the locusts and the springbok.'

Termites in the flying stage were a delicacy. Ants' eggs, often called 'Bushman rice', were collected too and were sieved on reed mats to remove the grit. Kannemeyer (1890) describes how this was done. 'To obtain them the women, using the weighted sticks as pounders, tapped the ground; their acute and practised sense of hearing enabled them, with unerring accuracy, to detect the "nests." The larvae of the anthills were also eaten. Let any of you break up an anthill and try to collect the "eggs" and you will find what an endless task it is. But Bushman ingenuity overcame the difficulty, they availed themselves of the overmastering instinct of the mature insects, which makes the care of their young their first object. They made them collect the larvae. The outer parts of the mound were broken away and stacked at a short distance around a central core, left intact for the purpose. Into this the workers hurried the "eggs" and when the contents of the whole anthill were closely packed into this circumscribed space, the core was removed, broken up and placed on the "*thkatsge*," or small reed mat, made for the purpose; this was then shaken with a peculiar twisting, jerking motion, which thoroughly winnowed and discarded the mature insects and earthy matter from the glistening white mass, known to the Dutch as ant, or Bushman rice.'

Ants' eggs were clearly a treat, a favoured food, as !Kweiten-ta-//ken related in *A Lion's Story* (Bleek & Lloyd 1911:259–61): 'A child cried for "Bushman rice" as her parents slept and her crying attracted a lion. When she realised that the lion was about to kill her parents, she set fire to some of the dry grass they were sleeping on and set the lion's hair on fire with it. The lion was killed. The mother praised her daughter for her bravery, for if she had not set the lion on fire, they would all have died: "Therefore it is, that we will break for thee an ostrich eggshell of 'Bushman rice'; for, thou hast made us to live." '

In another account, Dia!kwain drew attention to the need to dig up 'Bushman rice' in the right frame of mind. He said that when his mother was going to collect it, she would plunge a stone into the ashes of the fire 'while she wished that the evil things, about which she had been dreaming', should remain in the fire instead of going out with her. The 'Bushman rice' would not be favourable to her if she did not act in this way (Bleek & Lloyd 1911:365).

Caterpillars are seasonal but, when dried, offer protein throughout the year. The most widely used is the so-called mopane 'worm', which is still smoke-dried and sold widely today in the Northern Province and Mpumalanga as well as in Botswana and Zimbabwe. As there are no ethnographic records of Khoisan eating them, and as caterpillars leave no residue, we do not know whether they were prepared in the same way by Stone Age people.

Honey and salt were much sought after, the former having special medicinal and ritual uses in addition to being used as a sweetener. /Han#kass'o spoke of the joy when honey was brought home to the camp. The women would make a drum and clap and sing for the men so that they might dance all night until sunrise (Bleek & Lloyd 1911:355).

Honey was also used for exchange, as one of the early encounters between San hunter-gatherers and the Dutch illustrates. In April 1655 Van Riebeeck, who had arrived at the Cape in 1652 to set up a refreshment station for the Dutch East India Company, first noted that his men had first met Soaqua in the vicinity of present-day Malmesbury. In December 1660, he sent a party under the leadership of Jan Danckaert to search for the fabled land of Monomotapa. About 80 km north-east of Cape Town they had great difficulty in finding a way through the mountains, probably somewhere between Paarl and Tulbagh. With limited rations, two men in the party felt too unfit to proceed and returned to the Fort. The rest of them, accompanied by two Khoekhoe men called Doman and Bisente, supplemented their rations with fish from the rivers and by shooting three large eland. Danckaert reports that they met 'a poverty-stricken band of tiny people, who had helped them to cross the first range and had been very friendly to them, giving them some honey and dried fish. These small people, who have already been encountered somewhat nearer here by previous exploring parties, live in a state of poverty in shabby, low huts made of branches. Our explorers had found some of these standing empty here and there and it seemed to them that these little fellows use them during the night. They are well provided with bows and arrows, and they are adept at using these for shooting all kinds of game for food. Honey also forms part of their diet. They dress like the Hottentots, but they use very poor skins of wild animals. They are not so greasy as the Hottentots, for greasiness is a sign of prestige and of wealth in cattle, etc.' (Thom 1958: 299–300).

And again in April 1661 Van Riebeeck noted (Thom 1958:373): 'The Soaquas made promises to our men that they would bring down ivory, honey and wax.'

Women's artefacts

Dr D.R. Kannemeyer (1890), who practised as a medical doctor in Burghersdorp in the north-eastern Cape, spoke to 'Coranna-Bushmen' in the course of his work. He learned what some of the stone artefacts were used for, such as the *'ka'ka 'kouwie,* or stick stones, the round cobbles with a hole through the middle which we refer to as bored stones (Figure 8.13). As a child he remembered having collected some two hundred of them. They are used today as door stoppers in almost every farmhouse in the country. 'These perforated stones were used by the women to weight the

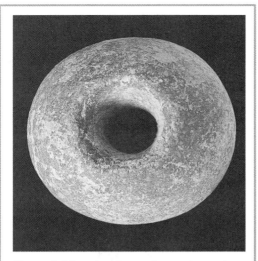

Figure 8.13: *A bored stone showing the marks caused by grinding to form the hole.*

Figure 8.14: *Photograph taken in Salt River, Cape Town, in 1884 at E.J. Dunn's home. He had collected the digging stick and its bored stone weight in Griqualand West a decade earlier. The photograph was posed for Lucy Lloyd by /Xaken-an, a /Xam woman from the vicinity of Kenhardt. The digging stick is now in the Pitt-Rivers Museum, Oxford. (Bleek & Lloyd 1911)*

"*cibi*" or sharp-pointed fire-hardened stakes employed in digging bulbs ... or termite larvae ... The pitfalls used for entrapping game were also dug by means of these weighted sticks.'

Bored stones intrigue the public more than any other Stone Age artefacts, with the exception of rock art. Many people refuse to believe that they were hand-made. Others question their use as digging-stick weights. And some cannot credit the Khoisan with their manufacture. These views are not new ones. E.J. Dunn (1931:77) remarked more than a century ago: 'In the early [eighteen] 'seventies an idea prevailed that these stones had been made by a race that preceded the Bushmen, and not by the Bushmen themselves, and that the latter merely made use of a tool they found ready to hand. This theory was disproved in Bushmanland in 1872, where I ascertained from the Bushman people themselves that they had made the perforated stones up to quite recent times' (Figure 8.14).

A 'Bushman' woman using a bored stone on her digging stick at Struis Pits on the Sak River near Brandvlei in the Northern Cape in 1872 explained to Dunn (1931:77–80) how the bored stones were made. 'She told me that first of all the stone was picked roughly into shape by means of hard pointed stones. Evidently it was recognised that the drilling of the hole was a very critical operation, and that there was a risk of wasting time over shaping the outside of the stone before this drilling was successfully accomplished ... The implement used for drilling was a long, hard, siliceous stone of lydianite, quartzite or chert ... The drills were held in the hand, and sharp strokes were required to make any progress with a rock like diabase. The hole was picked in from opposite sides of the surface until the two holes met in the centre ... As the outline of a hole fashioned in this way was very irregular, the implements that had been used as picks were now used as reamers, and were twisted in a circular manner in the hole so as to make it more regular in form. Twisting a hard but brittle stone in a hole of irregular form resulted frequently in the points of the reamers being broken off ... The final process in making the hole was to rasp it first with coarse, and then with fine sandstone rasps and files, until in some cases it was quite circular and polished and had a straight wall right through ... The outside surface of the stone was next reduced to more or less symmetrical form. First of all it was picked over the outside surface, thus getting rid of all surplus material; and then, in the better examples, sandstone rubbers were used to produce an even and smooth surface.'

Isaac Schapera (1930:141), in his summary of ethnographic information on the Khoisan, notes that digging sticks and their weights were used by both men and women, 'but whereas with the former it is incidental to their hunting, the latter are collectors only'. In 1812 William Burchell illustrated a weighted digging stick carried by a man who visited his camp in the Northern Cape.

The link between women and digging sticks and bored stones was more than simply functional, though. Bleek and Lloyd recorded that a /Xam woman from the Northern Cape would beat upon the ground with a bored stone if she wanted to communicate with a dead sorcerer (shaman) to ask for help when her husband had not been successful in his hunting. I heard a similar account from a farmer living in the same area of the Northern Cape in 1986. He said his grandfather had told him about a /Xam woman who lived on the farm and who used to place a sheepskin on the ground and beat it with a bored stone when she wanted rain to fall.

Apart from the artefacts they use for collecting plant foods, women also make ornaments like beads and pendants for themselves and their families and to give as exchange gifts. They are some-times found associated with burials. Ostrich eggshell is the most popular material, followed by shell, bone, reed and wood (Figure 8.15). To make beads, women break the ostrich eggshell first into small fragments, using either their teeth or a small hammerstone. A hole is drilled in each piece with a stone or metal borer. Some women drill only from the inside, others drill from both sides. The roughly shaped pieces are then threaded tightly onto a length of sinew and are ground into shape in a grooved stone or rolled across a grindstone so that they are all roughly the same size. They may then be rubbed with red ochre or left plain and threaded on sinew to make necklaces, bangles or anklets, or they may be sewn onto garments.

Shell pendants are found in a variety of shapes and designs, sometimes with notches around the perimeter and sometimes with a plain rim. Bone beads may be plain or may have a continuous groove around the outside (Figure 8.15).

Can gender roles be recognised archaeologically?

Archaeologists have become aware of the need to explore whether the relationships between men and women, and their respective roles in Stone Age society, have always been similar to the gender relations recorded amongst the present-day San. Even though San society is egalitarian, the balance

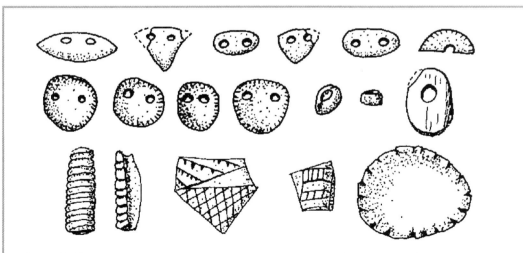

Figure 8.15: *Ostrich eggshell 'buttons' and pendants, shell pendants, bone beads, shell beads and decorated ostrich eggshell.*

of power may have been different in the past.

To test for such changes, archaeologists have assumed that they can identify the activities of men and women through their artefacts and in the food remains at occupation sites. If certain ethnographically observed correlations are valid, men and their activities should be recognisable by arrow parts (backed bladelets, segments, polished bone points) and bones of hunted and trapped animals. Women and their gathering activities should be evident from hearths, ostrich eggshell beads and other ornaments, digging sticks and bored stones, and the remains of plant foods and small animals. However, as most of these remains are seldom found in rock shelter sites, it has been assumed that the manufacture and maintenance of digging sticks can be identified by the presence of stone adzes.

Aron Mazel, working in the Thukela Valley of KwaZulu-Natal, has documented an increase in the incidence of the remains of small mammals, fish, fruits and corms after 4000 years ago in rock shelters there, an increase that coincides with a change in the formal stone tools. Using historical materialism as a theoretical base, Mazel explains the accompanying increase in the number of Later Stone Age sites over the period between 7000 and 2000 years ago, in terms of a population expansion. This expansion in turn affected alliance networks and the size and distribution of band and group territories. It also led to intensification in the search for food. Mazel argues that these adjustments – reflected in the larger number of adzes amongst the stone artefacts and in the plants and animals collected and hunted – were caused by a shift in gender relations, as a result of which women achieved the controlling power in decision-making for a period of several thousand years.

What also requires explanation is the changes in the relative abundance of artefacts, which could have been used in gift exchange. Mazel suggests (1989a:37) that Later Stone Age people who moved into the Thukela basin about 7000 years ago 'experienced uncertainty in the maintenance of social relations that are critical for social production and reproduction'. They therefore expended much time and energy in servicing these social relations. He suggests they strengthened the entire social network by intensifying the exchange of goods between groups.

In developing this explanatory model, Mazel quotes Sanday in her book on *Female Power and Male Dominance* (1981:181) where she states: 'It is easy to imagine that dependence on the male would evolve when expansionism, migration or social stress puts men in the position of fighting literally and figuratively to maintain an old or forge a new sociocultural identity in the face of pressures threatening to destroy this identity.' Mazel accepts this possibility and argues that when Later Stone Age groups first migrated into the new territory, men dominated the power relations. As social tensions relaxed and the people settled into their new environment, the status of women improved. The women then began to control production through increasing the amount of food generated by gathering rather than by hunting. Women became more self-sufficient and consequently less malleable as the importance of their contribution grew and as they took control over their working conditions and the distribution of the goods they produced. While making their own decisions more and more about reproduction and population growth, they raised their status accordingly.

With the relaxation of gender tensions, fewer gift exchange items were made between 5000 and 3000 years ago. However, after about 3000 years ago, Mazel considers that the archaeological remains suggest that 'population densities may have reached a point where they stimulated social contact to a degree which precipitated increased social stress and instability' (Mazel 1989a). This was reflected again in territorial expansion of the social groups and alliances, increased ritual activity, and greater expenditure on social relations through exchange.

Lyn Wadley has used another argument to identify patterns that result from the different behaviour of men and women. Instead of examining change through time, she has analysed the placement of artefacts around hearths. The decision to do so was stimulated by Lorna Marshall's observation that around the !Kung family hearth men sit to the right facing the entrance to the hut and women sit on the left. At Jubilee Shelter she found that beads and the debris from bead-making were concentrated to the left of the hearth as one faced the back wall of the shelter, whereas debris from the making of polished bone artefacts like bone points and arrowheads was located to the right.

A similar study of Holocene hearths at Rose Cottage Cave shows comparable patterning. However, artefact distributions are different in the terminal Pleistocene Robberg levels because the artefacts used to indicate activities of men or women are absent or rare in the Robberg. Rather, stone knapping, which generates a lot of small flakes and chips, was consistently carried out some distance from the hearth and in about the same place within the cave over a period of several thousand years. Activities that used grindstones, ochre and other pigments, and implements like backed tools and bladelets are not found with the flaking debris. Thus although there was some consistent patterning in the use of the space within Rose Cottage Cave, it cannot be interpreted in terms of either gender-related activities or aggregation and dispersal, using modern ethnographic parallels.

While Larry Barham (1992) and others consider the interpretations offered by Mazel and Wadley tenuous, they have nevertheless raised some interesting and challenging questions. Did gift exchange take place during the terminal Pleistocene? Was the work that men and women did during the Robberg different from that done during the Holocene? Did the people who made Robberg artefacts have a social system that involved aggregation and dispersal, or was the population too small and too dispersed to make this necessary? How do the changes in the Thukela basin differ from those in adjacent regions? These are questions that need to be answered through innovative research.

Environment and activity patterns

The view that people change their technology as an adaptive response to environmental factors has been one of the most popular explanations for the introduction of new artefacts or changes in the design and relative frequency of existing ones.

In his influential book *The Prehistory of Southern Africa*, published in 1959, Desmond Clark suggested that people adapted Later Stone Age technology for use in different environments and thereby created regional specialisations. However, the results from excavations since then have only partially supported this claim. Later Stone Age people in the dry Karoo made pretty much the same range of artefacts as did people on the

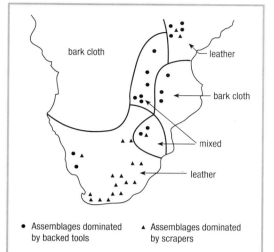

● Assemblages dominated by backed tools   ▲ Assemblages dominated by scrapers

Figure 8.16: *Diagrammatic summary of the distribution of hunter-gatherers making leather and bark clothing, and stone tool assemblages dominated by backed tools or scrapers. Leather clothing is clearly correlated with scrapers.*

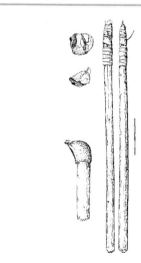

Figure 8.17: *The long metal-tipped tool was used by Nharo for the preparation of skins for leather. It is bound to a wooden handle with sinew. The stone scraper with mastic adhering to it comes from Boomplaas Cave and was mounted at right angles to a wooden or bone handle.*

southern Cape coast and in Kenya, Zimbabwe and Lesotho. This broad similarity is seen in the timing of changes in long sequence sites, too. The changes were thus driven by forces way beyond those at local and regional level.

All the same, at a regional level one can discern gross differences in the relative importance of certain activities during the duration of an artefact tradition. Faunal remains from Later Stone Age sites in the equatorial zone north of 20° South latitude show a much greater emphasis on the hunting of larger game animals in the Holocene, for example, than in sites to the south. This is reflected in a higher number of tools assumed to relate to hunting (such as segments and backed bladelets) in Wilton and Nachikufan industries in the northern sites (Figure 8.16).

Linked with this pattern is another one that goes some way towards explaining the higher incidence of scrapers in sites to the south. Ethnographic records summarised by Von Boeckmann (1921) show that the majority of hunter-gatherer peoples in South Africa make clothing from leather, whereas those to the north are more likely to make clothes from bark cloth. Assuming that scrapers were made mostly for the preparation of leather, we would expect to find more scrapers where more leather was worked. There is indeed such a coincidence, as can be seen in the map in Figure 8.16 (Deacon & Deacon 1980). However, the correlation does not seem to work when changes through time occur in the frequencies of backed tools and scrapers, presumably because in such instances technology is not held constant.

Ethnographic records outside of South Africa show no consistent pattern for linking gender with leather-working. In Steve Brandt's (1996) recent study of leather-working in Ethiopia amongst agricultural people who still use stone scrapers for this purpose, he records that in some groups it is done exclusively by men, in others exclusively by women, and in yet others it is done by both men and women. In South Africa and parts of Namibia and Botswana, the data collected by Von Boeckmann in 1921 show that leather-working was done exclusively by women (Figure 8.17). More recently, Lita Webley (1990) has recorded leather-working by Namaqua women, who still use stone tools (but not scrapers) in order to prepare skins.

Fishing and shellfish gathering

South Africa's coastline of 3000 km is dotted by literally thousands of shell middens that bear witness to the long-term exploitation of shellfish over the last 10 000–12 000 years, when the coastline was close to its present position (see Box 30). In a recent compilation by Jonathan Kaplan (1993), records are given for 3500 sites between the high-water mark and 5 km inland: this figure probably represents less than 10 per cent of the total. Shell middens are easily distinguishable from natural accumulations of shell because they include the bones of animals eaten by Later Stone Age people as well as artefacts (Figure 8.18).

We know from sites like Klasies River and Hoedjiespunt that shellfish were also collected during the Last Interglacial and so we assume that the practice was continuous for the last 120 000 years or more. Middens that accumulated during the time of lower sea level between about 100 000 and 12 000 years ago are not visible now because they have been covered by the rising sea.

Most Later Stone Age shell middens of the Present Interglacial also include remains of a wide range of fish species. Bones of sea birds dating back to 12 000 years ago are present at sites like Elands Bay Cave, Nelson Bay Cave and Matjes River Rock Shelter. Some sites also include the remains of crustaceans like crabs and crayfish and of marine mammals like seals, dolphins and, occasionally, whales.

As none of the San communities studied in depth by ethnographers and anthropologists lived along the coast, we have few detailed observations of the way in which hunter-gatherers collected shellfish and fish. An exception is a short study reported by Budack (1977) of two #Aonin (or Topnaar) bands, who are Khoekhoen living in the vicinity of Walvis Bay in Namibia. One of the bands is the !Khuiseb people, who come to the coast only during the season when !nara melons are ripe, but do not fish or collect shellfish. The Hurinin, on the other hand, live at or near the coast all year. They club seals, collect turtles, sea birds and their eggs, and shellfish, and they fish using spears, their bare hands or reed baskets.

Perhaps the lack of written records is one of the reasons for a popular misconception that there was a separate cultural, linguistic or even racial group

30 • A chain of inference: longshore drift, half-moon bays, rivers, shellfish, rattles and sheep •

Longshore drift moves inshore waters from west to east along the southern coast of South Africa. Parcels of sand are dumped in half-moon bays, are eroded again, and dumped again further along this dynamic coastline. At places like Cape St Francis, the sand takes a short cut overland in a dune by-pass. If houses are built on such a by-pass and the sand is stabilised, the next beach will be starved of sand and the sea will gradually erode the beach away.

Rivers contribute clay, silt and sand where they flow into the sea and, importantly, they bring nutrients that provide food for marine life. Larger rivers, like the Gouritz which flows into the sea near Vlees Bay, and the Sundays, which flows into Algoa Bay, are associated with rich communities of the Cape sand mussel, *Donax serra*. Also called the white mussel, it has a distribution from Lüderitz Bay in the north-west to Algoa Bay in the east. Like all mussels, the body is enclosed in two shells, so it is called a bivalve. It is a filter feeder that moves up and down the beach with the tide. The flesh is dense, almost rubbery, and is good eating. It is also used for bait. You find white mussels by digging down about half a metre in the sand at the water's edge.

Donax shells are found in most coastal Stone Age midden sites, where they would have been collected as food. They are also sometimes found at inland sites, where they are less likely to have been carried as food. At both places there are usually some with a large rough hole in the shell. Perhaps the piece that was broken out was used for making beads. The shell with the hole in it may also have been used. Some show damage around the edge of the shell, suggesting they may have been used as scraping tools, perhaps even to scale fish. *Donax* shells are hard and make a clatter when knocked together, rather like castanets. Ray Inskeep suggested that the ones he found at Nelson Bay Cave with holes in them

were strung together as ankle rattles to be worn when dancing, essential gear for a Stone Age rave. We cannot prove whether they were or not, but it is a possibility.

At Vlees Bay and Algoa Bay, where *Donax* shells are so plentiful, there are large patches of shells in the dunes behind the beach. Most of the patches include stone artefacts, and so we know that people were living there. Many middens also include pieces of pottery, called sherds – black and red earthenware made of clay tempered with sand grains to help bind it. Inland, grass is sometimes used as a temper. If the wind has not eroded the potsherds too much, features typical of Cape coastal pottery may be seen, such as lugs or handles, spouts and pointed bases. It is this type of pottery that is consistently associated with Khoekhoe herders. These observations of the presence of Cape coastal pottery with sand temper tell us immediately that the site was occupied within the last 2000 years and that the people who lived there were most likely herders. Pottery was introduced into South Africa by herders, who needed pots to store their dairy produce. Although it was quickly adopted by hunter-gatherers too, the herders retained the traditional bag-shaped pots with lugs that could be easily suspended on thongs slung over the backs of oxen.

Today, at Vlees Bay, off-road vehicles take fishermen to the beach and tyre tracks are imprinted on the patches of *Donax* shells. The potsherds are broken into smaller and smaller pieces each time. New legislation has been enacted to limit vehicles to below the high-water mark, but is difficult to enforce. Where no proper archaeological study of shell middens has been done, the damage inflicted on middens such as those at Vlees Bay is tragic and irreversible and can never be repaired. We rely on those who know the importance of such sites to tell those who do not.

Figure 8.18: *Left: A typical shell midden at Cape St Francis, showing the scatter of stone and shell on a sand dune. Right: The shell midden in Elands Bay Cave in section (photo: Cedric Poggenpoel).*

called the Strandlopers, who were responsible for all the shell middens along the entire coastline of South Africa. Michael Wilson's (1990) careful assessment of the historical and archaeological records dispels this myth.

As originally used by European writers, and in particular by Jan van Riebeeck in his reports to the Dutch East India Company, the term 'Strandloper' referred to a very specific and quite small group of about 50–80 people of Khoekhoe origin. They lived in the seventeenth century in the vicinity of Table Bay, where Cape Town was established. They called themselves the Goringhaicona or Watermen and had apparently abandoned their former lifestyle as herders to settle around the Table Bay anchorage. They did so in order to derive the maximum benefit from passing ships sailing between Europe and the East. One of the Strandloper men, Autshumao, also known as Herrie or Harry, was taken by an English ship to Bantam in the East Indies in 1630 and returned in 1631. During the voyage he learned English and on his return became a useful go-between for English travellers wishing to obtain provisions from the Khoekhoen. He and other Strandlopers later acted as brokers for Van Riebeeck and his settlement and negotiated on their behalf with the Khoekhoen for the exchange of cattle, sheep and other products.

The term Strandloper was used for the last time in the official Dutch records from the Cape in March 1681 (Moodie 1960:376n). There is no good reason to continue using it as a catch-all term for people who lived along the coast, as no distinct biological or cultural group had exclusive rights to the coastal resources. Both before and after the introduction of herding, Later Stone Age people visited the coast from time to time to enjoy a meal of seafood, and others stayed at or near to the coast all year. It is misleading to call them all by the same name.

There are two sources of archaeological information on the lifestyle of the people who accumulated Later Stone Age shell middens: the analysis of their food remains and the analysis of Later Stone Age human skeletons buried either in shell middens or within a kilometre or two of the coast.

The shellfish species represented in middens closely reflect the species available in the immediate vicinity. Middens above sandy shores will be dominated by the white sand mussel, *Donax serra*. Middens on isolated rocky promontories are likely to have mussels and limpets, while those along shores where rocks alternate with beaches and shallow water are likely to include a wider variety of species including perlemoen (abalone), alikreukel, periwinkles, whelks and barnacles.

Identification of shells in a midden will give information about environmental conditions too. The black mussel, *Choromytilus meridionalis*, is more likely to occur where the water is colder, as on the west coast where the Benguela current keeps temperatures low. The brown mussel, *Perna perna*, prefers the warmer waters of the south and east coast, where the Agulhas current flows. At times when the water temperatures on the south coast would have been cooler, for example between about 12 000 and 8000 years ago, the black mussel frequencies are higher.

The season at which certain shellfish were taken from the water can also be determined if the sea-water temperatures vary from summer to winter. The shell is sectioned for analysis to expose the growth rings or layers that form during the lifetime of the shellfish. A sample of shell is taken from each growth ring and the oxygen isotope ratio is measured to give a relative temperature reading. The annual pattern of summer and winter temperatures can then be plotted on a graph and, as long as the shell is older than a year, the time of death can be estimated. If a large enough number of shells is measured, one can work out the season of occupation of the site.

Middens protected by rock shelters, such as Matjes River and Elands Bay, have built up to depths of several metres. If the site was occupied over a long period, there will be changes through time in the species of shellfish in the midden. These reflect changes in the shoreline adjacent to the site and changes in sea temperature as well.

Women probably collected most of the shellfish, perhaps using digging sticks or a stone tool to dislodge them from rocks in shallow water. They would have carried the shellfish in leather bags back to the camp. When large quantities were collected they may have dried or smoked them for eating later. They were probably placed in the fire until the bivalve shells opened or the limpets were cooked, and were then removed and eaten. The shells accumulated on the midden where people were living and it must have become uncomfortable at times. At some sites eel grass (*Zostera* sp.), which grows in shallow estuaries, was brought in, probably for bedding.

Some shells were used to make mother-of-pearl ornaments like pendants, buttons and beads. Others, especially white mussel shells, were mod-

ified and used as scrapers.

Shell middens are also found inland, along rivers where the freshwater mussel *Unio* sp. occurs. These middens are not as large as the coastal ones because the freshwater mussels are less commonly found in large quantities. In the Eastern Cape they are more common in sites dating to within the last 3000 years.

Fish were probably caught with lines. At a few coastal sites, stones with a groove around them have been found, strongly suggesting they were used as sinkers (Figure 8.19), but fish hooks of the kind we use today were not apparently part of Later Stone Age fishing tackle. The high incidence of double-pointed polished bone points in the Albany and Robberg levels only at coastal sites like Nelson Bay and Elands Bay caves indicates, however, that they may have been used as fish gorges on lines made of vegetable twine (see Figure 7.15). Professor J.L.B. Smith showed us fishing tackle made by fishermen in Mozambique in the 1950s to support this idea. They were using long thorns from *Acacia* trees and tying twine around the middle of the thorn. The fish would be attracted by bait; when the thorn was in its throat the fisherman would pull it sideways and then land the fish.

Polished bone hooks have been found at a few inland sites in the Drakensberg range, but they are not clearly associated with fishing. Reed baskets may have been used in rivers and estuaries.

Along the southern Cape coast, large tidal fish traps were constructed in precolonial times. Several are still in use. Some are very complex

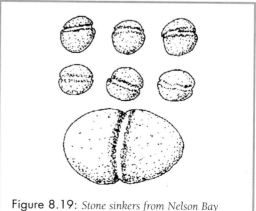

Figure 8.19: *Stone sinkers from Nelson Bay Cave dating to within the last 4000 years. (Redrawn from Inskeep 1987)*

31 ● Case study: Sequence of changes in west coast shell middens ●

● **4300–3500 BP** Only a few shell middens on the west coast between Elands Bay and Lamberts Bay have evidence for sporadic occupation before 4300 years ago. Shortly thereafter, climatic conditions and a brief regression of sea level seem to have favoured productivity in both the marine and terrestrial environments: this attracted people to the coast. No single type of site was preferred at this time. Middens were occupied by relatively small groups of people over relatively short periods, when they used both marine and terrestrial foods.

● **3500–3000 BP** The number of shell middens increased at this time and so did the quantity of shell at the sites. These changes suggest an increase in regional population density and in the length of time people stayed at each site. Marine and terrestrial environments were especially productive during another sea-level regression. People seem to have become less mobile, staying within defined territories. The economy was what Jerardino calls the 'immediate return' type, with an increasing focus on shellfish and on the snaring of small game, rather than on large-game hunting.

● **3000–2000 BP** Maximum population levels were reached during this millennium, but after 2400 BP marine and terrestrial productivity began to decline. People seem to have been even more sedentary and occupied large open sites, or megamiddens. Only one cave site is known to have been occupied in the area at this time. The food remains show that highly predictable and productive species were targeted to maximise low effort and low risk. Strategies included storage of smoked or dried fish and shellfish to tide people over periods when protein foods were difficult to obtain. Underground plant foods and tortoises were exploited more often than before, and large bovids were hunted only rarely. A variety of artefacts was recovered from Steenbokfontein Cave, perhaps indicating communal gatherings. After 2400 BP there seems to have been a breakdown of the old order, and by 2200 BP either different places were chosen for communal gatherings or smaller social networks may have formed.

● **After 2000 BP** There was change in all spheres of life after herders and domesticated livestock arrived in the Western Cape with pottery soon after 2000 years ago. The changes included a wide range of solutions to the population increase. Some groups favoured hunting and gathering, which gave them an 'immediate return' economy. Others stored foods and delayed the return. Small social units stayed for short periods at most sites, and shellfish were collected on a smaller scale than during the megamidden period. Protein came largely from non-marine resources (Jerardino 1996).

systems of enclosures covering several hundred square metres. Judging from the contents of middens in close proximity to the traps, they appear to have been made within the last 2000 years. Graham Avery (1975) has mapped 14 fish-trap sites along one 300 km stretch of coastline in the south-western Cape and interviewed local fishermen, some of them third-generation trap-users. The traps will remain efficient only if the walls are packed correctly and regular maintenance is thus essential. Better catches are made at night during spring tide and when there is a slight breeze to ripple the water, so the fish are not alarmed.

The bones of freshwater fish are found in Later Stone Age sites in the Eastern Cape and along the Orange River, and more occasionally elsewhere. Although the archaeological evidence suggests they were not eaten as more than a supplement when they were in good supply, this may not necessarily have been the case: they could have been caught and dried away from living sites.

Coastal birds, and probably their eggs as well, were also exploited by Later Stone Age people living on the coast. Jackass penguins, cormorants, albatrosses, gulls, terns, petrels, shearwaters and Cape gannets are all represented in Later Stone Age archaeological sites. Graham Avery (1987) analysed birds that had died naturally and were discovered washed up on the beaches of the west coast between 1977 and 1983. He found that all species were more common in the summer months. More than 80 per cent of the bird remains from Elands Bay Cave are those of jackass penguins, Cape gannets and Cape cormorants. Because the penguins and gannets do not normally come ashore unless sick or dying, Avery concludes that the Later Stone Age people ate these as beached birds. Cape cormorants could have been caught live on land, though.

Detailed studies of shell middens at open sites and in rock shelters along the coast between Elands Bay and Lamberts Bay have been made by John Parkington and the Spatial Archaeology Research Unit at the University of Cape Town since the early 1970s. This work has shown some interesting patterns in the foods eaten by coastal hunter-gatherers and the interplay between availability and exploitation. It has also stimulated the development of innovative analytical techniques designed to test hypotheses. They range from Judith Sealy's analysis of bone chemistry and stable carbon isotopes in bone, to changes in oxygen isotope ratios in marine shells and the meticulous plotting of spatial patterns at Dune Field Midden (Parkington *et al.* 1988, 1992).

Parkington (1987:8) interprets the changes over the last 14 000 years at Elands Bay Cave as indicating continuous modification of behaviour in each successive millennium. The people living in the sites used various combinations of food resources, in particular shellfish, fish and marine mammals in addition to land mammals and plant foods.

Occupation of the sites was not continuous through the last 12 000 years, and there remains a gap of several thousand years between about 7500 and 4500 years ago, when human occupation is all but invisible archaeologically in the area. Climatic change probably played a major role in this patterning. Evidence summarised in Chapter 2 from other southern hemisphere countries indicates

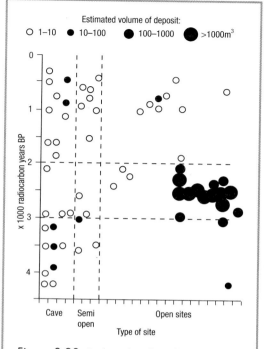

Figure 8.20: *Radiocarbon dates for Later Stone Age sites between Elands Bay and Lamberts Bay, summarising the nature and timing of changes in settlement pattern over the last 4000 years (Jerardino & Yates 1996).*

that it is only within the last 5000 years that the El Niño factor, which affects the rainfall regime in the Western Cape, has operated in its present mode.

As part of this long-term project, excavations have been carried out at shell middens at 29 sites, which together have 116 radiocarbon dates between 4300 and 300 BP (Figure 8.20). Antonieta Jerardino (1996) has correlated information from them to speculate about the complex relationship between changes in environment and social, economic and settlement processes. Her conclusions are summarised in Box 31.

Men's work: hunting

As in the vast majority of hunting and gathering communities worldwide, San men are responsible for hunting and thereby for supplying most of the protein and fat in the diet of an extended family. There is no reason to suppose any different

Figure 8.21: *Copy of a rock painting in the Western Cape showing a group of men with their hunting equipment. Note the size of the bows and arrows relative to the size of the people. (Tracing by Stephen Townley Bassett)*

arrangement prevailed during the Later Stone Age although the progressive trend towards the hunting of smaller mammals in more recent assemblages indicates that hunting patterns certainly changed.

What such a statement hides is the prestige of hunting and of being closely involved with animals. As Mathias Guenther (1986:237) writes about the Nharo: 'The mental attitude the Nharo hold about animals is more than mere intellectual curiosity; animals are also considered, in a certain sense, to be kindred to man and to the Nharo they are aesthetically captivating and beguiling. They are the characters of the stories told and retold evening upon evening. Such stories are either the myths or tales about the old animals or are based on observations and hunts of real animals, recently encountered. Animal sounds are skilfully imitated and the behaviour of specific animals is mimed. The tracks of specific animals can be identified and read. A set of hand signals is used for the hunt and represents yet another symbolic device of culture

for mentally processing animals and establishing them within the culture and minds of the people. Some of the important animals (giraffe, springbok) are also featured in trance dances. The eland antelope gives name and content to the most dramatic and symbolically pregnant ritual of Nharo culture, the dance of the old men and women during female initiation when the courtship behaviour of the powerful eland antelope is mimed by the old.'

Bows and poisoned arrows, spears and traps of various kinds were the main tools used for hunting. This is confirmed by early travellers' accounts, ethnography and rock paintings. A practice that is not recorded ethnographically but is apparently illustrated in rock art is the use of nets for hunting.

As we have summarised in the previous chapter, analysis of the bones of hunted animals at Later Stone Age occupation sites shows that while climatic and environmental factors certainly played a part in changing the vegetation and the range of animals available, the choices that the hunters made also changed. Some archaeologists believe that the changes were gradual, with small adjustments made every millennium or so, while others believe that adjustments were made in two major steps.

During the Last Glacial Maximum between about 20 000 and 12 000 years ago, grassland prevailed in the southern Cape. Faunal remains from sites dating to this period show that Later Stone Age people were successful in hunting not only small to medium-size antelope, but also very large ones including the now extinct giant buffalo, the giant Cape zebra and the giant hartebeest. When conditions grew warmer and bushier after 12 000 years ago, these giant species became extinct, possibly because of overkill aided by environmental change. Later Stone Age people then focused increasingly on smaller browsing species that did not migrate seasonally, although larger animals like elephant, hippo, buffalo, eland and wildebeest were still available. From about 4000 years ago, not only are the bones of large antelope very rare at Later Stone Age sites, but the medium-sized antelope are also less common than in earlier deposits.

Selecting increasingly smaller animals to hunt had implications for the tactics and weapons used by the hunters, as well as for dispersal of the meat and consequently the size and organisation of the group of people to be fed. When the dominant vegetation was bushy rather than grassy, Later Stone Age people seem to have preferred hunting the smaller solitary antelope that move around mainly at dusk and at night and do not migrate seasonally. These include grysbok, steenbok, mountain reedbuck and bushbuck. They were more easily taken with traps or even nets placed along routes which the hunters would have noticed them using. The relatively small parcels of meat that these animals represent would have provided for an extended family.

On the other hand, the larger migratory grazers like buffalo, wildebeest, hartebeest, gemsbok and zebra as well as the smaller springbok and impala are more visible during the day and are more easily taken by groups of hunters with bows and arrows or spears. Very large animals like elephant were taken in pit traps. The size of bows and arrows used during the Later Stone Age and by the San does not enable hunters to kill many animals outright. Rather, it is the poison that does the work, and the tracking of the animal after it is hit

is important for success. With larger animals, it is vital that hunters work together as a team, not only to find and shoot the game, but to track the wounded animal and then to cut up the meat and transport it to camp. As a buffalo has ten times the amount of meat that a bushbuck has, more people are required not only to hunt it but also to eat it, and plans need to be made accordingly.

The change in hunting pattern, like the changes in shellfish collecting described above, reflects a significant growth in population size. As the larger grazers became extinct, partly through over-predation as environmental change made them more vulnerable, so larger numbers of people concentrated their hunting strategy on more reliable smaller, non-gregarious browsers. The result of increasing pressure on easily obtainable meat resources was that more people were packed into the landscape, occupying smaller territories.

A /Xam perspective

Dr Bleek asked one or more of the men he interviewed in the Breakwater Prison in 1870 to make some arrows for him. Later, in 1878, /Han#kass'o explained the process of arrow manufacture to Lucy Lloyd and told her about the poison used and the way he and the other men in his group hunted springbok.

Reeds were collected for the arrow shafts and were stored in a porcupine hole. When dry, the

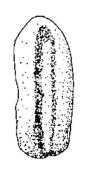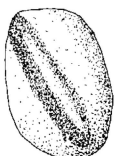

Figure 8.22: *Grooved stones of the kind used to straighten arrows, apply poison or smooth ostrich eggshell beads. From Nelson Bay Cave, dating to within the last 4000 years. (Redrawn from Inskeep 1987)*

papery outer skin was scraped off. If the reed was too curved, a grooved stone (Figure 8.22) or half a bored stone was heated in the fire and the reed was passed through it repeatedly until it was straight. One end of the reed was nocked to take the bow-string. Sections of a feather were cut to size and bound longitudinally with sinew and vegetable gum (called /kwai) to the reed just above the nock. Not all nineteenth-century San arrows in museum collections are feathered, however: those that are not are bound with sinew for 2 or 3 cm above the nock and are sometimes decorated with designs burnt, scratched or painted on the reed (Figure 8.23). Arrows were marked because the person who made the arrow that killed the animal was entitled to distribute the meat.

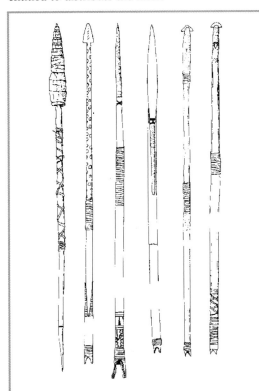

Figure 8.23: *Various types of arrow used by San in South Africa and Namibia in the nineteenth and twentieth centuries. On the left is a poison stick used to store poison for future use. The two on the right are tipped with iron and have quill barbs. The third arrow from the right can be reversed in the reed shaft to keep the poisoned tip safe.*

The design of the killing end of the arrow differed according to the kind of arrowhead that was to be fitted for particular prey. The main idea was to allow the arrow tip only to break the skin so that poison could be introduced into the bloodstream, and to allow the reed arrow shaft to fall away once the incision had been made. The stone and glass tips made by the Breakwater prisoners were pressed into a lump of vegetable gum or mastic. This was often made from an *Acacia* tree. Two stone flakes were placed with the sharp side outwards; while some were not trimmed, others do appear to have been backed like the backed bladelets and backed segments so characteristic of the Later Stone Age (Figure 8.24).

The most common type in museum collections has a wood or polished bone foreshaft with blunt points at both ends. The one end is inserted into the hollow reed reinforced with sinew binding. The other end is split and a small half-moon of metal inserted into it. Sinew binding keeps the split closed and secures a barb made of ostrich feather quill or porcupine quill. The sinew binding is then covered with a thick layer of gum and poison. Other designs have only a sharp bone point that could be reversed into the reed arrow shaft when not in use (Figure 8.23), or a piece of fencing wire that has been hammered into an arrow-point and inserted straight into the reed shaft.

/Han#kass'o's recipe for poison was the juice of the //kao plant (called #ku) mixed with saliva and cobra and puffadder venom, to which the gall of a cobra was added. It was mixed in a grooved stone or on a grindstone. After it had been applied to the arrows and left to dry, the poison that was left over was mixed with resin and stored on the end of a stick, to be heated and applied again when required (Figure 8.23). Other San used only vegetable poisons or poison grubs, depending on availability. In an experiment conducted by Margaret Shaw at the South African Museum in about 1960, poison on nineteenth-century arrows that probably came from the bulb of *Boophane disticha* killed white mice within three minutes when injected into their bloodstream (Deacon, J. 1992).

Dr Kannemeyer's (1890:126) informants mentioned a similar recipe, using snake or spider venom and caterpillars mixed with bland juices from a *Euphorbia* to make it plastic and with gall as a preservative. Despite his persuasive attempts, the

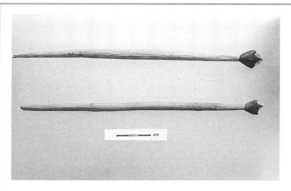

Figure 8.24: *Left: Arrows made by /Xam men for Dr Bleek in Cape Town in the early 1870s (South African Museum collection). Right: Close-up of the tips of two of the arrows (Pitt-Rivers Museum collection). Note the mastic (gum) holding the stone inserts on the left. One of the inserts has fallen out of the mastic in the example on the right. The remaining insert has been blunted like the stone segments typical of the Wilton industry.*

people Kannemeyer spoke to would not give him the recipe for the poison antidote. He confirms the use of 'a liliaceous bulb' in the poison, presumably *Boophane disticha*, and remarks: 'Its effects were not fatal, but acting rapidly and in a peculiar manner upon the cerebellum, it caused an animal wounded with it to run around in circles and thus kept the stricken quarry within easy reach of the hunter, till such time as the other poisonous, but more hardy, ingredients produced their fatal effects. The farmers called it "Dronkgift" [drunken poison].'

Apart from their use as hunting weapons, arrows were also an important item in the gift exchange system. The anthropologist Polly Wiessner examined the arrows in quivers belonging to 16 !Kung men in northern Botswana in the 1970s and found that only 57 per cent were made by the person who carried the quiver. About a quarter were made by exchange partners within a 20 km radius and the rest by men living between 20 and 200 km away. Exchange partners were entitled to sharing of resources, assistance and extended visiting.

All ethnographic and written records from the seventeenth century and later in southern Africa describe the bows used by San hunter-gatherers as a simple curve of wood. They usually use wood from a *Grewia* sp. tree, with a sinew string, but rock paintings in the south-western Cape suggest that a more elaborate bow with a triple curve may have been made at some stage in the past as well. Quivers to hold arrows were made of bark or

leather or from the hollowed-out stem of the quiver tree.

The /Xam men spoke eloquently about their hunting activities and the sentiments and beliefs that surrounded them. Hunters were taught to behave themselves 'nicely' and had to obey a series of rules and taboos so that the meat could be eaten safely. The hunter's actions could have a significant effect on the behaviour of the animal being hunted, and consequently both general and specific observances were required.

In an interview with Dr Bleek in 1873, //Kabbo explained that /Xam hunters would feel a presentiment in the form of a kind of 'beating' or 'tapping' in the body when certain events were about to happen. Ignorant or stupid people who did not understand what the tappings meant would get into trouble. They might be killed by a lion, for instance. But those who listened would discover which way not to go and which arrow not to use. If the migrating springbok herds were coming, a man would feel a tapping along the side of his ribs, in the place where the springbok has a black stripe. This 'springbok sensation' was felt also where the springbok has a black stripe on its face, where the horns are on the head, and at the back of the hunter's legs where the blood drips down as the dead springbok is carried home.

It was in the Northern Cape that springbok runs still took place in the nineteenth century. Literally millions of animals would migrate *en masse* and sometimes at great speed into new grazing

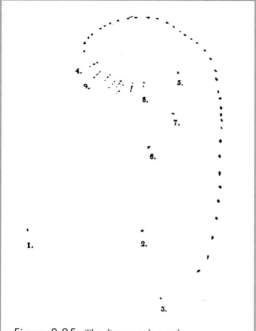

Figure 8.25: *The diagram drawn by /Han#kass'o to explain the method of springbok hunting to Lucy Lloyd. (Bleek & Lloyd 1911)*

grounds after rain. Young boys were sent to the top of the nearest hill to see where the springbok were and then signal those below. E.J. Dunn (1873) gave a graphic account of such an event that took place within /Xam territory in 1871. He described the migrating herd as extending for one hundred miles. Dunn drove a wagon through the herd for six hours and the animals were so mesmerised by their flight that they allowed Dunn and his party to within 40 metres of them.

The /Xam hunted the springbok by luring groups into a confined space and then shooting at them with bows and poisoned arrows. /Han#kass'o illustrated the way in which sticks, with ostrich feathers tied to them, were placed in the ground at about the height of a person, to steer springbok from the herd towards the waiting hunters, who would be facing them as they approached the cul de sac. A man held a smaller bunch of feathers at position 5 on the diagram to frighten the springbok. As they came close to him he stopped calling them and, as they turned aside, the hunters at positions 4, 8 and 9 would shoot

them (see Figure 8.25).

The manner in which the ostrich feathers and sticks were prepared was quite elaborate and underlines the perception that every step of the plan had to be prepared with ritual care. The feathers were tied to sticks with thongs of springbok skin and the sticks were smeared with red haematite or ochre. A certain root was dug up and put into a shallow hole in the ground over hot coals so that it smouldered gently, making smoke but not flame. The feather brushes were then placed over the smoking root, which was covered with a springbok skin to keep the smoke contained. The brushes absorbed the smell of the root and they were then ready to be used for springbok hunting.

The springbok were shot with a bow and poisoned arrow. After one was wounded, it would have to be tracked by the hunter and his companions as the poison took a while to act. During this period, the successful hunter had to be careful what he ate, for this would affect his prey. When he shot an animal he would only eat and touch meat of another animal that did not run as fast as his quarry. As Dia!kwain expressed it: 'they only give us food which they know ... will strengthen the poison, that the poison may kill the game ... [and] when we have shot gemsbok they do not give us springbok flesh [because springbok do not sleep at night].'

When the springbok was dead, the hunter whose arrow had killed it was not allowed to touch the meat with his hands because his hands had held the bow and arrow that killed it. He had to sit a little distance away while others cut up the meat and distributed it amongst the group. This distancing of the hunter emphasises sharing rather than hunting ability or, as Patricia Vinnicombe (1972:202) says, 'the efficacy of a hunting technique rather than the prowess of an individual hunter'.

The stomach contents were taken out and the blood from the springbok, including blood that had fallen on the ground, was scooped into the stomach. Later, the stomach, its contents and the blood, together with the bones that remained after the meat had been eaten, were put in a heap on the ground opposite the entrance to the hut of the man who had shot the springbok. If clay pots were being made at the time, the blood may have been used in curing the fired pot.

The hunter whose arrow had killed the springbok received the upper bones of the forelegs and the back of the neck. Women were not allowed to eat the meat of the shoulder blades or else the men would lose their aim next time they tried to shoot a springbok. The bones of the shoulder blades were not thrown away with the rest, but were hidden in the stick frame of the grass hut.

The wife of the successful hunter would be given the tail, which might be used in curing the springbok skin to make it soft and supple so that it could be made into a bag. The man and his wife would be able to exchange the bag for red ochre, specularite and arrows. The inner skin of the springbok's ears could be cured and dried and then sewn into little pouches; these were filled with dried seeds and strung together as dancing rattles worn by men on their feet.

The reason for these practices was that springbok were in possession of invisible magic arrows and if their bones, meat and skin were not handled correctly, the people would become ill and die. Several examples of this were cited by Dia!kwain and /Han#kass'o.

Springbok were believed sometimes to lure hunters towards lions, who would kill them, and also to act strangely before and after a person died. 'If we saw the sun setting while the springbok resisted us, we should leave it ... for it is a thing which smells from afar; therefore it knows all things' (Bleek 1932:241). Dia!kwain related how a springbok he had shot in the leg with a gun did not die immediately and bleated at him, yet he still killed it and took it home. A few days later his first wife died inexplicably. /Han#kass'o said springbok should also not be killed when the hunter's friend had died, for the hunter would miss his aim, and even if it was wounded, the springbok would appear to be alive. To counteract this, the women would smoke arrows for them by burning buchu (an aromatic herb). A woman could make a cut on the man's shoulder and suck out the blood, spitting it into a springbok horn. When the horn was full of blood, they would burn the buchu and put the blood on top of the buchu, 'for they want the springbok to lie down [to die] for us' (Bleek 1932:248). The women would also shave straight lines on the hunter's head from the temple backwards to make the springbok run straight to them.

And they did. Many times.

Romancing the stones?

Theory is part of the romance of archaeology and is vital if we want to breathe some life into the snippets of information drawn from stone and other artefacts. The process has sometimes been compared to squeezing blood from stone. But the blood comes from the squeezer, not the squeezed. The archaeologist builds up theories that can be tested against field observations, from analogies drawn from the ethnographic record; they are not inherent in the stones. To construct a believable history of the San from the stones and bones of archaeology, with or without romance, there must be an appropriate theory or else the analogies become mere speculations. This has been shown most clearly in South Africa in the study of rock art, as we shall see in the next chapter.

CHAPTER NINE

Rock art and religious beliefs

Of all the secrets learned from archaeological research, by far the most rewarding for me has been the one that unlocked the meaning of San rock art. The inspiration came from the research of Patricia Vinnicombe in her book People of the Eland, *which was published in 1976. It was reinforced by a lecture that I heard her give at about the same time, and by the lectures and articles of David Lewis-Williams, in particular his book* Believing and Seeing, *which was published in 1981. The revelation was not instantaneous. I had bought a copy of* Specimens of Bushman Folklore *by W.H.I. Bleek and L.C. Lloyd in 1961, but it dawned on me only gradually. I struggled to understand the strange phrases and expressions used by the /Xam that were metaphors for beliefs and ritual actions. As David Lewis-Williams pointed out, the keys to understanding these metaphors were to be found in the publications of twentieth-century anthropologists like Richard Lee, Megan Biesele and Richard Katz, and it took a while for me to digest these too.*

When I finished my Ph.D. in 1982 I was in need of a change. The analysis of the stone artefacts from Nelson Bay Cave, Boomplaas and Kangkara had been an interesting exercise, but I felt a certain frustration. It was difficult to move beyond the obvious and explain the kind of patterning we were observing in the stone artefact sequences in a way that was both intellectually satisfying and believable. There was much controversy at the time about whether all of the rock art was trance-related, or whether there were elements of myth and simple decorative art in it. I thought it might be worth while to locate places where the /Xam informants had lived and to examine the rock engravings in the same vicinity. The purpose was to compare the themes in the art with the characters and events in the /Xam folklore and myths recorded by Bleek and Lloyd. The results would help to evaluate the extent to which the rock art illustrated folklore.

A year later, having pored over a map drawn by Bleek with information from //Kabbo, extracted notes about places mentioned by //Kabbo, /Han#kass'o and Dia!kwain from the records in the Jagger Library at the University of Cape Town, spoken to numerous farmers and local people, and visited rock engraving sites known from surveys done by Dora and Gerhard Fock, Peter Beaumont and David Morris at the McGregor Museum in Kimberley, I stood on top of the Strandberg in the territory of the /Xam. The dry landscape, home of the accurately named Flat Bushmen, and the Bitterpits, where //Kabbo and /Han#kass'o had lived, lay in the distance. /Han#kass'o's mother had told him how the three hills that make up the Strandberg were formed. The agama lizard had intended to pass through the gap between the hills, but when he did so, the mountains squeezed and broke him. He fell over and his forelegs and head became the hills to the east, while his hind part became the hills to the north and west.

The death of the lizard, itself a messenger of the rain, was a metaphor for the 'death' in trance of a rain-maker. The rock engravings on the lizard mountain included elephant, eland and other rain animals, and were in turn metaphors for beliefs. Analysis of the themes in the rock engravings confirmed their primary association with rituals such as healing, rain-making and trance. It seemed plausible that the rock art had been deliberately positioned to enhance the power of the place for generations of shamans of the rain. The pieces of the puzzle were beginning to fall into place (Deacon, J. 1997). [JD]

The rock art of the San and their ancestors in South and southern Africa is one of the region's greatest cultural treasures. It is technically excellent, visually exquisite and, to many modern viewers, unexpected in its detail and depth of meaning. Although it has been greatly misunderstood in the past, its value has been considerably enhanced by research conducted in South Africa over the past two decades. We will probably never fully comprehend the meaning of all rock paintings and engravings, but the stereotype of the San as 'children of nature' who painted or engraved simple pictures just for the fun of decorating their homes has been convincingly debunked. Their art stands out as a sophisticated reminder of the depth of their religious beliefs and their ability to use art as part of ritual practices to mediate social conflict and record experiences in the spirit world.

Distribution

The pictures or images in southern African rock art are presented in two forms, as paintings and as engravings. When the first major survey of rock art sites was published as a map and list in 1952 by Van Riet Lowe at the Archaeological Survey, it appeared as if there was little or no overlap between the distribution of paintings and engravings. Further research has shown this not to be the case. The major divide is a geological one, so that in the western interior of the country where rock shelters with suitable surfaces for painting are not common, the solution was to engrave suitable rocks in the open. Paintings were sometimes done in landscapes where engravings predominate and can still be seen where the natural weathering process has not obliterated them completely, while engravings are found in the same area as paintings if the rock formations are suitable.

There is rock art of one form or another in more than half of the magisterial districts in South Africa and in all the neighbouring countries. Programmes to record the art and compile information on the location of sites have been undertaken by various people and organisations over the past 130 years or more in Tanzania, Zambia, Zaire, Malawi, Mozambique, Angola, Namibia, Botswana, Zimbabwe, Lesotho, Swaziland and South Africa. But a survey of official records of rock art sites in all these countries in 1996 showed a combined total of only 14 118 sites, of which South Africa contributed a little over 10 000. This is a gross underestimate of the actual number of sites. We know from recent surveys that when these records are checked in the field, even for small areas, the numbers can be quadrupled at least, and there are many areas in all the southern African countries that have never been surveyed at all. Peter Garlake believes that in Zimbabwe alone there are at least 30 000 sites, and there must be many more in South Africa.

The artists

Although most of the rock paintings and rock engravings were done by San, not all South African rock art was the work of hunter-gatherers. There are many sites, mainly in the north and east of the country, with paintings in a distinctive 'finger painting' or 'late white' style, as well as engravings that depict subjects different from those in the San art. It is highly likely that they were done by Xhosa, Zulu, Venda, Shona, Sotho and Tswana agriculturists and their ancestors within the last 2000 years. They include stylised images of the crocodile and of cattle, which are of ritual significance to agriculturists. Engravings often depict the plans of huts and villages (Figure 9.1). Although

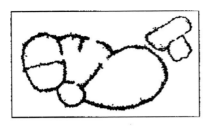

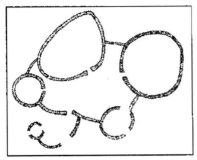

Figure 9.1: *Top: Rock engraving of a Tswana-style cluster of cattle pens from the Northern Cape. Below: Plan of stone-walled cattle pens at a pre-colonial Tswana settlement in the Free State. (After Maggs 1995)*

there is no clear evidence that the San influenced the agriculturists in their choice of art forms, Frans Prins and Pieter Jolly have documented a particularly close symbiosis between San rain-makers and southern Nguni people. This relationship persisted into the twentieth century in the Eastern Cape and Lesotho and affected the rock art, the economy and the ideology of both parties.

The Khoekhoe herders in the Northern, Eastern and Western Cape may also have contributed 'finger' paintings and some engravings, although in this case the subject matter is less easy to differentiate from art that is clearly attributable to the San. There are even engravings and paintings on rocks done by early European settlers, which are easily recognisable, especially if accompanied by names and dates!

Dating

The subject matter, dating and archaeological associations are the best evidence that most of the rock art was done by the San and their ancestors. Until

recently there was no reliable method to date rock paintings or engravings directly. A few rare finds have been made of portable art – paintings and engravings on small stones and rocks – recovered from excavated sites where they were buried beneath the surface in Later Stone Age occupation horizons. Radiocarbon dates on charcoal at the same level as the portable art from Apollo 11 cave in southern Namibia (Figure 9.2) show the remarkable antiquity of the rock art tradition and place it in the same general time frame as the earliest rock art of Western Europe and Australia.

Spalls of painted rock have been found at two caves in the Matopo Hills in Zimbabwe, and charcoal associated with them is dated to *c.* 10 500 BP and *c.* 9520 BP. The oldest dated rock art in South Africa is an engraving on a small slab of dolomite from Wonderwerk Cave south of Kuruman in the Northern Cape; this has a radiocarbon date of *c.* 10 200 BP (Thackeray 1983). Like one of the stones from Apollo 11, it was also broken and depicts part of a fine line engraving of a mammal. There are at least four other engraved stones in similar style from the upper levels at Wonderwerk that date to between *c.* 5180 and *c.* 3990 BP, confirming that the tradition of portable art was continued at the site throughout most of the Later Stone Age occupation.

There are at least seven further radiocarbon dates for painted stones, all from the southern

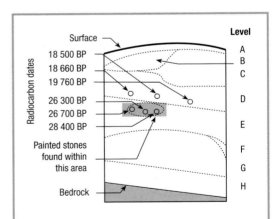

Figure 9.2: *Diagrammatic section through the Apollo 11 deposits showing the position of the painted stones (within the dashed and shaded oval) and selected charcoal samples (open circles) that were radiocarbon-dated.*

32 • Dating of rock art at Apollo 11 •

The oldest dated rock art in Africa was found at a rock shelter called Apollo 11 in the southern region of Namibia in 1969. Erich Wendt, a research archaeologist from Germany, was excavating there at the time of the Apollo 11 space mission and while listening to the drama unfold on his portable radio, he decided to name the site after this momentous event in world history. He did not know when he did so that he would also make one of the most important discoveries of the twentieth century, at least in the field of African archaeology. In the deposits that Wendt excavated, seven painted stones were found in all at Apollo 11, four in the first excavation season and three in the second in 1972. They are quite small slabs, hardly larger than the average adult's hand, and are of a rock type different from that of the walls of the rock shelter. Remarkably, one of those found in 1972 fitted one of the stones found in 1969. It completed a painting that had apparently been broken before the next occupation layer covered it. Equally remarkable is the fact that the artefacts associated with the painted stones are from the end of the Middle Stone Age sequence and pre-date the Later Stone Age. At first, this was a reason for some to doubt the association and

the date of 27 500 years for the art. The diagram in Figure 9.2 shows that the painted stones came from the top of Layer E. Three charcoal samples from the area surrounding them were radiocarbon-dated. Taken with the standard errors, the mean of these three dates is 27 500 BP. Five further charcoal samples were dated from the same layer, but below the painted stones. They were older than 27 500 BP, as would be expected. After the accumulation of Layer E and the covering of the painted stones, the site was not occupied for several millennia. The base of the overlying Layer D, which has Later Stone Age artefacts similar to the Robberg industry of the southern Cape, has three radiocarbon dates of *c.* 19 760, *c.* 18 660 and *c.* 18 500. Six further dates from the upper levels of Layer D gave younger dates. Some published reports therefore prefer to err on the cautious side and say that the Apollo 11 painted stones are 'at least 18 500 years old'. We are confident that the meticulous excavation procedure followed by Erich Wendt, and the fact that all but one of the dates are in stratigraphic sequence, gives as good evidence as one could hope for in this time range that the rock art tradition in southern Africa is at least 27 500 years old.

Cape. They range from *c.* 6500 to *c.* 1500 BP. A painted spall from a rock shelter in the Thukela Valley in KwaZulu–Natal and a fallen slab of painted rock in Steenbokfontein Rock Shelter near Lamberts Bay on the Western Cape coast date within this same time range. In the Cederberg in the Western Cape, N.J. van der Merwe and his colleagues collected a sample of black paint with charcoal as an ingredient that was radiocarbon-dated to *c.* 500 BP.

New techniques developed by the Australian Alan Watchman are now being applied to paintings from the Natal Drakensberg. The method involves removing samples of paint and testing them for organic ingredients like carbon and plant

fibres. These minute residues can then be dated by radiocarbon using the accelerator method. Aron Mazel and Alan Watchman have reported on two dated paintings so far, one at 330 ± 90 and the other at 420 ± 340 years before the present, both therefore before the colonial era, in the Drakensberg.

At the recent end of the timescale, there are also paintings in the Western Cape of people in European dress with mule wagons. There is at least one rock painting of a ship, and there are several others of people with guns and horses. All indicate they were painted in the last 300 years or less. In the Drakensberg in the Eastern Cape and KwaZulu–Natal there are paintings of British soldiers with horses and guns, which would date them securely to the nineteenth century.

This suite of dates from a variety of sources, sites and methods confirms the antiquity of rock art in South Africa. While most of the dates fall within the last 7000 years, the fact that both rock paintings and engravings were still being created in the nineteenth century gives the tradition a time span of at least 27 500 years.

Rock art analysis

The first major works on South African rock art to refer in detail to the religious beliefs of the Later Stone Age people of South Africa were Patricia Vinnicombe's book *People of the Eland*, which was published in 1976, and *Believing and Seeing* by David Lewis-Williams, published in 1981. Both books were directed primarily at the interpretation and contextual analysis of rock art. The separation in the minds of many archaeologists of the significance between what Stone Age people made and ate, on the one hand, and what they believed in, on the other, is gradually being bridged, and this owes a great deal to the research done by these two authors.

Central to understanding the San worldview and the extent to which their belief system permeated their lifestyle and their art have been the recorded testimonies of Dia!kwain, //Kabbo and /Han#kass'o, who lived in the Northern Cape, as well as that of a San man named Qing interviewed by James Orpen in Lesotho in the 1870s, and of numerous twentieth-century San informants in Botswana and Namibia. These testimonies have also shown that although neighbouring San groups may have emphasised their differences with language, their beliefs – like their hunting and gathering practices – were broadly similar. Changes in the belief system certainly took place through time, regional variations developed, and idiosyncrasies of individual artists are evident, but the ethnographic information suggests that there are enough consistent similarities to enable us to trace at least some elements of the tradition back in time and throughout southern Africa.

It was once thought that one of the ways in which the general principles could be discovered was by the careful analysis of rock art to reveal patterns that might be important for interpretation. This assump-

tion was not very different from the way in which archaeologists have analysed stone tools in the absence of direct information from the tool-makers. Tim Maggs counted the number of people in group scenes in the Western Cape paintings and worked out the average number in a group (Figure 9.3). He then compared the statistics with band size amongst twentieth-century San. His conclusion was that the hunter-gatherers in the Western Cape lived in bands of about 13 people. In another set of statistical analyses, Gerhard and Dora Fock, Patricia Vinnicombe, Harald Pager and David Lewis-Williams, amongst others, made detailed counts of animals and people in various postures and combinations. Between them they visited hundreds of sites and counted tens of thousands of individual paintings and engravings. The results of their labours showed that the eland is the most commonly painted antelope. In addition, men are much more commonly painted than women, though in many cases it is not clear whether the artist was depicting one or other gender. Certain animals like the wildebeest, springbok and zebra, although common in the veld, are rarely depicted; and eland are more commonly painted over humans and other eland than humans are painted over eland.

What such detailed analysis did not, and in fact could not, determine was what the art meant. In his book *Discovering Southern African Rock Art*, David Lewis-Williams explains why this is the case by distinguishing between three different approaches, which he calls the aesthetic, narrative and interpretative. He takes the example of Leonardo da Vinci's painting of *The Last Supper* to help one understand the distinction between the approaches, but almost any painting with a religious theme could be taken to make the point. Looking at *The Last Supper*, someone with no knowledge of Christian beliefs may see only a group of men seated at a table. Would counting the number of men help to understand the painting better? Would we assume that 13 was the average number of men who normally ate together? These questions may seem inappropriate, but they do highlight the difficulty of interpreting images without knowing anything about the beliefs of the artist.

In taking an aesthetic approach to the painting, one would look at the composition, the colours, the contrast between light and dark, and the

Figure 9.3: *Tracing of a rock painting of a group scene from the Western Cape. It is typical of those analysed by Tim Maggs for information about average group size. (Tracing by Stephen Townley Bassett)*

expressions on the faces of the men. Art historians use such techniques to classify artistic traditions and the method has been adapted for the classification of rock paintings into monochrome (one colour), bichrome (two colours on the same image), polychrome (many colours) and shaded polychrome (where the colours change gradually from one to another). At one time it was assumed that there was a gradual development in rock art through time from the simple monochrome to the more sophisticated shaded polychrome, but this has no factual basis. Rock engravings have been described by the way the engraving was made, for example with a fine-line outline, by pecking the inside of the image, or by scraping the image smooth.

Narrative description of *The Last Supper*, on the other hand, would examine how the table was set and how the men placed themselves at it, their style of dress, the interior décor, or the foods they ate. With rock art analysis this approach is widely used

in drawing attention to the equipment carried by the people depicted, to the way they are dressed, and to the range of animals in the art and to the question whether they were known in the region historically.

Finally, an interpretative approach towards *The Last Supper* would require some knowledge of the biblical account of the event it illustrates. One would consider the religious importance of the building and the room in Milan in which the painting is displayed, and the artistic conventions and codes that Renaissance painters like Leonardo used. The meaning of little details would be evident, such as Judas knocking over the salt (even today superstitious people believe this signals bad luck), and the significance of the money bag that he holds in his hand. It is only by knowing that this is an illustration of the birth of one of the most important Christian rituals, Holy Communion, that we can appreciate that it is not an ordinary dinner table with ordinary men. When applied to rock art, this approach requires a detailed knowledge of San beliefs and customs.

Anne Solomon's research suggests another stage and dimension to this process. She argues that the next logical step is what she has called intelligibility. In other words, rather than identifying only what an image represents, we should be inquiring how it is like it is. Rather than matching the pictures in the art with activities that ethnographers have described, we should uncover the narrative in the painting because in San thought all domains are interconnected. To understand *The Last Supper* by using this approach, we would combine aspects of the approaches described above. We may ask who the artist was, how he came to do the painting, and which aspects of it are biblically inspired. Or it may be relevant to ask which codes and conventions relate to the customs of the time at which the event took place, rather than to the time the painting was done – why the artist chose to do the painting the way he did. The reasons for the inquiry may also be significant. Such an approach takes into account not only the time and place in which the artist created the work, but also the historical position of the reader of both the art work and ethnography. Some of these lines of inquiry cannot be investigated in rock art, where we have few written records and little detail on dating.

The study of rock art in South Africa has passed through all of these approaches and no doubt more will follow. Some viewers continue to prefer the apparent safety of the aesthetic and narrative approaches because it allows them to give full rein to their imagination. However, in doing so they are perhaps learning more about themselves than about the rock art and the original artists.

It is now widely accepted that San rock art is essentially a religious art from a society in which the religion was shamanistic. It uses conventions and codes and it depicts subjects of significance to San religion and beliefs in the same way that Christian, Islamic, Classical Greek, Ancient Egyptian, Buddhist and other religious arts do. Once we recognise the artistic conventions and key metaphors of San religion, and take time to examine rock paintings and engravings in detail, it is possible to enjoy and understand them a great deal more.

San ethnography

There are several main sources of ethnographic information that have been helpful in providing keys to understanding the metaphors used in rock art. The most extensive is the nineteenth-century Bleek and Lloyd manuscript collection and the long account of a Lesotho rock painting by Qing. Twentieth-century anthropological studies include the Kalahari-based work of Lorna Marshall, Megan Biesele and Richard Katz. Interviews reported by Pieter Jolly and Frans Prins with Xhosa- and Sotho-speaking people are also important. One of these informants, known as 'M', told Jolly and Prins about her San father who had done paintings in the Transkei in the early twentieth century.

The links between the informants and the rock art are sometimes tenuous and inconclusive. Although Dia!kwain came from an area where rock engravings are common and said his father had done some 'chippings' of animals, Lucy Lloyd did not record any further interviews that might have shed light on why his father had selected these particular images or what the circumstances were surrounding the making of the engravings. However, both Bleek and Lloyd showed copies of rock paintings from the Eastern and southern Cape to Dia!kwain and /Han#kass'o and recorded their remarks about them. They have been illuminating especially for understanding rain-making images (Figure 9.4).

None of these written records, however, is more

Figure 9.4: *Rock painting at Ezeljagdspoort. A copy of this painting was shown by Lucy Lloyd to the /Xam San informant, /Han#kass'o, in 1878. He identified the people as the 'rain's sorcerers'. (Lewis-Williams et al. 1993)*

than 150 years old, and all were made after the rock art tradition had effectively ended. Furthermore, the surviving Kalahari San who were studied in the twentieth century had no tradition of rock art. The rock paintings in the Tsodilo Hills of Botswana and the Brandberg in Namibia are far from these hunter-gatherer communities and although they acknowledge that their ancestors did them, they have not been able to offer any deep insights into the meaning and motivation of the art. But all is not lost. San beliefs and rituals still form an important aspect of their lives. The basic structure and metaphors in this belief system have strong similarities with those used by the /Xam and Qing and it is these that have shed welcome light on the rock art. And because these similarities can be identified from information gathered a century ago and several thousand kilometres apart, we feel confident about using the general principles of the beliefs and rituals to interpret the rock art.

Healing

San religion, like many other religions, involves ritual practices that assist people to obtain supernatural power from God. The most common of these rituals is the trance dance, sometimes called the curing dance. It acts as a catalyst enabling all the people taking part to assist the healers amongst them to receive power or potency, which is then used mainly to cure sick people. Medicine people also need potency to enable them to make rain and to control game animals for the good of the group as a whole. As Lorna Marshall expresses it, this potency is like electricity. People who have learned to control and use it correctly find it beneficial, but if a person does not understand its intricacies and if it is uncontrolled, it can be harmful and even deadly.

Control and knowledge are important elements for medicine people, who were called sorcerers by Bleek and Lloyd, and are referred to as shamans by most present-day authors. A shaman will learn how to activate the 'electricity' in a period of apprenticeship. The first few experiences may be so frightening that the person will not wish to try again, but those who persist learn to control and use the power.

Amongst the Kalahari San it is usually the women who start a dance by singing and clapping the rhythm of special medicine songs believed to have supernatural potency. The men then gradually start dancing around the fire near the seated women, and the ritual begins in earnest. As the dance increases in intensity, supernatural potency is said to 'boil' in the stomach and up the spine of a shaman until it explodes in his or her head. People in the Kalahari bend forward at the waist when this happens, as the diaphragm contracts painfully. The potency is thought to exit at the *n/au* spot at the base of the neck (Figure 9.5). The person then enters trance – an altered state of consciousness or the spirit world – and may collapse into unconsciousness. They are said to 'die'; the word for 'death' amongst the /Xam and the Kalahari San is the same word used for deep trance. Dia!kwain (Bleek 1935:14) explained the concept by saying that sorcerers could bewitch people so that they 'die without feeling ill'.

Healers are able to control the level of their trance so that they do not fall unconscious. Kalahari healers take sweat from their armpits and

Figure 9.5: *Rock painting from the Western Cape showing lines coming from the nape of the neck, the* n/au *spot, of a cloaked figure. /Xam San informants remarked that the medicine men or shamans wore cloaks because they shivered.*

mucus or blood from the nose and lay their hands on the sick to draw out what is harming them. They then expel the sickness, sending it back to the spirits of the dead from whom it came. Some use the metaphor of 'arrows of sickness', believing that arrows causing illness are drawn out of the sick person. Some /Xam referred to them as 'sticks' or perceived the illness as having animal connotations. The words 'snoring' or 'sneezing' emphasise the use of nasal blood or mucus; biting and beating were also used to expel the illness.

//Kabbo gave the following graphic description of a healer (Bleek 1935:1–2): 'He (the sorcerer) sniffs at a person with his nose, as the man lies; then he beats (? the air). He bites people with his teeth; when other people seize him with their hands, then he bites the other people. The others hold him down and rub his back with fat, as he beats. Then he leaves off beating, because he is a sorcerer; that is why he beats when he is snoring a person with his nose (to cure the person). Lion's hair comes out on his back, people rub it off with fat, they rub pulling the hair out ... Then the man (the patient) gets up, because he is well ... They sit drinking there, he lies down, because he is well.'

/Han#kass'o gave further details (Bleek 1935: 2–3): 'A sorcerer acts like this, a sorcerer or sorceress, when he snores a person, takes a lion out (of the patient), and then he bites people ... Then people give him buchu to smell, and he sneezes the lion out. Then he takes out harm's things (from the other person). They call them bits of wood, for the things are like sticks. They were very pretty when I used to see them. These he sneezes out nicely.'

As Dia!kwain explained (Bleek 1935:23–4), the healer had to be helped by others when he returned from a 'magic expedition'. They would notice that his vertebral artery had risen up and that he was trembling: 'The people by singing make his vertebral artery lie down ... for he would turn into a lion if they did not ... for if a sorcerer's bloodvessels do not lie down, he grows hair, he becomes a beast-of-prey, he wants to bite people ... So they quickly make him smell buchu.'

These few extracts show how hair was closely associated in /Xam thought with lions and, by extension, with the activities of shamans. For example, they used their word for hair, /kuken, instead of the usual word for lion, //kha, when they

were hunting and also at night so that the lion would not know they were talking about him. In a similar association, Lorna Marshall (1969) notes that the !Kung believe that the potency which 'boils' up a shaman's spine goes into his hair. If a trancer, at the height of his frenzy, thrusts his head into the fire, the potency is released. She also found that the !Kung believe //Gauwa, or God, has long black or yellow hair, perhaps an expression of his potency (Marshall 1962). These associations of hair help to explain why rock paintings of trancing figures, especially those transformed or partly transformed into animals, often have hairs carefully drawn on their legs and backs.

Shamans who did not perform well lost the respect of others and were therefore not paid for their services. Dia!kwain (Bleek 1935:19–20) spoke about a sorceress named /Kwara-an who healed him 'when she snored me, took something out of my liver ... while blood came from her nose'. She told him that she had been weakened after a fight with her husband and as a result she could 'not smell out quickly where the mischief used to be'. Consequently, people no longer came to her to heal them and she had therefore lost much of her power.

Dancing and trance

In the 1950s and 1960s, typically almost half the men and about a third of the women in any group of Kalahari San would have said they were shamans. Shamans are treated like everyone else and have no special privileges, although they do enjoy considerable respect and may become well known for their powers beyond their immediate family. A person wishing to become a shaman goes to an experienced trancer and asks to be taught the techniques. For some years the pupil will learn from the mentor and may also receive potency from him or her. Qing spoke of this as 'initiation' and said that small, invisible 'arrows of potency' were shot into the novice. Dia!kwain (Bleek 1935:11–12) spoke of the sorcerer as a teacher when he gave his explanation of a copy of a rock painting from the Eastern Cape which George Stow had made in 1867 (Figure 9.6):

'They seem to be dancing, for they stand stamping with their legs. This man who stands in front seems to be showing the people how to dance; that is why he holds a stick, for he feels that he is a

Figure 9.6: *George Stow's copy of a rock painting near Tarkastad, published in 1930.*

great man. So he holds the dancing stick, because he is the one who dances before the people, that they may dance after him, for the people know that he is the one who always dances first, because he is a great sorcerer. That is why he dances first, because he wants the people who are learning sorcery to dance after him ... For when a sorcerer is teaching us, he first dances the *//ken* dance, and those who are learning dance after him as he dances. When a sorcerer is teaching us, when his nose bleeds, he sneezes the blood from his nose into his hand, he makes us smell the blood from his nose.'

There is no evidence that the Kalahari San use hallucinogens regularly, though a student shaman may smoke some marijuana to go into trance for the first time. Otherwise they achieve ecstasy through prolonged rhythmic dancing and singing, intense concentration and hyperventilation. An apt pupil will eventually be able to enter trance and visit the spirit world, but about half of those who try to become shamans fail. A northern San man explained to Richard Lee just how hard it is to break through the barrier: '*N/um* [potency] is not an easy thing. It is extremely difficult. As the *n/um* starts to build up inside you, the pain is

intense. You are gasping for breath. You feel as if you are choking. The boys are afraid; they fear what will happen to them next' (Lee 1979:111).

Although Qing did not know all the 'secret things' because he had not been initiated, his description of the dance has some interesting parallels with the record made by Lee, even though the two accounts are a hundred years and more than a thousand kilometres apart: 'It is a circular dance of men and women, following each other, and it is danced all night. Some fall down; some become as if mad and sick; blood runs from the noses of others whose charms are weak, and they eat charm medicine, in which there is burnt snake powder. When a man is sick, this dance is danced round him, and the dancers put both hands under their arm-pits, and press their hands on him, and when he coughs the initiated put out their hands and receive what has injured him – secret things' (Orpen 1874:10).

Pieter Jolly (1994) has examined Qing's statements, and the paintings to which he referred, in some detail and has compared them with information about initiation rituals amongst Sotho and Nguni men and with historical records of their mutual interaction. He concludes that the complex imagery of the paintings at Melikane and upper Mangalong in eastern Lesotho show postures, animal headdresses and artefacts that represent a mixture of San and Nguni–Sotho ritual concepts and practices. Such symbiotic relationships are likely to have occurred elsewhere in southern Africa as well and have certainly added to the regional variety in San rock art.

Altered states of consciousness

In the rock art, the curing dance and the sensations felt by shamans when receiving potency are encoded in the postures of the human figures and in associated images. John Parkington, Tony Manhire and Royden Yates have analysed the processions of people in cloaks that are common in the rock art of the Western Cape and interpreted them as initiates. Both in the Western Cape and elsewhere in southern Africa, there are paintings of women clapping and people dancing in a circle that illustrate the dance itself. Participants often carry fly-whisks; these are said to be indispensable for curing dances because they are used to remove the arrows of sickness. Bags are often placed next to clapping or dancing people, presumably because they contain 'medicine'. People shown bending forward from the waist are experiencing

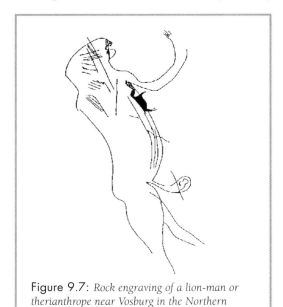

Figure 9.7: *Rock engraving of a lion-man or therianthrope near Vosburg in the Northern Cape. The original is nearly 1 m long.*

the boiling energy described to Katz. There are numerous paintings of people with blood, mucus or other liquid coming from the nose; potency from the *n/au* spot is depicted by a line drawn from the nape of the neck. Both tall, stretched-out figures and tiny people exhibit sensations felt during trance. People shown in a horizontal position are shamans who have collapsed into unconsciousness. People touching others are probably curing. The close association of birds and fish is indicative of the sensation that trancers report of feeling so light they could fly, or feeling as though they are under water. These metaphors are well illustrated in the Linton rock art panel on permanent display in the South African Museum in Cape Town. It was taken from a rock shelter in the Eastern Cape earlier this century and has been analysed by David Lewis-Williams (1988).

For the purposes of rock art interpretation David Lewis-Williams and Thomas Dowson have summarised Siegel's research into the experiences of people from a variety of ethnic backgrounds in different countries around the world who have taken hallucinatory drugs. They have described three stages of trance. In the first, the subject sees patterns of light, or 'entoptics', such as grids, wavy lines, dots, vortices, nested U-shapes and zigzags. In the second, animals or objects that have significance for the person will be seen. In the case of San it may be the eland or another source of potency; in the case of Native Americans it may be a bear or an eagle. In the third stage there is a merging of images in stages one and two; for example, zigzags may be imposed on eland, or the person feels drawn into the spirit world and believes that he or she is becoming an animal or is otherwise transformed. Dia!kwain, for example, said that the lion 'often turns into a person' (Bleek 1932:61) and the rock engraving in Figure 9.7 is one illustration of this phenomenon. Paintings of people with animal heads or hooves, or of animals with human legs, are fairly common and are referred to as 'therianthropes' (Figure 9.8).

Rain-making

Dia!kwain, /Han#kass'o and Qing all commented on paintings and engravings that illustrated rain animals, although the form of these animals varied from an enigmatic rain animal of ill-defined form

Figure 9.8: *Rock painting from the Western Cape: elongated black therianthropes with wildebeest heads bending from the waist. (Tracing by Stephen Townley Bassett)*

to a 'water-bull', a 'snake' and a 'caterpillar'. Swallows, locusts, snakes, tortoises, lions and the agama lizard were also linked with rain, but not necessarily to rain-making. Rain would not fall if frogs were killed or if a fire was made. //Kabbo differentiated between gentle 'she-rain', which was generally preferred, and the destructive 'he-rain', which was accompanied by thunder and lightning.

The common theme described by the /Xam was that a rain-maker would enter trance and collapse when his spirit left his body. His spirit would capture the rain animal in a water hole, in a kloof or on a mountain and lead it across the veld. He would kill it, and where the blood or milk fell, the rain would fall too. This was not a real event, but an hallucination in the mind of the rain-maker, who may have 'seen' any one of a variety of potent images during the quest for rain. Yet it was so convincing – and successful – that Nguni agriculturists in the nineteenth and early twentieth centuries are known to have consulted San rain-makers and to have paid them for their services. The paintings that illustrate such events show fat animals, sometimes being led by a thong, often surrounded by people, some of whom are therianthropes or are

otherwise transformed. Others illustrate both ordinary and fantastic creatures surrounded by zigzags, lines, fish, snakes and other images.

Animals with potency

The power or potency that the San wanted to acquire came from God. The trickster-deity who 'made everything' was /Kaggen (spelled 'Cagn' by Orpen), who could take many forms. Most of the time he was an ordinary man whose wife was the Dassie, his daughter the Porcupine and his son-in-law the Ichneumon or Mongoose, but he had supernatural powers and could change into many forms such as a mantis, snake, eland, hartebeest and even a hare. He was essentially beneficial, but also played tricks and caused trouble.

/Kaggen's favourite animal was the eland. The /Xam said he created it in a water pool and Qing said he created it in a secluded kloof, but essentially the event was closely connected to water. Supernatural power could be accessed through the eland because it was believed to have more fat than any other animal and for this reason it played a central role in rituals. For a boy to become a man

Figure 9.9: *Rock painting from the Eastern Cape showing a dying eland. Note that the eland is painted upside-down and there is blood coming from the nose.*

he had to kill an eland; for a girl to become a woman an eland dance was performed; and eland were closely connected with marriage rituals and rain-making.

The importance of the eland is reflected in the fact that it is the most commonly depicted animal in the rock paintings and engravings in South Africa. It is lovingly shown in a wide variety of postures, not because the artists wanted to kill and eat it, but because it was revered and respected. One of the postures commonly selected shows the eland with its head lowered, blood or mucus streaming from its nose or mouth, the hair on its neck standing erect, and flecks of paint suggesting that it is sweating profusely. It is a graphic portrayal of a dying animal which in real life would eventually collapse (Figure 9.9). Lewis-Williams regards the eland as a metaphor for the 'dying' shaman, who, when entering trance, will also stagger, may bleed from the nose, sweats profusely, feels a tingling sensation as if hair is growing on the body, and eventually collapses into an altered state of consciousness. Eland features are also most frequently combined with those of humans in images of therianthropes.

Research into the hallucinations experienced by people in altered states of consciousness gives some insight into the phenomenon of therianthropes. David Lewis-Williams and Thomas Dowson recount the experiences of a man who took drugs, and was subsequently interviewed by a psychologist as part of a research programme in the 1960s in the United States. Siegel and Jarvik (1975:105) described one of these experiences: 'I thought of a fox, and instantly I was transformed into that animal. I could distinctly feel myself a fox, could see my long ears and bushy tail, and by a sort of introversion felt my complete anatomy was that of a fox.' San shamans had much the same kind of experience, as indeed do all people wherever they live in the world. By concentrating on an animal which one believes to be important as a source of power, anyone who undergoes the appropriate training can feel that they are changing into that animal. One can also feel stretched out and taller than one really is, or feel that one is very tiny. Rock paintings illustrate these hallucinations in a wide variety of combinations of animal and human features, in images of very tall thin people (see Figure 9.8), as well as in paintings of very tiny figures.

Placement of rock art

The placement of most religious art is as significant as its content. By virtue of its situation in a place such as a temple, church or mosque, both the message and the importance of the place are enhanced. San rock art is no exception, although the details of this significance are not always evident. In general both the rock paintings and rock engravings are placed in positions that are easily visible. Occasionally a painting will be found tucked under a boulder, or in a dark crack in the rock, or even on the ceiling of a rock shelter. Even more rarely, an engraving may be found in the dark recesses of a limestone cavern or on a boulder far removed from others on the slope of a hill.

Not all rock shelters that are painted were occupied by Stone Age people, and not all occupied shelters have paintings. By the same token, one does not invariably find evidence of people having camped at or near to rock engravings in the open veld. This suggests that the images were meant to be seen and that there were no taboos that limited access to them. The decision about where to place them seems, though, to have been made at two levels.

The first of these is the decision to use rock as the 'canvas'. David Lewis-Williams and Thomas Dowson have argued that this was no accident. The rock is seen as a 'veil' between the artist and the spirit world, onto which the images that are first perceived in hallucination are later painted or engraved. During training to become shamans, some Native Americans described a period of initiation known as a vision quest, when they would undergo a period of seclusion and sensory deprivation, often enhanced by hallucinogenic drugs, in order to 'see' the animal that would become their spirit helper. When they concentrated on rock or on the wall of a rock shelter, the images would appear to come out of the rock and were later painted on it to re-create the vision.

Lewis-Williams and Dowson (1990) cite a number of examples of San rock paintings in which images of snakes, eland, other antelope and even humans come out of, or go into, cracks in the rock. In other instances both rock engravings and paintings are given a three-dimensional quality by the clever incorporation into the image of bumps, hollows and even natural stains in the rock. The placement of paintings on top of others may support the notion that images were 'seen' to come out of the rock.

The second decision is which rock or rock shelter in the landscape to engrave or paint. There is good reason to believe that certain sites were regarded as well placed for rituals like rain-making, while others may have been used for initiation ceremonies or were places where visions were seen or important events took place. The great variety of images in some places suggests that they may have been important for different reasons at different times in the past and may have been used as aggregation sites. As the example from the Strandberg shows, however, we will not know the reasons for these decisions without some written records.

Rock art conservation

Rock paintings and rock engravings are especially vulnerable to vandalism because they are so visible and accessible. For this reason they need special consideration in conservation programmes, particularly if they occur in public parks and reserves where large numbers of people visit them. Visitors to rock art sites should be careful not to kick up dust and should never touch painted or engraved surfaces. Never put water or any other substances onto either paintings or engravings. Although water may enhance the colour of paintings for the benefit of photography, it ultimately leads to the deterioration of the paint.

CHAPTER TEN

Khoekhoen and the introduction of domestic animals

In 1961 Dr Tom Barry took over as Director of the Albany Museum in Grahamstown from the zoologist Dr John Hewitt, who had been at the museum since 1910. Archaeology had been a hobby of Dr Hewitt's and he had done some valuable pioneering work in the 1920s and 1930s. After a devastating fire in the museum in the 1940s, the archaeological collection had been literally stuffed into a back room. When we joined the staff of the museum in 1963, it was our job to unpack this 'chamber of horrors' and to create some order in the collection. Although the lack of information about many of the boxes was frustrating, we learned a great deal about the archaeology of the Eastern Cape from Hewitt's collection and were especially impressed with the number of sites at which plant remains had been preserved.

In July 1963 the Department of Water Affairs began planning a dam on the Gamtoos River west of Port Elizabeth. The engineer in charge, Mr Alexander, reported to the Historical Monuments Commission the existence of a cave that was in the path of a new road to the dam, and Mr Berry Malan inspected it. He noticed a rich horizon of plant material in the cave deposit and asked Dr Barry if we could do a test excavation. We camped in an orchard belonging to the landowner, Mr Scott, and spent two weeks excavating a lens of occupation debris that had been preserved almost as well as a herbarium collection because it was sandwiched between layers of rockfall. As a result of our first joint research report, published in the Annals of the Cape Provincial Museums *a few months later, the road was realigned to save the deposit.*

We were fortunate that the herbarium of the Botanical Research Institute was housed at the Albany Museum because it brought us into contact with the botanist Michael Wells. He was amazed to discover that some of the plant fragments from Scott's Cave were better preserved than the scientifically pressed specimens of much lesser antiquity in the herbarium. His meticulous identifications and analysis pioneered the study of archaeological plant remains.

Although we did not realise it at the time, the Scott's Cave excavation was the first in South Africa to yield the remains of sheep in a stratified Later Stone Age context. As with many sites of its kind, the small number of sheep remains makes it difficult to say categorically whether it was occupied by herders who owned the sheep or by hunter-gatherers who acquired sheep from their neighbours. However, it does demonstrate without a doubt that people with domesticated sheep and pottery were living in the Eastern Cape more than a thousand years ago. This chapter summarises the archaeological evidence for the change from hunting and gathering to herding.

It comes as a surprise to many to realise that the Khoekhoe herders had been in South Africa for almost 1500 years before the first European sailors rounded the Cape in the late fifteenth century. Their sheep and cattle were a major attraction for the Dutch East India Company when they set up a supply station at the Cape of Good Hope in 1652.

From the archaeological and linguistic record it appears that the herding way of life was adopted quite rapidly once it was first introduced. People moved southwards from Botswana and gradually acculturated hunter-gatherer people living in South Africa (Figure 10.1). Sheep and pottery reached the southern end of Africa within a few centuries.

These first herders introduced sheep and, later, cattle and domesticated dogs as well as the art of pottery-making. They recruited some of the hunter-gatherers with whom they came in contact, and they established a working relationship with those who preferred to remain hunter-gatherers. They would also have come in contact with siNtu-speaking Iron Age agriculturists in the eastern half of the country. Figure 10.2 gives a broad overview of the distribution of the main Khoekhoe groups and the documented trade links between them and some of the siNtu- (Bantu-) speakers in the late seventeenth century.

Some early historians and anthropologists speculated that the Khoekhoen had migrated from East and even North Africa, and others said that Chinese travellers had contributed to their gene pool. Biological tests show no evidence to support either these or more recent claims of influence from India. Instead, they strengthen the view that the Khoekhoen and San shared the same ancient southern African genetic heritage. Furthermore, linguistic information studied by Ernst Westphal, Tony Traill and others shows unequivocally that the Khoe or 'Hottentot' languages are more closely related to the hunter-gatherer San languages than to languages spoken by any other people. We can confidently state that the ancestors of the Khoekhoen and the San were an indigenous population that originated and diversified within southern Africa.

Despite common roots, language remained one of the traits that set most San hunter-gatherers apart from the Khoekhoe herders, even in colonial times. There were only two variations of Khoe, the

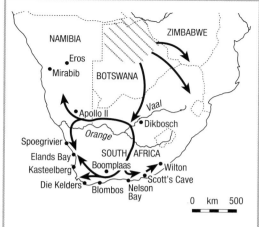

Figure 10.1: *Possible routes taken by herders moving southwards from Botswana. (After Elphick 1977)*

Western and Eastern, and of these only three languages in the Western group, Nama, !Ora (Korana) and Xiri, were still spoken by a small number of people in the mid-twentieth century.

Because of the biological and linguistic similarities between San and Khoekhoen, early European settlers and travellers were often unable to classify individuals they met as 'Bushman' hunters or 'Hottentot' herders and sometimes took the easy way out by referring to them as Bushman-Hottentots. The stereotype of a 'Hottentot' was someone who was taller than a 'Bushman' and who lived mainly on the products of herding sheep and cattle. The person would have been a member of a group of between 50 and 200 or more people who lived in mat-covered houses and moved with their stock to obtain the best grazing in an annual round, carrying their possessions on the backs of oxen. The stereotype of a 'Bushman' was of a short, even tiny person with a small face and high cheekbones who lived in a brush shelter with a nuclear family group of 12–25 people. Such a person was said to live 'close to nature', and either existed entirely on hunting and gathering or stole sheep and cattle from farmer neighbours. The reality was much more complex, not only amongst people who lived as neighbours or in different geographical regions, but also amongst successive populations that were affected by social and other factors.

As the historian Shula Marks, the archaeologist

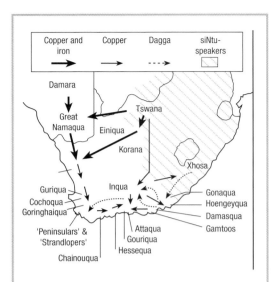

Figure 10.2: *Distribution of Khoekhoe 'tribes' in the seventeenth century. Arrows indicate the trade network amongst and between the Khoekhoen and siNtu agriculturists such as the Tswana and Xhosa. (After Elphick 1977)*

Carmel Schrire and others have pointed out, the 1500-year period of living alongside each other brought about a very different social and economic situation from that which had prevailed when herders first moved southwards. As the written records show, Europeans met a wide spectrum of people, who at one extreme were dedicated hunter-gatherers and wanted to maintain their status without accumulating wealth, and who at the other extreme were well established as successful herders. In the middle were individuals in an intermediate situation. Sometimes they were hunters working for herders so as to obtain meat for their families. Sometimes they had married out of a hunting and into a herding group or vice versa. And sometimes they were herders who had lost their livestock and were in the process of acquiring animals again.

If there was such a broad range of identities between herder and hunter-gatherer, what is the purpose of trying to recognise one or the other? Categorisation of people as herders or hunter-gatherers was a historical trend that polarised and stereotyped Khoisan economies at a time when it was considered interesting to do so. Oppositions

like these are devised so that comparisons can be made when cultural and economic changes are evaluated, for example when testing for the presence of hunters or herders. But the method is complicated by the fact that there is no invariable correlation between the physical appearance of a person, the language he or she speaks, and the economy and social structure of the group to which he or she belongs. It is also questionable whether hunters and herders are invariably recognisable by the artefacts they made. Thus, although individuals chose the lifestyle they preferred, there were both hunter-gatherer and herder groups that kept separate identities in the western half of South Africa for at least a thousand years. This implies that there were indeed social and economic differences between herders and hunter-gatherers that many people chose to maintain, but that there was also a wide range of choices open to individuals.

What it means to be a herder

The change from being a hunter-gatherer to becoming a herder is much more than a change in diet from venison to lamb. Karl Marx called it a change in the 'means of production' and it has a number of important social and economic consequences.

Perhaps the most significant consequence is the accumulation of wealth in the form of livestock, which could be and was inherited by the next generation. Most herding communities do not breed their animals only for food. Many will use them primarily for milk and exchange and will slaughter them only for ritual and ceremonial occasions, relying instead on game and wild plant foods for their staple diet. By investing time and effort in breeding and caring for their flocks and herds, the Khoekhoen were postponing the returns from this investment so that the benefits could be felt by their children and by the community as a whole. It gave them a form of security that hunter-gatherers did not have, even if they regularly acquired a few sheep or cattle for the pot. It is not quite the same as the difference between sharing your entire salary every month with your family and friends and setting aside a portion to invest for your pension and your children, but such an analogy helps to highlight some of the adjustments required.

One of the social adjustments is that some

people will accumulate more wealth than others; this wealth will bring them prestige and standing in the community. These individuals achieve status while others remain workers without the power to make decisions for the group as a whole. This is very different from an egalitarian hunter-gatherer community in which everyone has an equal say because they all have equal access to resources. A man moving from a hunter-gatherer to a herder community would therefore have to accept subservient status until he could work to accumulate wealth and prestige. It was especially difficult to break into the system. Most of the men in a village community were descended from the same male ancestor and they married women from other clans. A man who was unrelated to them would therefore have been a stranger. A woman from a hunter-gatherer group, on the other hand, would have stood a better chance of breaking into herder society than a man would. It was socially acceptable (and a lot cheaper) for Khoekhoe men to marry San women, but San men could only marry Khoekhoe women if they had acquired sufficient cattle to pay the bride price.

In the Western Cape in the seventeenth century, we know from historical records that men from hunting and gathering groups who wished to become herders could become servants or 'clients' of a Khoekhoe family. They were responsible for looking after the flocks, especially during seasons when these had to be taken to grazing lands some distance from the camp. They were paid for their labour in sheep or goats and may in this way have accumulated a few animals of their own. Emile Boonzaier and his co-authors of the book *The Cape Herders* have suggested, however, that it was in the interests of the rich and powerful to keep the poorer people poor. As a result not many hunter-gatherers would have been able to switch successfully to herding without subterfuge. They conclude that it was this poorer class of people – who did not want to remain hunter-gatherers, but who had not yet acquired the wealth and status to be herders – that was initially exploited most successfully for labour by the European colonists.

The accumulation of wealth and the consequent stratification of society are accompanied by a fundamental change in mind-set. Herders, just like hunter-gatherers and all other communities, need to justify their actions through beliefs and rituals that specify what is right or wrong and acceptable or unacceptable behaviour. This belief system or

Figure 10.3: *A typical mat-covered hut used by Nama in the Northern Cape in the 1980s.*

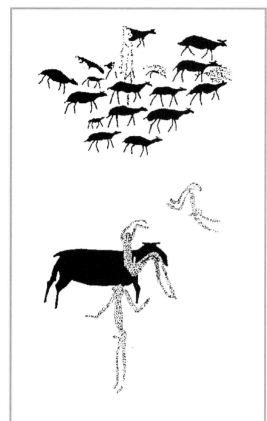

Figure 10.4: *Rock paintings of fat-tailed sheep from the Western Cape (above) and thin-tailed sheep from the Northern Province (below). (Tracings by Stephen Townley Bassett and Ed Eastwood)*

ideology is seen by many as the major barrier that discouraged and even prevented people brought up as hunter-gatherers from switching to herding. It is used as an argument against the suggestion that individuals were able to move within their lifetime from hunting and gathering to herding and back again as their economic situation changed. Yet the history of the world is full of examples of human adaptability and entrepreneurship alongside examples of conservatism and resistance to change. There is no need to imagine that the history of the Khoekhoen and the San was any different. At the level of individual choice there were probably many people who made the change effortlessly from San hunter-gatherer to Khoekhoe herder. At a community level, however, the integ-

rity of the two economies, social organisations and belief systems remained largely intact. This is eloquent evidence that a form of symbiosis worked successfully to sustain both the hunter-gatherer and herder lifestyles in some parts of the South African landscape for at least 1500 years after the first herders brought sheep south of the Limpopo and Orange rivers.

A similar symbiosis did not work as well between the Khoekhoen and European colonists for any length of time. As historians like Hermann Giliomee, Richard Elphick, Susan Newton-King and Robert Ross have shown, it took less than a century for Khoekhoen to be integrated into the wider Cape colonial society. Individuals joined either the underclass as labourers or became indistinguishable members of the burgher community through intermarriage. Herder groups, however, lost their leaders, stock and cohesion. Within the borders of South Africa today, a few Nama communities still retain some of their old traditions and language (Figure 10.3), while in Namibia there are about 100 000 Nama-speakers. Only a handful of elderly South Africans still remember words and sentences in !Ora, Griqua and #Khomani.

Aside from the social and economic results of herding, another important consequence is the effects of a change in diet. In well-managed herding communities, dairy products like milk, butter and cheese are available almost throughout the year. All hunter-gatherers, on the other hand, suffer from seasonal scarcities and nutritional stress. Milk enables herders, and especially their children, to overcome such shortages and to develop continuously. The Dutch settlers remarked on the fact that the Soaqua hunter-gatherers were generally much shorter than their Khoekhoe counterparts in the Western Cape. This difference in stature could be largely eliminated when children had the benefit of milk. The knowledge that herding could overcome seasonal stress must have been a major reason for individuals to change their economic status.

The details of the process of integration of the Khoekhoen into both urban and frontier colonial environments have been investigated at length by the historians already mentioned and are therefore not discussed further in this book. We focus instead on those aspects of Khoekhoe lifestyle that are visible archaeologically or that help us to interpret what has been found through archaeological methods.

Domesticated animals of the Khoekhoen

Sheep, which are indigenous to North Africa and the Near East but not to southern Africa, seem from the archaeological record to have been domesticated in Africa north of the Sahara between 8000 and 7000 years ago. In East Africa they have been found in deposits dating to about 4000 years ago, and in South Africa in sites of about 2000 years old. This means that it took about 5000 years for the practice of herding to filter southwards across the equator over a distance of about 2500 km. Once in Botswana and Zimbabwe it seems to have been adopted with alacrity and to have spread southwards to the southern Cape coast within 500 years or less over a similar distance.

Both the breeds that were seen in the Western Cape by the early European sailors were fat-tailed, with hair rather than wool. The Ronderib Afrikaner – the rams have a live weight of 60–80 kg – was kept by all Khoekhoe tribes except the Namaqua, and is closely related to the modern sheep breeds in East Africa. The Namaqua breed – the rams have a live weight ranging between 50 and 64 kg – was better adapted to drier conditions and sparse vegetation. The sheep kept by Iron Age farmers in the eastern half of South Africa had thin tails and genetically had more in common with the Namaqua breed than with the Ronderib Afrikaner. Rock paintings of both thin- and fat-tailed sheep can be seen in the Soutpansberg district of the Northern Province, but only the fat-tailed breed is represented in the rock art of the Northern, Western and Eastern Cape (Figure 10.4). The implication is that the Ronderib Afrikaner may have been introduced earlier than the Namaqua through a more direct route from East Africa than the later breeds kept by the Namaqua and the Iron Age farmers.

Young boys tended flocks of sheep during the day, driving them to suitable pasture and bringing them back in the evening. Khoekhoe women were responsible for milking ewes. Organisation of the flocks followed standard animal husbandry prac-

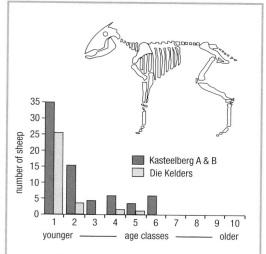

Figure 10.5: *The age distribution of sheep from Kasteelberg A and B and Die Kelders, showing that the majority in both cases were less than two years old when slaughtered. (After Klein 1986)*

tice: young rams were castrated and young lambs were kept penned away from their mothers except during milking times in the mornings and the evenings. They were allowed into the flock only after they had been weaned.

Written sources record that sheep were slaughtered only on special occasions. Archaeological evidence from Boomplaas Cave, Kasteelberg and Die Kelders shows that between 75 and 80 per cent of the sheep were less than 18 months old and most of these were lambs less than a year old. Angela von den Driesch and H.J. Deacon have compared the Boomplaas data with figures for the Maitland abattoir in Cape Town, where 70 per cent of the sheep delivered are less than a year old. Selective slaughtering of young animals is a viable management practice, and production of lamb is economic at this level. The archaeological evidence indicates therefore that Khoekhoe flocks were managed for maximum return from the earliest stages of herding in South Africa (Figure 10.5).

In rock paintings and engravings, sheep are the most commonly depicted domesticated animals. Images of sheep are found in small numbers in most areas where rock art occurs (Figure 10.6) and clearly show the fat tails in the west and thinner tails in the east. They are depicted in rock art

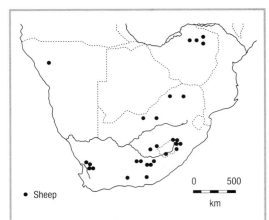

Figure 10.6: *Distribution of engravings and rock paintings showing sheep in southern Africa.*

attributable to the San as well as in the more recent 'late white' and 'finger' paintings attributed to herders and farmers. Unfortunately the art includes no insights into animal husbandry.

Cattle were domesticated in Anatolia and southeastern Europe between 9000 and 8000 years ago. There is also evidence for cattle in the eastern Sahara as early as 9000 years ago or even earlier. The faunal remains found here have been identified as *Bos primigenius*, which is indigenous to North Africa, where the non-domesticated species is known as the auroch or wild ox. Although it is not possible to be certain that the remains in archaeological sites are of domesticated animals,

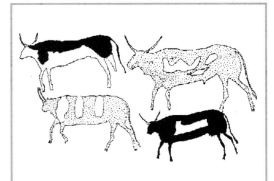

Figure 10.7: *Rock painting of Sanga-type cattle from KwaZulu-Natal. Compare the horns with the Afrikaner ox belonging to Namaqua in the painting by Daniell at the end of this chapter. (Tracing after Manhire* et al. *1986)*

Fred Wendorf and Romauld Schild conclude that they probably are. As with sheep, they were well established in herding communities in East Africa before they were adopted by people south of the equator about 2500 years ago.

There is historical and archaeological evidence for two breeds of cattle in South Africa at the time of European contact, the Afrikaner and the Sanga, both of which tend to be reddish brown with a pronounced hump behind the head and very large horns. The horns of the Afrikaner turn downwards as they leave the skull whereas the Sanga horns turn upwards. The Sanga seems to have been more common in the eastern half of South Africa amongst the siNtu-speaking agriculturists whereas the Afrikaner is associated mostly with the Khoekhoe herders (Figure 10.7).

Despite the fact that thousands of cattle were kept by Khoekhoen in the Western Cape in the latter half of the seventeenth century, they do not feature at all in rock paintings in the region, but are fairly common in the eastern half of South Africa (Figure 10.8). The archaeological evidence for cattle in the form of bones and teeth is sparse in the Western Cape, and the earliest evidence for cattle is found in deposits that are a few hundred years younger than the earliest deposits with sheep.

Early written records remark on the great affection the Khoekhoen had for their cattle; breeding stock was highly prized. Each animal had a name and was trained to answer to a whistle. Oxen were used as pack animals and were ridden as well. H.P. Steyn has estimated that although communally owned stock numbers were high, each Cochoqua family of eight would probably have had less than 45 head of cattle and about 90 sheep.

Goats and dogs were rarely painted or engraved. Goats seem to have been introduced into Khoekhoe herding practice later than sheep, and possibly also later than cattle, although they are present in Iron Age sites in the eastern half of the country from as early as AD 800. The bones of domesticated dogs have been found in several Iron Age sites but have seldom been positively identified in Khoekhoe sites. However, the remains of a dog from a shell midden dated to c. 1150 BP at Cape St Francis indicate that the Khoisan kept dogs. Some of the earliest of the European visitors to the Cape heard dogs barking and saw them working with the stock. Drawings and descriptions, as well as a few rock paintings, indicate that they were related to the same greyhound strain kept by Iron Age farmers in eastern and southern Africa.

Material culture

The material culture of the Khoekhoe herders can be regarded as the final stage of the Later Stone Age in archaeological terms, although if European technological terms are applied, it may be regarded as early Neolithic. Unlike the portion of the Later Stone Age previous to 2000 years ago, herder material culture included transitional elements between Stone Age and metal age technology, and would no doubt have developed independently into an 'Iron Age' had European settlement been unsuccessful.

Khoekhoen who were living in the Western Cape at the time of first European contact in the late fifteenth century possessed metal spears and arrowheads. From the evidence we have to date, it appears that the Khoekhoen did not mine and smelt iron themselves, but mined and worked copper. They acquired iron in the form of nuggets or ingots from neighbouring siNtu-speaking Iron Age agriculturists north of the Orange River and east of the Sundays River, and learned how to heat and beat it into the artefacts they wanted. Had they not known how to use iron, they might not have been so willing to exchange their sheep and cattle for a knife or a handful of tobacco or nails from passing ships. Khoekhoe guides took Governor Simon van der Stel in 1685 to the rich Namaqualand copper mines, where they had been exploiting the ore for some time; these mines were still yielding ore 300 years later.

In an attempt to recognise sites that were occupied by hunter-gatherers or herders, archaeologists over the past century have tried to identify traits that are exclusive to one group or the other. This has not been entirely successful because there is a wide spectrum of variation. In the middle of this spectrum are artefacts that were used by both. They included digging sticks and bored stone weights to retrieve underground plant foods, grindstones and mullers to grind harder plant foods, traps, bows and arrows for hunting, stone scrapers to work skins, twine for string and netting, and ornaments of ostrich eggshell, bone,

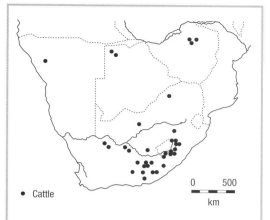

Figure 10.8: *Distribution of engravings and rock paintings showing cattle in southern Africa.*

ivory and marine shells. In addition, both groups collected shellfish, and fished and exploited seals and other marine mammals. The Khoekhoen had metal-tipped spears and arrows, but so did the San by the eighteenth century. Leather sandals made of thick hide were worn by Khoekhoen in several illustrations drawn by European visitors to the Cape. It is not possible to say with certainty, though, whether a child's sandal found in a rock shelter near Oudtshoorn was of San, Khoekhoe or early European manufacture (Figure 10.9).

The artefacts favoured more often by the Khoekhoen than the San were those connected with animal husbandry, such as pots for storing dairy produce. Herding was also reflected in the more extensive use of metal artefacts, in the layout of camp sites and features associated with the use of mat-covered huts, and of course in the associated faunal remains.

Stone tools

A question that has been posed by several archaeologists is whether there was also a consistent and detectable difference in the kinds of stone tools made by herders and hunter-gatherers. Andrew Smith has concluded that there are some suggestive correlations in the sites dating to between about 1800 and 300 years ago, which he has excavated in the west coast region of the Western Cape. At sites where formal stone tools are common, faunal assemblages have few or no sheep bones

Figure 10.9: *A child's leather sandal found in a rock shelter near Oudtshoorn early in the twentieth century.*

and a low incidence of pottery. It is therefore assumed they were occupied by hunter-gatherers. By contrast, sites with stone tool assemblages with few formal tools tend to correlate with large numbers of domesticated animal bones and quantities of pottery. The conclusion is that herders lived there. At these same sites there is also an interesting pattern in the size of ostrich eggshell beads: the 'hunter-gatherer' sites tend to have small beads, while the 'herder' sites tend to have larger ones.

This pattern does not seem to hold for all sites in South Africa, though. Formal tools occur with relatively large numbers of sheep bones and potsherds at Die Kelders and Byneskranskop; so it is not clear whether the sites were occupied by herders or by hunters. At Boomplaas Cave in the Cango Valley, however, the site was certainly used by early herders as a kraal, and here the artefacts are microlithic although there are few formal tools. On the other hand, Peter Beaumont and David Morris have shown a consistent correlation between their microlithic Swartkops industry and backed bladelets and grass-tempered (hunter) pottery, and between their Doornfontein informal industry and herder pottery.

To the south and east in the Seacow Valley in the Karoo, some 5000 Later Stone Age open sites with

pottery were studied by Garth Sampson and his students. They have established a sequence of changes in economic and social patterns and in pottery manufacture and decoration through time. Sampson concludes that herders were established in the valley between 1400 and 400 years ago. Making distinctive pottery with quartz temper, lugs, spouts, pointed bases and a red slip, they lived in the open around stone kraals. Their pottery is also found in a few rock shelters, where it is associated with Interior Wilton artefacts. The stone artefacts associated with Khoekhoe pottery at open kraal sites tend to be more informal. Formal Smithfield-type artefacts dating to the last 1000 years tend, on the other hand, to be associated with grass-tempered hunter-gatherer pottery.

The patterning may therefore be more complicated than simple correlations between a hunter-gatherer economy and formal stone artefacts, and between a herder economy and informal artefacts. There is the additional factor that both formal and informal stone tool assemblages are found without pottery well before the advent of herding, as has been documented by Lyn Wadley in the Magaliesberg, by Ray Inskeep at Nelson Bay Cave and by Johan Binneman in the Eastern Cape.

Instead of assuming that herders and hunters would have made different stone tools, we may more profitably ask what circumstances led to Stone Age people making informal stone tools rather than formal ones. One reason, as Lyn Wadley suggests, is that the activities carried out at a site may have required a different range of tools. Within the last 2000 years, another reason may have been that iron was preferred for making arrowheads and cutting tools. As with other artefacts, there was a spectrum of choices. Most situations required making choices in the middle of the range, regardless of whether the people were herders or hunter-gatherers. At a smaller number of sites the choice was making formal tools, whereas at an equally small number of sites the opposite choice was made.

Pottery

Pottery was introduced into southern Africa later than in any other part of the continent. The earliest dated potsherds in the continent come from north-eastern Africa nearly 10 000 years ago and

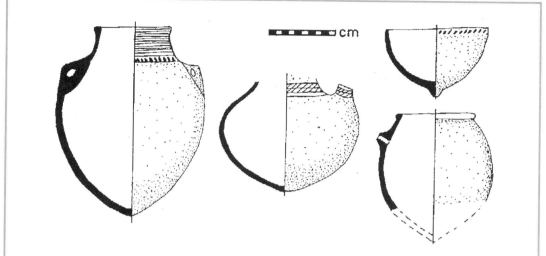

Figure 10.10: *Pottery commonly associated with herders in the western half of South Africa. Note the pointed bases, lugs, spouts and rim or neck decoration. (After Rudner 1968)*

about 7000 years ago from East Africa, where they are associated with early herding communities. Thereafter, pottery-making spread to West and Central Africa in the next two millennia, but it was only after 2500 years ago that it began to spread more than 5° South latitude.

Doubt has been cast on the assumption that the earliest pottery and sheep were associated. We know that herders used pots for cooking, for the preparation of seal oil and for storing their dairy produce, and that hunter-gatherers also made pots to cook their food. The style and manufacture of their pottery differed, though. Khoekhoe pots often had a pointed base and lugs and were made with quartz temper (Figure 10.10), but those made by hunter-gatherers were usually bowl-shaped and were often made with grass temper (Figure 10.11). It has been assumed that pottery was introduced into South Africa by the herders and that hunter-gatherers learned the technique from them. One might therefore expect that the earliest pottery and the earliest sheep would be broadly contemporary. Indeed until recently the archaeological evidence seemed to support this.

There was much excitement in the late 1960s when Frank Schweitzer excavated the Klipgat Cave at Die Kelders about 80 km west of Cape Agulhas, the southernmost tip of Africa. Here, in layer 12, he discovered the first stratified horizons

with sheep bones in South Africa. Only a few teeth and bones positively identifiable as sheep were found, but they were apparently associated with about 1000 potsherds. Radiocarbon dates were obtained on charcoal at the same level as the pottery and sheep, and suggested an age of about 1960 BP, or 10 BC. These dates were far earlier than had been expected for herding in this part of South Africa. During the 1970s several other sites

Figure 10.11: *A bowl with stamped decoration and grass temper typical of those associated with settlements of San hunter-gatherers.*

in the region also gave dates of around 1800 and 1900 years ago, but in each case there were only a few sheep teeth and bones in the lowest levels.

After excavating at Nelson Bay Cave, Ray Inskeep challenged these early dates. He checked the association between the sheep and the dated charcoal found at the same level, by dating the sheep bone directly. The result showed a discrepancy of 800 years between the charcoal at *c.* 1930 BP and the sheep bone at *c.* 1100 BP.

Similar tests were subsequently done on the earliest sheep remains from Die Kelders, Kasteelberg, Byneskranskop, Blombos and Spoegrivier and were reported by Judith Sealy and Royden Yates. All but Spoegrivier and Blombos showed a similar discrepancy, with Die Kelders sheep some 600 years younger than the apparently associated charcoal. But this discrepancy was not found at all sites. Despite these anomalies the earliest sheep are dated at *c.* 2105 BP in a rock shelter excavated by Lita Webley at Spoegrivier on the Namaqualand coast (Vogel *et al.* 1997). The next oldest are from Blombos on the southern Cape coast, at 1880 BP and 1960 BP. Paradoxically, Chris Henshilwood reports, the Blombos layer 6 sheep remains were not associated with pottery, although in the overlying layer 5 he found potsherds that radiocarbon dates showed were broadly contemporary. This is likely to be the result of sampling rather than a real absence of pottery at this time.

It is a bit more difficult to date potsherds directly, unless grass has been used for temper. As grass was used only with more recent pottery, we still rely on charcoal associated with potsherds for dates, although Sampson and Vogel (1995) have demonstrated that we can trust thermoluminescence dating on quartz grains in pottery that has been buried. The most reliable early dates for pottery are on associated charcoal from stratified sequences in which pottery occurs in quantity. Aron Mazel has summarised the early dates for pottery from ten rock shelters in the eastern half of South Africa. He concludes that although the oldest dates are between 2200 and 2300 years ago, it would be prudent to say that pottery was certainly being made in KwaZulu-Natal between 2100 and 2200 years ago. Yet not one of these early pottery assemblages is associated with sheep bones.

Another interesting anomaly is that the potsherds found in the oldest layers, both in the west-

ern and the eastern half of the country, are different from those in the more recent layers. The oldest sherds are not, as one might expect, more crudely made. They are finely made and generally quite thin and hard, with quartz temper and sometimes with a red slip. In the east the mean thickness of the early sherds is about 7 mm, whereas the more recent sherds that are associated with early Iron Age farming communities are on average about 12 mm thick. In the west, the contrast in thickness is not as marked, but the characteristic pointed bases and reinforced lugs tend to be less common in the earliest assemblages although the sherds themselves are thin and finely made.

The possibility of identifying different groups of people from the way in which they signalled their individuality with decorative patterns on their pottery has been the subject of a long-term study by Garth Sampson in the Seacow Valley between Richmond and Middelburg in the Karoo. He analysed nearly 66 000 potsherds from about 1000 Interior Wilton, Smithfield and Khoekhoe open sites and excavated rock shelters in the upper Seacow Valley, an area of about 2000 square kilometres. The Khoekhoe sites were identified by potsherds with a red slip, pointed bases, lugs and rims that usually had quartz temper. They were represented by nearly 10 000 sherds. The 7000 Smithfield potsherds were decorated and had grass temper or mixed grass and quartz. The rest of the sherds were undecorated and could not be clearly classified as either Khoekhoe or Smithfield. Sampson regards most of these as having been made and used by Interior Wilton hunter-gatherers.

Sampson and his colleagues have not only analysed the decoration on the potsherds, but have also examined the clays from which they were made. Grass-tempered cooking bowls were made of clays derived from dolerite, whereas the Khoekhoe pots with lugs and pointed bases were made with clays derived from shales (Bollong *et al.* 1997). There is clearer spatial patterning of these two types in the landscape than there is with the decorative motifs. This observation further supports the conclusion that the two kinds of pots were made by hunter-gatherers and by herders.

If Sampson's assumption is correct that the Khoekhoe sherds were made and used by the earliest herders in the valley, then herders were present in the Karoo at least by AD 700. They do not

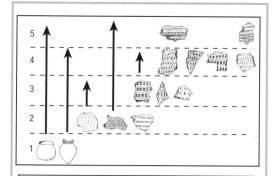

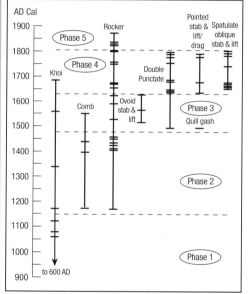

Figure 10.12: *Summary of pottery decoration phases (top) and of the direct radiocarbon and thermoluminescence dates for them (below) in the Seacow Valley between c. AD 600 and AD 1850. (After Bollong & Sampson 1996)*

appear to have stayed there permanently, however. Dating of the rock shelter sites with pottery and sheep bones, and of potsherds themselves, suggests that during the cold period known globally as the Little Ice Age in the late sixteenth century AD, conditions in the Karoo may have become unsuitable for both herders and hunter-gatherers. There are few traces of their presence in the valley. After conditions improved, only the hunter-gatherers appear to have returned permanently to the valley. By this time the herders were well estab-

lished on the coastal plain and in the southern Karoo. In the late seventeenth century Khoekhoe herders who called themselves Inquas were in control of the region to the south of the Seacow Valley known as the Camdeboo, and the Gonaquas were living further east in the Zuurveld.

The hunter-gatherers in the Seacow Valley, however, had steadfastly resisted change to a herder economy. European farmers began settling in the Seacow Valley from the late eighteenth century; by the mid-nineteenth century the takeover was all but complete. Thermoluminescence and radiocarbon dates on Khoekhoe-style pottery reported by Sampson show that it was made between AD 700 and AD 1700 in the Seacow Valley while grass-tempered hunter-gatherer pottery was made until the late nineteenth century (Figure 10.12).

Clothing

Another way in which herders signalled their identity in relation to hunter-gatherers was in their dress. If we can rely on illustrations and descriptions by early European visitors, the Khoekhoen were more likely to wear cowhide or sheepskin hats and cloaks whereas the San used the skins of indigenous animals. Illustrations of Khoekhoen around Cape Town in the early eighteenth century show them wearing sheepskin cloaks, heavy copper bracelets, anklets and necklaces. Khoekhoe 'chiefs' such as the Chainouqua leader Soeswa, who was in power at the time that the Dutch first settled at the Cape, wore a leopard-skin cloak. In the eighteenth century, Robert Gordon illustrated Namaqua wearing cloaks made of penguin pelts, which must have been spectacular to look at as well as a challenge to design and make (Figure 10.13).

H.P. Steyn's research on historical illustrations and texts has shown that, in general, most Khoekhoe men wore a loin cloth of soft leather with another piece of leather hanging down the back that looked a bit like a tail. The Dutch colonists called it a *staartriem* and it was sometimes decorated with copper or brass buttons. They also wore a string of ostrich eggshell, shell or, later, glass beads around the waist and, more occasionally, around the neck. Caps were quite common and were made of fur or leather, while many men threaded beads or small plates of copper in

Figure 10.13: *A painting by Robert Gordon in 1779 of Khoekhoe dancers and musicians in the Northern Cape. Note the mat-covered houses in the background. (Cape Archives)*

their hair. Other ornaments were worn round the wrists and ankles and were made of leather, iron or copper, ivory or beads. Leather sandals were made of thick hide. Fly-whisks, made from the tail of an animal like a jackal and occasionally from ostrich feathers, were sometimes carried as a sign of status. Leather bags held items of value.

Women tended to wear more clothing than men. They usually had two or three aprons in front, one of which was often decorated with beads, and a longer and wider skirt at the back. Their karosses were designed to carry children. They seem to have worn caps less often than men, but wore more ornaments in their hair. Many were richly adorned with beaded or decorated waist bands, necklaces, earrings, bangles and anklets made of ostrich eggshell beads, copper, ivory, shells, leather and seed pods (Figure 10.14).

Both men and women rubbed their skin with butter and fat, often mixed with ochre and buchu. They also painted their faces with red, black and white or yellow lines and spots. The fat was a sign of wealth and set them apart from hunter-gatherers. As Van Riebeeck expressed it in his diary after a meeting with the chief of the Cochoqua, fat was

the highest mark of distinction. This and the elaborate dress styles Van Riebeeck observed were undoubtedly an important reflection of the social transformation not only of hunter-gatherers to herders, but of herders to trading partners with Europeans.

Herder living sites

Apart from the presence or absence of the bones of domesticated animals, the size of ostrich eggshell beads and the style of pottery, the most obvious difference between living sites of herders and hunter-gatherers is their location. There were two kinds of herder sites. The main stations were situated where relatively large numbers of people could set up mat-covered houses and where kraals could be built for sheep and cattle. The location of these sites has been difficult to predict, however, and few have been found and excavated in detail. Large sites that were regularly revisited by the Khoekhoen were probably situated close to reliable water sources and were therefore subsequently used by Europeans for towns and mission stations. As a result any evidence of an earlier Khoekhoe presence has been destroyed. The second type of herder site, the stock posts, were much smaller and were occupied by small groups of people, mostly young men, who would care for the stock when they were sent out to better grazing. They were even more ephemeral than the main stations, but as they were sometimes in rock shelters a number of them have been found.

Garth Sampson's work in the Seacow Valley has linked Khoekhoe-style pottery with sites that have the remains of stone kraals; the majority of these do not have evidence for occupation by hunter-gatherers. Andrew Smith's research in the Western Cape has linked herders with open sites on the coastal plain where the grazing is good. The best-known of these is the site of Kasteelberg in the shelter of granite boulders near St Helena Bay.

Boomplaas Cave in the Cango Valley is one of the few cave or rock shelter sites where there is unequivocal evidence for herder occupation. The topmost deposit is a thick accumulation of burnt sheep dung with no cultural material associated with it. It is believed to date to the late eighteenth and early nineteenth centuries, when historical records indicate that the first European farmers in the valley used the cave as a sheep kraal. Beneath the burnt sheep dung is what has been called the DGL Member. This is composed of a series of thinner layers of burnt sheep dung interleaved with cultural units. The cultural units contain not only the burnt bones of sheep and small game animals, but also late Wilton stone artefacts, typical Khoekhoe-style pottery with lugs and pointed bases, ostrich eggshell beads, a copper bead and other artefacts, and large hearths packed with stones. A radiocarbon date on charcoal from a hearth in the uppermost of these herder levels places the occupation at about 1700 years ago. Perhaps this was a time when herders first came into the region and, under pressure from resident hunter-gatherers, or for want of a ready shelter, used the cave to protect their lambs at night.

Other cave sites like Scott's Cave, Die Kelders, Spoegrivier and Elands Bay have Khoekhoe pottery and the bones of sheep amongst the faunal remains, but there is no clear evidence that the sites were occupied by herders as stock posts or by hunter-gatherers. They likewise fall into the middle range of the spectrum of sites in the time period of the last 2000 years.

Figure 10.14: *Two seventeenth-century illustrations by European visitors of Khoekhoen in the Western Cape. Note the iron spear, copper leg bands, the pot and the cloaks. (Cape Archives)*

Herder ethno-archaeology

A valuable insight into the way in which Khoekhoe herders organised their camp sites was documented in a research project in Namaqualand in the 1980s. It was initiated by H.J. Deacon and H.P. Steyn through the Department of Archaeology at the University of Stellenbosch to obtain ethnographic information that could extend the research into the herder layers at Boomplaas. The work was completed by Lita Webley as an MA project. She focused on the Leliefontein Communal Reserve, which is based around a mission station established by the Rev. William Shaw in 1820 to protect the land rights of the Khoekhoen in Little Namaqualand. The descendants of the original

Figure 10.15: *Above: Painting by Samuel Daniell (1804) of Namaqua dismantling a mat-covered house and packing the mats and other goods on the back of an ox. Note the milk pails on the forked stick and the horns of the ox, which turn downwards. The photograph (below) is all that remained after a twentieth-century Nama family had moved their mat-covered house. (Photo: Lita Webley)*

Namaqua herders used to move with their sheep and goats during the year in a pattern dictated by scarce water resources and seasonally available pastures. In summer they lived in larger encampments, called stations or *stasies*, based around reliable water points; in winter they broke up into smaller groups and lived at stock posts, or *veeposte*. This pattern was modified with the establishment of the mission churches, schools and shops at some of the station sites. In some communities in the 1980s only the people responsible for the stock moved around in the winter.

The Leliefontein community used a series of stock posts within a radius of 15 km of the stations so that the herdsmen could visit their families at weekends. Although in the past between ten and fifteen huts may have been set up at a stock post, in the 1980s only one or two were noted. In addition to the huts, which were traditionally made with reed mats, each camp had a *kookskerm* or cooking shelter, usually a round enclosure made of small bushes packed together and kept in place with upright poles fixed in the ground. The cooking fire would be made there and the people would sit round the fire at mealtimes. Longer forked poles, called *n//a*, were stuck at the entrance to the enclosure and were used to hang belongings and meat out of reach of animals. In 1804 the artist Samuel Daniell visited the Namaqua and illustrated milk pails hanging from these poles too (Figure 10.15).

Stock posts generally had two kraals and a smaller one for lambs, all demarcated either by wire or by bushes. In some instances the walls were made of stone. Lita Webley excavated two old stock posts. Very little remained visible at either of them, but at both summer and winter sites she could trace stone for anchoring the huts, baked mud and dung hut floors, raised hearths in the cooking shelters, and dung in the kraal floors, if local conditions permitted. At Bethelsklip, in the shelter of large granite boulders reminiscent of Kasteelberg, there were traces of calcined dung like the deposit at Boomplaas, and hearth stones were found packed together. These observations reinforced what we already suspected from archaeological fieldwork in the south-western and southern Cape. Open stock-post sites seldom retain the traces of use. Evidence of the presence of herders in the landscape will probably continue to elude archaeologists unless their camps were located at sheltered places in rock shelters or around granite boulders that were visited and revisited many times.

A radiocarbon date from Bethelsklip of about 800 years ago suggests that it has been used as a stock post regularly for the past 1000 years. Both Kasteelberg and Boomplaas were used, however, for shorter periods. As Lita Webley has pointed out, the change in site use may well reflect a change in herding practices after the introduction of cattle.

The herder legacy

The ancestors of the people of Leliefontein were only one of hundreds of groups of Khoekhoen whose society was transformed once European traders, missionaries and farmers moved onto their land. In spite of the changes this brought to their material culture, Nama descendants have retained many customs from the past. Their herding practices still work as well today as they did hundreds of years ago. Adaptability has enabled them to switch to new tools and materials. This is testimony to their ability to make changes that improve the quality of life while retaining those elements of their living heritage that make life worth while.

Regrettably, very few Khoekhoe communities were as fortunate. The vast majority were unable to keep the integrity of their family units, and communities were destroyed. An inevitable consequence was the loss of knowledge of their language, customs and heritage. Since the Government of National Unity came to power in 1994, there has been a rekindling of interest in Khoekhoe heritage. We trust that when this matures, the results of archaeological research will become recognised as the most detailed information we have on the history of the earliest stock farmers in South Africa.

CHAPTER ELEVEN

Conserving heritage for the future

Promotion of Stone Age history as a legitimate field of study in schools was never a priority in former European colonial countries. Even now the perception has lingered that if something was not written down, it cannot be taught in schools.

This was a frustration for us as archaeologists in South Africa too, as we wanted to make the results of our work known to the public, but the opportunities were limited (see Mazel & Stewart 1987). Tim Maggs made a contribution in this respect during the 1980s when he advised the publishers Shuter and Shooter to include a more significant precolonial section in their Discovering History series (Sieborger et al. 1985). Other publishers have now broadened their vision and educational programmes on television include archaeology more often than in the past. The effects are beginning to snowball.

Appreciation and conservation of the archaeological heritage come through education, understanding and action. Interaction is important too because if Stone Age sites are to be promoted as tourist and educational facilities, both funding and management infrastructure are required.

Our personal interest in site museums was born when the Tsitsikamma National Coastal Park was established in the 1960s. It was a departure from the usual game reserve. There were no big animals to see, just a wild rocky coast fringed with mountains and having lots of fish in the sea. This was the beginning of ecotourism. At the mouth of the Storms River, there is a narrow cave that was occupied for a short period in the last few thousand years. We cut a section through the shell midden near the entrance to show the layers that formed as shells were piled on the heap. The artist and technician at the Albany Museum built a rust-proof display case and an information board was designed and completed.

Some twenty years later, Janette visited Nelson Bay Cave with archaeologists attending a post-conference excursion. When Richard Klein finished his excavations there in 1971, he had left the cutting open. The 4 m section had stood up well on one side, but on the other there was collapse that threatened to destroy some of the in situ *deposit. Richard obtained funding from the National Science Foundation to fill in the excavation, but the prospect of carrying enough sand down the hill to do the job was so daunting that the project was postponed.*

By happy coincidence, Mike Brett, the nature conservation officer in charge of the Robberg Nature Reserve in which the cave is situated, wanted to create a site museum there. When we went to assess the damage and the possibilities in 1991, his father, a retired building contractor, took a look round and said laconically, 'What this place needs is a brick wall.' Horrifying as the idea seemed at the time, it was an excellent solution. The wall supports three sides of the excavation and steps lead down into the excavation on the fourth side. Displays and a peel of the section explain the stratigraphy and describe the changes in artefacts, hunting patterns and shellfish collecting linked to sea-level changes over the past 120 000 years. The visitors' book shows that at least 80 per cent of the more than 10 000 people who signed the book in the past five years came from South Africa and about 10 per cent from Europe.

The Langebaan footprints presented a very different problem. In 1995 the geologist David Roberts found two and a half footprints preserved in Last Interglacial dune rock on the shore of the Langebaan Lagoon. As the oldest footprints of anatomically modern people yet found, they were featured in the September 1997 issue of National Geographic, *and then on the national news on SABC television. Initially, the National Monuments Council considered it unwise to move the rock to a museum as much of its significance lies in the setting. Unfortunately, however, the National Parks Board was unable to guard the site adequately during the holiday season and some damage was done to the surface.*

Luckily, the local press drew attention to the dilemma and the Engen petroleum company offered to assist. They sponsored the salaries of two security guards as well as the cost of an information board and pamphlet until a long-term solution could be found. It is gestures like these that make us hopeful for the sustained conservation of our Stone Age heritage. [JD]

The clues to South Africa's Stone Age history can be found in the hills and valleys, in the ground, and even in our genes and contemporary customs. This book is an introduction to the ways we can use to read those clues. They are secrets from the past that can be unravelled and interpreted through a learning process that is continually refined by research and debate.

One key to unlocking information about the history of our planet is uniformitarianism. This is the simple idea that the earth has been shaped in the past by the same geological processes that operate in the present. We can see wind and water etching away rocks and we can see streams and rivers carrying loads of soil down to the sea to form new sedimentary layers. There are volcanoes belching forth molten lava from deep in the hot earth. With drills we can probe into the crust of continents and the ocean floors and use the travel time of the shock waves of earthquakes to explore the innards of the earth to its very core. From all this has come an appreciation that over the aeons of geological time the surface of the earth, where plants and animals live, has been constantly changing. Continents have drifted on plates of the earth's crust across its surface and oceans have widened and shrunk. A knowledge of earth history is necessary to understand how habitats developed and provided for life in the sea, on land and in the air.

The key to unlocking information about life on earth is the idea of evolution. Again a simple idea, it proposes that there is a unity among all living organisms and that the great variety of life forms have developed in time through natural selection. It is logical to assume that creatures that look alike share more recent common ancestors than those that are not so alike. This can be shown to be the case by comparisons of gross anatomy and genes. Natural selection, which is descent with modification, produces the diversity we see in life, but without purposeful direction. A difficult pill to swallow is that rational humans are not the goal of evolution. Evolution is a game of chance with many twists and turns.

One of the twists in the history of life on earth highlights information unlocked by another key, fossil plants and animals. A missile from space struck the earth 65 million years ago and, as discussed in Chapter 2, the dust clouds thrown high into the atmosphere possibly caused the extinction of the dominant large vertebrates on earth, the dinosaurs, and heralded the rise of the mammals. Mice and men are mammals and the fact that the zoological order of the primates, to which people belong, has a mammal ancestry is something we cannot deny. We look like monkeys and apes because in the not-so-distant past we shared common ancestors with those animals.

Fossils allow us to track some of the turns that evolution has taken. Here again, chance plays a role as unusual conditions are needed for the preservation of fossils. There can never be enough fossils to give us an understanding of the full range of human ancestors, but crucial gaps are being filled by conscious search. Also providing details and complementary evidence are comparative studies of living primates. Evolutionary biology seeks answers to questions like why there was selection for larger brains in animals as different as baboons, chimpanzees and humans, and seeks to explain the benefits over the costs in survival and success of the species. In the example of brain size, Robin Dunbar has argued from evolutionary principles that the benefit of increased brain size lay in coping with the stresses of living in large groups and in the protection large groups afforded.

A concept central to the message of this book is that humans were not created different from other primates. Humans *became* different. There was a long apprenticeship as a two-legged ape-like australopithecine during the rise of humankind. If we had not found and dated the relevant fossils, who would have thought that such creatures once roamed the highveld of South Africa? Yet they did. Still fleeing to the trees in the face of danger, the australopithecines had not crossed the hurdle of dedicated ground-living. That is the rubicon that separates the man-apes from true humans. It was a precarious existence on the ground, but was enforced by Ice Age aridity, which reduced the diversity of forests and woodlands and expanded the shrublands and grasslands. Our ancestors who adopted stone artefacts as the means to cope have left a trail of evidence in the African landscape. As the oldest stone artefacts occur in Africa, we know that this is the continent where true humans emerged. The archaeological study of artefacts left in the landscape provides further keys to discovering the past.

At the earliest stage, true humans were restricted in their distribution to the African continent and only ventured into Eurasia little more than a million years ago. Africa continued to be the evolutionary centre of humankind and to contain the bulk of the world's population until the explosive global expansion of our species, *Homo sapiens*, in the last 50 000 years. Those modern people who moved out of Africa were inventive and aggressive colonisers who spread to all the continents of the Old and New Worlds, and more recently to the Moon, Mars and beyond. *Homo sapiens* has also colonised all the habitats on earth, altering them to such a degree that the survival of the species in the next hundred years has become a serious concern. This is a message that politicians and the wider public have still to take seriously.

South Africa has provided primary evidence for the emergence of modern humans. Sites like Klasies River and Border Cave have preserved remains of the ancestors of modern humans, and more specifically the ancestors of Khoisan peoples, who lived there more than 100 000 years ago. The initial divergence of regional African populations was followed by expansion and local and inter-regional migration. These processes have contributed to the genetic make-up of contemporary South Africans. The implications of DNA studies are that everyone in the world today can trace their ancestry back to an African origin. The unity of the human species is remarkable.

Unlike conventional histories, the nature of archaeological evidence does not allow us to identify the names of the people whose remains we study, but we can see where and how they lived and what they did, from the artefacts and other things they discarded. Stone artefacts are the most durable of these, and much effort has been spent on what archaeologists have referred to as 'drawing blood from stones', or working out patterns of behaviour from stone tool technology. Where preservation has been good, we can also see what kinds of plants and animals our ancestors ate. When human bones have been preserved, we may be able to reconstruct a face, decide whether the person was male or female, how tall and how old he or she was, and what foods were commonly eaten, and even sample an individual's DNA.

From the time when rock paintings and rock engravings were made, we obtain a glimpse of the beliefs and thoughts of the artists, and these are illuminated by the memories of a small number of hunter-gatherers who survived the onslaught of colonialism. The rock engravings from Wonderwerk and the painted stones from Apollo 11 in Namibia show that southern African people were creating works of art in the same time range as people living in Europe and Australia 30 000 years ago. The sophistication of the southern

African San rock art and the interpretations of its meaning from rich sources of oral testimony have in turn inspired the re-evaluation of rock art in Europe and the Americas. These interpretations have also challenged old stereotypes, revealing that popular perceptions of the San as small and insignificant populations of 'primitive' people are uninformed and inaccurate.

Within the last 2000 years, great changes have taken place in southern Africa. The southward movement of siNtu-speaking African farmers with domesticated plants and animals brought pottery, mining and metal-working technology and introduced the Iron Age. At about the same time, Khoe-speaking hunter-gatherers in Botswana acquired pottery, sheep and, later, cattle from the Iron Age farmers and migrated across the Limpopo and Orange rivers into South Africa. In a gradual process, some local San were drawn in as herders while others remained hunter-gatherers. By the time the first European sailors rounded the Cape in search of a sea route to the East, the eastern half of South Africa had been populated by Iron Age people for about 1000 years. Hunter-gatherers had developed a working relationship with them as well as with the Khoekhoe herders who had been settled along the west and southern coast for at least 1500 years. The Stone Age effectively came to an end when both hunter-gatherers and herders stopped using stone as the main source for tool-making. In areas like the south-western Cape this happened soon after 1652 when the Dutch East India Company established a trading post at Cape Town. In areas remote from European contact and Iron Age farmers, this happened only in the nineteenth century.

For some people such information about the first inhabitants of South Africa opens new and exciting doors for self-discovery; for others it is too tantalising and impersonal to qualify as 'history'. Yet others regard it as a dark secret either because they think it is undignified to acknowledge that one's ancestors were from the Stone Age, or because they are afraid that knowledge about human evolution may be against the word of God. Faith in God need not outlaw an understanding of the physical evidence for genetics and evolutionary biology. Religion and science are not in conflict.

Whatever direction we come from, the fact remains that the evidence we draw together using archaeological methods is the only information we have about the people who lived in South Africa before the late fifteenth century AD.

Archaeological sites are often referred to as fragile 'non-renewable' resources. In other words, they cannot be re-created or made again after they have been excavated, damaged or destroyed. In this sense they are unlike natural resources such as plant communities or animals threatened by extinction, which can be cloned or reintroduced by careful cultivation and breeding programmes. Archaeological sites represent behaviour patterns that are no longer practised.

For these reasons alone it is important that there be some form of effective protection of archaeological sites so that they are not damaged or destroyed during modern development and so that what is disturbed and recovered is properly documented and looked after. Such a system must transcend the interests of individuals and particular interest groups for the benefit of the nation as a whole.

Legislative protection

The National Monuments Act (Act No. 28 of 1969), and the National Heritage Act that will come into force in 1999 or 2000, protect all Stone Age and other archaeological sites. The definition includes caves, rock shelters, middens and other places in the open that were occupied by Stone Age people, as well as rock-art sites and graves. It is an offence to destroy, damage, alter or excavate sites, or to remove or export artefacts and fossils without a permit from the National Monuments Council. Such permits are normally issued only to professional archaeologists or to developers who have already hired an archaeologist to excavate and sample all or part of the site that will be affected by the development.

Archaeological sites can also be given special protection if they are declared as national monuments, but of the approximately 4000 buildings and places declared national monuments in South Africa, fewer than 40 date to the Stone Age. Experience has shown that unless such national monuments are looked after and maintained by a museum or nature reserve, they are quickly vandalised.

The National Heritage Act will protect all

archaeological sites in much the same manner as the National Monuments Act. An important change, however, is that it becomes mandatory for developers to ensure that an archaeological impact assessment is made of any property before major development takes place. This enables archaeological sites to be identified and assessed so that places of significance can be sampled well ahead of any earthmoving that may be required.

Another innovation in the National Heritage Act that affects all heritage sites is that it devolves decision-making about the significance of places to the lowest level of government with the competence to make such decisions. Municipalities and rural councils are charged with setting up heritage committees responsible for liaison with communities to undertake surveys in their area and to identify sites that are of significance to them. Where such committees cannot be established, it is the task of the Provincial Heritage Authority to undertake the surveys. These identified sites can then be assessed in terms of their local, provincial, national and international significance and the information will be available to planners and developers.

While this system will work well for buildings and places of significance to modern communities, it does not always suffice for archaeological sites. Firstly, there are at present no municipalities or rural councils in the country that employ professional archaeologists, and so the competence to identify and assess such sites is lacking. It will therefore be important for non-governmental organisations like archaeological and historical societies and Khoisan groups to register their interest in Stone Age sites. If they do so, they must be consulted during surveys and the assessment of significance.

Secondly, many archaeological sites are below the surface of the ground and are found only once development begins. At this stage it is often costly for the developer to stop work, so as to allow archaeologists to rescue information and artefacts. The National Heritage Act therefore makes provision for archaeological impact assessments before development takes place so that sites can be identified. It also allows the new South African Heritage Agency or its provincial equivalent to stop a development in order to enable information and to recover artefacts if they are found accidentally.

Damage to Stone Age sites is not only done as a result of property development, mining or engineering activities. It is also caused by vandalism (particularly at rock-art sites) and by people collecting artefacts and taking them away from their site of origin. Vandalism is an international problem. In some countries it is connected to illicit traffic in cultural property because people in wealthier countries are willing to offer large sums of money for antiquities from countries like Egypt, Greece, Turkey, Ethiopia and Mali. In countries like South Africa where Stone Age artefacts have little perceived monetary value, and indeed the National Heritage Act explicitly forbids their sale without a permit, the problem is not yet critical but nevertheless requires control.

Many people who pick up stone artefacts and take them home are not aware that in doing so they are destroying information about the original inhabitants of the site. Once the artefact has been removed from its place of origin, its context is destroyed and cannot be retrieved. This information has lain undisturbed sometimes for thousands or even tens of thousands of years, but it takes just one careless or thoughtless person to destroy it.

The National Heritage Act therefore makes all archaeological material and fossils the property of the State. Anyone found in possession of them without a permit may be liable for a fine and the artefacts or fossils may be confiscated. Anyone who already has a collection of archaeological artefacts or fossils must register the collection with the South African Heritage Agency or a provincial heritage authority within two years of the Bill being enacted. The registration of these collections will not change their ownership, but will make provision for the curation of the artefacts or fossils after the death of the present owner.

The philosophy underlying the registration of artefact collections in private hands and the protection of sites in both general and specific ways emphasises that this heritage belongs to the nation and not to individuals. This is a philosophy shared by many former British colonies and is rooted in nineteenth-century legislation and practice. When it was adopted in the colonies, however, it failed to make provision for indigenous peoples to contribute their own philosophy of heritage protection. As a result the 'one legislation fits all' concept makes us all equally responsible for our own heritage and that of everyone else. The descendants of the indigenous people who occupied Stone Age sites in the past therefore have no particular legal claim to them and have equal status regarding the protection of this heritage with any other interested party.

Indigenous people in other former colonial countries have challenged what they perceive as the theft of their heritage and have had considerable influence in changing and shaping legislation. In Australia, for example, several laws explicitly acknowledge the continuing interest of Aboriginal peoples in places significant to their tradition and grant groups responsible for a site certain rights with respect to that site, regardless of the underlying land tenure. Such rights may include a right of access, a right to deny access to others, and a right to determine what may or may not happen at the site (Ritchie 1996).

Public participation in controlling heritage resources

The National Heritage Act recognises that community participation in shaping a philosophy for heritage conservation is vital if people are to feel a true sense of ownership of that heritage. This has been demonstrated recently at Thulamela in the Kruger National Park in the Northern Province of South Africa. Before reconstructing ruined Late Iron Age stone walling so that the site could be used for educational purposes, all local communities with hereditary links to the original inhabitants of the site were consulted. When graves were found within the stone enclosures, a collective decision was made that allowed the remains to be studied, but also made provision for their replacement.

Will solutions like this one be negotiated for Stone Age sites as well, as Khoisan people become aware of their heritage? Claiming this heritage after more than a century of forgotten ties has raised and will raise a series of moral, ethical, political and social issues. One of the issues already hitting the headlines is the question of the return of the remains of the Khoekhoe woman Saartje Baartman, who died in Paris in 1815. A wax cast of her body was exhibited there for many years after her death. It is no longer on display, but her skeletal remains have been in the Musée de l'Homme for more than 180 years. Negotiations, spearheaded by the Griqua National Conference and encour-

aged by the Unesco International Decade of Indigenous Peoples, were initiated in 1995 to have Saartje Baartman's remains returned for burial in South Africa. If the Musée de l'Homme agrees to the proposal, a decision will have to be made about where she should be buried and by whom.

Would it be appropriate for similar requests to be made for the restitution of the remains of other Khoisan people that were sent to museums in Britain, Germany and other European countries as well? Alan Morris has documented a number of similar cases both in South Africa and abroad, and he and Carmel Schrire, in papers published in the book *Miscast* edited by Pippa Skotnes, raise some questions that are difficult to answer. Morris is an anatomist who studies human remains from the present as well as the past. He asks whether the shared genetic origin of present-day Khoisan descendants entitles them to reclaim the remains of people who may be biologically similar but who did not speak the same language and whose cultural and economic backgrounds have little in common. He argues that 'a balance must be struck between the search for knowledge and the need for moral sensitivity. The dead are not at issue here. It is the disposition of the living toward the dead that concerns us' (1996:79).

Writing from a broader perspective, Carmel Schrire (1996) draws attention to the social and intellectual climate of the nineteenth century which led Europeans to collect skulls and other memorabilia from 'native' peoples in other parts of the world. South Africa was not the only country to be targeted, nor were Europeans the only culprits. When Captain Cook was killed by Hawaiian islanders, some of his cooked and defleshed bones were formally returned to his men the following evening. But the reason for his death may have been Hawaiian religious beliefs about the disposal of the remains of gods rather than a desire to measure his bones for comparative purposes.

Whatever the reasons that people may give for collecting the human remains of others, Carmel Schrire points out that the ultimate aim is power and control. Because the ways of enforcing power can be both damaging and beneficial, this inherent factor needs to be acknowledged in legislation and regulations that protect the Stone Age heritage of South Africa. The stated purpose of legislative control is to ensure that both the tangible and intangible remains of the people of the Stone Age are protected against damage and destruction so that they remain accessible for inspection and study by anyone with an interest in them, regardless of genetic ancestry. Implicit in these principles is that ownership rests with the State, with the further implication that it is the duty of the State to pay for their protection. The decision about what is to be protected and what is not is therefore a political one that will change as political agendas come and go.

Public awareness and its implications

A long-term insurance policy needs to be established so that the heritage of the Stone Age people of South Africa is not neglected. An essential element of this policy is to increase public awareness of the importance of this legacy to the nation as a whole. One way to achieve this is to include Stone Age history as an integral part of the school curriculum. Another is to promote our Stone Age heritage as part of the cultural signature of South Africa and to develop places of significance both for local and for foreign tourists.

Museums are key institutions for the conservation of our Stone Age heritage. This book could not have been written without the aid of collections held in trust by local, provincial and national museums and by a few university departments of archaeology and anatomy in South Africa. The integrity and safety of these collections must be ensured at all costs because the items from our Stone Age cultural heritage held in them are irreplaceable. Their individual monetary worth is not high, but collectively they represent a legacy of more than two million years of human endeavour. Museums have a great advantage too because, as public places, they make the items in their collections available to anyone with an interest in studying them. This would not be the case if such collections were in private hands.

What museums cannot always do adequately is convey the ambience of places where Stone Age people lived and, as a result, there is often a lack of understanding of how archaeological information is accumulated. There are a few archaeological sites that are open to the public. The Sterkfontein Cave can be visited although facilities are not well developed. There are several caves and rock shelters along the southern Cape coast: Nelson Bay Cave on the Robberg peninsula at Plettenberg Bay and the small cave at the mouth of the Storms River in the Tsitsikamma National Park are open all year. The Matjes River Rock Shelter at Keurboomstrand east of Plettenberg Bay is accessible at low tide. Cape St Blaize Cave at Mossel Bay is easy to visit and so is Peers Cave near Fish Hoek in Cape Town. In other parts of the country, Wonderwerk Cave near Kuruman receives hundreds of visitors a year and so does the spring site at Florisbad near Bloemfontein. Rock paintings can be seen in Main Caves and at other sites around Giant's Castle in the Natal Drakensberg Park. Rock engravings are on display at Nooitgedacht near Kimberley. There are also many smaller rock-art sites that individual landowners allow people to visit and information about them is usually available at museums.

This short list needs to be extended, and will be, once public interest demands it. It is essential, however, that entrepreneurs seek advice on site protection and management because without a management plan sites are rapidly destroyed. Such advice is available at the National Monuments Council or at any museum or university that employs professional archaeologists.

The future of our Stone Age heritage

Does the Stone Age have a future in South Africa? We believe that the information on the Stone Age that has been gathered over the past century or more is at last accessible enough for the general public to enjoy and acknowledge as a rich source of inspiration. This history, because it is based on objects and features that people have created rather than on the successes and failures of individual 'great' men or women, is a history of the collective achievements of all the anonymous people who have lived here in the past. We trust that our contribution will enable present and future generations to value theirs.

Bibliography

Ardrey, R. 1958. *African Genesis*. London: Geoffrey Bles.

Avery. D.M. 1982. Micromammals as palaeoenvironmental indicators and an interpretation of the late Quaternary in the southern Cape Province, South Africa. *Annals of the South African Museum* 85:183–374.

Avery, G. 1975. Discussion on the age and use of tidal fish-traps (visvywers). *South African Archaeological Bulletin* 30:105–113.

Avery, G. 1987. Coastal birds and prehistory in the Western Cape. In: Parkington, J. & Hall, M. (eds.) *Papers in the Prehistory of the Western Cape, South Africa*: 164–191. Oxford: British Archaeological Reports International Series 332(I).

Bailey, W.J. 1993. Hominoid trichotomy: a molecular overview. *Evolutionary Anthropology* 2:100–108.

Balinsky, B.I. 1962. Patterns of animal distribution on the African continent. *Annals of the Cape Provincial Museums* 2:299–310.

Barham, L.S. 1992. Let's walk before we run: an appraisal of historical materialist approaches to the Later Stone Age. *South African Archaeological Bulletin* 47:44–51.

Barham, L.S. & Smart, P.L. 1996. An early date for the Middle Stone Age of central Zambia. *Journal of Human Evolution* 3:287–290.

Barnard, A. 1992. *Hunters and Herders of Southern Africa: A Comparative Ethnography of the Khoisan Peoples*. Cambridge: CUP.

Barnard, A. 1996. Laurens van der Post and the Kalahari Debate. In: Skotnes, P. (ed.) *Miscast: Negotiating the Presence of the Bushmen*: 239–247. Cape Town: UCT Press.

Barrow, J. 1801. *An Account of Travels into the Interior of Southern Africa in the Years 1797 and 1798*. London: Cadell and Davies.

Bar-Yosef, O. 1992. The role of western Asia in modern human origins. *Philosophical Transactions of the Royal Society, London* B 337: 193–200.

Beaumont, P.B. 1978. Border Cave. Unpublished MA thesis: University of Cape Town.

Beaumont, P.B. 1980. On the age of Border Cave hominids 1-5. *Palaeontologica Africana* 23:21–33.

Beaumont, P.B. & Vogel, J.C. 1989. Patterns in the age and context of rock art in the Northern Cape. *South African Archaeological Bulletin* 44:73–81.

Belfer-Cohen, A. & Goren-Inbar, N. 1994. Cognition and communication in the Levantine Lower Palaeolithic. *World Archaeology* 26:144–157.

Benefit, B.R. & McCrossin, M.L. 1995. Miocene hominoids and hominid origins. *Annual Review of Anthropology* 24:237–256.

Berger, L.R. & Clarke, R.J. 1995. Eagle involvement in accumulation of the Taung child fauna. *Journal of Human Evolution* 29:275–299.

Biesele, M. 1993. *Women Like Meat: The Folklore and Foraging Ideology of the Kalahari Ju/'hoan*. Bloomington: Indiana University Press.

Binford, L. 1981. *Bones: Ancient Men and Modern Myths*. New York: Academic Press.

Binneman, J. 1985. Research along the South Eastern Cape coast. In: Hall, S.L. & Binneman, J. (eds.) *Guide to Archaeological Sites in the Eastern and North Eastern Cape*: 117–134. Grahamstown: Southern African Association of Archaeologists Conference Excursion.

Bishop, W.W. & Clark, J.D. (eds.) 1967. *Background to Evolution in Africa*. Chicago: University of Chicago Press.

Bleek, D.F. 1932. Customs and beliefs of the /Xam Bushmen. Part III: Game animals. *Bantu Studies* 6:233–249.

Bleek, D.F. 1933. Beliefs and customs of the /Xam Bushmen. Part V: The rain. *Bantu Studies* 7:297–312.

Bleek, D.F. 1935. Beliefs and customs of the /Xam Bushmen. Part VII: Sorcerors. *Bantu Studies* 9:1–47.

Bleek, D.F. 1936. Beliefs and customs of the /Xam Bushmen. Part VIII: More about sorcerors and charms. *Bantu Studies* 10:131–162.

Bleek, W.H.I. & Lloyd, L.C. 1911. *Specimens of Bushman Folklore*. London: George Allen.

Blumenschine, R.J. 1986. *Early Hominid Scavenging Opportunities: Implications of Carcass Availability in the Serengeti and Ngorongoro Ecosystems*. Oxford: British Archaeological Reports International Series 283.

Boesch, C. & Boesch, H. 1990. Tool use and tool making in wild chimpanzees. *Folia Primatologia* 54:86–99.

Bollong, C.A. & Sampson, C.G. 1996. Later Stone Age ceramic stratigraphy and direct dates on pottery. *Southern African Field Archaeology* 5:3–16.

Bollong, C.A., Jacobson, L., Peisach, M., Pineda, C.A. & Sampson, C.G. 1997. Ordination versus clustering of elemental data from PIXE analysis of herder-hunter pottery: a comparison. *Journal of Archaeological Science* 21:319–327.

Boonzaier, E., Malherbe, C., Smith, A. & Berens, P. 1996. *The Cape Herders. A History of the Khoikhoi of Southern Africa*. Cape Town: David Philip.

Bousman, C.B. 1991. Holocene paleoecology and Later Stone Age hunter-gatherer adaptations in the South African interior plateau. Unpublished PhD dissertation: Southern Methodist University, Dallas.

Brain, C.K. 1967. Hottentot food remains and their meaning in the interpretation of fossil bone assemblages. *Scientific Papers of the Namib Desert Research Station* 32:1–11.

Brain, C.K. 1981. *The Hunters or the Hunted? An Introduction to African Cave Taphonomy*. Chicago: Chicago University Press.

Brain, C.K. (ed.) 1993. *Swartkrans: A Cave's Chronicle of Early Man*. Pretoria: Transvaal Museum Monograph 8.

Brandt, S. 1996. The ethnoarchaeology of flaked stone tool use in Southern Ethiopia. In: Pwiti, G. & Soper, R. (eds.) *Aspects of African Archaeology*. Papers from the 10th Congress of the PanAfrican Association for Prehistory and Related Studies: 733–738. Harare: University of Zimbabwe Publications.

Bräuer, G., Yokoyama, Y., Falquères, C. & Mbua, E. 1997. Modern human origins backdated. *Nature* 386:337.

Broecker, W.S. & Denton, G.H. 1990. What drives glacial cycles? *Scientific American* January 1990: 43–50.

Bromage, T.G. & Dean, M.C. 1985. Re-evaluation of the age at death of immature fossil hominids. *Nature* 317:525–527.

Broom, R. & Robinson, J.T. 1952. Swartkrans ape-men, *Paranthropus crassidens*. *Memoirs of the Transvaal Museum* 6:1–23.

Brunet, M., Beauvilain, A., Coppens, Y., Heintz, E., Moutaye, A.H.E. & Pilbeam, D. 1995. The first australopithecine 2 500 kilometres west of the Rift Valley (Chad). *Nature* 378:273–275.

Budack, K.F.R. 1977. The #Aonin or Topnaar of the lower !Kuiseb valley and the sea. In: Traill, A. (ed.) *Khoisan Linguistic Studies* 3:1–42. Johannesburg: African Studies Institute, University of the Witwatersrand.

Bunn, H.T. & Ezzo, J.A. 1993. Hunting and scavenging by Plio-Pleistocene hominids: nutritional constraints, archaeological patterns, and behavioural implications. *Journal of Archaeological Science* 20:365–398.

Cann, R.L., Stoneking, M. & Wilson, A.C. 1987. Mitochondrial DNA and human evolution. *Nature* 325:31–36.

Cartmill, M. 1992. New views on primate origins. *Evolutionary Anthropology* 1:105–111.

Cashdan, E. 1985. Coping with risk: reciprocity among the Basarwa of Northern Botswana. *Man* 20:454–474.

Clark, J.D. 1959. *The Prehistory of Southern Africa*. Harmondsworth: Penguin.

Clark, J.D. 1992. African and Asian perspectives on the origins of modern humans. *Philosophical Transactions of the Royal Society*, London B 337:201–215.

Clarke, D.L. 1968. *Analytical Archaeology*. London: Methuen.

Clarke, R. 1994. On some new interpretations of Sterkfontein stratigraphy. *South African Journal of Science* 90:211–214.

Clarke, R.J. & Tobias, P.V. 1995. Sterkfontein Member 2 foot bones of the oldest South African hominid. *Science* 269:521–524.

Conroy, G.C., Pickford, M., Senut, B. & Mein, P. 1993. Diamonds in the desert: the discovery of *Otavipithecus namibiensis*. *Evolutionary Anthropology* 2:46–52.

Coppens, Y. 1994. East Side Story: the origin of humankind. *Scientific American* May 1994:62–69.

Dale, Langham. 1870. Stone implements in South Africa. *Cape Monthly Magazine* 1:23–239.

Dart, R.A. 1925. 'Australopithecus africanus': the man-ape of South Africa. *Nature* 115:195–199.

Dart, R.A. 1957. The osteodontokeratic culture of *Australopithecus prometheus*. *Memoirs of the Transvaal Museum* 10:1–105.

Darwin, C. 1859. *On the Origin of Species by Means of Natural Selection, or the Preservation of Favoured Races in the Struggle for Life*. London: John Murray.

Deacon, H.J. 1972. A review of the post-Pleistocene in South Africa. *South African Archaeological Society Goodwin Series* 1:26–45.

Deacon, H.J. 1976. *Where Hunters Gathered: A Study of Holocene Stone Age People in the Eastern Cape*. Claremont: South African Archaeological Society.

Deacon, H.J. 1979. Excavations at Boomplaas Cave: a sequence through the Upper Pleistocene and Holocene in South Africa. *World Archaeology* 10:241–257.

Deacon, H.J. 1992. Southern Africa and modern human origins. *Philosophical Transactions of the Royal Society, London* B 337:177–183.

Deacon, H.J. 1993. Planting an idea: an archaeology of Stone Age gatherers in South Africa. *South African Archaeological Bulletin* 48:86–93.

Deacon, H.J. 1995. Two Late Pleistocene-Holocene archaeological depositories from the southern Cape, South Africa. *South African Archaeological Bulletin* 50:121–131.

Deacon, H.J. & Deacon, J. 1963. Scott's Cave: a late Stone Age site in the Gamtoos Valley. *Annals of the Cape Provincial Museums* 3:96–121.

Deacon, H.J., Deacon, J., Brooker, M. & Wilson, M.L.

1978. The evidence for herding at Boomplaas Cave in the southern Cape, South Africa. *South African Archaeological Bulletin* 33:39–65.

Deacon, H.J. & Deacon, J. 1980. The hafting, function and distribution of small convex scrapers with an example from Boomplaas Cave. *South African Archaeological Bulletin* 35:31–37.

Deacon, H.J., Deacon, J., Scholtz, A., Thackeray, J.F., Brink, J.S. & Vogel, J.C. 1984. Correlation of palaeo-environmental data from the Late Pleistocene and Holocene deposits at Boomplaas Cave, southern Cape. In: Vogel, J.C. (ed.) *Late Cainozoic Palaeoclimates of the Southern Hemisphere*: 339–352. Rotterdam: Balkema.

Deacon, H.J. & Wurz, S. 1996. Klasies River main site, cave 2: a Howiesons Poort occurrence. In: Pwiti, G. & Soper, R. (eds.) *Aspects of African Archaeology*: 213–218. Harare: University of Zimbabwe.

Deacon, J. 1972. Wilton: an assessment after 50 years. *South African Archaeological Bulletin* 27:10–45.

Deacon, J. 1974. Patterning in the radiocarbon dates for the Wilton/Smithfield complex in southern Africa. *South African Archaeological Bulletin* 28:1–18.

Deacon, J. 1978. Changing patterns in the late Pleistocene/early Holocene prehistory of southern Africa as seen from the Nelson Bay Cave stone artefact sequence. *Quaternary Research* (NY) 10:84–111.

Deacon, J. 1984a. Later Stone Age people and their descendants in southern Africa. In: Klein, R.G. (ed.) *Southern African Paleoenvironments and Prehistory*: 221–328. Rotterdam: Balkema.

Deacon, J. 1984b. *The Later Stone Age of Southernmost Africa*. Oxford: British Archaeological Reports International Series 213.

Deacon, J. 1988. The power of a place in understanding southern San rock engravings. *World Archaeology* 20:129–140.

Deacon, J. 1992. *Arrows as Agents of Belief amongst the /Xam Bushmen*. Cape Town: South African Museum, Margaret Shaw Lecture 3.

Deacon, J. 1997. 'My heart stands in the hill': rock engravings in the Northern Cape. *Kronos* 24:18–29.

Deacon, J. & Lancaster, N. 1988. *Late Quaternary Palaeoenvironments of Southern Africa*. Oxford: OUP.

DeMenocal, P.B. 1995. Plio-Pleistocene African climate. *Science* 270:53–59.

De Waal, F.B.M. 1992. Intentional deception in primates. *Evolutionary Anthropology* 1:86–92.

Diamond, J. 1991. *The Rise and Fall of the Third Chimpanzee*. London: Radius.

Dugard, J. 1993. The Taung 'trial' of 1925. *South African Journal of Science* 89:54–57.

Dunbar, R.I.M. 1992. Neocortex size as a constraint on group size in primates. *Journal of Human Evolution* 20:469–493.

Dunbar, R.I.M. 1995. *The Trouble with Science*. London: Faber and Faber.

Dunn, E.J. 1873. Through Bushmanland: Part 2. *Cape Monthly Magazine* 6:31–42.

Dunn, E.J. 1880. Stone implements of South Africa. *Transactions of the South African Philosophical Society* 2:6–22.

Dunn, E.J. 1931. *The Bushman*. London: Griffin.

Eastwood, E. & Fish, W. 1996. Sheep in the rock paintings of the Soutpansberg and Limpopo River valley. *Southern African Field Archaeology* 5:59–69.

Elphick, R. 1977. *Kraal and Castle: Khoikhoi and the Founding of White South Africa*. New Haven and London: Yale University Press.

Elphick, R. & Giliomee, H. (eds.) 1979. *The Shaping of South African Society 1652–1820*. Cape Town: Maskew Miller Longman.

Fagan, B.M. 1960. The Glentyre shelter and Oakhurst re-examined. *South African Archaeological Bulletin* 15:80–94.

Falk, D., Hildebolt, C. & Vannier, M.W. 1989. Reassessment of the Taung early hominid from a neurological perspective. *Journal of Human Evolution* 18:485–492.

Fock, G.J. 1968. Rooidam, a sealed site of the First Intermediate. *South African Journal of Science* 64:153–159.

Fock, G.J. 1979. *Felsbilder in Südafrika. Teil I*. Cologne: Böhlau Verlag.

Fock, G.J. & Fock, D. 1984. *Felsbilder in Südafrika. Teil II*. Cologne: Böhlau Verlag.

Fock, G.J. & Fock, D. 1989. *Felsbilder in Südafrika. Teil III*. Cologne: Bühlau Verlag.

Foley, R. & Lahr, M.M. 1997. Mode 3 technologies and the evolution of modern humans. *Cambridge Archaeological Journal* 7:3–36.

Gooch, W.E. 1881. Stone Age of South Africa. *Journal of the Anthropological Institute* 11:124–182.

Goodwin, A.J.H. 1930. A new variation of the Smithfield Culture from Natal. *Transactions of the Royal Society of South Africa* 19:7–14.

Goodwin, A.J.H. & Van Riet Lowe, C. 1929. *The Stone Age Cultures of South Africa*. Annals of the South African Museum 27:1–289.

Grine, F.E. 1986. Dental evidence for dietary differences in *Australopithecus* and *Paranthropus*: a quantitative analysis of permanent molar microwear. *Journal of Human Evolution* 15:783–822.

Groves, C.P. 1989. *A Theory of Human and Primate Evolution*. Oxford: OUP.

Groves, C.P. & Lahr, M.M. 1994. A bush not a ladder: speciation and replacement in human evolution. *Perspectives in Human Biology* 4:1–11.

Grün, R., Brink, J.S., Spooner, N.A., Taylor, L., Stringer, C.B., Franciscus, R.G. & Murray, A.S. 1996. Direct dating of Florisbad hominid. *Nature* 382:500–501.

Guenther, M. 1986. *The Nharo Bushmen of Botswana*. Hamburg: Helmut Buske Verlag.

Guenther, M. 1989. *Bushman Folktales*. Wiesbaden:

Franz Steiner Verlag.

Hall, S.L. 1990. Hunter-gatherer-fishers of the Fish River Basin: a contribution to the Holocene prehistory of the Eastern Cape. Unpublished D.Phil. thesis: University of Stellenbosch.

Hall, S.L. & Binneman, J. 1987. Later Stone Age burial variability in the Cape: a social interpretation. *South African Archaeological Bulletin* 42: 140-152.

Harpending, H.C., Sherry, S.T., Rogers, A.R. & Stoneking, M. 1993. The genetic structure of ancient human populations. *Current Anthropology* 34: 483–496.

Heaton, T.H.E., Talma, A.S. & Vogel, J.C. 1986. Dissolved gas paleotemperatures and oxygen-18 variations derived from groundwater near Uitenhage, South Africa. *Quaternary Research* 25:79–88.

Hedenström, A. 1995. Lifting the Taung child. *Nature* 378:670.

Henshilwood, C. 1995. Holocene archaeology of the coastal Garcia State Forest, southern Cape, South Africa. Unpublised PhD thesis: University of Cambridge.

Henshilwood, C. 1996. A revised chronology for pastoralism in southernmost Africa: new evidence of sheep at *c.* 2000 b.p. from Blombos Cave, South Africa. *Antiquity* 70:945–946.

Hewitt, J. 1921. On several implements and ornaments from Strandlooper sites in the Eastern Province. *South African Journal of Science* 18:454–467.

Hewitt, J. 1955. Further light on the Bowker implements. *South African Archaeological Bulletin* 10:94–95.

Hill, K. 1993. Life history theory and evolutionary anthropology. *Evolutionary Anthropology* 2:78–88.

Hrdlicka, A. 1925. The Taungs ape. *American Journal of Physical Anthropology* 8:379–392.

Humphreys, A.J.B. & Thackeray, A.I. 1983. *Ghaap and Gariep: Later Stone Age Studies in the Northern Cape.* Cape Town: South African Archaeological Society Monograph Series 2.

Hunt, K. D. 1993. The mosaic lifeways of our australopithecine ancestors. *AnthroQuest* 47:3–7.

Imbrie, J. & Imbrie, K. 1979. *Ice Ages: Solving the Mystery.* Cambridge, Mass.: Harvard University Press.

Inskeep, R.R. 1986. A preliminary survey of burial practices in the Later Stone Age, from the Orange River to the Cape coast. In: Singer, R. & Lundy, J.K. (eds.) *Variation, Culture and Evolution in African Populations: Papers in Honour of Dr Hertha de Villiers*: 221–239. Johannesburg: Witwatersrand University Press.

Inskeep, R.R. 1987. *Nelson Bay Cave.* Oxford: British Archaeological Reports International Series 357(i) & (ii).

Isaac, G. 1971. The diet of early man: aspects of archaeological evidence from Lower and Middle Pleistocene sites in Africa. *World Archaeology* 2:279–299.

Isaac, G. 1984. The archaeology of human origins: studies of the Lower Pleistocene in East Africa: 1971-1981. In: Wendorf, F. & Close, A.E. (eds.) *Advances in World Archaeology* 3:1–87. New York: Academic Press.

Jerardino, A. 1996. Changing social landscapes of the Western Cape coast of southern Africa over the last 4 500 years. Unpublished PhD thesis: University of Cape Town.

Jerardino, A. & Yates, R. 1996. Preliminary results from excavations at Steenbokfontein Cave: implications for past and future research. *South African Archaeological Bulletin* 51:7–16.

Johanson, D. & White, T. 1979. A systematic assessment of early African hominids. *Science* 202:321–330.

Jolly, P. 1994. Strangers to brothers: interaction between south-eastern San and southern Nguni/Sotho communities. Unpublished MA thesis: University of Cape Town.

Jolly, P. 1995. Melikane and Upper Mangolong revisited: the possible effects on San art of symbiotic contact between south-eastern San and southern Sotho and Nguni communities. *South African Archaeological Bulletin* 161:68–80.

Jones, S. 1996. *In the Blood: God, Genes and Destiny.* London: HarperCollins.

Kannemeyer, D.R. 1890. Stone implements of the Bushmen. *Cape Illustrated Magazine* 1:120–130.

Kaplan, J. 1990. The Umhlatuzana rock shelter sequence: 100 000 years of Stone Age history. *Natal Museum Journal of Humanities* 2:1–94.

Kaplan, J. 1993. *The State of Archaeological Information in the Coastal Zone from the Orange River to Ponta do Oura.* Pretoria: Department of Environment Affairs.

Katz, R. 1982. *Boiling Energy: Community Healing among the Kalahari !Kung.* Cambridge, Mass.: Harvard University Press.

Kimbel, W.H., Johanson, D.C. & Rak, Y. 1994. The first skull and other new discoveries of *Australopithecus afarensis* at Hadar, Ethiopia. *Nature* 368:449–451.

Klein, R.G. 1972. The late Quaternary mammalian fauna of Nelson Bay Cave (Cape Province, South Africa): its implications for megafaunal extinctions and environmental and cultural change. *Quaternary Research* (NY) 2:135–142.

Klein, R.G. 1974. Environment and subsistence of prehistoric man in the southern Cape Province, South Africa. *World Archaeology* 5:249–284.

Klein, R.G. 1975. The mammalian fauna of the Klasies River Mouth sites, southern Cape Province, South Africa. *South African Archaeological Bulletin* 31:74–98.

Klein, R.G. 1978a. Stone Age predation on large African bovids. *Journal of Archaeological Science* 5:195–217.

Klein, R.G. 1978b. A preliminary report on the larger mammals from the Boomplaas Stone Age cave site, Cango Valley, Oudtshoorn District, South Africa. *South African Archaeological Bulletin* 33:66–75.

Klein, R.G. 1980. Environmental and ecological implications of large mammals from Upper Pleistocene and Holocene sites in southern Africa. *Annals of the South*

African Museum 81:223–283.

Klein, R.G. 1986. The prehistory of Stone Age herders in the Cape Province of South Africa. *South African Archaeological Society Goodwin Series* 5:5–12.

Klein, R.G. 1989. *The Human Career: Human Biological and Cultural Origins*. Chicago: University of Chicago Press.

Klein, R.G. & Cruz-Uribe, K. 1983. Stone Age population numbers and average tortoise size at Byneskranskop Cave 1 and Die Kelders Cave 1, southern Cape Province, South Africa. *South African Archaeological Bulletin* 38:26–30.

Klein, R.G. & Cruz-Uribe, K. 1987. Large mammal and tortoise bones from Elands Bay Cave and nearby sites, Western Cape Province, South Africa. In: Parkington, J. & Hall, M. (eds.) *Papers in the Prehistory of the Western Cape, South Africa*: 132–163. Oxford: British Archaeological Reports International Series 332(I).

Klein, R.G. & Cruz-Uribe, K. 1991. The bovids from Elandsfontein, South Africa, and their implications for the age, palaeoenvironment, and origins of the site. *African Archaeological Review* 9:21–79.

Klein, R.G. & Cruz-Uribe, K. 1996. Exploitation of large bovids and seals at Middle and Later Stone Age sites in South Africa. *Journal of Human Evolution* 31: 315–334.

Klein, R.G. & Scott, K. 1974. The fauna of Scott's Cave, Gamtoos Valley, south-western Cape Province. *South African Journal of Science* 70:186–187.

Kuman, K. 1994. The archaeology of Sterkfontein: past and present. *Journal of Human Evolution* 27:471–495.

Leakey, L.S.B. 1961. New finds at Olduvai Gorge. *Nature* 189:649–650.

Leakey, L.S.B., Tobias, P.V. & Napier, J.R. 1964. A new species of the genus *Homo* from Olduvai Gorge, Tanzania. *Nature* 202:308–312.

Leakey, M.D. 1971. *Olduvai Gorge: Excavations in Beds I and II, 1960–1963*. Cambridge: CUP.

Leakey, Meave G., Feibel, C.S., McDougall, I. & Walker, A. 1995. New four-million-year-old hominid species from Kanapoi and Allia Bay, Kenya. *Nature* 376: 565–571.

Lee, R.B. 1979. *The !Kung San: Men, Women and Work in a Foraging Society*. Cambridge: CUP.

Lee-Thorp, J. A., Van der Merwe, N.J. & Brain, C.K. 1994. Diet of *Australopithecus robustus* at Swartkrans from stable carbon isotopic analysis. *Journal of Human Evolution* 27:361–372.

Leslie, M. 1989. The Holocene sequence from Uniondale rock shelter in the Eastern Cape. *South African Archaeological Society Goodwin Series* 6:17–32.

Lewis-Williams, J.D. 1981. *Believing and Seeing: Symbolic Meanings in Southern San Rock Paintings*. London: Academic Press.

Lewis-Williams, J.D. 1987. A dream of eland: an unexplored component of San shamanism and rock art. *World Archaeology* 19:165–177.

Lewis-Williams, J.D. 1988. *The World of Man and the World of Spirit: An Interpretation of the Linton Rock Paintings*. Cape Town: South African Museum.

Lewis-Williams, J.D. 1990. *Discovering Southern African Rock Art*. Cape Town: David Philip.

Lewis-Williams, J.D. & Dowson, T.A. 1988. Signs of all times: entoptic phenomena in Upper Palaeolithic art. *Current Anthropology* 29:201–245.

Lewis-Williams, J.D. & Dowson, T.A. 1989. *Images of Power: Understanding Bushman Rock Art*. Johannesburg: Witwatersrand University Press.

Lewis-Williams, J.D. & Dowson, T.A. 1990. Through the veil: San rock paintings and the rock face. *South African Archaeological Bulletin* 45:5–16.

Lewis-Williams, J.D., Dowson, T.A. & Deacon, J. 1993 Rock art and changing perceptions of southern Africa's past: Ezeljagdspoort reviewed. *Antiquity* 67: 273–291.

Lichtenstein, H. 1810. *Travels in Southern Africa*. Translated and reprinted 1928–29. Cape Town: Van Riebeeck Society.

Lorius, C., Merlivat, L., Jouzel, J. & Pourchet, M. 1979. A 30,000-yr isotope climatic record from Antarctic ice. *Nature* 280:644–648.

Louw, J.T. 1960. *Prehistory of the Matjes River Shelter*. Memoir of the National Museum, Bloemfontein 1:1–143.

Maggs, T. 1967. A quantitative analysis of the rock art from a sample area in the Western Cape. *South African Journal of Science* 63:100–104.

Maggs, T. 1995. Neglected rock art: the rock engravings of agriculturist communities in South Africa. *South African Archaeological Bulletin* 50:132–142.

Manhire, A. 1993. A report on the excavations at Faraoskop rock shelter in the Graafwater district of the south-western Cape. *Southern African Field Archaeology* 2:3–23.

Manhire, A.H., Parkington, J.E., Mazel, A.D. & Maggs, T.M.O'C. 1986. Cattle, sheep and horses: a review of domestic animals in the rock art of southern Africa. *South African Archaeological Society Goodwin Series* 5:22–30.

Marks, S. 1972. Khoisan resistance to the Dutch in the seventeenth and eighteenth centuries. *Journal of African History* 13:55–80.

Marshall Thomas, E. 1959. *The Harmless People*. Harmondsworth: Penguin.

Marshall, L. 1962. !Kung Bushman religious beliefs. *Africa* 32:221–252.

Marshall, L. 1969. The medicine dance of the !Kung Bushmen. *Africa* 39:347–380.

Marshall, L. 1976. *The !Kung of Nyae Nyae*. Cambridge, Mass.: Harvard University Press.

Mason, R.J. 1962. *Prehistory of the Transvaal*. Johannesburg: Witwatersrand University Press.

Mason, R.J. 1967. The archaeology of the earliest surficial deposits in the Lower Vaal Basin near Holpan,

Windsorton District. *South African Geographical Journal* 49:39–56.

Mason, R.J. 1988a. Cave of Hearths, Makapansgat, Transvaal. Johannesburg: Archaeological Research Unit, University of the Witwatersrand, Occasional Paper 21.

Mason, R.J. 1988b. Kruger Cave, Late Stone Age, Magaliesberg. Johannesburg: Archaeological Research Unit, University of the Witwatersrand, Occasional Paper 17.

Mazel, A. 1989a. Changing social relations in the Thukela Basin, Natal 7000-2000 BP. *South African Archaeological Society Goodwin Series* 6:33–41.

Mazel, A. 1989b. People making history: the last ten thousand years of hunter-gatherer communities in the Thukela Basin. *Natal Museum Journal of Humanities* 1:1–168.

Mazel, A. & Parkington, J. 1981. Stone tools and resources: a case study from southern Africa. *World Archaeology* 13:16–30.

Mazel, A. & Stewart, P.M. 1987. Meddling with the mind: the treatment of San hunter-gatherers and the origins of South Africa's black population in recent South African school history textbooks. *South African Archaeological Bulletin* 42:166–170.

Mazel, A.D. & Watchman, A.L. 1997. Accelerator radiocarbon dating of Natal Drakensberg paintings: results and implications. *Antiquity* 71:445–449.

McBrearty, S., Bishop, L. & Kingston, J. 1996. Variability in traces of Middle Pleistocene hominid behaviour in the Kapthurin Formation, Baringo, Kenya. *Journal of Human Evolution* 30:563–580.

McGrew, W.C. 1991. *Chimpanzee Material Culture: Implications for Human Evolution.* Cambridge: CUP.

McHenry, H.M. 1991a. Petite bodies of the 'robust' australopithecines. *American Journal of Physical Anthropology* 86:445–454.

McHenry, H.M. 1991b. Femoral lengths and stature in Plio-Pleistocene hominids. *American Journal of Physical Anthropology* 85:149–158.

McHenry, H.M. 1992. Body size and proportions in early hominids. *American Journal of Physical Anthropology* 87:407–431.

McKee, J.K. 1993. Faunal dating of the Taung hominid fossil deposit. *Journal of Human Evolution* 25:363–376.

Mehlman, M.J. 1989. Later Quaternary archaeological sequences in northern Tanzania. PhD thesis, University of Illinois at Urbana-Champaign. Ann Arbor: University Microfilms International.

Mellars, P.A. 1996. *The Neanderthal Legacy: An Archaeological Perspective from Western Europe.* Princeton: Princeton University Press.

Milo, R.G. 1998. Evidence for hominid predation at Klasies River Mouth, South Africa, and its implications for the behaviour of early modern humans. *Journal of Archaeological Science* 25:99–133.

Milton, K. 1993. Diet and primate evolution. *Scientific American* August 1993:70–77.

Mitchell, P.J. 1994. Understanding the MSA/LSA transition: the pre-20 000 BP assemblages from new excavations at Sehonghong Rock Shelter, Lesotho. *Southern African Field Archaeology* 3:15–25.

Mitchell, P.J. 1995. Revisiting the Robberg: new results and a revision of old ideas at Sehonghong Rock Shelter, Lesotho. *South African Archaeological Bulletin* 50:28–38.

Moodie, D. 1960. *The Record.* Reprint edition. Cape Town: Balkema.

Morell, V. 1994. Will primate genetics split one gorilla into two? *Science* 265:1661.

Morris, A. 1992. *Skeletons of Contact.* Johannesburg: Witwatersrand University Press.

Morris, A. 1996. Trophy skulls, museums and the San. In: Skotnes, P. (ed.) *Miscast: Negotiating the Presence of the Bushmen:* 67-79. Cape Town: UCT Press.

Morris, D. 1988. Engraved in place and time: a review of the variability in the rock art of the Northern Cape and Karoo. *South African Archaeological Bulletin* 43:109-120.

Mossop, E.E. (ed.) 1935. *The Journal of Hendrik Jacob Wikar (1779) and the Journals of Jacobus Coetse Jansz (1760) and Willem van Reenen (1791).* Cape Town: Van Riebeeck Society.

Movius, H.L. 1948. The Lower Palaeolithic cultures of southern and eastern Asia. *Transactions of the American Philosophical Society* 38:329–420.

Newton-King, S. 1992. The enemy within: the struggle for ascendancy on the Cape Eastern frontier 1760–1799. Unpublished PhD thesis: School of Oriental and African Studies, University of London.

Oakley, K.P. 1957. Dating the australopithecines. In: Clark, J.D. & Cole, S. (eds.) *Proceedings of the Third Pan-African Congress on Prehistory, Livingstone, 1955:* 155–157. London: Chatto and Windus.

Opperman, H. 1987. *The Later Stone Age of the Drakensberg Range and its Foothills.* Oxford: British Archaeological Reports International Series 339.

Opperman, H. 1996. Strathalan Cave B, north-eastern Cape Province, South Africa: evidence for human behaviour 29 000–26 000 years ago. *Quaternary International* 33:45-53.

Opperman, H. & Heydenrych, B. 1990. A 22 000 year-old Middle Stone Age camp site with plant food remains from the north-eastern Cape. *South African Archaeological Bulletin* 45:93–99.

Orpen, J.M. 1874. A glimpse into the mythology of the Maluti Bushmen. *Cape Monthly Magazine* 9:1–13.

Pager, H. 1971. *Ndedema.* Graz: Akademische Druck.

Parkington, J. 1972. Seasonal mobility in the Late Stone Age. *African Studies* 31:223–243.

Parkington, J. 1976. Coastal settlement between the mouths of the Berg and Olifants rivers, Cape Province. *South African Archaeological Bulletin* 31:127–140.

Parkington, J. 1980. Time and place: some observations

on spatial and temporal patterning in the Later Stone Age sequence in southern Africa. *South African Archaeological Bulletin* 35:73–83.

Parkington, J. 1981. The effects of environmental change on the scheduling of visits to the Elands Bay Cave, Cape Province, South Africa. In: Hodder, I., Isaac, G. & Hammond, N. (eds.) *Pattern of the Past: Studies in Honour of David Clarke*: 341–359. Cambridge: CUP.

Parkington, J. 1987. Changing views of prehistoric settlement in the Western Cape. In: Parkington, J. & Hall, M. (eds.) *Papers in the Prehistory of the Western Cape, South Africa*: 4–23. Oxford: British Archaeological Reports International Series 332(i).

Parkington, J., Nilssen, P., Reeler, C. & Henshilwood, C. 1992. Making sense of space at Dunefield Midden campsite, Western Cape, South Africa. *Southern African Field Archaeology* 1:63–70.

Parkington, J., Poggenpoel, C., Buchanan, B., Robey, T., Manhire, A.H. & Sealy, J. 1988. Holocene coastal settlement patterns in the Western Cape. In: Bailey, G. & Parkington, J. (eds.) *The Archaeology of Prehistoric Coastlines*: 22–41. Cambridge: CUP.

Peabody, F.E. 1954. Travertines and cave deposits of the Kaap Escarpment of South Africa and the type locality of *Australopithecus africanus* Dart. *Bulletin of the Geological Society of America* 65:671–706.

Penning, W.H. 1886. Notes on a few stone implements found in South Africa. *Journal of the Anthropological Institute* 16:68–70.

Péringuey, L. 1900. Notes on stone implements of Palaeolithic (Old Stone Age) type found at Stellenbosch and vicinity. *Proceedings of the South African Philosophical Society* 11:xxiv–xxv.

Plug, I. 1978. Die Latere Steentydperk van Boesmansrotsskuiling in Oos-Transvaal. Unpublished MA thesis: University of Pretoria.

Potts, R. 1988. *Early Hominid Activities at Olduvai*. New York: Aldine de Gruyter.

Prins, F.E. 1990. Southern Bushman descendants in the Transkei: rock art and rainmaking. *South African Journal of Ethnology* 13:110–116.

Rayner, R.J., Moon, B.P. & Masters, J.C. 1993. The Makapansgat australopithecine environment. *Journal of Human Evolution* 24:219–231.

Rightmire, G.P. 1990. *The Evolution of* Homo erectus: *Comparative Anatomical Studies of an Extinct Human Species*. Cambridge: CUP.

Rightmire, G.P. 1995. Geography, time and speciation in Pleistocene *Homo*. *South African Journal of Science* 91:450–454.

Rightmire, G.P. 1996. The human cranium from Bodo, Ethiopia: evidence for speciation in the Middle Pleistocene? *Journal of Human Evolution* 31:21–39.

Rightmire, G.P. & Deacon, H.J. 1991. Comparative studies of Late Pleistocene human remains from Klasies River Mouth, South Africa. *Journal of Human Evolution* 20:131–156.

Ritchie, D. 1996. Australian heritage protection laws: an overview. In: Finlayson, J. & Jackson-Nakano, A. (eds.) *Heritage and Native Title: Anthropological and Legal Perspectives*: 28–39. Canberra: Australian Institute of Aboriginal and Torres Strait Islander Studies.

Robinson, J.T. 1954. The genera and species of the Australopithecine. *American Journal of Physical Anthropology* 12:181–199.

Rogers, A.R. & Jorde, L.B. 1995. Genetic evidence on modern human origins. *Human Biology* 67:1–36.

Rose, L. & Marshall, F. 1996. Meat eating, hominid sociality, and home bases revisited. *Current Anthropology* 37:307–338.

Ross, R. 1993. *Beyond the Pale: Essays on the History of Colonial South Africa*. Hanover and London: Wesleyan University Press.

Rudner, J. 1968. Strandloper pottery from South and South West Africa. *Annals of the South African Museum* 49:441–663.

Ruvolo, M., Disotell, T.R., Allard, M.W., Brown, W.M. & Honeycutt, R.L. 1991. Resolution of the African hominoid trichotomy by use of a mitochondrial gene sequence. *Proceedings of the National Academy of Sciences, USA* 88:1570–1574.

Sampson, C.G. 1972. *The Stone Age Industries of the Orange River Scheme and South Africa*. Memoir of the National Museum, Bloemfontein 6:1–283.

Sampson, C.G. 1974. *The Stone Age Archaeology of Southern Africa*. New York: Academic Press.

Sampson, C.G. 1988. *Stylistic Boundaries among Mobile Hunter-Foragers*. Washington: Smithsonian Institution Press.

Sampson, C.G. 1996. Spatial organization of Later Stone Age herders in the upper Karoo. In: Pwiti, G. & Soper, R. (eds.) *Aspects of African Archaeology: Papers from the 10th Congress of the PanAfrican Association for Prehistory and Related Studies*: 317–326. Harare: University of Zimbabwe Press.

Sampson, C.G. & Vogel, J.C. 1995. Radiocarbon chronology of Later Stone Age pottery decorations in the upper Seacow Valley. *Southern African Field Archaeology* 4:84–94.

Sampson, C.G., Bailiff, I. & Barnett, S. 1997. Thermoluminescence dates from Later Stone Age pottery on surface sites in the Upper Karoo. *South African Archaeological Bulletin* 52:38–42.

Sampson, C.G., Hart, T.J.G., Wallsmith, D.L. & Blagg, J.D. 1989. The ceramic sequence in the upper Seacow Valley: problems and implications. *South African Archaeological Bulletin* 44:3–16.

Sarich, V.M. & Wilson, A.C. 1967. Immunological time scale for human evolution. *Science* 158:1200–1204.

Savage-Rumbaugh, S. & Lewin, R. 1994. *Kanzi: The Ape at the Brink of the Human Mind*. New York: John Wiley.

Schaller, G.B. 1972. *The Serengeti Lion*. Chicago: Chicago University Press.

Schapera, I. 1930. *The Khoisan People of South Africa: Bushmen and Hottentots.* London: Routledge and Sons.

Schick, K.D. & Toth, N. 1993. *Making Silent Stones Speak.* New York: Simon and Schuster.

Schrire, C. 1962. Oakhurst: a re-examination and vindication. *South African Archaeological Bulletin* 17: 181–195.

Schrire, C. 1980. An inquiry into the evolutionary status and apparent identity of San hunter-gatherers. *Human Ecology* 8:9–32.

Schrire, C. 1984. Wild surmises on savage thoughts. In: Schrire, C. (ed.) *Past and Present in Hunter Gatherer Studies*: 1–25. New York: Academic Press.

Schrire, C. 1996. Native views of Western eyes. In: Skotnes, P. (ed.) *Miscast: Negotiating the Presence of the Bushmen*: 343–353. Cape Town: UCT Press.

Schwarcz, H.P., Gr,n, R. & Tobias, P.V. 1994. ESR dating studies of the australopithecine site of Sterkfontein, South Africa. *Journal of Human Evolution* 26:175–181.

Schweitzer, F.R. 1974. Archaeological evidence for sheep at the Cape. *South African Archaeological Bulletin* 29:75–82.

Schweitzer, F.R. 1979. Excavations at Die Kelders, Cape Province, South Africa: the Holocene deposits. *Annals of the South African Museum* 78:101–233.

Schweitzer, F.R. & Wilson, M.L. 1982. Byneskranskop 1: a late Quaternary living site in the southern Cape Province, South Africa. *Annals of the South African Museum* 88:1–188.

Sealy, J.C. 1986. *Stable Carbon Isotopes and Prehistoric Diets in the South-western Cape Province, South Africa.* Cambridge: British Archaeological Reports International Series.

Sealy, J.C. & Van der Merwe, N.J. 1986. Isotope assessment and the seasonal mobility hypothesis in the south-western Cape, South Africa. *Current Anthropology* 27:135–150.

Sealy, J.C. & Van der Merwe, N.J. 1988. Social, spatial and chronological patterning in marine food use as determined by $\partial^{13}C$ measurements of Holocene human skeletons from the south-western Cape, South Africa. *World Archaeology* 20:87–102.

Sealy, J.C. & Yates, R. 1994. The chronology of the introduction of pastoralism to the Cape, South Africa. *Antiquity* 68:58–67.

Sealy, J. & Yates, R. 1996. Direct radiocarbon dating of early sheep bones: two further results. *South African Archaeological Bulletin* 51:109–110.

Sept, J.M. 1992. Was there no place like home? *Current Anthropology* 33:187–207.

Seyfarth, R.M. & Cheney, D.L. 1992. Meaning and mind in monkeys. *Scientific American* December 1992: 78–84

Shackleton, N.J. 1987. Oxygen isotopes, ice volume, and sea level. *Quaternary Science Reviews* 6:183–190.

Shackleton, N.J. & Opdyke, N. D. 1976. Oxygen-isotope paleomagnetic stratigraphy of Pacific Core V28-239 late Pliocene to latest Pleistocene. *Geological Society of America Memoirs* 145:449–464.

Shaw, E.M., Woolley, P.L. & Rae, F.A. 1963. Bushman arrow poisons. *Cimbebasia* 7:2–41.

Sieborger, R., Nisbet, J., Machin, I. & Kingwill, R. 1985. *Discovering History: Standard 5.* Pietermaritzburg: Shuter and Shooter.

Siegel, R.K. & Jarvik, M.E. 1975. Drug-induced hallucinations in animals and man. In: Siegel, R.K. & West, L.J. (eds.) *Hallucinations: Behaviour, Experience and Theory*: 81–161. New York: Wiley.

Sigmon, B.A. 1995. J.T. Robinson and W.E. le Gros Clark and their influence on thought in early australopithecine research. *South African Journal of Science* 91:425–430.

Silberbauer, G.B. 1981. *Hunter and Habitat in the Central Kalahari Desert.* Cambridge: CUP.

Sillen, A., Hall, G. & Armstrong, R. 1995. Strontium calcium ratios (Sr/Ca) and strontium isotopic ratios ($^{87}Sr/^{86}SR$) of *Australopithecus robustus* and *Homo* sp. from Swartkrans. *Journal of Human Evolution* 28: 277–285.

Singer, R. & Wymer, J.J. 1968. Archaeological investigations at the Saldanha skull site in South Africa. *South African Archaeological Bulletin* 23:63–74.

Singer, R. & Wymer, J.J. 1982. *The Middle Stone Age at Klasies River Mouth in South Africa.* Chicago: Chicago University Press.

Skotnes, P. 1996. *Miscast: Negotiating the Presence of the Bushmen.* Cape Town: University of Cape Town Press.

Smith, A.B. 1986. Competition, conflict and clientship: Khoi and San relationships in the Western Cape. *South African Archaeological Society Goodwin Series* 5:36–41.

Smith, A.B., Sadr, K., Gribble, J. & Yates, R. 1991. Excavations in the south-western Cape, South Africa, and the archaeological identity of prehistoric hunter-gatherers within the last 2 000 years. *South African Archaeological Bulletin* 46:71–91.

Smith, B.H. & Tompkins, R.L. 1995. Toward a life history of the Hominidae. *Annual Review of Anthropology* 24:257–279.

Solomon, A. 1995. Rock art incorporated: an archaeological and interdisciplinary study of certain human figures in San rock art. Unpublished PhD thesis: University of Cape Town.

Solomon, A. 1997. The myth of ritual origins? Ethnography, mythology and interpretation of San rock art. *South African Archaeological Bulletin* 52:3–13.

Soodyall, H. & Jenkins, T. 1992. Mitochondrial DNA polymorphisms in Khoisan populations from southern Africa. *Annals of Human Genetics* 56:315–324.

Soodyall, H. & Jenkins, T. 1997. Khoisan prehistory: the evidence of the genes. Khoisan identities and cultural heritage. Arts and Culture Trust: Cape Town.

Spratt, D.A. 1982. The analysis of innovation processes. *Journal of Archaeological Science* 9:79–94.

Stanley, S. 1996. *Children of the Ice Age: How Global*

Catastrophe Allowed Humans to Evolve. New York: Harmony Books.

Steyn, H.P. 1971. Aspects of the economic life of some nomadic Nharo Bushman groups. *Annals of the South African Museum* 56:275–322.

Steyn, H.P. 1990. *Vanished Lifestyles. The Early Cape Khoi and San*. Pretoria: Unibook.

Stoneking, M. 1993. DNA and recent human evolution. *Evolutionary Anthropology* 2:60–73.

Stoneking, M. & Cann, R.L. 1989. African origin of human mitochondrial DNA. In: Mellars, P. & Stringer, C. (eds.) *The Human Revolution: Behavioural and Biological Perspectives on the Origins of Modern Humans*: 17–30. Edinburgh: Edinburgh University Press.

Story, R. 1964. Plant lore of the Bushmen. In: Davis, D.H.S. (ed.) *Ecological Studies in Southern Africa*. The Hague: W. Junk.

Stow, G.W. 1905. *The Native Races of South Africa*. Reprint edition. Cape Town: Struik.

Stow, G.W. 1930. *Rock-paintings in South Africa: From Parts of the Eastern Province and Orange Free State*. London: Methuen.

Stringer, C. & Gamble, C. 1993. *In Search of the Neanderthals: Solving the Puzzle of Human Origins*. London: Thames and Hudson.

Stringer, C. & McKie, R. 1996. *African Exodus*. London: Jonathan Cape.

Susman, R. 1988. Hand of *Paranthropus robustus* from Member 1, Swartkrans: fossil evidence for tool behavior. *Science* 240:781–784.

Swisher III, C.C., Rink, W.J., Anton, S.C., Schwarcz, H.P., Curtis, G.H., Suprijo, A. & Widiasmoro. 1996. Latest *Homo erectus* of Java: potential contemporaneity with *Homo sapiens* in Southeast Asia. *Science* 263: 1118–1121.

Talma, A.S. & Vogel, J.C. 1992. Late Quaternary paleotemperatures derived from a speleothem from Cango Caves, Cape Province, South Africa. *Quaternary Research* 37:203–213.

Tattersall, I. 1995. *The Last Neanderthal: The Rise, Success, and Mysterious Extinction of Our Closest Human Relatives*. London: Macmillan.

Tattersall, I. 1997. Out of Africa again ... and again? *Scientific American* April 1997:46–53.

Thackeray, A.I. 1983. Dating the rock art of southern Africa. *South African Archaeological Society Goodwin Series* 4:21–26.

Thackeray, A.I. 1989. Changing fashions in the Middle Stone Age: the stone artefact sequence from Klasies River Main Site, South Africa. *African Archaeological Review* 7:33–58.

Thom, H.B. (ed.) 1958. *Journal of Jan van Riebeeck. Volume III: 1659–1662*. Cape Town: Balkema.

Tobias, P.V. 1984. *Dart, Taung and the 'Missing Link'*. Johannesburg: Witwatersrand University Press.

Toth, N. 1985. The Oldowan reassessed: a close look at early stone artifacts. *Journal of Archaeological Science* 12:101–120.

Toth, N., Schick, K.D., Savage-Rumbaugh, E.S., Sevcik, R.A. & Rumbaugh, D.M. 1993. Pan the tool-maker: investigations into the stone tool-making and tool-using capabilities of a Bonobo (*Pan paniscus*). *Journal of Archaeological Science* 20:81–91.

Traill, A. 1995. The Khoesan languages of South Africa. In: Mesthrie, R. (ed.) *Language and Social History. Studies in South African Sociolinguistics*: 1–18. Cape Town: David Philip.

Traill, A. 1996. *!Khwa-Ka Hhouiten Hhouiten* 'The rush of the storm': the linguistic death of /Xam. In: Skotnes, P. (ed.) *Miscast: Negotiating the Presence of the Bushmen*: 161–183. Cape Town: UCT Press.

Trinkhaus, E. & Shipman, P. 1993. *The Neandertals: Changing the Image of Mankind*. London: Jonathan Cape.

Tuan, Y. 1974. *Topophilia: A Study of Environmental Perception, Attitudes and Values*. Englewood Cliffs, NJ: Prentice-Hall.

Turner, A. 1985. Extinction, speciation and dispersal in African larger carnivores, from the late Miocene to recent. *South African Journal of Science* 81:256–257.

Van Andel, T.H. 1989. Late Pleistocene sea levels and the human exploitation of the shore and shelf of southern South Africa. *Journal of Field Archaeology* 16:133–55.

Van der Merwe, N.J., Sealy, J. & Yates, R. 1987. First accelerator carbon-14 date for pigment from a rock painting. *South African Journal of Science* 83:56–57.

Van der Ryst, M.M. 1996. The Later Stone Age prehistory of the Waterberg, with special reference to Goergap Shelter. Unpublished MA thesis: University of the Witwatersrand.

Van Riet Lowe, C. 1936. The Smithfield 'N' Culture. *Transactions of the Royal Society of South Africa* 23:367–372.

Van Riet Lowe, C. 1937. The archaeology of the Vaal River basin. In: Söhnge, P.G., Visser, D.J.L. & Van Riet Lowe, C. *The Geology and Archaeology of the Vaal River Basin*. Geological Survey Memoirs 35:61–164. Pretoria: Government Printer.

Van Riet Lowe, C. 1952. *The Distribution of Prehistoric Rock Engravings and Paintings in South Africa*. Archaeological Survey Series 7. Pretoria: Government Printer.

Van Wyk, R. 1979. Technological change: a macro perspective. *Technological Forecasting and Social Change* 15:281–296.

Vinnicombe, P. 1972. Myth, motive and selection in southern African rock art. *Africa* 42:192–204.

Vinnicombe, P. 1976. *People of the Eland*. Pietermaritzburg: Natal University Press.

Vogel, J.C. 1983. Isotopic evidence for past climates and vegetation of South Africa. *Bothalia* 14:391–394.

Vogel, J., Plug, I. & Webley, L. 1997. New dates for the introduction of sheep into South Africa: the evidence from Spoegrivier Cave in Namaqualand. *South African*

Journal of Science 93:246–248.

Volman, T.P. 1984. Early prehistory of southern Africa. In: Klein, R.G. (ed.) *Southern African Prehistory and Palaeoenvironments*: 169–220. Rotterdam: Balkema.

Von Boeckmann, K. 1921. Stoffe der tracht. In: Frobenius, L. & von Wilm, L.R. (eds.) *Atlas Africanus 1*. Munich: Beck.

Von den Driesch, A. & Deacon, H.J. 1985. Sheep remains from Boomplaas Cave, South Africa. *South African Archaeological Bulletin* 40:39–44.

Vrba, E.S. 1975. Some evidence of the chronology and palaeoecology of Sterkfontein, Swartkrans and Kromdraai from the fossil Bovidae. *Nature* 254:301–304.

Vrba, E.S. 1985. Environment and evolution: alternative causes of the temporal distribution of evolutionary events. *South African Journal of Science* 81:229–236.

Vrba, E.S. 1988. Late Pliocene climatic events and hominid evolution. In: Grine, F.E. (ed.) *Evolutionary History of the 'Robust' Australopithecines*: 405–427. New York: Aldine de Gruyter.

Vrba, E.S. 1992. Mammals as a key to evolutionary theory. *Journal of Mammology* 73:1–28.

Vrba, E.S. 1996. Climate, heterochrony, and human evolution. *Journal of Anthropological Research* 52:1–28.

Wadley, L. 1987. *Later Stone Age Hunters and Gatherers of the Southern Transvaal: Social and Ecological Interpretations*. Oxford: British Archaeological Reports International Series 380.

Wadley, L. 1989. Legacies from the Later Stone Age. *South African Archaeological Society Goodwin Series* 6:42–53.

Wadley, L. 1993. The Pleistocene Later Stone Age south of the Limpopo River. *Journal of World Prehistory* 7:243–296.

Wadley, L. 1995. Review of dated Stone Age sites recently excavated in the eastern Free State, South Africa. *South African Journal of Science* 91:574–579.

Wadley, L. 1996a. The Bleek and Lloyd records on death and burial, and the problems that these present for archaeologists. In: Deacon J. & Dowson, T.A. (eds.) *Voices from the Past*: 271–286. Johannesburg: Witwatersrand University Press.

Wadley, L. 1996b. The Robberg industry of Rose Cottage Cave, eastern Free State: the technology, spatial patterns and environment. *South African Archaeological Bulletin* 51:64–74.

Wainscoat, J., Hill, A., Boyce, A., Flint, J., Hernandez, M., Thein, S.L., Old, J.M., Lynch, J.R., Falusi, Y., Weatherall, D.J. & Clegg, J.B. 1986. Evolutionary relationships of human populations from an analysis of nuclear DNA polymorphisms. *Nature* 319:491–493.

Webley, L. 1986. Pastoralist ethnoarchaeology in Namaqualand. *South African Archaeological Society Goodwin Series* 5:57–61.

Webley, L. 1990. The use of stone 'scrapers' by semi-sedentary pastoralist groups in Namaqualand, South

Africa. *South African Archaeological Bulletin* 45:28–32.

Wendorf, F. & Schild, R. 1994. Are the Early Holocene cattle in the eastern Sahara domestic or wild? *Evolutionary Anthropology* 3:118-128.

Wendt, W.E. 1976. 'Art mobilier' from the Apollo 11 Cave, South West Africa: Africa's oldest dated works of art. *South African Archaeological Bulletin* 31:5–11.

Westphal, E.O.J. 1963. The linguistic prehistory of southern Africa: Bush, Kwadi, Hottentot and Bantu linguistic relationships. *Africa* 33:253–256.

Wheeler, P. 1988. Stand tall and stay cool. *New Scientist* 12 May 1988:62–65.

Wheeler, P.E. 1990. The significance of selective brain cooling in hominids. *Journal of Human Evolution* 19:321–322.

White, F.J. 1996. *Pan paniscus* 1973–1996: twenty-three years of field research. *Evolutionary Anthropology* 5:11–17.

White, J.P. & Thomas, D. 1972. What mean these stones? Ethnotaxonomic models and archaeological interpretations in the New Guinea Highlands. In: Clarke, D.L. (ed.) *Models in Archaeology*: 275–308. London: Methuen.

White, T.D. 1987. Cannibalism at Klasies? *Sagittarius* 2:6-9.

White, T.D., Suwa, G. & Asfaw, B. 1994. *Australopithecus ramidus*, a new species of early hominid from Aramis, Ethiopia. *Nature* 371:306–333.

Wiessner, P. 1982. Risk, reciprocity and social influence on !Kung San economics. In: Leacock, E. & Lee, R. (eds.) *Politics and History in Band Societies*: 61–84. Cambridge: CUP.

Wiessner, P. 1983. Social and ceremonial aspects of death among the !Kung San. *Botswana Notes and Records* 15:1–5.

Wilson, M.L. 1986. Notes on the nomenclature of the Khoisan. *Annals of the South African Museum* 97:251–266.

Wilson, M.L. 1990. Strandlopers and shell middens. Unpublished MA thesis: University of Cape Town.

Wolpoff, M. & Caspari, R. 1996. *Race and Human Evolution: A Fatal Attraction*. New York: Simon & Schuster.

Wrangham, R. & Peterson, D. 1996. *Demonic Males: Apes and the Origins of Human Violence*. New York: Houghton Mifflin.

Yellen, J. 1977. *Archaeological Approaches to the Present: Models for Reconstructing the Past*. New York: Academic Press.

Zihlman, A. 1996. Looking back in anger. *Nature* 384:35-36.

Zihlman, A., Cronin, J.E., Cramer, D.L. & Sarich, V.M. 1978. Pygmy chimpanzee as a possible prototype for the common ancestor of humans, chimpanzees and gorillas. *Nature* 275:744–745

Index